THE STORY
OF A
FAMILY

Saint Thérèse, the Little Flower (1873-1897), shortly before she entered the Carmelite Order at age 15. Although she lived to be only 24, Pope Saint Pius X described Thérèse as "the greatest saint of modern times."

THE STORY
OF A
FAMILY

The Home of St. Thérèse of Lisieux
(The Little Flower)

By

FR. STÉPHANE-JOSEPH PIAT, O.F.M.

Translated by
A Benedictine of Stanbrook Abbey

DEFINITIVE EDITION

*"God gave me a father and a mother more
worthy of Heaven than of earth."*
—St. Thérèse of the Child Jesus

TAN BOOKS AND PUBLISHERS, INC.
Rockford, Illinois 61105

Nihil Obstat: Justin McCann, O.S.B.
                 Censor Deputatus

Imprimatur: Herbert Byrne, O.S.B.
                 Ab. Praes.
                 June 19, 1946

In obedience to the decrees of Pope Urban VIII and other Sovereign Pontiffs, the author declares that all the graces and other supernatural facts related in this volume rest upon human authority alone, and that in regard to such, as in the use of all terms and in the opinions expressed, he submits himself without reserve to the infallible judgment of the Holy Apostolic See.

Library of Congress Catalog Card No.: 93-61562

ISBN: 0-89555-502-6

Cover design by Peter Massari, Rockford, Illinois.

Printed and bound in the United States of America.

TAN BOOKS AND PUBLISHERS, INC.
P.O. Box 424
Rockford, Illinois 61105
1994

"When we had our children, our ideas changed somewhat. Thenceforward we lived only for them; they made all our happiness and we would never have found it save in them. In fact, nothing any longer cost us anything; the world was no longer a burden to us. As for me, my children were my great compensation, so that I wished to have many in order to bring them up for Heaven."

—ZÉLIE MARTIN

Letter from His Lordship, Monseigneur Picaud, Bishop of Bayeux and Lisieux.

Bayeux.
April 6th, 1945.

Reverend Father,

I have read with the keenest interest the M.S. of *The Story of a Family*, which you have been kind enough to send me. Your undertaking fulfils a wish I expressed many years ago, and which an excessive modesty persistently hesitated to grant. At last, you are about to reveal to the Catholic public the exemplary lives of M. and Mme. Martin.

I am firmly convinced that this book will do much good by setting before its many readers its vivid portrayal of a Christian marriage. At a time when so many unhealthy influences have attacked the indissolubility, the union, and the fertility of the home, what an attractive and persuasive sight, despite the seeming austerity of duty and sacrifice, was that household of M. and Mme. Martin! At a time when the inadequate home training of the children so frequently witnesses to the remissness of so many parents, even baptised Catholics, what a charm and what a benefit it is to note in the correspondence of Mme. Martin in particular the tender affection, and constant watchfulness of an ideal Christian mother! When priestly and religious vocations so often meet with an unfavourable reception and even with formal opposition in family circles, what an eloquent reminder of the hierarchy of vocations is empha-

Letter

sised by the noble aspirations and holy desires confided to God by the lace-maker of Alençon and the patriarch of *Les Buissonnets!* Would we find many parents today leading, as did M. Martin his "little Queen," to the Bishop of Bayeux in order to hasten her entry into a convent, even though this step must at the same time hasten the wounding and solitude of his fatherly heart?

To these examples of conjugal and family life, you have not omitted to add those of a laborious existence and of high professional conscientiousness, which, again, today it is very timely to recall in order to enlighten and readjust the attitude of many readers.

To sum up in a word, it is the portrait of two incomparable models—I was nearly saying two holy patrons —which you set before us for our admiration and for the imitation of Catholic parents.

Need I add that the author's skill in such writing, and the obvious enthusiasm that has guided his pen, well add to the prestige of the subjects to charm and edify the reader. I would suggest, Reverend Father, that, over and above these, well chosen and abundant illustrations should still further enhance pages already so attractive by adding life and local color.

I believe that a success comparable to that of the Autobiography of the Saint will reward your labors, and that an immense good will result from this publication. It is in this hope that I bless your undertaking with all my heart, and am

Yours devotedly in Our Lord,

Francis Picaud.

Bishop of Bayeux and Lisieux.

PREFACE

ON JULY 13th, 1858, Louis Martin and Zélie Guérin were united in the Sacrament of Marriage. On July 13th, 1927, Pius XI extended to the Universal Church the Office and Mass of St. Thérèse of the Child Jesus. The coincidence of the dates emphasises in its own way the spiritual kinship which, repeating the blood relationship, united the wonder-worker and her parents even in glory.

"If I had not had this, you would not have had that," said significantly Signora Sarto pointing to her wedding ring and to the episcopal ring of the future Pius X. Without the patriarchal atmosphere of the *Rue Saint Blaise* and the *Buissonnets*, the ascension of the Carmelite would have been from a less pure lineage. She herself is careful to inform us of this in the opening pages of her Autobiography: "The little Flower that now tells her tale, rejoices in having to publish the wholly undeserved favors bestowed upon her by our Lord . . . He allowed her to grow up in holy soil enriched with the odor of purity, and preceded by eight lilies of shining whiteness."

"Nature does not make sudden leaps." It is by stages that the level of the ground rises to its culminating point. Though sudden interventions and thunderbolts are not unknown, preferably grace also proceeds by slow stages. In order to cause a peak of sanctity to emerge, God works at and raises up a whole series of generations. Giants of holiness who rise up in isolation

Preface

and detached, as it were, from the family territory, are rare. Alexis, "the saint under the staircase," who ran away on his wedding night; Francis of Assisi, whom his father cursed and disinherited; Jane de Chantal, who stepped over the body of her own son to reach the convent, remain exceptional cases. Normally, the saint receives his early fashioning in the home circle.

Called as she was to teach the world the sovereign art of rendering the ordinary routine of life a divine thing, Thérèse of Lisieux could not escape from the general rule. At the source of her greatness there is a twofold lineage of thoroughbred Christians; bent over her cradle are two saintly faces. Cardinal Mercier rejoiced at this as a providential sign. "Ah," he exclaimed, "how glad I am to know that she is the recompense of an exemplary family. We must never weary of repeating that everywhere."

The Church is readily accused of reserving liturgical honors for virgins, martyrs, bishops and religious. Married folk only find grace in her eyes on condition of having secured a certain rehabilitation by widowhood. Joking apart, and without taking it upon ourselves to research into the Roman Calendar, we must admit that a current prejudice, for which the Sacred Congregation of Rites is by no means responsible, condemns married couples to a "reduced" fervor which does not reach the altars. The greater number of spiritual books exude a monastic perfume. They would feel themselves out of place at a married bedside. Is marriage, to quote the celebrated words of Lacordaire, so wittily recalled by Pius IX, "the snare into which every ideal of perfection fatally stumbles"?

By praising in their allocutions and in the breviary lessons the parents who gave the world "the greatest

Preface

saint of modern times," the Sovereign Pontiffs have given a timely correction to these erroneous opinions. The home which produced Thérèse today enters into her way of glory. The halo surrounds the child's head, but in its radiating light it includes the father and mother bending over her. Are not parents called upon to efface themselves, to forget themselves, to know no triumphs save those of the dear beings to whom, together with life, they have given all that was best in themselves?

Looked at from this standpoint, the publication of a biography of the Martin couple is not without its usefulness. All over the world, naturalism has sapped the foundations of the family, and at the same time shaken the foundations of the State. All over the world, a return to the principles set forth by Pius XI in the Encyclical *Casti Connubii* is the necessary condition of public safety. What more effective in helping on this result than the lesson of facts, of an heroic family?

Humanity is emerging from the war, bloodless and mangled. Europe is but an immense area of ruins. At Lisieux itself, the ten bombardments which between June 6th and August 22nd, 1944, rained down a hurricane of iron and fire, have demolished 2100 houses out of 2800, beaten to the ground two parish churches out of three, razed likewise the majority of the religious houses, and caused to perish, together with sixty religious, more than a tenth of the population. By a veritable miracle, which leaps to the eye of the passer-by, the Theresian iselet constituted by the Carmel, the *Hermitage*, and the *Maison Saint Jean*, has escaped the destruction and lost none of its inhabitants. An invisible hand checked the sea of flame which entirely destroyed the buildings in the neighborhood of the mon-

Preface

astery. The eighty-five incendiary bombs that fell in the convent garden, the high explosive bombs and shells that struck the roofs and walls, caused only damage which can be repaired. The personnel of the *Mission de France* was able in time to confine the area of the fire which, from the Outsisters' quarters, threatened the chapel of the shrine. The Basilica was, in its turn, ringed round by several enormous columns of smoke and flame without being damaged in its vital parts. The Carmelite nuns, having taken refuge in the crypt, there continued beneath the shrapnel, their mission of prayer and sacrifice until Sunday, August 27th, when, escorting the relics of their glorious Protectress, they regained their convent. *Les Buissonnets*, also, came through almost untouched by the universal ruin, whilst at Alençon the house where the saint was born and the Pavilion suffered only very slightly.[1]

Historic Lisieux is almost annihilated. Spiritual Lisieux remains standing. Is it presumptuous to see in this a symbol of the restoration which is a necessity for wounded humanity? St. Theresa of the Child Jesus is not only the special Patron of France; for the whole world she scatters her roses. She teaches us that from the vast area of material ruins a spiritual renaissance may rise, if the regenerated soul rules the broken body. She tells us that nothing is lost so long as faith in Christ remains. She reminds us that a nation's essential wealth is the blood that flows generously in the veins of its sons. Many monuments that were our pride now litter the ground as débris. Unfortunately there are other

[1] The devastation that has stricken Lisieux has, nevertheless, not wholly spared the institutions consecrated to the Saint's glory. The offices concerned with the pilgrimages have been severely affected. Twelve buildings were lost including the Chaplains House and the Central office of the *Editions de Sainte Thérèse* and certain accessories of the Basilica damaged.

Preface

devastated regions to which our heedlessness pays too little attention: the churches without priests, the godless schools, the childless homes.

Thérèse points to those red districts in which our decay is writ large. She tells us in her way: "Civilisation is in peril. Society is tottering. Hasten to return to Him who is the Way, the Truth, and the Life! Restore with all speed that dismantled sanctuary which is the family. Thence will come your salvation."

It is to serve this crusade that the *Annales de Sainte Thérèse* have published the correspondence of Mme. Martin. It is to contribute our share that we have tried to sketch the portrait of the ideal home in which Thérèse grew up. Principles are not enough to galvanise men's courage. Living examples have power of another sort. They illustrate the principle by bringing it into the realm of the concrete. They fasten on to the real. They shake off cowardice by showing what can be done. The provocative thought that haunted St. Augustine on the threshold of his conversion is never out of date: "Cannot I do what these men and women did?"

Documents have not been wanting in order to render possible the biography of the parents of the Little Theresa. The letters of Mme. Martin and the Autobiography are the primary sources. We have drawn largely upon the Life of the saint by Mgr. Laveille. The Lisieux Carmel has been willing to yield to our entreaties and, for the sake of the general edification, hand over to us certain papers which filial piety might have wished to hide in a perpetual silence. This trusting collaboration, besides constituting for our modest work a guarantee of inestimable value, will count among the choice graces for which we give thanks to Providence. The work we give to the public might have

Preface

gained in interest had it been presented in a more graphic form, with the *parti pris* of anecdote and setting of the romantic biographies so fashionable today. The honesty of the historian, the desire also to lighten the labors of psychologists and propagandists of the family crusade, have led us to undertake the production of a complete Life of a somewhat austere aspect. Some will perhaps regret these developments. Such as it is, in its attempt to seize upon the soul of a beautiful home, to reconstitute the outward appearance, to place the subjects, this book, we hope, will be able to offer many an example to those, among all classes, who are fighting and trying to give to society not only children but also, and above all, men and women of character, Christians, apostles, and—why not?—saints.

Roubaix. October 3rd, 1944.
Feast of St. Thérèse of the Child Jesus, and Vigil of the Feast of St. Francis of Assisi.

FR. STÉPHANE-JOSEPH PIAT, O.F.M.

CONTENTS

Contents

Contents

COMMON FRENCH WORDS
AND ABBREVIATIONS

M.	Monsieur	Mr.
Mme.	Madame	Madam, Mrs.
Mlle.	Mademoiselle	Miss
Mgr.	Monsignor	Bishop
S.	Saint	Saint (masculine)
Ste.	Sainte	Saint (feminine)
	Abbé	(priest's title)
	Mère	Mother
	Père	Father
	Frère	Brother
	Soeur	Sister
	Rue	Street
	Maison	House

ILLUSTRATIONS

THE STORY
OF A
FAMILY

MAP OF FRANCE

CHAPTER 1

ORIGINS AND FIRST STEPS

Ancestry and early years of Louis Martin and Zélie Guérin.

NOT far from the *Alpes Mancelles*, in the heart of a bright countryside, overlooked by the high trees of the forests of Perseigne, Multonne, and Écouves, Alençon lies displayed in its careless, rather aristocratic grace. Its old medieval houses, with their projecting upper stories painted balconies with bare beams, the later mansions in a plain, severe style, the streams with places for public washing beside them, the quiet streets crossed by the muddy waters of the Briante and the Sarthe, give it a picturesque and peace-giving aspect. It is a lordly city where the stones sing; a dream city where the wood prays; there is a certain natural air of distinction about it, a penetrating charm and a nobility marked with the seal of old France. There are silent hours when, in its almost deserted streets, you might think you heard the footfall of the watchmen of yore going their rounds and see pass by the shy ghost of the "Good Duchess Margaret." [1]

[1] Margaret of Lorraine was the niece of Margaret of Anjou, queen of Henry VI of England. Her mother, Yolande, married Ferri of Lorraine. Left an orphan, Margaret was brought up at her grandfather's court and married René, Duke of Alençon. She was greatly beloved and after she became a widow founded the convent of Poor Clares of Argentan and

3

The Story of a Family

Modern urban development has not robbed it of its mystery. Willy-nilly, it has respected the old-world aspect of the *Maison d'Ozé*; it has left to the *Tribunal de Commerce* its hoary splendor described in the *Cabinet des Antiques* of Balzac. The *Hôtel-Dieu*, the *Tour Couronnée*, the local government offices—the *Préfecture* —attract the notice of the tourist, whilst the historian loves to question the façades, troubled and weighted with their secrets, of the *Rue Bonette* and the shops in the Ghetto.

Three churches stand open to the pilgrim; the tottering sanctuary—now rebuilt—of Saint Pierre-de-Monsort, Saint Léonard, which owes its restoration to the Blessed Margaret of Lorraine and, above all, Notre-Dame, an example of the flamboyant style which, unlike the King's daughter, is more glorious without than within. Its triple arcaded porch is indeed a veritable masterpiece, with its octagonal towers, its corniced balustrades, its slender gables and the thousand arabesques which recall the exquisite art of the Alençon lacemakers. We forget the over heavy choir, and the inelegant tower, both rebuilt after the fire of 1744. The traveller almost forgets to admire the soaring grace of the nave, the magic of the painted windows, the subdued light of the aisles, so fascinated is he at the sermon in stone written on the threshold of the building at the dawn of the 16th century by the genius of Jean Lemoyne. There beats the real heart of the city. It is there, before Our Lady of the Assumption or, as certain competent authorities say, the Transfiguration, facing the gaping niches and the holy personages mutilated by the Huguenots, that we really enjoy the intimacy of the

herself took the habit. Though never formally beatified, she bears the title of *Blessed*, and her cultus has been sanctioned in her Order. (Tr.)

Book Request Form:

Author:

Title:

Requested by:

Apt # or Cottage #

Origins and First Steps

"changeless province," as Balzac called it, and love to reread the lines in which Paul Harel has drawn poetically the portrait of the city over which the Spirit breathes:

> "Twixt slope abrupt and forest high,
> And a plain widespread, she rose
> Bathed in the brightness of the dawn,
> Her lace-like spires, her pale cathedral,
> And her homestead roofs, some high some low."[2]

But behold how, its present glory now linked with the splendors of its past, Notre-Dame, so rich in memories, enters once more into history. On Tuesday, July 13th, 1858, at midnight—the custom was not unusual at the period—Louis Martin and Zélie Guérin crossed the threshold of its imposing entrance, accompanied by a few intimate friends. Simply, without the least parade, they were united before God. Fifteen years later, on the 4th of January, 1873, the last child of their marriage, Thérèse, entered beneath the gothic vault in her turn, in order to receive holy Baptism. Yet another half-century will go by, and the statue of the Carmelite nun, beatified on April 29th, 1923, then triumphantly canonised, will take its place amid those portrayed in stone by the chisels of the sculptors of long ago. Alençon will be the cradle of "a spiritual renaissance."

*　　*　　*

Preparing the way for this renaissance there was, providentially arranged, a whole family heritage of courage, soldierly honor and faith. Legend is ever roaming round sainthood, and legend has tried to blacken the ancestry of Thérèse of the Child Jesus. The result

[2] Cited by René Jouanne, in his remarkable literary and artistic guide: *Promenade à travers le Vieil Alençon.*

5

The Story of a Family

has merely been to encourage certain delvers in archives, and these have promptly disposed of the calumnious insinuations. To the cultus rendered to her "incomparable parents" the Carmelite could add a legitimate pride in her forbears.

It is at Athis-de-l'Orne, a good-sized market town in the Domfront district, that the church registers, which mention several families of the name of Martin, record on April 2nd, 1692, the appearance of a whole undoubted progeny of Jean Martin, terminating at the date of April 16th, 1777, with the baptism of a little Pierre-François Martin. The parents, who were subsequently to settle in the neighborhood of Saint Quentin, lived at that time close to the church. The maternal uncle and godfather of the infant, François Bohard, "Bon Papa Bohard," as he was called in the neighborhood, owed to the honorable distinction of his family of fourteen children, and his dauntless courage, a popularity which was one day to cause him to be chosen mayor of the town. It was he who, at the height of the Revolution, braved the proscriptions of the Jacobins and hid the church bells in his own house. There the spirit of the old countryside still lived. Amidst persecution the Faith entered more deeply into men's souls. To make up to him for the glories of the liturgy of which he was thus early deprived, Pierre Martin was able to learn by experience what it meant to be supported by the example of a faith that would not die. A military career did not weaken his convictions.

On August 26th, 1799, he was drafted to the 65th infantry of the line, and from the army of the Rhine to Belle-Ile-en-Mer, from Brest to the Belgian frontier, then in Prussia, Poland and through the campaign in France, he followed eagerly after the tricolor and the imperial Eagle. After the Restoration, he gained his commission and, as an officer, passed into the departmental regiment of the Lower Loire, then to the 19th light infantry, and finally, to the 42nd infantry of the line, then doing garrison duty at Lyons.

It was in that city that he made friends with the Captain Nicholas Boureau whose daughter he was to marry. Nicholas Boureau, who had volunteered for the army at the age of seventeen, had lived through the tragic events of the revolutionary campaigns from 1791 to 1796. In 1812 and 1813 he had taken part in the vicissitudes of the *Grande Armée*, and experienced the hard captivity in Silesia, in which his son, captured with him, perished at the age of twelve and a half. Twice in the course of his career, he was the victim of odious accusations which forced him to withdraw from the camps. The records which witness to these allegations refute them triumphantly. The Marquis d'Averin, peer of France, M. de Grandmaison, chaplain to the Catholic and royalist army of the Vendée, both testify with many others to the perfect rectitude of the life of the accused. The parish priest of Ainay attests that "M. Nicholas-Jean Boureau, Captain, domiciled in this parish at no. 4, Rue Vaubecourt, with his wife and two daughters, had led a life grounded upon principles of honor, right conduct and religion, and that on account of its virtues this honorable family is worthy of the esteem and admiration of the citizens of this town."

During the years 1816 and 1817, Pierre Martin was frequently a guest in this Christian home, and became engaged to the Captain's second daughter, Marie-Anne-Fanie, aged eighteen. Reverses of fortune having swallowed up the dowry then obligatory for an officer's wife, the noble-hearted soldier would not on that account forsake the woman of his choice, but furnished the requisite sum out of his own resources. Of the marriage, which took place on April 7th, 1818, five children were born: Pierre, destined to be lost in a shipwreck when still very young, Marie, who died in her twenty-sixth year, Louis, who was to give to the world Thérèse of the Child Jesus, Fanny, whose earthly life closed at twenty-seven, and lastly Sophie, who died as a child of nine.

Louis-Joseph-Aloys-Stanislaus Martin[3] was born on August 22nd, 1823, in the Rue Servandoni, Bordeaux. He was immediately baptised privately, the completion of the ceremonies in church being deferred until his father's return home. The latter, then attached to the 19th light infantry, was taking part in the Spanish campaign, from which he returned decorated with the cross of a Knight of St. Louis. As the military operations were prolonged, however, the Abbé Martegoute, then prison chaplain, performed the baptismal ceremonies on October 28th, 1823, in the church of Sainte Eulalie, where one day a monument would commemorate the father of the Saint. Had the holy Archbishop of Bordeaux, Monseigneur d'Aviau du Bois de Sanzay, some vague intuition of that day, when he said to the relations of the infant: "Rejoice, this is a child of destiny!"

The unpredictable chances of camp life led the Martin family to Avignon and thence to Strasburg, where the Captain was acting as town Adjutant on the general staff. When, on December 12th, 1830, he retired,

---

[3] From devotion to the Apostle of the Indies, in later years Louis Martin liked to add the name of Xavier to his Christian names.

it was to the land of his ancestors that he returned to seek rest. He wished to see again his Normandy, Athis, and the church tower, for which in secret he had been homesick. A right concern for his children's education led him to prefer Alençon, where he would find greater resources for their training and settlement in life, and he took up his residence in the *Rue des Tisons*, and in 1842 the *Rue du Mans*, whilst waiting to join his son, Louis in the house attached to the clock and watchmaker's shop, which the latter opened in the *Rue du Pont Neuf*.

For a professional soldier retirement is the crucial trial, which may launch him into civil society deprived of occupation, without ideal or object in life. Captain Martin was proud of his Faith and a great character. The daguerreotype which has preserved his portrait for us shows features strongly marked, as though hacked out with a hatchet: thin, compressed lips, and an expression in the eyes which is keen and almost imperious. The face expresses, in fact, the inflexible energy and intransigent uprightness that becomes an officer of the Napoleonic wars. A lady moving in the leading circles of Alençon, who had often met him at close quarters, in after years thus described him to the Carmelites of Lisieux, his granddaughters: "He won our admiration by his immaculate appearance; he looked very fine in his greatcoat, decorated with the red ribbon which one did not meet in the streets in those days. What a lineage of saints you have in your family!" Those who knew Captain Martin intimately have owned to the emotion with which they listened as he recited the *Pater Noster*. When the regimental chaplain once remarked to him that some of the men were astonished at

The Story of a Family

Mass to see him remain so long on his knees after the Consecration, he replied without flinching: "Tell them that it is because I believe!"

For a man of this stamp the return to civil life could mean merely a change of scene. As a Christian, he appreciated the peaceful environment of the Norman countryside. He occupied himself in the more vigilant fulfilment of his family duties, as also in a more intense practice of his religion, and in works of charity, in which he was supported by his admirable wife. In the latter, her daughter-in-law, Thérèse's mother, was one day to recognise "an extraordinary courage and very fine qualities." An example of the principles which animated the Martin household may be found in this letter of congratulations addressed by the Captain to M. Nicholas Moulin, who was to become his nephew by marriage:

"Praised be Jesus Christ!"

Alençon. August 7th. 1828.

Monsieur,

I have received your letter from which I learn that, by my communication, the consent to your marriage has safely reached you. At last, thank God!, my task is fulfilled to the best of my ability; now I desire, with all my heart, that our divine Master may deign to bless your union with my beloved niece, and that you may be as happy as one can be in this world, and that when you draw your last breath God may receive you into His mercy and place you among the number of the blessed, there to live forever. Kindly greet your estimable parents and ours. We all send you affectionate greetings.

Yours sincerely in Jesus and Mary.

MARTIN.

Origins and First Steps

Surely such a letter reveals a soul of high spiritual lineage! Who today would think of writing in such a strain to a young engaged couple?

*   *   *

Little Louis was only seven and a half when he left Strasburg. He had early known the elation produced by the measured tread of marching soldiers, the delights of the mess and camp fires, the hubbub of the maneuvers. Lulled to sleep by the stories of the Napoleonic epic, brought up amid the sounds of fifes and drums, he was to retain a fondness for travel, an esteem for the military profession, and laid aside his childish uniform with regret.

His parents, whose best-loved child he was, provided carefully for his education. If he does not seem to have had the advantage of secondary schooling at this time, he was sufficiently initiated into the study of French to appreciate good books and, of his own accord, enter upon a course of reading in the classics of the language, a study that would enable him in the future to enrich his conversation with reminiscences culled from his reading and to furnish his library with sound literary taste.

By what miracle was this soldier's son, adventurous by inclination, directed to a completely sedentary profession? Personally, Louis would have preferred a military career, but what harvest of laurels could be gathered, now that "the Other" had died on the rock of Saint Helena? His artistic instinct, which was evident from the sure touch that marked his drawings, attracted him to work of delicate quality. He would have been happy carving precious objects. A sojourn at Rennes initiated him into the delicate mechanism of clock and watchmaking. From family papers, we learn that during the course of the years 1842 and 1843 he lived in the Breton capital with a first cousin of his father's, M. Louis Bohard, who carried on this craft at no. 1, *Rue Bourbon.*

It was during this temporary residence that Louis Martin became enamored of the spirit of Brittany. He loved, like a son of Armorica, the "oak-covered, granite land." The simplicity of manners, the wild poetry of its scenery, the fire of its mystical temperament, enchanted him. He gladly wore the national costume and studied the secrets of its folklore. In his fine, sonorous voice, he would sing *Le Breton exilé* and the hymn to Brittany:

"Hail, mother of the valiant! Glory be to thy diadem!" His mother would reply to his enthusiastic missives by letters in which she gave him wise advice in the phraseology and style dear to the period. On the 23rd of August, when sending him greetings for his feast day, she writes:

"Dear son, you are the subject of my dreams by night and the chief charm of my memories. How often I think of you when my soul, upraised to God, follows my heart's longing, and soars to the foot of His throne! There I pray with all the fervor of my love That God may pour out upon all my children the happiness and peace which we need in this stormy world . . . Be ever humble, my dear son."

In a more sober tone, the father speaks the same language, and prefaces his message with a proud profession of faith: ' May God be ever glorified and loved above all things!"

A curious document survives from this period, which witnesses to Louis' studious activity, running parallel with his technical training. It is a collection of cho-

Origins and First Steps

sen extracts, entirely written out by hand, copied and bound by him, under the title of *Literary Fragments*, into two thick notebooks, of which one is unfortunately mutilated. The work is perfectly set out; the paper of excellent quality, with lines patiently ruled in pencil. It is written in a good hand, with titles and subtitles in round hand, carefully kept margins, pages precisely numbered, references clearly shown and index carefully drawn up. Everything is eloquent in order, neatness and method. The choice of verses and prose passages shows a somewhat disconcerting eclecticism. Moderns elbow ancients, insignificant outpourings mingle with pure masterpieces. We recognise the work of a self-taught student, not yet initiated into literary criticism, who has not had a classical training, and appreciates the loftiness of the themes and the nobility of the thoughts rather than the perfection of the form.

Fénelon, Lamartine, and Chateaubriand seem to enjoy his preferences. He likes the large, highly colored pictures of the author of *Atala*, with their power to evoke past memories. Without offering sacrifice to the *mal du siècle*, he takes pleasure in quoting the epitaph that closes the description of the *Tombeaux champêtres:*

"Here, sheltered at last from this world's storms
He sleeps who long the plaything of their fury lived.
Grief made his heart its home,
And in the forest's deep retreat he needs must dwell."

Some heroic maxims of Duglesclin wander amid these pages of classical literature; some prayers also which, in their emotion and love of nature, closely resemble the upward flights of the *Génie du Christianisme*. On the other hand, it is the solid, candid piety of Louis Martin which bursts out in the last sentence: "Glory be to God

The Story of a Family

Almighty and the Blessed Virgin! May God be glorified by the whole earth!"

Was it to satisfy this need of glorifying God in His works, or was Louis Martin aware of some anxiety concerning his destiny when, in September 1843, he reached the Swiss mountains? A passport, signed by the Prefect of the Ain, dated September 6th, 1843, and which, with its many seals and visas makes a conspicuous ornament for an archive, lets us know that he crossed the Saint Moritz bridge on the 13th, reached Berne ten days later, and arrived at Strasburg by way of Bâle. During this interval, from a traveller he became a pilgrim in order to establish contact for the first time with the celebrated monastery of the Great St. Bernard, whence one day the spark of a religious vocation would be kindled. Among some family records, a small flower, marked with the date 1843, recalls this short visit without divulging the secret that lay behind it. No doubt, the young man wished to recruit his strength anew in an intensely religious atmosphere, before setting out on a new stage of his career.

Clock-making is an art that calls for close application, a long apprenticeship, and repeated experiments in practical workmanship. Profiting by the connections which his family had kept up with Strasburg, Louis Martin betook himself to that city, where a friend of his father's, Aimé Mathey by name, had a business. At his leisure he was able to study that masterpiece of precision and ingenuity, the cathedral clock and, at the same time, to acquire a knowledge of German.

Of this period, which lasted about two years, he retained delightful memories. Forty years later, we find him still talking of them to a friend of his youth and recalling the practical jokes and the happy days spent

14

LOUIS MARTIN
Age 58

MADAME MARTIN
Age 35

together in the city. Together, they tramped in the most picturesque part of beautiful Alsace, and plunged into its clear waters. On one occasion, their bathing nearly ended tragically. M. Mathey's son got out of his depth. Louis, who was an excellent swimmer, went to his assistance promptly but the other, already carried away by the panic of drowning, clung to his neck, seriously hindered his movements, and nearly dragged him to the bottom. But for the rescuer's perfect coolness, two dead bodies would have been recovered.

Welcomed as a son of the house, Louis Martin was to cherish a lasting sense of gratitude towards his hosts. He gladly returned thither and twenty-five years later, when on his way to Paris, he paid a flying visit to the Rhineland. Seeing in a shop window a keyless watch of the latest pattern, he entered to buy it, as an ordinary customer, to be received with open arms by M. Mathey and his family.

He had only one regret, namely to see these folk who, though Catholics, did not practice their religion, "pursuing their earthly way without casting a thought to what awaits them at the end." He had tried so hard to bring about their conversion! Such spiritual indifference struck a chill to one who whilst busy at his work table was now beginning to consider giving himself wholly to God.

But before relating this fresh incident, we must introduce the reader to her whom God destined for Louis Martin as his life's companion.

* * *

Zélie Guérin had also received in her cradle the heritage of religious traditions and military bravery. Her father was born at the very dawn of the Revolution, on July 6th, 1789, at Saint-Martin-l'Aiguillon, in the department of the Orne. He loved to recall among his earliest childish memories the sacrilegious incursions of the Republican troops, the locked and barred church, the masses celebrated in secret, and the thousand and one subterfuges resorted to in order to save the proscribed clergy. His own uncle, the Abbé Guillaume-Marin Guérin, was of their number. They concealed him in the family homestead and the little Isidore was given the duty of guiding him on his long, apostolic journeys over the countryside. One day, when the furious soldiers burst into the house and searched it from garret to cellar, the priest, driven to hide himself in the kneading trough, only escaped with his life thanks to the presence of mind of the small boy who, almost before the lid was closed, sat upon it as though nothing were amiss, spread out his toys, and by his merriment put the searchers off the scent. The confessor of the Faith was not wanting in bold resourcefulness. Taken to task by three rascals, one day when carrying the Viaticum to a cottage, he put down the Blessed Sacrament on a pile of stones, murmuring softly, "My God, take care of Yourself alone, whilst I settle these fellows." Then, hastening towards his attackers, he knocked them down, one after the other, and threw them unceremoniously into a shallow pond, whence they emerged dripping and crestfallen, whilst he took up again his divine Burden and quietly proceeded on his way.

Hunted on all sides, the Abbé Guérin was at last arrested near Écouché, on the 4th Germinal, in the year 4 (1793). Imprisoned at Bicêtre, and deported to the isle of Rhé, where he experienced the horrors of the régime of reprisals reserved for those clergy who had refused the oath to the Civil Constitution, he doubtless

Origins and First Steps

owed his release to the July reaction. We find him parish priest at Boucé, in the Orne, from 1802 to 1835.

As for Isidore Guérin, he found himself conscripted the day before his twentieth birthday, and assigned to the 96th infantry on June 6th, 1809, he had his first experience of fighting at Wagram. Transferred to the Oudinot division, he took part in the hard campaigns of the army in Spain, in the defeat at Vitoria and the battle of Toulouse. It was in virtue of this that he subsequently received the St. Helena medal from Napoleon III. The fall of the Emperor restored him to his family, but he liked the activity, the pageantry and the hard life of the soldier. He joined the foot constabulary, passed into the mounted section in 1823, and after a period in the Company of the Vendée, was attached on February 3rd, 1827, to the Orne—the 2nd legion—then in garrison at Saint Denis-sur-Sarthon.

More than once, his superiors wished to promote him to captain's rank, but he persisted in his refusal. At that period a commission meant more honor than profit, and his slender income would not suffice to cover the expenses involved. The fact was that he had set up a home and had no intention of escaping the responsibility of a young family. On September 5th, 1828, in the humble church of Pré-en-Pail, in Mayenne, he had wedded Louise-Jeanne Macé. She was to bear him three children, Marie-Louise and Zélie, who followed each other within two years, and Isidore who, born ten years later, was to become the spoiled child of the household.[4]

[4] A short account, published by Canon Chantepie, parish priest of *Notre Dame de Laval*, gives us one branch of the genealogical tree of St. Thérèse of the Child Jesus, beginning with Louise-Jeanne Macé and ending with Nouël Macé, who died at Horps in 1715, aged sixty-five. This branch belonged entirely to the Mayenne district.

The Story of a Family

Their home was at Pont, in the village of Gandelain, on the main road from Paris to Brest. Since the hamlet, being near to Saint Denis-sur-Sarthon, was served from that parish—from which it has since been detached—it was in the church of the latter that on Christmas Eve, 1831, the day after her birth, the future mother of Thérèse, Zélie-Marie Guérin, was baptised. In 1931, there were erected, as a single memorial, a statue of the saint and a tablet on the font commemorating the birth into the world of grace of the mother from whom she would one day receive natural life.

*   *   *

A shadow hangs over the child's earliest years. Of delicate constitution, she was nearly always ill between the ages of seven and twelve. She experienced the suffering of incessant headaches, which made her head heavy and stabbed it with pain, and subsequently went through a more serious illness. Did she always find at home all the delicate attentions, born of affection, which her sensitiveness, rendered the keener by suffering, craved?

M. Guérin was the type of good man, proverbially upright, and not wanting in Christian outlook on life. A photograph of him survives and from the curl of the lips, and surly expression of countenance, we may imagine a somewhat obstinate and difficult character. No doubt, the rough life of the *gendarmerie* had developed in him, as a sort of professional deformity, a domineering manner and morose demeanor. Nevertheless, he loved his daughters and was loved by them.

It was from her mother that Zélie had to suffer. Madame Guérin was endowed with the faith that moves mountains but she was wholly lacking in the sense of psychology essential for the training of young people,

18

and this want of the educative sense led her and that notwithstanding real motherly affection—to mishandle seriously an exceptionally sensitive character.

To some extent, the child seems to have been deprived of a mother's caresses. She who would so lovingly cradle, dress and fondly tend her nine live dolls, never knew, like her little friends, the delights of playing at motherhood. Perhaps the reason is to be sought in the spirit of rigid economy that governed the family budget in every department. Perhaps also, a certain rigorism systematically deprived Zélie of those thousand "nothings" which enchant our first years and fill them with poetic dreams. "My childhood and youth," she acknowledged subsequently in a letter to her brother, "were shrouded in sadness; for if our mother spoiled you, to me, as you know, she was too severe. Good as she was, she did not know how to treat me, so that I suffered deeply." [5]

Isidore was more indulgent than was wise. Of lively temperament, very decided, merry and quite ready to be combative, he knew how to win affection and incline his elders to give in to him. They readily forgave him many a piece of mischief and act of naughtiness. Did it not happen on one occasion, when he had been shut up in the cellar, as punishment for some misdemeanor, that he ran the cider onto the ground, and then proclaimed his misdeed at the top of his voice in order to hasten his liberation? On another day, when wandering in the market place, he saw fit to rob the stall of an apple seller. However that time he did make unpleasant acquaintance with the maternal hand and had to restore the fruit without delay. Nevertheless, if the régime of preferential treatment established in his

[5] Letter from Madame Martin to her brother, November 7, 1865.

favor did not alter the deep affection which Zélie always bore him, it continued, no less surely, to create in the home a sort of atmosphere of discomfort which the girl felt cruelly. She sought consolation in the particularly confiding friendship which existed between her and her elder sister, Marie-Louise.

She found help also in those who were chosen to be her teachers. M. Guérin, who took the highest view of his responsibilities, had not hesitated to make great sacrifices in order to assure his children's future. In 1843, seeing his retirement drawing near, after thirty-five years' service, he had sold his property at Saint-Denis and on February 9th he had bought at Alençon, *no. 36*—today *42*—*Rue Saint Blaise*, a comfortable though rather small house, which he proposed to enlarge sooner or later. Thither he moved on September 10th, 1844, when he retired with a pension of 297 francs per annum. Whilst he occupied himself as an amateur with woodwork, his wife opened a modest café for some time. However, it did not pay, Madame Guérin's fondness for sermonising not being calculated to attract or retain customers.

This change from an uninteresting small town to the capital of the department helped to settle the schooling problem for the better. There were several schools in Alençon. When old enough, Isidore attended the Lycée; the two sisters were entrusted as day-boarders to the religious of the Sacred Hearts of the *Picpus Congregation*, who had the convent of Perpetual Adoration. This house had been founded in 1828 by the Reverend Mother Henriette Aymer de la Chevalerie, whose Cause of Beatification has now been begun in Rome. It enjoyed a good reputation in the district and Zélie received a sound education to which the good style of her letters would witness later on. She owns to this to her brother, when playfully recalling her former successes. "I won the first prize for French composition. Out of eleven, I won first place ten times, and I was also placed in the first division of the top class. So judge of the capacity of the others!"[6]

But besides the elements of human learning the girl took away from this convent of teaching nuns the spirit of faith and the thorough religious instruction of which she would give such ample proof when presiding over her own home. At one time, thanks to her contact with this fervent community, she even conceived the hope of consecrating herself to God in the religious life. Providence, which was preparing from afar the cradle of Thérèse, guided Zélie Guérin to Louis Martin by subjecting both to the same preliminary experience of aspiring after complete detachment from the world.

[6] Letter from Mme. Martin to her brother, Nov. 12, 1863.

CHAPTER 2

IN PURSUIT OF AN IDEAL

Louis Martin at the Great St. Bernard—the
watchmaker of the *Rue du Pont Neuf*—
Zélie Guérin, the lacemaker—the
providential meeting.

I T WAS in early autumn of 1845—without our being
able to assign a precise date to the incident—that
Louis Martin resolved to carry out his project of
entering upon a more perfect state of life. He was just
twenty-two, and it was time for him to enter upon either
married life or the service of the altar. He chose the
cloister.

His religious training had been thorough. From
Captain Martin he had learnt to yield himself to God
without reserve, in a complete self-oblation, as becomes
a soldier or, better still, a warrior. His piety had been
deepened and rendered more delicate by as frequent
reception of Holy Communion as the custom of the
time allowed. His faith could not but be strengthened
by his contact with that of the Bretons and Alsatians.
His naturally thoughtful temperament inclined him
towards communing with the Master of the interior
life, who seizes upon the soul as upon a prey, and he
allowed himself to be thus borne away.

Whither should he turn his steps? Having witnessed

the early rise of the Romantic school, Louis had been initiated into the cult of nature. The splendor of a sunset, the sighing of the wind among the forest trees, the roar of the waves moved him to an interior recollection akin to contemplation. This ardent admirer of Chateaubriand and Lamartine was, moreover, a Catholic brought up on the Bible. Sensitive to the beauties of earth, he rose above them in order, Franciscan fashion, to voice the praise of all creation. He longed to fix his retreat in one of those impressive spots where the very landscape raises the mind to God. Let someone but point out to him, in addition, some institute the activities of which, whilst being impregnated with prayer would be capable of satisfying his knightly ardor, his instinct for adventure, and even his taste for risks—and his choice would be made.

Was he informed concerning this journey by his spiritual director or by some tourist who had come down from the mountains? Was he urged on irresistibly by the memory of his expedition two years previously? Whatever it may have been, he believed that he would find his ideal fully realised at the hermitage of the Great St. Bernard. Towering aloft in the chain of the Pennine Alps, some eight thousand feet high, at the head of the pass separating the Swiss Valais from the Val d'Aosta, the hospice of Mount-Joux belongs to the Order of Canons Regular of St. Augustine, established there nine centuries ago by Bernard of Menthon. After singing the praises of God in the heights, in a fairy-like setting, the rescue parties of religious, guided by the scent of their dogs, go through the snow in an average winter temperature of twenty degrees centigrade below freezing-point, to succor travellers who have fallen victims to avalanches or lost their way in the storms.

The Story of a Family

Was not this mingling of the life of the cloister, of prayer which is at the same time poetry, and of heroic charity, just the realisation of Louis Martin's dreams?

So it was that in September 1845, he took up the pilgrim's staff[1] and from Strasburg where, doubtless, he was still living, partly on foot and partly by coach he reached the Swiss frontier. The devout wayfarer was entranced as he passed by the many natural glories so lavishly scattered on his way. The spirit of praise within him was so moved that at times he had to pause and even shed tears of joy. World-weary like Dante, though without having known the troubled existence of the great Florentine, what he came to beg at the monastery gate was *Peace*.

The Prior kindly received this young man, whose expression conveyed something at once fervent and frank. He questioned him concerning the motives which had led him to take this step, inquired about his family and antecedents. Edified by his replies on these heads, he asked him concerning his studies and soon learned that the visitor had not had a classical education. Had Louis Martin hoped to make up this deficiency in the monastery? In any case, he was extremely disappointed when the religious answered that a knowledge of Latin was indispensable for his admission to the community, and suggested that he should return home to complete his studies.

It was with the feelings of an exile that Louis made his way down the mountain side. To the end of his life he was to retain in his heart a regret for the hermitage

[1] On the evidence of the passport, mentioned above, the preface to the Saint's autobiography had assigned the request of Louis Martin to be admitted to the Great St. Bernard to September 1843. The recent discovery of some private papers obliges us to date it two years later, his first visit having been only as a traveller.

and a nostalgia for the silent cell where the religious lives "alone with Him who is alone."

For the moment, he thought it meant only a delay. Returning to Alençon, he placed himself in the hands of the Dean of *Saint Leonard*, M. Jamot, who consented to help him to realise his project. The pages of his account book, meticulously filled in daily, make mention between the 16th of October 1845 and the beginning of January 1847 of frequent purchase of text books and Greek, Latin and French authors. There is evidence that he followed a regular course of study at one-and-a-half francs per lesson with a certain M. Wacquerie. We can count one hundred and twenty lessons, with an interruption—precisely noted down like all the rest—from May 18th to June 23rd, 1846. The pages referring to the first six months of 1847 contain no further mention of fees for coaching or purchases of books. The allusion to the bartering of a Latin-French dictionary suggests, on the contrary, that the studies must have been given up. It was at this time that illness compelled the young man to bid farewell to his dear books and take up less exacting occupations. He saw in this a providential sign and returned to his craft of clock-making.

*   *   *

It was then, doubtless, that in order to complete his apprenticeship, he went to Paris, where he had some relatives and friends: his grandmother, Madame Boureau-Ney, then seventy-four years of age, who lived on an allowance from her family, and his uncle by marriage, Louis-Henri de Lacauve, a retired Staff officer, who usually lived at Versailles, and the son of this latter, Henry de Lacauve, then a cadet at the military school, between whom and Louis Martin there existed a brotherly affection, but who left for Africa on December 14th, 1848.[2]

The sojourn at Paris, which appears to have been prolonged for two or three years, was a strong test of Louis Martin's faith. The Voltairean spirit, which had ushered in the July Monarchy, still flourished in intellectual circles, despite the vigorous counter-offensive of Lacordaire and Montalembert. The ruling classes, obeying Guizot's order, "Get rich!" remained deaf to the murmurs of revolt that were rising from the working men. In vain did Frederic Ozanam raise the alarm. In order to draw attention to the danger to society, and the spiritual and material needs of the proletariat, the upheaval, bloodshed and barricades of the June days of 1848 would be needed. For the moment Paris gave itself up to scepticism and amusement.

Louis Martin came very near to danger. Taking advantage of his natural generosity, some strangers invited him to join a philanthropic club, apparently devoted to works of charity. He inquired more closely concerning them and discovered that the club was in

[2] At twenty-six, the Staff-Colonel Henry de Lacauve had, by an action of conspicuous bravery gained his commission, and been awarded the decoration of a Knight of the Order of St. Louis. He fought in the Royalist army of the Vendée, was taken prisoner by the English on board the privateer *Duguay-Trouin*, of which he had become second Master-at-Arms, and during the Empire remained faithful to the Legitimist cause. He resumed active service at the Restoration, where we find him playing a brilliant part in the Spanish campaign. A series of letters of his remain, in good French style, wherein he inculcates upon his son the cultus of the military virtues and the Catholic Faith. These lessons were not lost. Henry-Charles de Lacauve, in his turn, had a distinguished career, shared in divers African campaigns, was wounded at Saint-Privat, and retired an officer of the Legion of Honor with the rank of Major. The patriotic tradition was nobly perpetuated in the family that gave to the world St. Thérèse of the Child Jesus. A great grand-nephew by marriage of M. Louis Martin, Squadron-Leader Bruneau, after having won the Croix de Guerre at the age of twenty-one, fell gloriously on May 31st, 1940, at the defence of Dunkirk, and was the subject of a highly laudatory mention in despatches.

reality a secret society. His loyal nature was indignant. He cared only for what was open and above board. Only evil works seek for darkness. He firmly refused the acquaintanceship and preserved his freedom.

His distinguished appearance and personal charm exposed him to temptations of another sort which only his robust faith enabled him to surmount. Later on, he mentioned them to his wife in confidence, and the latter profited thereby to put her young brother on his guard, since he also had gone to the capital to study medicine. "I am very anxious about you," she writes. "My husband utters gloomy forebodings daily. He knows Paris, and he tells me you will be exposed to temptations which you will be unable to resist because you are not sufficiently religious. He has told me what he experienced himself, and the courage he needed to emerge victorious from all these struggles. If you only knew what he has been through!" [3]

It may be imagined how joyfully Louis Martin withdrew from such surroundings to breathe once more the healthy air of Normandy. He was now completely master of his craft. He liked the careful attention to detail which it involved, the sense of exactitude, the delicate skill which sets the seal of the artist upon it. He who would gaze entranced at the harmonious beauty of the starry heavens, wherein the omnipotence of the divine Artist is displayed, handled no less lovingly the tiny wheels of a delicate mechanism. His professional conscience drew therefrom a delight which, together with his fondness for beautiful workmanship, make him akin to the proud craftsmen of the middle ages.

A saintly lady in Alençon, Mlle. Félicité Baudouin, who esteemed him very highly, helped him to set up

[3] Letter to her brother, January 1st, 1863.

business in that town. On November 9th, 1850, he became the owner of a house, no. 15 *Rue du Pont Neuf*, and there established his premises as clock and watch-maker, to which he subsequently added a jeweller's shop. It was situated in the parish of *Saint Pierre*, close to the bridge that crosses the Sarthe on the way to Monsort. The district, rather a quiet one, livens up on market days. Even then, there is no feverish business activity, for the old town rarely sheds its tranquil dignity. The house was very large and provided with a small garden. The Martin parents lived there with their son.

He began then the hard-working, orderly and almost monkish life which he was to lead for almost eight years. Tall of stature, of imposing appearance, good-looking with high, open forehead, bright complexion, a fine oval face framed in chestnut hair, and in his brown eyes a light both soft and deep, there was something about him that partook of both the gentleman and the mystic, and which could not fail to make an impression. A young woman, very wealthy and a family friend, had planned to marry him, but he found means to escape the proposal. He intended to keep himself free for God. His workshop had become for him a sort of monastic retreat, where he prolonged intensely the dream so early broken. The minutiae of his craft required close attention and silence. What conditions better calculated to raise his mind to the Most High?

On Sunday, the shop door remained obstinately shut and with his parents Louis attended to his religious duties. By way of recreation, he gladly joined an association of friends belonging to the Alençon middle class, which was familiarly known as the *Vital-Romet Club*, from the name of one of its presidents, and met

In Pursuit of an Ideal

in premises in the *Rue de Mans*, close to the chapel of *Our Lady of Loreto*. In company with the Abbé Hurel, Dean of *Saint Léonard*, he contributed his distinctive characteristics, namely an uncompromising faith and an overflowing charity.

On a certain occasion in a drawing room, whether from frivolity, a desire to appear daring, or some infiltration of the free-thinking spirit, the company tried some experiments in table turning. Louis' presence prevented the seance from degenerating into anything serious. He held that even supposing that all such spiritualistic manifestations did not originate from diabolic intervention, on account of the morbid attraction for the marvellous, they nevertheless all furnished him with an opportunity of intervening, so difficult is it to draw the line between natural phenomena and the activity of the prince of darkness. At first he declined the invitation and only finally consented to be present on condition that he remain a passive spectator. His attitude of disapproval disturbed certain of those present who, alleging the harmlessness of the proceedings, pressed him to join in. He refused absolutely, and began to pray interiorly that the attempt might fail if the evil spirit were to be involved in it. That day, the table remained obstinately steady and some irresponsible members of the party accused "the holy man" of having played the part of a kill-joy, although the more thoughtful wisely took a lesson from the incident.

But although he did not withdraw himself from social gatherings, where his frank gaiety and perfect manners were appreciated by all, Louis Martin preferred long walks. The artist in him delighted in the roads. He made his way to the district of Saint-Cénery, dear to celebrated painters, on beneath the royal trees of the Perseigne forest. Even more readily, turning to sedentary pastimes, he would settle down on the bank of a lake or stream and patiently cast his fishing line.

Angling was his favorite recreation, and none of its secrets were hidden from him. In the seclusion of the Norman undergrowth, in front of calm waters where sometimes the swans would glide by, with his contemplative temperament enjoyed himself to his heart's content. As a child of God, he rejoiced in the trills and songs of the birds, to the accompaniment of the wind sighing in the foliage. He tore himself away only in the evening from nature's symphony, to take to the convent of the Poor Clares of Alençon the abundant catch that testified to his skill. In the season he would also bring back some items of game; a gun licence attests the fact that he was no stranger to the huntsman's exploits.

There came a day when he wished to provide himself with a "retreat" where he could keep his fishing tackle, garden when he wished—even though he had little taste for it—and give himself to the delights of serious reading and thought at leisure. In the neighborhood of the *Sénatorerie*, in the *Rue des Lavoirs*, right in the south of the town, near the spot where the waters of the Sarthe separate into several branches, on April 24th, 1857, he bought the charming property known as the *Pavilion*. It stands beside the road, surrounded by a pretty patch of ground, and consists of a hexagonal tower, containing a ground floor and two stories above, to which access is gained by an outside staircase reaching as far as a terrace at the level of the first floor, and thence by an inside wooden spiral staircase.

Let us enter the little building. The furniture is

In Pursuit of an Ideal

scanty; a few chairs, a table upon which lie some austere spiritual books, their markers showing; in a corner, the fishing lines, a net and a basket; a crucifix, some pious pictures and sentences which the young man had put up himself. "God sees me. Eternity draws nigh and do we think about it! Blessed are they who keep the commandments of the Lord! May God preserve me from His judgements!" There is nothing of the bachelor's snuggery about the place. It is rather the shrine of austerity. A rather worldly lady, who had to visit it one day with M. Martin's eldest daughter, quickly came out. "Oh, Marie, it sends a chill down my spine! Let us go into the garden."

The solitary had for company only a greyhound, which one day, scenting his arrival, climbed to the terrace, and jumped about so much that it fell into the street and broke its legs. The surrounding garden bears the same stamp. Louis sowed some flowers, and later on he planted a walnut tree which grew up beside the fir already there. At the far end, he placed a statue of the Blessed Virgin, given him by Mlle. Baudouin. It was a not inelegant copy of that wrought in silver by Bouchardon for the church of *Saint Sulpice* in Paris and which disappeared during the horrors of the Revolution. This statue, about 36 inches high, but sufficiently heavy to fatigue a strong man, represents Our Lady Immaculate, clad in skillfully carved, clinging robes, the hands outstretched as though scattering graces, was destined to play a highly important part in the history of the Martin family. After having presided at the miracle of Thérèse's cure, it was enthroned triumphantly above the chasse enshrining her relics, under the title of "Our Lady of the Smile."

For the moment—and that was the one anxiety

which he caused his mother—Louis had no thought of founding a family. Labor, prayer, good works, healthy recreation and serious reading amply sufficed to occupy his life. Who knows whether his inner eye was not still gazing upon the snows, the crevasses and the peaks where his ardent courage aspired to seek out the victims of accidents in the mountains? Did he not keep with jealous care the wild flower once gathered on the slope of the Great St. Bernard, which for him symbolised so much?

* * *

Zélie Guérin was to experience a disappointment of a similar kind. Unusually sensitive, her heart might have yielded prematurely to the call of human affection. The home training which she had received, the somewhat suspicious vigilance with which she was surrounded and, still more, the instinct of a nature spontaneously upright and pious, effectively protected her. It was towards God that she directed all her power of loving. Marie-Louise, her intimate friend and confidante, told her of her own dreams of a religious vocation, temporarily hindered by the duty of helping her mother to run the home. Being more free than her sister, Zélie wished to enter religion before her. Her eager temperament inclined her to the active religious life; her gentle sympathy attracted her to the sick and unfortunate. She ambitioned the habit of St. Vincent de Paul.

Thus it came about that, accompanied by her mother, she presented herself at the hospital of Alençon to discuss her intentions. Was there some suggestive reticence in the mother's words and demeanor? Did the health of the aspirant seem too precarious? Or was it

In Pursuit of an Ideal

simply that some supernatural intuition enlightened the Superior concerning God's real designs for the young woman before her? To put it briefly, the interview failed in its object. To Zélie's request for admission, the religious replied without hesitation that such was not the will of God. Faced with such a categorical statement, the girl yielded, though not without sadness. Thenceforth she would limit herself to uttering this ingenuous prayer: "Lord, since, unlike my sister, I am not worthy to be your bride, I will enter the married state in order to fulfil Your holy will. I beg of You to give me many children and to let them all be consecrated to You." Nevertheless, she was to suffer for a long time the nostalgia for the cloister, and many a time in the course of her life men might have imagined her wearing the white *cornette* of the Sisters of Charity— so dearly did she love to serve the lowly.

Thenceforth she had to prepare for the future. The slender means of the retired officer of the gendarmerie would not suffice to provide his younger daughter with a dowry and pay for the education of the youngest of the family who, being destined for one of the learned professions, was about to enter the Lycée. Zélie entrusted this uncertainty about her future life to Our Lady. The answer came to her on December 8th, 1851, and took the form of an interior locution. She was absorbed in some work that was far from calculated to favor any auto-suggestion, when she very distinctly heard the words: "See to the making of Point d'Alençon." The girl took this as an order from on high and forthwith set about carrying it out. During her school days, she had already learnt the first elements of the industry for which the town is noted. In order to master it thoroughly, she entered a lace-making school where she would be methodically initiated into the many secrets of the craft.

It is indeed an art, and one of the most delicate. Napoleon and, still more, Marie-Louise, were astounded when the imperial coach brought them to Alençon in 1811. They admired those craftswomen with their fairy fingers who, all day long, as sings the poet, Vavasseur:

> Still without shuttle's facile aid
> With finger skilled slip thread within the loop
> To clothe the empty net with flowers.

The beginning of the history of the celebrated Point d'Alençon dated back to the Blessed Margaret of Lorraine. This ancestress of Henry IV, the daughter by marriage of the *Gentil Duc* who was the companion of Joan of Arc, was not content with ruling her duchy during twenty years with a wisdom and mildness that earned her the title of "Mother of all charity." Before ending her days as a Poor Clare at Argentan, on November 2nd, 1521, she enriched churches and monasteries with costly treasures, and in particular with priceless embroideries, lovingly worked with her own hands, which make her the legitimate forerunner of our modern lacemakers. Technically, the honors of patron of the craft belong undoubtedly to Colbert who, about the year 1664, sent for thirty expert craftswomen from Venice.

The lace is made in strips of from 15 to 20 centimetres, on vellum on to which the design is perforated, and which is then lined with linen. Very fine linen thread of high quality is used in the making. Once a pattern is finished, the piece of work passes from hand to hand, according to the number of stitches to be included. There are nine of these latter, each of which is a speciality in itself. Each "piece" must then be detached, the useless ends of thread removed and the inevitable breaks repaired and then follows the process of "assembling" them. This a delicate task if ever there was one. It is carried out with almost invisible needles and still finer thread. The incredible variety of the processes, the fine shades of difference in the designs and their arrangement have caused Point d'Alençon to be in demand as an unrivalled trimming for royal robes.

Zélie Guérin quickly mastered this marvel of feminine handiwork. Really wonderful specimens of her work remain, almost as fine as cobwebs. She seems, indeed, to have left the school before the usual time required. Her good looks, her lively intelligence, and the gift of sympathy which she possessed in a high degree, could not pass unnoticed. When she became aware that one of her instructors was assiduously paying her attention, she decided to end the situation and set up on her own account whilst, doubtless, she continued to perfect her training by following one of the many courses of instruction available in the town.

Towards the close of 1853, therefore, she went into business as a "Maker of Point d'Alençon," as she was henceforth styled in the town Directory. That does not mean that she opened a workroom. The lace is a "collective" masterpiece, but the makers do not all work simultaneously as a team. All that is needed is the initiative and diligent direction of a master of the craft, who deals with the customers, assigns the orders, procures everything requisite for each lacemaker to work at home at her speciality, sees that the "pieces" are passed on from one to another, and coordinates and corrects it all so as to assure its final lucrative sale.

The Story of a Family

Alençon is the seat of the industry but all around, in the neighboring districts, at Damigny, Gandelain, Roche-Mabile, the graceful arabesques are sketched out, the fairy-like forms of which are in marked contrast to the rustic environment.

> "In the old wooden houses,
>   The spindles are forsaken,
>   But the needles, pricking pretty fingers, hasten on."[4]

Zélie Guérin established her office in the front room of the house in the *Rue Saint Blaise*. On Thursdays, she remained at the disposal of her employees, distributing, receiving and arranging the work. She usually reserved to herself the repairs, mending the damage which occurred unavoidably in the course of the constant handling and, when necessary, carried out the invisible joining of the pieces, a task that is both the snare and the triumph of the craftswomen. It is no exaggeration to say that she excelled in this delicate process of assembling, which calls for an observant eye, skill and good taste. It was with real pleasure that she devoted herself to it, she who wrote one day, "I am never happier than when sitting at my window assembling my Point d'Alençon." Ere long, the strips of her handiwork were classed among the finest specimens and sold at a high price, thereby assuring her both credit and prosperity.

The strictly commercial side interested her less, which no doubt explains why between 1853 and 1863, she ceased to produce for herself directly and worked for the firm of Pigache. When negotiations were opened with this end in view with the Paris salesmen, Zélie

---

[4] Verse from Gustave Le Vavasseur, quoted by René Jouanne, op. cit.

In Pursuit of an Ideal

Guérin's youth took fright. It was her elder sister who, overcoming her personal repugnance, gallantly offered to replace her. Accompanied by her father, Marie-Louise paid a business visit to the capital. Her arrangements were crowned with success and assured the launching of the enterprise, but on this occasion she caught a chill which was very nearly fatal, if we may judge from this paragraph of a letter, dated March 22nd, 1877, which, shortly before her death, Mme. Martin wrote to her daughter, Pauline:

"I trust that God will do for me what He did for your aunt, for it is twenty-four years now since she was condemned to death. The doctor had told my mother that she could hardly live more than three months. She prayed and made a novena to Our Lady of La Salette, to obtain the grace of dying a nun. The disease never disappeared but she lived twenty-two years longer."

* * *

From this year 1853 the paths of the two sisters were to divide without any change in the friendship and confidence that reigned between them. Marie-Louise or, to call her by the name familiarly given her at home, Élise, was making a determined effort to enter religion. Ever since her childhood, she had with indomitable energy avoided even a shadow of evil. The harping upon the preemptory phrase "that is a sin" had even developed in her a delicacy of conscience which came near to degenerating into servile fear and scrupulosity.

She was taught to read in the Apocalypse. When she went to church with her mother, she thought she was obliged to attend to her missal without raising her eyes, and so she spent High Mass repeating the prayers of the Ordinary over and over again. Her youth was deprived of the freedom to develop that is the outcome of a training predominantly influenced by love.

Two years spent with the religious of Perpetual Adoration had opened to her the prospect of the religious life, and she would have gladly have set out on the quest of perfection. But she had first to finish her work as a second mother to Isidore, her brother. Then in 1853 after her journey to Paris, came the first onset of consumption, of which the traces would always remain. Her moral health was no less shaken. During five or six years, she was assailed by doubts and scruples which contributed in no light degree to shatter her health. They seemed to wither her up. Desirous as she was at that time to embrace the austere Rule of the Poor Clares, she was in addition so imprudent as to shoulder a burden of corporal penances which exhausted her strength. Consequently, about 1856, she had a serious relapse.

Heroically tenacious, she overcame all the obstacles and, free at last from family duties, delivered from her interior trials, and sufficiently recovered physically, on April 7th, 1858, she was able to knock at the door of the Visitation convent at Le Mans, and adopted for herself this all-inclusive watchword: "I have come here to be a saint!" She was age twenty-nine. One last trial—and the worst—awaited her. Informed that the young woman had shown signs of tuberculosis, in the preceding years, the Superior told her that it was impossible for her to remain in the community. Once again, Marie-Louise asked and obtained a miracle. During the few days' respite allowed her, she gave herself so energetically to her work in the linen room, prayed so fervently and tried so earnestly to keep the Rule, that Mother Thérèse-Gonzague de Freslon allowed herself to be softened and admitted the aspirant to her novitiate among the Associate Sisters, who are not bound to keep choir. Madame Guérin, who had hastened from Alençon to take her home, was herself likewise disarmed by such courage. The battle was won.

Zélie had followed all its phases with sisterly anxiety. Not understood by her mother, she had cast herself with a sort of impetuosity into her affection for the elder sister who was so thoughtful and kind, to whom she confided her secrets. In the strict sense of the word, they were inseparable. Twenty years later, when the Visitandine was dead, Mme. recalled these memories in a letter to Pauline: "I could not do without her. I loved her so, that darling sister! One day, shortly before she left for the convent, I was working alone in the garden. I could not remain without her and went to look for her. 'What will you do when I am no longer here,' she asked. I replied that I would go away also. In fact, I did go three months later, but not by the same road." [5]

It was at the time of the distressing separation from her who was in truth the "soul of her soul," that Zélie Guérin suddenly saw the prospect of marriage open up before her. Was she seriously thinking about it, or did she still feel, albeit unawares, the attraction of the nun's veil and the life which it confers? Rather below middle height, with a very pretty face and a very innocent expression, brown hair simply dressed, a long well-shaped nose, black eyes, sparkling with decision, into which now and then there came a shade of melancholy, she was an attractive girl. She was all vivacity, refinement and good nature. Possessed of a lively, cultivated intelligence, very sound practical good sense, a noble

[5] Letter of Mme. Martin, March 4, 1877.

The Story of a Family

character and above all intrepid faith, she was a woman above the ordinary who could not but attract attention.

A lady living in Paris wanted her to come and live with her, and offered to bring her out into society. Zélie smiled at the proposal. She had no intention of throwing herself at anyone. But now it was that Providence intervened and, firstly, by means of a strong-minded woman anxious to marry off her son, a holy man but too much in love with bachelorhood.

Captain Martin's wife did not resign herself to seeing Louis, who would soon be thirty-five, burying himself in the pious solitude of the watchmaker's shop in the *Rue du Pont Neuf* and the Pavilion. She rallied him pleasantly without apparently making any impression. At some professional classes, which she was attending in her free time in order to specialize in one of the stitches of the famous lace, and so add to her domestic resources, she had met Zélie Guérin at close quarters and observed her solid qualities combined with many attractions. Was this not the wife of whom she had dreamed for her son? She made overtures to her, and succeeded in overcoming a restraint that had appeared invincible.

A mysterious incident facilitated the acquaintance. One day, when Zélie Guérin was crossing the bridge of Saint Léonard, she passed a young man whose distinguished appearance, dignified bearing, and reserved manner struck her. At the same moment, an interior voice murmured, "This is he whom I have prepared for you." His identity was soon revealed to her and she came to know him more intimately.

The two young people did not take long to learn to appreciate and become fond of each other. Their mutual moral harmony was so quickly established that

In Pursuit of an Ideal

their private engagement was sealed by a formal, religious betrothal without delay, and three months after their first meeting they were able to be united together before God. On July 13th, 1858, not to take account of the civil marriage which, in their eyes, was merely an odious anomaly, and in reality an empty formality, they plighted their troth in the splendid church of *Notre Dame*. The Abbé Hurel, Dean of Saint Léonard, who had doubtless lent to the project the support of his authority as a spiritual director, received the vows of the pair. The ceremony took place at midnight, as quietly as possible, as though to enjoy only the sacred, Christian aspect of the ceremony; perhaps also because the great works of God are accomplished in the night silence, and this was a work of greatness from which was to be born the Saint of Lisieux.

The house in the *Rue du Pont Neuf* had been hastily arranged to receive the newly married couple. As it was large, and had a private entrance, it was possible for two families to live there quite separately, and that without encroaching upon the space taken up by the workshop and the jewelry business. Louis' parents were installed on the first floor. Zélie transferred her business to her new home. She lived there close to her own people, since only a short section of the main road separated her from the *Rue Saint Blaise.*[6]

[6] Perhaps it may not be out of place, in this sketch of a model French family, to mention that Zélie Guérin brought her husband a dowry of 5000 francs, and 7000 francs saved from her personal earnings. As for Louis Martin, in addition to his two properties, that in the *Rue du Pont Neuf* and the Pavilion, both entirely free of debt and furnished, he possessed his complete professional outfit, and 22,000 francs invested.

CHAPTER 3

A VOCATION TO HOME-MAKING

Virginity in the married state—the call to life—
Marie, Pauline, Léonie and Hélène—Mme.
Martin as a letter-writer—her relations
with her brother, M. Guérin.

THE history of the Martin family opens with a scene reminiscent of the *Golden Legend*, so delicate in its lines that even the telling would seem to rob it of its freshness.

We have seen in what dispositions the young man faced married life. He had liked his bachelor existence, not merely because it allowed him to enjoy his independence and be selfishly wrapped up in himself, but as an ascetic discipline allowing him to lead a life more purely spiritual.

If he had finally yielded to his mother's arguments, in the depths of his being he remained attracted to the ideal of a dedicated, celibate life. The spiritual nobility of which he had caught a glimpse in the soul of his betrothed, led him to cherish the hope of contracting with her one of those purely fraternal unions, after the fashion of the martyr Cecilia and Valerian, or the Franciscan Tertiaries, SS. Elzéar de Sabran and Delphine de Glandève, wherein rising above the pleasures of the senses, the souls alone are united in order to tend

A Vocation to Home-Making

towards God with all the energy of a love divinely purified.

He had closely studied the theological value of such a marriage, as witnesses the following note, copied by his own hand at this time, and found among his private papers: *Concerning the doctrine of the Church on the Sacrament of Matrimony.* The bond which constitutes this Sacrament is independent of its consummation. We have a striking proof of this truth in the case of the Blessed Virgin and St. Joseph who, although they were truly married, observed perpetual continency. These illustrious spouses have since had as imitators several saints who, living as virgins in the married state, have limited themselves to a perfectly pure union of hearts, renouncing by common consent the physical union which was permitted to them. These marriages contained everything essential to their validity; they had even this advantage over the others that they represented more perfectly the chaste and wholly spiritual union between Jesus Christ and His Church.

Did Zélie Guérin share her husband's views? As soon as she had been obliged to give up hope of the religious life, without for all that losing her secret attraction to it, a strong maternal instinct had awakened within her. Her one ambition was to bear many children and, in the precise sense of the words, to "bring them up," that is to uplift their souls to God. Nevertheless, unusual as it may seem to our modern minds, she understood the mystery of life only incompletely. Books written in preparation for married life were then wholly lacking. The problem of sexual initiation did not belong to the order of the day. It was a subject banished from consideration in schools, and was supposed to be forbidden to the curiosity of the young people in the hermetically

43

The Story of a Family

sealed circles of the Catholic middle class. Nor had the austere up-bringing to which the Guérin parents had subjected their daughters been calculated to facilitate the frank confidences necessary for the purpose.

Under these conditions it can be understood—we have known such cases among our grandparents—that it was possible for a crystal-clear soul to enter upon married life without being previously warned of all the duties and responsibilities involved thereby.

The complete revelation made to her on this occasion, aroused in Zélie Guérin a modest terror of the things of sense, and inclined her to correspond with her husband's private aspirations. She forthwith confided this decision to her Visitandine sister. On their wedding day, for everything in this union was "impregnated" with religion, the couple journeyed to Le Mans to recommend themselves to the prayers of her whom they would readily speak of as "the saint." This first visit to the convent, immediately following upon such a psychological shock, revived in Mme. Martin the longing for the religious life, and called forth an outburst of tears which, nineteen years later, in a letter to her daughter, Pauline, she would own to in touching words:

"I can say that I had my cry out, that day. I cried as I had never cried in my life and as I was never to cry again. My poor sister did not know how to comfort me.

"For all that, I was not grieving at seeing her there; on the contrary, I should have liked to have been there also. I compared my life with hers, and my tears flowed more than ever. In short, for a very long while my thoughts were in the Visitation. I often went to see my sister, and there I breathed a peace and calm which I could not describe. When I returned home, I felt so unhappy at being in the world that I yearned to hide myself and share her life.

A Vocation to Home-Making

"You, Pauline, who love your father so much, will think, perhaps, that I was making him unhappy and that I had spoilt our wedding-day for him. But no, he understood me and consoled me as well as he could, for he had similar inclinations. I even think that our mutual affection was increased. We always thought alike, and he was always my comfort and support."[1]

Indeed, the couple daily appreciated more the charm of their supernaturalized love, and, in a letter dated July 27, 1858, the elder sister expressed her satisfaction thereat.

"I am very glad that you are happy, I could not say how grateful I am to the excellent family you have entered for all their kindness to you." And alluding to the secret entrusted to her, she rejoices to see Zélie and him whom she henceforth regarded as her brother, "embrace so perfect a state."

Before concluding this gracious episode, perhaps it will not be without interest to examine the reasons underlying it. No doubt, we may see in it only a dream and a somewhat utopian one, added to an excessive distrust of everything related to the senses, and we may even venture to censure severely the inadequate system of education prevailing at that period. Is it not wiser, considering the wonderful example of sanctity that would spring from such a union, to draw attention to the supernatural fitness of its prelude?*

[1] Letter of Mme. Martin to Pauline, March 4, 1877.

* In order to mark the extent of the absence of egoism in the agreement of M. and Mme. Martin to abstain from conjugal relations, it is sufficient to remember that from the very beginning of their marriage, and for several years thereafter, they took into their home a little five year old boy whose father had just become a widower, and the sole head of a family of eleven children.

The Story of a Family

Marriage has a personal objective: the complete development of the parties concerned, who mutually assist each other to fulfil their destiny in the unity of the family. What more powerful to attain this end than the transition period provided to both by a temporary sojourn on the peaks of continence? There, free from other cares, the husband and wife can fully realise the moral union between them. Marriage has a social objective: the support brought to the national solidarity by those powers, yesterday individualised, today energised tenfold by being welded together. And further, and above all—for this is the essential end which dominates and precedes all the others—the bestowal of life, the rearing of the child, the training of the man. What more effective novitiate in this order than that period of recollection, prayer and sacrifice wherein the mind restrains the instinct and suspends its activity?

The resolve of the Martin couple was not the false start of an idyll cut short. It was a providential preparation for an exceptionally holy progeny. God, who willed for His Son a virgin birth, willed to entrust Thérèse of the Child Jesus only to parents who were capable of understanding the grandeur of virginal life because they had practiced it.

* * *

After ten months of life together, the timely intervention of a confessor led M. and Mme. Martin to modify their views, and carry out God's plans for them after another fashion. Their concept of marriage widened. They came to understand that, in the words of Père Sertillanges, "when kept in its place, the flesh does not offend the spirit; it serves it." The early repugnance gave place to the full comprehension of the

46

ZÉLIE GUÉRIN (Madame Martin), left, before her marriage
LOUISE GUÉRIN, before her entrance into the Convent of the
Visitation at Mans
Their young brother, ISIDORE

LOUIS MARTIN

About
40 years
of age

LITTLE
MARIE HÉLÈNE

Fourth child of
M. and Mme.
Martin

Died February
22, 1870,
at the age of five

A Vocation to Home-Making

work of life, wherein Catholic theology sees not only the means ordained by God for the perpetuation of the human race and the peopling of heaven with chosen souls, but also the concrete symbol of conjugal union, the final expression of the love without reserve that binds husband and wife together, in a word, the outward sign of the perfect gift, each to the other, of his and her whole being, in order to "carry each other to God," as St. Francis de Sales well expresses it.[2]

What above all decided them to end their pious experiment was the longing to give sons and daughters to the Lord. The visions of the cloister and the altar which had charmed their youthful days—could they not live again in a posterity fashioned by their hands for God's service? What a joyful compensation would such a destiny be! The children, the pledge and fruit of their love, the living incarnation and synthesis of their characteristics, in fine the objects of their joint devoted care, would replace them, would consecrate themselves

[2] Thérèse would later know an analogous evolution. "When I was very little," she writes, "I was troubled at having a body. I was not at ease in it; I was ashamed of it." Her sister, Marie had related that at the age of nine, the child could hardly bear to be undressed in order to undergo the hydrotherapic treatment ordered by the doctor. In time, she came to think more nobly of the relations between "Sister soul" and "Brother body." The Révérend Mère Agnès de Jésus—her "little mother"—made the following statement on this subject at the Process of Canonization:

"The Servant of God was very simple, completely ignorant of evil, and afraid of discovering it, as she acknowledges in her autobiography.

"She had entrusted the safeguarding of her purity to the Blessed Virgin and St. Joseph. Later on, she learnt that to the pure all things are pure. When I saw that she was informed concerning the facts of life, I asked her who had given her this knowledge. She replied that, without seeking for it, she had found it out for herself in nature, by watching the flowers and the birds, and she added: "But Our Lady knew everything fully. Did she not ask the Angel on the day of the Annunciation, 'How shall this be done, seeing that I know not man?' It is not the knowledge of things that is evil. Everything that God has made is very good and very noble. For those whom God calls to that state, marriage is a beautiful thing. It is sin which disfigures and defiles it."

to the Most High, and bestow upon the parents' marriage a priestly and religious permanency! It was an inspiring prospect and one calculated to make their Christian hearts thrill. Dare we say that it reconciled them to the many material constraints of married life. Can we not sense this rectifying of their ideas when, at the end of the letter cited above, the mother thus concludes her confidences to Pauline:

"When we had our children, our ideas changed somewhat. Thenceforward we lived only for them; they made all our happiness and we would never have found it save in them. In fact, nothing any longer cost us anything; the world was no longer a burden to us. As for me, my children were my great compensation, so that I wished to have many in order to bring them up for Heaven."

Thenceforth the husband and wife had found their centre of equilibrium and their source of perfection. Gradually the desire to escape to a higher state of life shaded off. It was not *in spite of* marriage, it was *in* and *by* marriage that they were to sanctify themselves, setting at a more accessible level than that formerly envisaged a no less heroic example. They were to prove that married life is not a "cape of storms," off which devotion and desire of holiness founder, but the starting point of an ascent ever more eager because it is made in each other's company. When nature is attuned to the rhythm of grace, far from hindering the flight of the latter, it aids it. It is because original sin has upset the harmony of the divine plan that we have been led to take a gloomy view of the Creator's work. Mutilated and debased when rendered sterile by egoism, married life is ennobled when it is lived as God meant it to be

A Vocation to Home-Making

lived, and the family responsibility is raised to the height of a vocation.

M. and Mme. Martin were now equipped for the great adventure. In the evening, after their busy days, their thoughts, their conversations, their prayers, turned all towards the little being who was about to arrive. The mother lived a more than usually recollected life. Spontaneously, she followed out the line of conduct which Monsignor Gay was then sketching out for Christian matrons.

"Above all, during the months immediately preceding the birth of her child, the mother should keep close to God, of whom the infant she bears within her is the image, the handiwork, the gift and the child. She should be for her offspring, as it were, a temple, a sanctuary, an altar, a tabernacle. In short, her life should be, so to speak, the life of a living sacrament, a sacrament in act, burying herself in the bosom of that God who has so truly instituted it and hallowed it, so that there she may draw that energy, that enlightening, that natural and supernatural beauty which He wills, and wills precisely by her means, to impart to the child she bears, and to be born of her."

The decisive turning in the life of the pair had been taken. They were to experience the joyful stage, marked out by four cradles; the laborious stage: five more births, six deaths, sorrows mingled with smiles; the sorrowful stage: the calvary and the sublime sacrifice of the parents; to end at last with the glorious stage—the day when Thérèse, the last conquest of their love, would carry their name to the altars.

* * *

It was on February 22nd, 1860, that Mme. Martin knew the pride of being a mother. She was still thrilled

The Story of a Family

with it when, seven years later, in order to encourage her sister-in-law, she recalled the event:

"Is not what you confide in me the first hope of becoming a mother? Now the little worries are coming, but amidst all that are mingled many joys. I heard from my father that you had been ill. I went through the same thing when my first little girl was on the way. I thought all was lost and I cried; I who so longed for a child! But that did not prevent the little one from coming in due time and she was a very strong child."[3]

During the anxious waiting period, they had decided, in detail as young parents know how to do, upon the future tradition of the family, the code or, if you like, the Christian ritual which was to govern the births of their children. The Queen of Heaven was to be the patron of the eldest daughter, and Her name should be given, likewise, to all the other children, irrespective of sex, although for convenience they would, of course, be called by the names of their secondary patrons. The first boy was to be placed under the patronage of St. Joseph. Apart from these general rules, out of respect they would choose the name of one of the god-parents. This rule, which was scrupulously observed, compelled M. Martin to sacrifice the name of "Yvonne," which he would have liked to assign to one of his girls, in memory of the Brittany he loved.

The baptism was to take place on the day of the birth or, at the latest, on the following day, conforming to the law of the Church which aims at avoiding the risk of newly born children dying without hope of enjoying the Beatific Vision, and also on account of the

[3] Mme. Martin to her sister-in-law, January 13, 1867.

50

A Vocation to Home-Making

parents' desire to see their children become as soon as possible the children also of God. When M. Martin presented himself with Marie-Louise, his firstborn, at the baptistry of the old church of S. Pierre-de-Monsort, the curate was struck with his radiant expression. "It is the first time that you have seen me here for a baptism," exclaimed the happy father, "but it will not be the last!"

In fact, on the following feast of the Immaculate Conception, remembering the grace obtained nine years previously on that day, the mother turned to Our Lady to ask of her the favor of a second child. On September 7th, 1861, Marie-Pauline made her entry into this world. Then, on June 3rd, 1863, Marie-Léonie was baptised the day after her birth, which happened to be the feast of Corpus Christi. With her began the mother's anxieties. She was a little blonde, with blue eyes and a very frail constitution, a complete contrast to her predecessors, eager little brunettes and full of life.

From the mother's letters, we can judge of the ecstasy of the first kisses, we can see her bending over the little folk, watching their tiny gestures, the first lispings, which the parents discuss endlessly in the evening lamp light. Already we sense the cares of sick-nursing. And what of the sufferings of childbirth? She has no dread of them. If she worried over them for the sake of others, she could say in all truth that "when it was her turn, she did not even think about them."

But to see her little ones stricken with suffering and hanging between life and death, was a torture to which she could never become accustomed. "I was very fortunate," she writes, "when I reared my firstborn. She had such good health. I was too proud of her and

The Story of a Family

God did not will that to last. All the children I had subsequently were difficult to rear and have given me plenty of uneasiness." [4]—"Little Léonie is over nine months old and is not nearly so steady on her feet as Marie was at three months. The poor child is very delicate. She has a sort of chronic whooping cough, happily less violent than that which attacked Pauline, since she would never get over it, and the good God gives her only as much as she can bear." [5]

When Marie-Hélène arrived on October 13th, 1864, her mother was no longer able to enjoy the pleasure—which she had so highly appreciated—of partly nursing her herself. Her health gave out at times and the first symptoms of the malady that was to carry her to her grave were soon to show themselves. She had to put the child out to nurse—a cruelly perplexing problem! In this matter her husband was particularly exacting. In his opinion, when choosing nurses their moral character ought to be the subject of as strict inquiry as the condition of their physical health. Is not the soul of every infant like an extremely sensitive plate, which the first touches mark indelibly for life?

The visits paid to the child counted henceforth among the happy hours when Mme. Martin savored all the delights of her motherhood. Her account to her brother must be read: "Last Tuesday, I went to see my little Hélène. I set off alone at seven in the morning, in rain and wind which accompanied me there and back. Imagine how tired I was on the road, but I was upheld by the thought of soon holding my treasure in my arms. She is a dainty little jewel, enchantingly pretty." [6] "I

---

[4] Mme. Martin to her sister-in-law, May, 1868.
[5] Mme. Martin to her brother, March 5, 1864.
[6] Mme. Martin to her brother, March 5, 1865.

A Vocation to Home-Making

never remember experiencing such a thrill of happiness as when I took her in my arms, and she smiled so charmingly at me that I seemed to be looking at an angel. In short, I cannot describe it. I do not think I have ever yet seen, or will ever see again such an enchanting little girl. Oh, when shall I have the pleasure of possessing her completely? I cannot realise that I have the honor to be the mother of such a delightful little creature! Oh indeed, I do not repent of having married! If you had seen how well the two elder ones looked in their pretty frocks. Everyone admired them and could not help looking at them. And I was radiant, and saying to myself: 'They are mine! I have still two others who are not here, one pretty and one less pretty, whom I love as much as the others, though she will not do me so much credit." [7] The last words refer to Léonie, whose difficult disposition was already making her mother uneasy, but who would yet, in her turn, falsify the prognostic by a splendid reaction and enrich that mother's crown with her virtues.

This profession of faith, which equals in sincerity if not in artistic value the best pages of Victor Hugo, attests how Mme. Martin would have pitied the type of woman who, simply a doll, dreads to lose her appearance, and takes every care of her complexion and her figure. How she would have smiled at the luxury flat, wherein everything gravitates around the only child, who is at one and the same time an idol and a tyrant! One day, when someone told her the surprising news that a woman in the neighborhood had given birth to triplets, she exclaimed, "Oh, what a happy mother! If I had only had twins! But I shall never know that joy." What she loved supremely was the cradle song,

[7] Mme. Martin to her brother, April 28, 1865.

the cry of the newly born child, the awakening of the intelligence of these little mites with its promise; to see them toddling, prattling and frolicking around her, never leaving her alone for a minute, peppering her with questions and smothering her with kisses.

Her correspondence is full of the pretty sayings and simple gestures, which in her eyes are worth more than the discovery of a world. Isidore Guérin used to inquire eagerly about everything concerning Pauline, his goddaughter. A letter of New Year's Day 1863 describes her for him. "You do not know how attractive and caressing she is. She kisses you every few minutes without being told to do so. She blows kisses to 'the good Jesus.' She does not talk yet, but she understands everything. In short, she is a phoenix." Later, we have some amusing items. In the middle of the Good Friday office, the little girl had brandished a small paper doll, dressed as a Visitandine, which had been given her, and had proclaimed at the top of her voice, "this is my aunt!" Then with a photograph of her uncle in her hand, she teased her elder sister over a question of æsthetics. "There is my godfather; he is beautiful, my godfather! He has hair on his head and yours has no hair."[8] Marie's godfather was her grandfather, old M. Guérin. "Would you believe it," writes the happy mother elsewhere, "she is already fond of dress! When she is told that she is going for a walk, she runs quickly to the wardrobe where her prettiest frock is kept, holds up her little face and says, 'Wash me.' I think it all wonderful, as though it were not quite natural . . ."[9]

For this woman, who never spared herself in her life, motherhood was not a burden to be dreaded or a last

[8] Mme. Martin to her brother, January 12, 1865.
[9] Mme. Martin to her brother, April 5, 1863.

A Vocation to Home-Making

shift to be endured. It was a renewal, a development, a transfiguration. The woman's masterpiece is the child.

* * *

On this subject, Mme. Martin has left us something better than a learned work, namely a human document; the admirable correspondence wherein she sets down, day by day, her impressions, her plans and her dreams. There are about two hundred letters, which filial affection has carefully collected and which range from January 1863 to August 16th, 1877. The family spirit alone has dictated them. She lived at a distance from Isidore Guérin, who was kept first at Paris by his studies, and then at Lisieux by his chemist's business; from "the saint of Mans," shut up in her convent, and later from Marie and Pauline, who became boarders at the Visitation. She must needs send them "some sparks from the hearth." The father being, like men in general, very lazy when it came to writing letters—his wife would occasionally reprimand him for it, but in vain—the mother took up her pen. This explains why throughout this period her personality will appear conspicuously in our account, rather relegating to the second place the no less fruitful activity of M. Martin and his all-important part in the direction of the household.

There are blanks in the collection of letters. We have lost those written to prepare Marie for her first Communion, those concerning the death of little Marie-Joseph-Louis, and finally—and this is the most regrettable of the disappearances—all the correspondence addressed to Zélie's elder sister.

As has been stated, thanks to her heroic courage, Marie-Louise Guérin—Élise, as she was called for short —had obtained her admission to her novitiate. On

February 24, 1859, she had received the religious habit with the name of Sister Marie Dosithée. She had made her profession on March 12, 1860, after which, during the following six years, she fulfilled the duties of Assistant Novice Mistress with thoroughness and devotion. In the convent as in the world she continued to be for her younger sister more than a sister—a friend. Zélie confided in her in all simplicity. With the years, their intimacy was to reach the highest level. In essence it was wholly spiritual if we may judge of it from this allusion which, almost playfully, in a tone half serious half teasing, slips into a note from Mme. Martin to her brother.

"I have no more news to give you. However if you saw the letter I have written to my sister at Mans, you would be jealous; there are five pages. But I say things to her which I do not tell you. We talk to each other of a mysterious, angelic world above the mire of this earth."[10]

Alas! the Visitandine never temporized with a sacrifice once contemplated. She must have put the precious collection into the fire, for not a trace of it has been found. We find it hard not to deplore a too radical detachment which has deprived us of an unique source of information with respect to the mother of Thérèse.

Notwithstanding these lacunæ, Mme. Martin's correspondence is a treasury of which it is difficult to estimate the value. We are not discussing its literary merit. Written hastily, all at a stretch, without erasures, by a woman worn out with fatigue at the end of weeks of crushing work, these letters make no pretensions. They

[10] Mme. Martin to her brother, March 5, 1865.

do not aim at being works of art, yet even from this standpoint they do not lack a certain merit. Often marked by really happy expressions, there is movement, fire, life in them. Here and there, they foreshadow those of the saint of Carmel, with her flowing style, her gift of imagery, the elegant precision and supernatural sadness wherewith she sings the lament of the soul in exile on earth.

The mother's letters owe their value to something else: to the freshness and delicacy of their anecdotes, the charming spontaneity and artless frankness, their tone of unaffected tenderness and eager sensitiveness; in a word, to the kind of peculiarly feminine facility for clothing the concrete happenings of daily family life with the finest feelings. The Christian mother stands portrayed in them, with all her nobility, lovable, lively, practical, indefatigable; an enemy to dilettantism and complication, humbly acknowledging her impatiences and fears; her feet firmly planted on the ground and her inward eye fixed upon God. She is a woman of faith without exaggeration, fervent but free from illuminism, above all good, intensely loving yet, withal, never allowing her love to degenerate into weakness. Her spirit of faith underlies everything yet never intervenes openly save with perfect discretion, as a sheet of water awaits an appropriate movement of the ground to well up and gush forth. If there are times when she has to give Isidore a lecture, she does so expertly and without sickly, affected terms. We find nothing of the sanctimonious unction which renders the letters of pious humbugs so intolerable. There is nothing of that desire to give edification which, to quote the neat phrase of St. Thérèse the Great, makes some correspondences

into an exchange of false coin. Already it is the Autobiography of the saint of Lisieux, or better still, *the
picture of a home*.

* * *

Perhaps her letters to her brother are the most characteristic of Mme. Martin's style. For him, Zélie was
the loved sister with whom he was ever ready to joke
and argue. Between them there reigned the healthiest
of friendships and an absolute frankness. They liked to
exchange home truths, and only loved each other the
better after the curtain lecture. Therein lies the charm
of a correspondence which for its freshness and fraternal
affection might be compared with the letters of Louis
Veuillot to his sister, Élise.

When, on becoming a nun, the elder sister was obliged
to curtail her correspondence with her family, the
younger claimed the right to admonish Isidore the least
bit in the world. He had plenty of need of it. His heart
was generous enough, but his religion quite superficial.
He was thoughtless and still a schoolboy. He liked
company and his lively character soon made him somewhat of a social success. His medical studies kept him
in the sceptical and pleasure loving circles of Paris,
which were not without their dangers for a youth of
scarcely twenty-two. On January 1st, 1863, Mme.
Martin sends him a message that sounds a note of
alarm.

"I wish you a happy New Year. I heartily wish you success in your undertakings, and I am sure you will do well if
you wish. It only depends upon yourself. God protects all
those who trust in Him. Not one has ever been forsaken.

"When I think of what this good God, in whom I have
put all my trust, and into whose hands I have resigned the

A Vocation to Home-Making

care of my affairs, has done for me and for my husband, I cannot doubt that His divine providence watches over His children with especial care."

After having instanced the experience of her husband, who had come through like dangers, she concludes with this urgent advice: "I beg of you, dear Isidore, to do as he did; pray, and you will not let yourself be carried along with the stream. If once you give in, you will be lost. It is only the first step that costs, on the way of evil as on that of good. After that, you will be borne along by the current.

"If you would only consent to do one thing I am going to ask of you, and which you may well give me for a New Year's gift, I should be happier than if you sent me all Paris. Here it is: You live close to *Our Lady of Victories*. Very well! Go in, just once a day, to say an *Ave Maria* to her. You will see that she will protect you in a quite particular way, that she will make you succeed in this world and give you an eternity of happiness hereafter. What I am saying to you is not just an exaggerated and unfounded pious statement on my part. I have good reason to trust in Our Lady. I have received graces from her of which I alone know.

"You know well that life is not long. We shall soon be at the end, you and I, and we shall be glad to have so lived as not to render our last hour too bitter.

"Now if you are not right-minded, you will laugh at me; if you are, you will admit that I am right."

Isidore Guérin was not bad at heart. Perhaps he joked a little about the kill-joy eloquence of his preacher, but he accepted her exhortations no less gracefully. With still greater pleasure, he received the "potted goose and jam," which tempered the frankness of the scolding. Since his mother's death, it was Zélie who

59

supplied him with all sorts of dainties and indulgences. In return, at each calling to order he went to *Notre-Dame des Victoires* to put up a candle for her.

His examination successes were greeted at Alençon with tears of joy and Mme. Martin, who had mobilised the prayers of the Poor Clares on his behalf, claimed her share in the triumph. A family feast was held in his honor. They longed for the happy graduate to return. "Come soon, if you can, as you say you intend to do. We shall enjoy ourselves together and we shall argue a little, as usual, but that will be entertaining. It is a little pastime." [11]

Nor did Isidore fail to take it into his head to marry a girl whose qualities were superficial rather than solid, and who was, moreover, indifferent to his advances. An item of another sort in the Alençon chronicle furnished the opportunity to point a moral and remind him how fragile is human happiness. We quote it at length. The specimen will enable the reader to appreciate the solid faith and ready pen of the writer:

"I do not know whether you knew M. Ch. who kept the large mill and married the sister of Mme. L. Well, he and his wife were having a very fine house built, just opposite the *Renaissance* café. They were delighting in this house in advance, they were to move in on St. John's day and not move out until they died. The wife, in particular, was so overjoyed at the prospect of living there that she was telling everybody, 'Oh, I am so happy about it! I have nothing left to wish for. I have health, means, and can have all I want, and have no children to worry me. In fact, I don't know anyone better off than I.'

"I have always heard say, 'Woe and triple woe to such as speak like that,' and, my dear, I am so convinced of the

[11] Mme. Martin to her brother, Jan. 17, 1864.

truth of the saying that at certain times of my life, when I could testify that I was happy I could not think about it without trembling, for it is certain, and verified by experience, that happiness is not to be found on this earth. No, it is a bad sign when all goes prosperously, and happiness is not to be found here below. God, in His wisdom, has willed it so, to make us remember that earth is not our fatherland.

"But to return to my story. About six o'clock on Saturday evening, M. and Mme. Ch. went to visit their grand home and spend the evening with their relatives at the *Renaissance*. About half-past-eight, the husband said to his wife, 'I have a letter to post, and it is already late. Come with me.' They set off together and on returning said, 'To save time, let us take a short cut by crossing the garden.' Their garden bordered on this spot, and abutted just in front of the café where they were awaited. But at the bottom of the garden a ditch was being made and it had to be crossed on planks. As it was impossible to see clearly, the husband stepped too near the edge and fell into the ditch; the wife fell in after him and in her fall dragged down a stone which killed her husband instantaneously. She called for help and her cries were heard. She was seriously injured, was carried to her sister's home and expired ten minutes later.

"About half-past-nine, I heard the steps of many people outside our house and loud talking. I looked out and the two bodies were being carried past on stretchers. There you have the lamentable story of this so-happy couple."[12]

The gruesome picture with which the account closes did not have the effect of correcting Isidore's frivolous thought. He still dreamt of a brilliant marriage. Mme. Martin would have liked him to have been a priest, and would gladly have sacrificed all her share of the family heritage for that end, but she had to admit that her desire was chimerical. "That will never be. In fact

[12] Mme. Martin to her brother, March, 1864.

The Story of a Family

miracles as great have been worked, but none greater!"
As for the alliance of which he was caressing the idea,
it was playing for a high stake. The sister was thoroughly angry about it, and it furnished her with the
opportunity of sketching the portrait of the ideal wife,
in which, all unknowingly, she describes herself, feature
for feature.

"You are still thinking about Mlle. X, it seems. I think
you are crazy; I am persuaded of it! You will come to grief,
either over her or over someone else, for the only considerations that weigh with you are futile ones: beauty and money.
You do not trouble yourself about the qualities that make
a husband's happiness or the defects that cause his sorrow
and ruin. As you know, all that glitters is not gold. The
principal thing is to seek out a really home-making woman,
who is not afraid of soiling her hands with work and cares
for dress only as much as it must be cared for; who knows
how to train her children to labor and piety. Such a woman
would frighten you; she would not be brilliant enough in the
eyes of the world; but sensible men would love her better
with nothing than another with a dowry of 50,000 francs,
who lacks the qualities I have mentioned. However, we
shall speak of that later."[13]

No doubt the lecture would have been in vain, had
not Providence intervened by a timely diversion. In
1865, to the great disappointment of his family, Isidore
suddenly interrupted his medical studies, and decided
to set up as a chemist. He arranged to take over the
Fournet premises at Lisieux. At first his sister was
sorry. She would have liked to have him close to her at
Alençon, or else at Mans, near the "holy nun." A distance of a hundred and seventy miles was an insur-

[13] Mme. Martin to her brother, July 14, 1864.

mountable obstacle to one who was overwhelmed with business orders and had four children on her hands. "Then I must say good-bye for good. We shall hardly see each other again, save in the next world. I shall never in my poor life, which I do not think will be very long, have time to go and see you . . . I shall look at your photograph, which is very poor consolation . . . However that must not make you take the wrong road. You must settle where you have reason to think you can build up a good business . . ." [14]

The matter solved itself so perfectly that the supernatural part therein was evident. At one and the same time, Isidore Guérin found both a business and a wife. On April 22nd, 1866, he settled at Lisieux in very large premises at the corner of the *Place Saint Pierre* and the *Grande Rue*—known today as *Place Thiers* and *Rue Henry Chéron*—in a thoroughfare where—as an authentic list testifies—ever since 1550 apothecaries and chemists have succeeded one another in an unbroken line.[15] On September 11th, 1866, he married the daughter of the house, Céline Fournet, who was related to the best families in the neighborhood and, in addition to great sweetness and piety, possessed a surprising maturity of judgement and a moral balance that enhanced the charm of her nineteen years. From the outset she acquired a decisive influence over her husband, helped him to develop and discipline the as yet unexplored resources of his rich nature, and contributed in no small degree to make of him the exemplary Catholic and active worker who was to play a leading part at Lisieux.

[14] Mme. Martin to her brother, Nov. 7, 1865.

[15] The Guérin pharmacy has unfortunately disappeared in the course of the bombardments of 1944, which destroyed whole districts of Lisieux.

The Story of a Family

Kept at home by the imminent arrival of a fifth child, Mme. Martin could not attend the wedding. She sought compensation in arranging an enthusiastic reception for the newly married couple. The qualities of her young sister-in-law won her heart at once, and she was never tired of eulogising her. Henceforth Isidore was in good hands. She would have no further need to admonish him. At the very most, she would good humorously launch a shaft to tease him, and so as not to lose the old customs. For the moment she had but one thought; to extend to the new home the warm friendship that united her to her brother. It is in this tone that she writes to him on November 18th, 1866:

"It hurts me that you should still be thinking about the little trumpery quarrels we have had together. All that is nothing, and I have forgotten it long ago. I know you of old, and I know the goodness of your heart and that you love me. If I needed you, I am sure that you would not fail me. Our friendship is sincere; it does not consist in pretty speeches, it is true, but it is not less solid and built upon a rock. Neither time nor man, nor even death will ever destroy it.

"Marriage must not set a distance between our hearts, and I am quite convinced that your affection for me is still the same.

"As for mine for you, it is doubled. I still love you very much and my little sister-in-law as much as you. You do not know how happy I am to think that you have chosen so well. Before your marriage, as I often told you, I was very anxious about your future; now I think your happiness is assured. As my dear sister at Mans says so often, I think you were always the lucky one, and that God has never ceased to protect you visibly."

Between the two families the bonds were to be drawn

A Vocation to Home-Making

ever closer. A regular correspondence was established which brought them together and made to live again, on both sides, the thousand scenes of common life. Those pages, wherein will pass, as it were, a film of home life, will constitute an unequalled source of information for the following chapters.

CHAPTER 4

THE GREATNESS OF FAMILY LIFE
AND ITS SERVICE

Professional work—first symptoms of Mme.
Martin's illness—birth and death of the two
sons—death of M. Guérin the elder—
illness of the Visitandine—birth of
Céline and death of Hélène.

T HOSE who are not afraid of cradles must be
fond of work. To face conjugal duties cheerfully
means making up one's mind to many cares, long
busy days in an age when all the conditions of social
life are envisaged and arranged according to the nig-
gardly measure of the individual. With a heedlessness
which, to such as are prepared to reflect upon it seriously is terrifying, "the eternal France" of the poets
and of official speeches settled down comfortably to a
policy of reducing the birth rate as though she had re-
nounced the right to perpetuate herself. In such an
atmosphere, to accept a large family meant a call to
heroism.

M. and Mme. Martin did not shrink from this prospect. To tell the truth, if the difficulty existed, it did
not constitute a problem for them. They had not read
Malthus. Ogino was not yet talked about. For a time
they had been able to experience the greatness of a

The Greatness of Family Life

union sanctified by voluntary continence. The idea never occurred to them to defraud nature or meddle with the divine plan. The children were born; they welcomed them as a blessing from heaven. Then, in view of the charge entrusted to them, they took measures to feed, clothe, educate and dower them. God, who imposed the duty, would provide the means to fulfil it.

In the meantime, they labored unceasingly. The jewelry business attracted more customers than ever. Sensible people liked this courteous craftsman, whose probity was a byword, who would not desecrate the Sunday for a fortune. In other jewellers' shops, Sunday was the busiest day, when business was in full swing. The country folk came into Alençon to do their shopping, prepare for weddings and buy presents. They readily entered the large knife-grinder's shop in the *Rue du Pont Neuf,* and then turned instinctively towards the watchmaker's just opposite. There they found the door shut. It was in vain that they showed impatience; the order was inviolable. They might go elsewhere, if they liked, to buy trinkets, watches and gems; here they were answered in the words of Joan of Arc, slightly modified: "It is the Lord's Day; God *only* must be served."

M. Martin's friends thought his conduct exaggerated. One does not defy the laws of competition to such a degree as that! His house had a private entrance. Let the good man have a side door put into the passage, and open it quietly for special customers; he would thus serve his interests and save appearances at the same time. He replied unceremoniously that he would rather lose some good custom and draw down the protection of God upon his family. His confessor—no doubt approached by some intimate friend, impressed by the arguments put forward—urged in his turn that the shop should not be shut, at least in the morning. He had no more success than the rest and could not but admire this intransigent fidelity to the third Commandment.

On her part, Mme. Martin steadily carried on her lacemaking business. In her case, as in that of her workers, who brought their "pieces" every Thursday, it was a domestic industry, perfectly compatible with family duties. Otherwise, she would not have undertaken it, for she held that a mother's place is always in the home, and that if the mother bird flies off there is no longer either nest or nestlings.

The cooperation of M. Martin, notably after the year 1863, when his wife seems to have begun again to work on her own account, quickly enabled her to extend her connections. He did not like writing business letters, but he willingly took over the book-keeping. He frequently went to Paris, where he arranged with the salesmen, bought the working materials, took orders, and saw to the delivery of specially expensive goods. His thoughtful tastes had not destroyed his capabilities as a practical business man, and his successes astonished his wife. The artist in him had quickly appreciated the lace. The skill and practice required in this work made it not so far removed from that of clock-making. There also, the worker is dealing with exquisitely tiny things. He busied himself in choosing patterns and drawing designs. In his leisure moments, he reserved for himself the task of "pricking," which consists of perforating the vellum according to the pattern, the former being first tinted green in order to lessen the fatigue for the eyes. The actual pricking is done on a pillow, with a specially mounted needle which enables the worker to perforate

The Greatness of Family Life

the vellum without tearing it, and requires a keen eye and sure hand. It may be seen that it was not unreasonable that the commercial notepaper should bear the heading: "Louis Martin, Maker of Point d'Alençon."

Nevertheless, his wife bore the leading part. In the dead season, she worried about her workers. When orders poured in—and with such luxury trades, it is always a question of urgently required orders—she sat up late until she lost count of the nights. "It is this wretched Point d'Alençon that makes my life difficult," she sighs. "When I have too many orders, I am a slave, and it is the worst kind of slavery. When business is less good, and I see myself liable for twenty thousand francs, on my own account, and obliged to send workers whom I have had such difficulty in finding to other firms, I have some cause to worry and even to have nightmares! But what is one to do? I must make up my mind to it and do my part as well as possible."[1]

M. Martin took it still more philosophically. His sole concern was to keep out of debt, and pay ready money. He considered it a crime against society to delay in paying, to the detriment of the workers and tradespeople, whose credit is limited, and that such practices led to ruin. At a later day, his daughter testified that he had often quoted and had taken as a motto, the words addressed by the elder Tobias to his son: *If any man hath done any work for thee, immediately pay him his hire: and let not the wages of thy hired servant stay with thee at all.*[2] In support of his contention he used to relate the lamentable story of a dressmaker who was entirely

[1] Letter of Mme. Martin to her brother, Nov. 7, 1865.
[2] Tob. IV, 15.

dependent upon her daily labor. She was a widow who was finding it difficult to bring up her four children, the youngest of whom was only two years old. Day and night, she plied her needle, like the shirt maker of the well-known English *Song of the Shirt* who was making her own shroud. Unfortunately, the fine ladies for whom she sewed, whether from thoughtlessness or bad management, put off paying their bills indefinitely. In vain she knocked at their doors. They turned her away; they put her off. There came a day when her resources reached an end and she was reduced to dire poverty. To the last she sacrificed herself for her little ones, and finally died of consumption, the victim of her debtors.

M. Martin's voice used to tremble with anger when he told this true story. His upright nature revolted at it. Thus he insisted upon always paying on the spot in order, as he said, not to retain unjustly a sum due or a salary earned, and not to expose himself to inadvertently living beyond his means.

Mme. Martin's relations with her employees were marked by the same social sense. On Sundays she would visit any who were sick and provide for their needs. The couple rivalled each other in transfiguring the monotonous daily round into a divine work through the supernatural spirit which they brought to it. The daily Mass taught them to refer all the duties of their state to God and transform them into real prayer or, as someone has boldly said, "into an eighth sacrament."

That traveller from a northern land had grasped this by intuition when, on his return from Alençon, he said to his daughter: "Here is a watch for you which I bought from a Mr. Martin, who made a great impression upon me. He is a saint!" The watch in question—

The Greatness of Family Life

it is to a missionary of a religious order that we owe this striking story—was to prove exceptionally long lived, for it owed its destruction to the bombardment of Merville in 1917.

This rectitude, this professional conscientiousness, brought prosperity to the household. These Catholics did not care for it for its own sake, they who liked to quote the words of the *Imitation:* "A man's happiness does not consist in having an abundance of temporal goods; moderation is sufficient for him." They saw therein only a means of assuring to their children a thorough education. A fortune slowly accumulated by labor, not liable to the danger of suddenly melting away, was less liable to tempt the possessor to increase it easily by speculation. At that period of financial stability, it was possible, once the yearly budget was balanced, to invest the surplus in safe family concerns and secure a return which guaranteed security in old age. The part assigned to the poor, to works of charity, God's portion, was entered into the account book in large figures. The spirit of economy and thrift, as may be seen ran parallel with that of the most liberal generosity.

*   *   *

Side by side with the record of work there now begins that of sorrow. In May, 1864, we find the mother writing to her brother: "Little Léonie is not thriving; she does not seem to want to walk. She is extremely small and thin, yet she is not ill; just very feeble and undersized. She just had measles and has been very ill, even having violent convulsions." The symptoms of ill-health increased: continual palpitations, intestinal inflammation. Then came running eczema which spread all over her body and reduced her to a pitiable condi-

71

tion. During sixteen months, the child hovered between life and death.

To obtain her recovery the parents moved heaven and earth. They pressed into the service M. Guérin's medical knowledge—not his prayers, for at this period Mme. Martin could still write to him mischievously that she "would hardly have faith in his relics!" They cried out to God when the little one seemed doomed: "If she is to become a saint some day, cure her!" The father, one of whose favorite hobbies was long walks, who loved to make his way through the beautiful country roads of France like a medieval traveller, revelling in healthy exercise, wide spaces and prayer, undertook a pilgrimage on foot to the shrine of Our Lady of Séez. Help came from Mans in the shape of a novena to the seer of Paray-le-Monial, then recently beatified. And at the end of the nine days—thanks be to the Blessed Margaret-Mary and Sister Marie Dosithée!—Léonie, who had hitherto been unable to stand on her feet, was "running about like a little rabbit" and "incredibly agile."

It was the mother's health that now caused uneasiness. On April 23, 1865, she confides this to her brother in her usual simplicity and courage.

"You know that when I was a girl I received a blow in the breast, through striking the corner of a table. No notice was taken of it then, but I have now a glandular swelling in the breast which makes me anxious, especially since it has begun to be a little painful. However, it does not hurt when I touch it, although every day, and frequently during the day, I feel a numbness. I can scarcely describe it, but what is certain is that it is worrying me. What can I do? I am rather perplexed. It is not that I would shrink from an operation. On the contrary, I am quite ready to undergo it, but I have not full confidence in the doctors here. I should like to profit by your stay in Paris, for you could help me so much under the circumstances. There is only one thing that prevents me; how would my husband manage during that time?"

What was the reply of him who in these matters carried authority in the family? From the tone of subsequent letters we gather that M. Martin, anxious himself, sought advice, and was anxious to see his brother-in-law soon in order to consult him as to the best treatment. Then silence falls, until the fatal development of the mischief eleven years later. Why this procrastination? What arguments were used to dismiss the idea of an operation? We can only conjecture. No doubt the surgery of that day produced only precarious and disappointing results. Sometimes it was perilous, and in many cases very painful. Doctors had not yet found in X rays an instrument capable of completing the work of the scalpel by methodical healing of the hidden tissues. In short, they hesitated, waited, perhaps made use of some external remedy at the time and let the vital moment pass by.

Doubtless, a family mourning helped to divert attention from the matter. At the time that Mme. Martin noticed the warning signs of the terrible malady that was to cause her death, her father-in-law quietly expired in the flat reserved for him in the house in the *Rue du Pont Neuf*. Robust as an old oak, the Captain carried the burden of his eighty-eight years lightly, edifying the whole town by the dignified bearing of his patriarchal figure, as by his charitable zeal and piety. In April, 1865, he was suddenly struck down with paralysis and the doctor gave him a fortnight to live. The last stage was prolonged for ten weeks during which the old man, half paralyzed, showed an astounding lucidity and an admirable spirit of faith.

On June 27, 1865, Mme. Martin informed her brother of the death:

"My father-in-law died yesterday at 1 p.m. He had received the sacraments last Thursday. He had a holy death and died as he had lived. I should never have believed it could have affected me so much. I am overwhelmed.

"My poor mother-in-law spent her nights nursing him during two and a half months, refusing to have anyone to help her. It was she who prepared him for death and watched him day and night. Indeed, she possesses extraordinary courage and very fine qualities.

"I own to you that I am terrified of death. I have just been to see my father-in-law. His arms are so stiff and his face so cold! And to think that I shall see my loved ones like that, or that they will see me!

"If you are used to looking upon death, I have never seen it at such close quarters."

Did the writer think as she wrote these lines that she, more than any other, would have to become familiar with "that to which no man willingly opens his door," as Dante said? Six times, between 1865 and 1870 she would have to stand over a grave.

* * *

For the moment, it was to another life that her thoughts turned. Every evening, at her bidding, the little girls folded their hands to ask St. Joseph for a little brother, who should one day offer the Holy Sacrifice and go to far off lands to convert the heathen. The good Saint let himself be won over and gave his name to the newly born child. On September 20, 1866, Marie, Pauline, Léonie and Hélène welcomed with cries of rapture the arrival of Marie-Joseph-Louis.

The Greatness of Family Life

The mother could not contain herself for joy and communicated her enthusiasm to M. Guérin with charming simplicity.

"Oh, it is a lovely little boy; so big and strong. I could not wish for a finer child and, excepting Marie, I never had one born so easily. If you knew how I love him! My darling little Joseph! I think my fortune is made."[3]

To her husband, who shared her pride and her hopes, she said with maternal satisfaction, "Look how beautifully his hands are formed. Won't it be lovely when he goes to the altar or preaches!" Already she saw herself making a grand alb, with Point d'Alençon for the ordination day, which should be a masterpiece worthy of the occasion.

Alas! the rosy prospect was soon to vanish. She was obliged to put the child out to nurse with a good countrywoman of Semallé, Mme. Taillé, known as "little Rose," a few kilometres distant from Alençon. On New Year's Day, he was brought home for a few hours, to be caressed by the family and the mother, who had never had any dolls, amused herself delightedly with him.

"As a New Year gift, I dressed him like a little prince. If you knew how nice he looked, and how he laughed! My husband said I treated him like a wooden statue of a saint! I exhibited him, it is true, like a curiosity. But, oh the emptiness of this world's joys! Next day, at 3 a.m. we heard a loud knock at the door. We got up to open it, and someone said, 'Come quickly. Your little boy is very ill. They are afraid he will die.' You can imagine that I did not take long to dress, and there I was on the way to the country on an intensely cold night, in spite of snow and a slippery frost.

[3] Mme. Martin to her brother, Nov. 18, 1866.

75

I did not ask my husband to come with me, for I was not frightened and would have crossed a forest alone, but he would not let me go without him."[4]

It was a case of erysipelas and the danger was very soon averted. Nevertheless, the child soon began to waste away. On February 14, 1867, under circumstances of which we know nothing, for there are lacunæ in the correspondence at this date, Mme. Martin experienced her first bereavement as a mother. Crushed with sorrow, she shared the supernatural resignation of her husband, whose strength and serenity never forsook him even amidst the most tragic trials.

On the following day, these consoling lines left the Visitation convent:

"Dear little sister. I received your telegram yesterday evening, at half-past five. Our little angel was then already in Heaven. How shall I comfort you, dear? I greatly need comfort myself. I am all shaking but, for all that, quite resigned to God's will. The Lord gave and the Lord hath taken away; blessed be the name of the Lord! Whilst I was praying to Our Lord this morning, at Holy Communion, to leave us the poor little one, whom we wished to bring up only for His glory and the salvation of souls, I seemed to hear interiorly this answer: that He wished to have the first fruits, and would give you another child, later on, who would be such as we desire."

These sterling Catholics were capable of understanding such language. They would accustom themselves to live as a matter of course with their departed, whom they hailed as "the real living." When Hélène was suffering from an attack of otitis which would not yield

[4] Mme. Martin to her sister-in-law, Jan. 13, 1867.

The Greatness of Family Life

to the doctor's treatment, the mother sought a remedy from another source.

"The inspiration came to me," she writes, "to turn to my little Joseph, who had died five weeks previously. So I took the child, and made her say a prayer to her little brother. The next morning, the ear was perfectly healed, the discharge had stopped all at once, and the little one has not felt any pain since. I have obtained several other graces also, but less obvious than this one."[5]

What she longed for above all was "her priest," "her missionary." To this end she turned to St. Joseph and made a novena which ended on his feast, March 19, 1867. On December 19th of that same year—he could not have been more punctual—a beautiful baby, Marie-Joseph-Jean Baptiste, came to increase the family. His birth was not easy. "He is very strong and lively," writes Mme. Martin, "but I had a terrible time and the infant was in the greatest danger. I suffered for four hours more severely than I have ever done, the poor little creature was nearly asphyxiated and the doctor administered clinical Baptism." [6] The child was delightful, having a pretty, bright smile, expressive gestures, and an intelligent way and interest in the noisy games of Marie and Pauline. The latter was his young godmother who was wild with delight over her godson.

He rapidly went the way of his elder brother. "Little Rose," who carried him off to her cottage, did not conceal her apprehension. His mother was torn between hope and fear. "He is as pretty as a little flower, and

[5] Mme. Martin to her sister-in-law, Oct. 17, 1871.
[6] Mme. Martin to her brother and sister-in-law, Dec. 21, 1867.

laughs like a cherub, till he chokes. I do so wish God would let me keep him. I pray and beseech Him daily to do so. If, however, He wills otherwise, we must resign ourselves."[7] Despite domestic and business duties capable of over-taxing three such women, she looked forward to the time when the infant would be weaned and return to her. "It is so sweet to attend to little children. If I had only that to do, I think I should be the happiest of women. But their father and I must work to earn enough for their dowries, otherwise when they are grown up they will not be pleased."[8]

The illusions were soon dispelled. From week to week the nursling failed. Three months of bronchitis ended by exhausting his frail constitution. Mme. Martin, who took the road to Semallé twice a day, at 5 a.m. and 8 p.m. watched, powerless to help, whilst the child suffered from fits of coughing and oppression. Towards mid-July, taking advantage of a slight improvement, she brought him home, where intestinal disorder promptly made its appearance. "I am really discouraged," laments the poor mother. "I no longer feel even the strength to nurse him; it breaks my heart to see a baby suffer like this. He only utters a pitiful wail. He has not closed his eyes for forty-eight hours, and he is doubled up with the violence of the pain."[9]

The end is announced on August 24, 1868, in this note, poignant in its sobriety:

"My dear little Joseph died in my arms at 7 o'clock this morning. I was alone with him. He had a night of cruel suffering, and I begged for his deliverance with tears. My

[7] Mme. Martin to her brother, Feb. 14, 1868.
[8] Mme. Martin to her sister-in-law, April 14, 1868.
[9] Mme. Martin to her brother, Aug. 23, 1868.

The Greatness of Family Life

heart felt lighter when I saw him breathe his last." She put a wreath of white roses round his head, laid him in a tiny coffin and, valiant in her faith, kept him to the end beside her, in the room where she received her workers. "Oh God," she groaned at times, "must I put that in the ground! But, since You will it, may Your will be done!"

The nun at Le Mans was immediately informed and comforted them in this sorrow with the same prophetic hope of a mysterious compensation.

"Oh yes, God's ways are inscrutable and life is full of woe. You, dear sister, know something of that, but the end will come and the measure of your joy will be that of your sorrow. Do believe this without any doubt. Now you are sowing in tears, but you will reap abundantly of the joy of the Lord. A poetic figure, borrowed from St. Francis de Sales, urges clinging without reserve to the hand of God who hurts only to heal. 'When the owner of the dovecot goes to take the young of the doves, they make no resistance; but if it were another than he, they would protest.' Now it is indeed the Master of the dovecot who has come to take His little dove, to place it in His Paradise. So let us acquiesce in His will with all the energy that is in us."

Taught by their double bereavement, M. and Mme. Martin advanced continually more in conformity to the designs of Providence. They would not impose their views upon the Lord. They ceased to ask for the apostle they so coveted. They counted upon having other children. "I do not despair," writes Zélie, speaking of her children, "of having still three or four." [10] But henceforth they would trust blindly in the discretion of "the Master of the dovecot" alone. St. Joseph retained their confidence, even though, in view of an-

[10] Mme. Martin to her sister-in-law, May, 1868.

other event, the Visitandine might plead for the name of "Francis," as though the gentle saint of Nazareth were in some way responsible for the premature deaths of his two protégés. Mme. Martin, who recounts her sister's intervention in view of a future boy, concludes in her strongest way: "I have answered her that he might die as a result or he might not, but that he should be named 'Joseph.' " [11] Surely simplicity and *abandon* could not be carried further!

*   *   *

A new anxiety was looming ahead on the horizon. In 1865, M. Guérin, senior, had received a warning, quickly forgotten, in the shape of the swelling of a leg with a threat of paralysis. When the second little Joseph was born, he was *in extremis*. In his daughter's life he counted considerably. In a sense she had never left him. When in 1859 he had lost his wife,[12] Zélie had installed him in a house in the *Rue du Pont Neuf*, close to her own home, had provided for his needs, and surrounded him with thoughtful attention. On his part, the old man, who had once made his own furniture, put his talent for carpentering at his youngest daughter's service. Six months later, when he planned to go back to his house in the *Rue Saint Blaise* which had just again become vacant, she hatched a real conspiracy to dissuade him. Not being able to put it before him tactfully that he needed his children, she declared convincingly that she could not do without him. M. Martin supported her; Isidore backed her up in a carefully expressed letter, and the Visitandine with her prayers. At last, pestered by his daughter, "weary and

[11] Mme. Martin to her brother, March 1, 1873.
[12] Mme. Guérin died of congestion of the lungs on Sept. 9, 1859, at the age of fifty-five years.

overcome with the deluge of words," the old, retired gendarme gave in and agreed in these words, softened with a smile, "Do leave me some peace!"

In December, 1866 a more radical measure was in question. There was a difficulty over the domestic service in M. Guérin's house. There was only one solution; he must come and live with his relations. This arrangement could not fail but upset the ways of the household, but daughterly affection did not stop at that sort of consideration. There we have an example of the noble service involved in family life, from which a Christian has no right to shrink. Isidore was commissioned to do the persuading. He had his father's ear.

"Suggest to him," writes Mme. Martin, "not to engage another housekeeper, but to come and live with us, for you cannot imagine all the trouble I have had to find persons who are trustworthy and devoted. My husband agrees with this arrangement. You would not find one in a hundred so good as he is to a father-in-law. As you know, our father is an excellent person. If he has now some of an old man's little whims, his children must bear with them and I have quite made up my mind. If you lived here, he would go to live with you, for he loves you better than me, but he will not change towns now, so he must remain with us to the end of his days." [13]

Henceforth we find the proud old soldier, who had a tender heart beneath the domineering manner of the ex-gendarme, in the household. He loved his daughter, although he did not show it much to her, and he was eager to help in every way. He spoilt the children, above all little Hélène, who reserved very special

[13] Mme. Martin to her brother, Dec. 23, 1866.

caresses for him. Occasionally he scolded and became annoyed when the little girls bewildered him with their noise or squabbled over the unpacking of a box of presents. In the evening, sitting in the chimney corner, smoking his pipe, he recalled the dazzling career of the "*Petit Caporal*," together with his own adventures. His sensitiveness, ordinarily concealed under a somewhat rough exterior, was revealed when he received the letter in which Isidore informed him of his budding romance. He fell under the spell of his young daughter-in-law's attractions at once and, delighted with such a marriage, never ceased to thank God.

He was about to keep his seventieth birthday when attacks of oppression, complicated with anthrax, brought him to the verge of the tomb. When sending the health bulletin to her brother, the daughter added: "Do not be anxious. I am with him constantly and scarcely ever leave him, so to speak. It is I who attend to his dressings twice a day, and I give him everything I can think of to help him . . . We are deeply sorry for our poor dear father." [14] After a few weeks of improvement, the patient's condition suddenly took a turn for the worse, and Isidore was hastily summoned. The Visitandine sent a sacred picture on which she had written these words: "Dear Father, death is a sleep; it is the close of the day, when the soul goes to receive the reward of its labors. It is the end of our exile, when the child finds again the Father it has so dearly loved." As for the last Sacraments, they had already been administered. To quote her own words, Mme. Martin "was worried about the case, even before the doctor had declared its gravity." The fear of frightening the patient by sending for the priest was unknown to these

[14] Mme. Martin to her brother, June 8, 1868.

The Greatness of Family Life

stalwart believers. The only fear they had was to see the sacrament of Extreme Unction unduly delayed, and their loved one dying unexpectedly without having received Holy Viaticum.

On September 3rd, 1868, the nurse informed her sister-in-law that the end had come that same morning. She sorrowed for the dead. "My heart is bruised with grief and at the same time filled with heavenly consolation. If you knew, dear sister, in what holy dispositions he prepared for death! At 3 A.M. he was still making the sign of the Cross. I have the hope, and even the certitude, that our dear father has been welcomed by God. I hope my death may be like his."

In vain did she describe herself as being "used to suffering"; this fresh blow, coming at the same time as the loss of her second son, left her shaking and as though stunned.

"Yesterday," she writes, "I went to the cemetery. Anyone seeing me would have said, 'There is the most unmoved woman in the world!' I knelt by my father's grave but I could not pray. A few steps away I knelt by that of my two little angels; still the same apparent indifference. I had trodden the road by which I had come five weeks previously with my little son and my father, and I could not tell you all I felt. I paid no attention to what was going on around me. I was looking at the spots where my father had sat. I stood there almost without thinking. Never in my life did I feel such heart-rending grief. When I reached home, I could not eat. It seems to me now that no matter what troubles came, I should not feel them." [15]

Her reactions, however, were wholly Christian. She

[15] M. Guérin was interred in the cemetery of Notre-Dame, Alençon, whence his remains were transferred to the vault of M. Martin at Lisieux in 1894.

at once asked for a hundred and fifty Masses for the souls of her parents, and intended to have others said. She offered all the satisfactions of her good works and sufferings throughout her life as suffrages for the dead. She even made the heroic offering. Her correspondence with her brother never ceases to recall him whom they were both mourning. "I often wish you were here to talk to me about our father. Poor Father! What a holy death he had! Do you remember how the night before he died, when he clasped our hands, what an air of holiness there was about him? If God hears me, He would place him in Heaven today; if it were I, I certainly would! Poor Father was not used to suffering. Suffering seems to me quite natural, and I am not afraid of going to Purgatory. If God so willed, I would promptly make the bargain to do Father's purgatory as well as my own. I should so love to know that he is happy." [16]

* * *

It was written that this heroine of family duty should never be able to enjoy her memories at leisure or dwell upon her crosses. Life bore her on at a dizzy pace, each day bringing new situations to be faced. This time it was her sister, Élise, her "second self," and faithful companion from childhood, who was concerned.

At the beginning of October, 1865, although he keenly felt the separation however brief, from a member of his family, M. Martin decided to place the two elder girls, then aged respectively eight and a half and seven years, at school as boarders. His intention in this was to lessen the work of his wife, whose health had not ceased to make him anxious. He wished, also, to take advantage of his sister-in-law's presence at Le Mans to

[16] Mme. Martin to her brother, Nov. 1, 1868.

assure to his children the advantage of a thoroughly good education under the direct influence of "the holy nun." A boarding school was attached to the Visitation convent, which was attended by pupils from the highest social circles, and Marie and Pauline owed it to their aunt's influence that they were admitted among these. Nothing less than the motherly tenderness of Sister Marie Dosithée succeeded in softening the hardly felt sacrifice of the departure from Alençon, and now, when the end of the first term sent Mme. Martin to bring her daughters home for the New Year holidays, and she was promising herself the pleasure of seeing her sister at the same time, she found the latter in a pitiable state of weakness, her voice gone, and worn out by a succession of bronchial attacks which could not but eventually prove fatal. "I am very troubled indeed at seeing this," she writes at once to Lisieux. "In losing her, I shall lose everything, for she is very dear to me and very useful to my children. I feel sad at heart when I think about it. My courage will fail me when I have to go to the convent and she is not there any longer." [17]

The truth was that it was a case of slowly developing consumption which left hopes of some respite. The sick nun, as a last consolation, took advantage of preparing Marie for her first Communion, which was thus hastened. During this time the mother wrote her child a series of letters so beautifully expressed and filled with such deep spirituality, that the nuns themselves learnt of them and read them with pious eagerness. Marie considered this collection as her greatest treasure and, refusing to leave it behind, took it home with her in the holidays. Alas, one day she found, to her distress, that the precious package had disappeared. Louise, the

[17] Mme. Martin to her brother and sister-in-law, Jan. 1869.

maid, without looking at it closely, had used it to light the fire!

Among the most urgent counsels which her mother gave Marie was that of winning from heaven the cure of Sister Marie-Dosithée. "On a first Communion day," she loved to repeat, "we obtain all we ask." The child considered it as settled. She learnt her catechism unusually easily. She marshalled a veritable "offensive" of prayers and sacrifices. "In my inmost heart," she owned later, "I thought that Jesus had made everyone believe that my aunt was going to die because He longed to give Himself to me, and that thought put the crown upon my happiness. As for the miracle, she felt sure of it. The infirmarian almost scandalised her by urging her to accept the will of God. Where should we be with that kind of reasoning? We should never get any further! What Marie wanted, in the obstinacy of her child's logic, and indeed, apart from the form in which she expressed it, theologians would not have much difficulty in agreeing with her, was "to change the will of God if necessary." St. Joseph became her advocate. Every time there appeared signs of a change for the worse, fever, blood-spitting, attacks of suffocation, Marie would look at his statue with gentle reproach.

The great day came at last; it was the second of July, 1869. Marie was nine and a half. Her mother was in the front row. She felt repaid for all her labors, and tasted one of the purest joys of a Catholic mother. "If you knew how well prepared she was," she writes of her daughter. "She looked like a little saint. The chaplain told me he was very pleased with her, and had awarded her the first prize for Catechism. I spent two of the happiest days of my life at Mans; rarely have I felt so joyful. My sister was better. Marie told me she had prayed so hard for her aunt that she was sure God would hear her." [18] In fact, the lesions in the lungs healed rapidly. The nun, who had not seen the danger pass without a certain sadness, would later be able to say to her niece, "It is to you that I owe seven years of life." The little girl gave all the credit to St. Joseph, and in token of her gratitude took "Josephine" as her Confirmation name.

*　　*　　*

This first Communion opened a series of ceremonies and feasts, of which each of the children in succession was the central figure, and which, linked by happy birthdays, constituted for the parents a perpetual renewal and for the family a permanent source of nourishment, even a sort of liturgical cycle, in which the "soul" of the whole household was set and gained renewed strength.

Four months later, M. Vital Romet and Mme. Guérin accompanied little Marie-Céline to church for her baptismal ceremonies, the baby having been privately baptised on the day of her birth, April 28, 1869 in virtue of a custom tolerated by the Church at the time. Deeply distressed by her recent losses, Zélie wrote to her brother before the birth: "Whatever you say, we shall have another child. That is certain, unless some misfortune happens to me beforehand. But if God wills once more to take this one from me, I pray that it may not die unbaptised, so that at least I may have the comfort of three little angels in Heaven." [19] "You could not imagine how I fear for the future as regards the little one I am expecting. I feel as though the fate of the last

[18] Mme. Martin to her sister-in-law, July 11, 1869.
[19] Mme. Martin to her brother, Nov. 1, 1868.

The Story of a Family

two will be its fate also. I think the dread is worse than the misfortune. It is a continual nightmare for me. When the sorrows come, I resign myself fairly well, but fear is a torture to me. During Mass this morning my thoughts were so gloomy that I was thoroughly upset. The best course is to leave everything in God's hands, and await events in calm and *abandon* to His will. That is what I am going to make myself do."[20]

Nevertheless, the longing and pride in her motherhood were so strong that, when announcing the coming of Céline to her husband, then away on business, she could not help adding: "You have no need to be anxious over the children. Unfortunately, I shall never have any more; that is certain. Yet I always hoped for a little boy. But if God wills otherwise, I accept His will." [21]

How it cost her to be separated from the little daughter, just when the latter was beginning to prattle and "take steps." This time again she had to seek help outside and resume her maternal pilgrimages on the road to Semallé. "I have already been very uneasy over this child. I feel worn out, and I have the impression that I shall not live long. During the week I had the baby to look after, I was feverish every day." [22]

At last, all seemed safely over. Her health was restored, her worries ceased, business was fairly good, and the doctor's visits to the *Rue du Pont Neuf* came to an end. At peace again, and astonished at this seemingly unclouded happiness, Mme. Martin writes to her sister-in-law: "For the moment, I have everything but trouble!" [23] The calm was to be short lived.

[20] Mme. Martin to her sister-in-law, Feb. 1869.
[21] Letter to M. Martin, 1869.
[22] Mme. Martin to her brother and sister-in-law, Aug. 29, 1869.
[23] Mme. Martin to her sister-in-law, Oct. 1869.

The Greatness of Family Life

Among the small daughters who enlivened the home, Hélène seemed marked with some mysterious sign. She was "enchanting," "fresh as a rose at morning," as affectionate as could be wished and her precocious intelligence gave her chatter a charm all her own. Her photograph shows refined, delicate features, with something in her countenance of a gentle gravity that makes one think of the world beyond. Almost unknown to her parents, a sort of languor was silently undermining her health; and on February 22, 1870, after scarcely a day's illness, and without the doctor having realised the gravity of the case, the dark wing of the angel of death touched her in her turn.

Her mother, who bitterly reproached herself for this unexpected end, draws a pathetic picture of the last hours.

"I was looking at her sadly. Her eyes were dull, there was no more life in her, and I began to cry. Then she put her little arms round me and did her best to comfort me. All day she kept saying, 'My poor little mother has been crying.' I sat up with her, and she had a very bad night. In the morning, I asked her if she would take her *bouillon*. She said yes, but could not swallow it. However, she made a last effort, saying to me, 'If I eat it, will you love me better?'

"Then she took it all but suffered dreadfully afterwards, and I did not know what was happening. She looked at a bottle of medicine which the doctor had ordered, and wanted to drink it, saying that when it was all drunk, she would be better. Then about a quarter-to-ten, she said to me, 'Yes, I shall soon be well again . . . yes, very soon . . .' and at that very moment her little head fell on my shoulder, her eyes closed, and five minutes later she was dead . . .

"I shall never forget the impression it has made upon me. Neither I nor my husband expected this sudden end. When he came in and saw his poor little daughter dead, he burst out sobbing, and crying, 'My little Hélène My little Hélène!' Then we offered her to God together . . . I spent the night beside the poor little darling. She was even lovelier in death than in life. I dressed her myself and laid her in her coffin. I thought I should die myself, but I did not want others to touch her."[24]

It was an overwhelming grief to the whole family. At school the elder children cried over their favorite sister; the father was cut to the heart. The image of the absent child never left him. Long years afterwards he was still heard humming the mournful lines of Chateaubriand's romantic poem:

"Ah, who will give me back my mountain,
    And the ancient oak and my Hélène?
    Their memory fills my every day with pain."

As for Mme. Martin, her lament is heart-rending.

"Sometimes I imagine myself slipping away very gently, like my little Hélène. I assure you I scarcely cling to life since I lost that child. I am aware of an ardent longing to see her again. However, those who remain need me, and for their sakes I pray God to leave me a few years longer on earth.

"I feel deeply the loss of my two little boys, but I have suffered still more at losing this child. I was beginning to rejoice in her. She was so good, so loving and so advanced for her age. There is not a moment of the day when I do not think of her. The Sister who taught her in school, told me—and it was well said—that children like her do not live. Well, she is in Heaven, far happier than here below, but for me it seems as though all happiness has flown."[25]

[24] Mme. Martin to her brother and sister-in-law, Feb. 24, 1870.
[25] Mme. Martin to her sister-in-law, March 27, 1870.

The Greatness of Family Life

However, she got the better of it. From the Visitation she received a message of hope which, looking back, sounds like an early foretelling of the glory of Thérèse: "Oh, my dear little sister! How glad I am to see your deep faith and your resignation! You will soon find again those you mourn. Yes, your crown will be beautiful—very beautiful. Just now your heart is broken but by your acquiescence in all that God wills, there will come a fragrance which will delight the Heart of God!

"One day your faith and trust that never flinch will have a magnificent reward. Be sure that God will bless you, and that the measure of your sorrows will be that of the consolations reserved for you. For after all, if God is pleased with you and wills to give you the great saint you have so desired for His glory, will you not be well repaid?"

In a large household there was no time to bury herself in her grief. The stream of life rose and surged ever forward. The gaps were gradually filled and the parents, while keeping before their eyes the beloved features of those who were gone, spent themselves upon those who remained, uniting in a magnificent solidarity the family on earth and the family beyond the tomb, the latter watching over the former.

One day, Mme. Martin had an intuition, even a physical impression of this communion with the world beyond. Recalling how a little fib had once escaped Hélène's lips, she harshly reproached herself for not having thought to make her go to confession. The idea that by her involuntary negligence the child was perhaps undergoing the suffering of Purgatory was unbearable. To shake off this obsession she turned to the family statue of Our Lady, the fingers of which, having been broken with much kissing, had been more than once replaced. The answer of the Immaculate Mother came forthwith: "She is here with me," tenderly murmured a mysterious interior voice. At these words the mother's anguish vanished and an indescribable joy arose in her heart, making her conceive a redoubled esteem for her high calling.

Again tranquil, she turned with all her affection to the little Céline and brought her home. "It will console us a little to have her here," she writes. "Besides, I cannot settle down to seeing myself in the streets without a child beside me." [26] M. Martin was delighted. The mite had a curious preference for him. "When he is there no one else may hold her. She cries to go to him with all her might, and when I want to take her again, I have to remove her forcibly from his arms." [27]

Was it a far-off foreshadowing of that painful eventide of life when in his humiliation the father would find in Céline the guardian angel of his old age?

[26] Mme. Martin to her brother, March 6, 1870.
[27] Mme. Martin to her sister-in-law, June 10, 1870.

CHAPTER 5

THE HOUSE AMIDST THE STORM

Birth and death of Marie-Mélanie-Thérèse—
Alençon during the war of 1870—threats
of a social crisis—a mother's courage.

THE year 1870 opened in France under gloomy horizons. Worn out with adventures, utopias and defeat, the Empire now became "Liberal," had lost in authority without gaining in popularity. Napoleon III, his health undermined by disease and more fanciful than ever, was nothing more than the plaything of his illusions. Catholics were looking anxiously from the side of the Alps where the heirs of Cavour's political ideas were dreaming of building Italian unity on the ruins of the Papal States. Clear-sighted patriots watched questioningly the line of the Rhine behind which Prussia, in the grip of the Iron Chancellor, hummed like an arsenal, working at full strength. Those more intelligent observers of social life feared as they saw increasing around Paris a hostile proletariat given up to squalor, immorality and irreligion, and thrown as a prey to the preachers of revolution. Formerly men had said, "France is bored"; the saying of the moment was, "France is uneasy!"

Mme. Martin left to the men the task of pondering over these disquieting problems. She was absorbed with her own duty, above all others, that of being "the mother of the living." She was thrilled with hopes of another arrival.

"I am rejoicing," she writes, to her sister-in-law, "that next August we shall each have a little son; at least I hope so. But, girl or boy, we must accept gratefully what the good God gives us, for He knows better than we what is best for us."[1] What troubles me is the thought of having once more to put the child out to nurse. It is so difficult to find good persons. I should also like to have the nurse here at home, but it is impossible. I have already enough in the house. After all, I think how God will help me. He well knows that it is not laziness that prevents me from nursing my children, for I am not afraid of trouble. I was speaking of you, yesterday, to Mme. Y. She thinks you very happy and told me she wished she were in your place. Some of her friends advise her to make a pilgrimage to Lourdes, to obtain the grace of having children, but she declares that she does not want to, for she would be afraid of having too many, and as she is extremely fond of pleasure, she would rather have none at all than be a slave to them."[2]

Beneath the gentle irony of the words we can feel how this cowardice in face of life calls forth the writer's disapproval. Neo-Malthusian calculations seemed to her as though marked with a curse. They meant the abdication of a dignity, the mutilation of an ideal. She took to herself, Victor Hugo's earnest words:

"Preserve me, Lord; preserve those whom I love,
Kin, brethren, friends, and e'en mine enemies,
Triumphant in their evil,

[1] Mme. Martin will return to this idea in a letter addressed to her sister-in-law on August 23, 1870, after the births of her own little Marie-Thérèse-Mélanie and Marie Guérin. It mattered little that a daughter had arrived instead of the longed-for boy. "If you are like me, you will not be saddened, for I have not had a moment's regret on this account."

[2] Mme. Martin to her sister-in-law, Feb. 12, 1870.

The House Amidst the Storm

From seeing ever, Lord, the summer lack its scarlet
flowers,
The cage bereft of birds, hives void of bees,
The home without its children."

It was in the high fever of war that Marie-Thérèse-Mélanie was born on August 17, 1870. The very next day the cousin, Henry de Lacauve, who was to have been her godfather, was wounded at the battle of Privat. He was not to see his godchild, and would express his sadness in a touching letter addressed as a prisoner of war to him whom he called "my good brother, Louis."

The mother, braver than ever at this eighth birth, tried in vain to nurse the child herself. At the least, she wanted to find someone who would come and live in the house so that she might watch over her treasure herself. Her search was fruitless. She was forced to have recourse to a woman living in the *Rue de la Barre* at Alençon, who disgracefully abused her confidence and let the infant starve. The latter had to be brought home. In the middle of the night, the father went to Héloup to find another nurse. She was confined to bed by sickness. Poor Mme. Martin, who relates all these disasters, and saw her Thérèse expire on her lap, after two and a half hours of agony, herself describes the death, which came on October 8, 1870.

"You could not imagine what she suffered. I am utterly desolate. I so loved this child. At each new bereavement I seem always to love the one I lose more than the others. She was as pretty as a flower, and then I looked after her all by myself. Oh, I wish I could die also! I am utterly worn out these last two days. I have eaten practically nothing and been up all night in mortal anguish."[3]

[3] Mme. Martin to her sister-in-law, Oct. 8, 1870.

The Story of a Family

She speaks out more freely in a letter to her brother.

"It was such a pretty little girl. She had eyes such as one never sees in babies of that age, and such delicate features. And to think that she was allowed to die of hunger! Is it not terrible? You do not know what a delight it was going to be to bring up this little one all by myself. I was as glad to have her as though it was my first child. Ah well! it is all over and there is no remedy, and the best thing I can do is to resign myself. The child is happy and that consoles me."[4]

Her mother's instinct knitted her the more closely to those who were left, and she continues charmingly: "Little Céline is very winsome, and is beginning to talk prettily. Every day I was mourning the loss of little Thérèse, and saying 'My poor little girl!' All at once, Céline came to cling to me, thinking that I was speaking to her. She looks everywhere for her little sister and demands *"la sesoeur."* "

Those who did not know Zélie Martin might have thought she was wanting in sensitiveness. When suffering from great shocks, she was incapable of weeping. She mastered her sorrow so well that she attended to her duties as though nothing had happened. Only her intimates perceived her interior anguish. Henceforth, when the family went to the public park known as *Les Promenades*, she would avoid passing on the side of the *Rue de la Barre*. The very name and sight of it, by reminding her of the guilty nurse, renewed all the mother's wounds to the point of becoming hateful to her. Her relatives were alarmed at this avalanche of troubles which might well destroy her health which was already uncertain. On All Saints Day of this sorrowful

[4] Mme. Martin to her brother, Oct. 1870.

96

The House Amidst the Storm

year the nun sister sent her a few comforting quotations, culled in the course of her spiritual reading:

"I want to write you something that will help you. The Venerable Margaret of the Blessed Sacrament, a Carmelite of Beaune, says that the Holy Innocents are very powerful in Heaven, and that children who die after Baptism form their court. Father Faber declares that in the Catholic Church they form a group apart, wherein God is continually loved and served in a wonderful manner which we cannot understand, but which is very near to that of the kingdom of the angels. And elsewhere, the same writer says: 'Some children belong only to God. They are those whom He takes from this world. They love their Mother in Heaven more than other children do. Those mothers are blessed who have such children, whom we call 'God's spring flowers.'

"So, dear sister, be valiant. Your dear little ones are today, up yonder with all the saints, and stand before the throne of the Lamb full of joy at having left the world without having known its perils."

Mme. Martin fully shared this supernatural outlook. "Four of my children are already well provided for," she will write one day, "and the others, yes, the others will also enter into the heavenly kingdom, laden with more merits, since they will have fought longer." [5] It was in a letter to her sister-in-law that she fully expressed her thought in respect to this. Mme. Guérin had just given birth to a son who died immediately. To console the sorrowing mother, Zélie writes in terms of incomparable tenderness and beauty.

"I am deeply grieved at the misfortune that has just struck you. Truly, you are sorely tried! It is one of your first troubles, my poor, dear sister. May our good Lord grant

[5] Mme. Martin to Pauline, March 4, 1877.

The Story of a Family

you resignation to His holy will. Your dear little child is with Him. He sees you, he loves you, and you will find him again one day. That is the great comfort I felt and still feel.

"When I closed the eyes of my dear children and buried them, I felt the sorrow indeed, but it has always been resigned sorrow. I did not regret the pain and cares I had borne for them. Several people said to me, 'It would have been better if you had never had them,' but I could not endure this sort of language. I did not think that the sufferings and anxieties could be weighed in the same scale with the eternal happiness of my children. Then they were not lost forever; life is short and full of miseries, and we shall find them again up yonder.

"It was especially at the death of the first that I was most vividly aware of the happiness of having a child in Heaven. For God showed me in a sensible manner that He accepted my sacrifice. Through my first little angel, I obtained a very extraordinary grace."[6]

Here she relates the cure, already mentioned in the course of our account, of little Hélène, by the intercession of her brother who had recently died. The conclusion follows as a matter of course: "You see, dear sister, it is a great advantage to have little angels in Heaven, but it is not less painful to nature to lose them. These are the great sorrows of our life."

Sully-Prud'homme will seize upon this theme. He will set it to music, and clothe it in the magic of rhythm and bright imagery to sing of the eternal after-life of dead children:

> "Blue eyes or black, all loved, all fair,
> Wide ope'd on some vast dawn
> Beyond the tomb, across the stream of death
> The eyes we closed still see."

[6] Mme. Martin to her sister-in-law, Oct. 17, 1871.

98

The House Amidst the Storm

Despite all the prestige of art, the vague spirituality of the poet fails to attain to the attitude of this Christian mother who, looking at the Cross, finds her dead again.

*　　*　　*

Soon it was over for the fatherland and it behoved them to mourn and weep. The military machine skillfully constructed by Bismarck, von Roon and von Moltke, had promptly crushed the infantry, despite their wild valor. The siege of Metz, the surrender of Sedan, the fall of the Second Empire, marked the stages of disasters. To relieve beleaguered Paris, the Government of National Defense improvised regiments with disconcerting speed. Thus it came about that progressively the West came within the zone of operations, following the varied fortunes of the two armies of the Loire. It was a matter of enemy incursions and raids, rather than an occupation on a large scale. The implacable procedure of total war had not then been reached.

From the middle of November, the department of the Orne was on the *qui vive*. Mme. Martin explains it to her sister-in-law in a letter that might be dated June 1940, so truly does history repeat itself. This document, written in the light of the invasion and in which we can feel a real, patriotic anguish, is yet enlivened by a touch of humor. Even in extreme peril the French wit loses none of its rights.

"On the 22nd of this month we had a notorious alarm at Alençon. We were expecting the Prussians next day; nearly half the populace had left. I never saw such desolation. Everyone was hiding his valuables. A gentleman near us hid his so well that he could not put his hand upon them

99

again. It took three people, digging for a whole morning, to find the hiding place.

"I was not much afraid. I no longer fear anything. Had I wished to take flight, I should have come straight to you, but my husband would have been in great difficulties all alone and I very uneasy. It was better to remain.

"The Prussians went to Bellême and made no light requisitions in the surrounding villages, but one of these turned out comically. Just imagine! They took the pig of a poor farm laborer, who defended his beast with unexampled courage; he could not have fought better had it been his child. When the pig had been tied on to a horse, the good man began to pull on the animal's tail with all his might. He had to be content with that, however, for in order to make him release his hold, a soldier struck it a blow with his sabre, so that the tail remained in the peasant's hand.

"Leaving Bellême, to march on Alençon they passed by Mamers. Then they turned aside in the direction of Mans. There were 20,000 of them."[7]

The maternal anxieties turned to Marie and Pauline. The children were at school there and it was impossible to go for them. The railway was requisitioned by the troops, the road was not safe and was encumbered by convoys.

M. Martin had soldier's blood in his veins. He deeply felt his country's humiliation and at times he regretted that, despite his forty-seven years, he was not fighting in the regular army. "It is still quite possible," writes his wife, "that men between forty and fifty will have to go. I am almost waiting for it. My husband is not at all upset. He would not ask for exemption and often says that if he were a single man he would soon join the sharp-shooters."[8] This was a painful prospect to Mme.

[7] Mme. Martin to her sister-in-law, Nov. 30, 1870.
[8] *Ibid.*

The House Amidst the Storm

Martin; nevertheless she proudly accepted the sacrifice. Hearing that a lady in the town had managed to hide her husband to avoid his being mobilized, she exclaimed, "Is it possible anyone could do such a thing!" She, also heiress to a military tradition, was naturally courageous and had a horror of cowardice.

However, the authorities put Alençon into a state of defense. Scout patrols were stationed in the forest to watch enemy movements. These were those sharpshooters whom the pen of Déroulède would celebrate. At the risk of being shot, if captured, M. Martin accompanied them, joined himself to them and returned only when the need for them no longer existed, the threat of German inroads having been removed for the time being.

Events soon moved rapidly. Having regrouped the army of General d'Aurelles de Paladine, which had been defeated at Beaune-la-Rolande and at Loigny, Chanzy led during five weeks, from Marchenoir to the Sarthe, those lightning attacks to which the German General Staff paid tribute by calling them "a hellish retreat." Mme. Martin could bear it no longer; she wanted to bring her daughters home, considering them no longer safe at the convent. On December 30th, she gives her sister-in-law an account of her expedition:

"There is nothing to be seen but sadness and desolation on every side, and my heart is aching. Truly we have never been so unfortunate as we are now. But it is nothing as yet in our towns. To form an idea of the desolation which this sad war has brought in its train you must go to Mans. My sister told me things that would make your heart bleed; the poor sick are lying in thousands; in the hospital at Mans alone, they are burying up to eighty daily, and there are auxiliary hospitals everywhere. The Lycée, and all the religious communities are obliged to house them. A quarter of an hour before I arrived at the convent, the municipal authorities had sent to inform the nuns that they were sending them thirty sick . . . In addition to these hospitals at Mans, you see Red Cross stations in every street. Nearly all the rich people have sick in their houses, even to Mme. D. who has received a soldier dying of dysentery. Smallpox also is raging on all sides."

The iron ring tightened around Alençon. The second army of the Loire had been crushed before Le Mans on January 11, 1871. The remnants of it fell back on Laval, where a supernatural intervention was to check the enemy advance. The department of the Orne was invaded in its turn, and in its capital they prepared to fight. The Prefect ordered the three bridges to be mined and the preparations—which a petition was soon to arrest—were promptly undertaken. In view of the explosion the Martin family, who lived only a few yards from the *Pont Neuf*, took up their quarters in the cellar whither the little girls carried down their stools and school books.

The National Guard was called out. They still believed then in "mass levies," and that to ward off a hostile offensive it sufficed to arm hastily men ill prepared to be soldiers. In a letter of January 17th Mme. Martin speaks of this unequal struggle.

"The whole populace is in consternation. Our poor men were mobilized and sent off to fight the Prussians who were about three miles from the town. We heard cannon in three different directions, on the roads to Mamers, Aunay and Mans, until six o'clock in the evening.

"It was pitiable to see our poor soldiers return, some without feet, others without hands. I saw one whose face was all covered with blood. In short, there are very many wounded

The House Amidst the Storm

and every auxiliary hospital is full. They do not know the number of the dead, among whom are many of the sharp-shooters.

"When there is such a shortage of men, is there any sense in sending them to be slaughtered by such an army as we have seen? No one had any idea what the Prussian army was like; it is a very formidable war machine. There is something sinister in the sight of their battalions, with the black flags and the death's head on their helmets. How is it that everyone does not recognise that this war is a chastisement?"

There was a short bombardment, a timber yard and several houses burnt. The Martin family took refuge in the basement whilst the fragments of shell fell in the near neighborhood, and one shell crashed through a shop window across the road. The Germans lost no time in entering the town, and during several hours they marched along the *Pont Neuf*, about twenty-five thousand in number. Exasperated by the resistance, they condemned the town to deliver an enormous war contribution. The Mayor, Eugène Lecointre, refused stoically. Since they threatened to pillage Alençon by way of reprisals, he replied, blusteringly, "Here are the keys of my house. Begin with me. Might is right!" Impressed by this attitude, the victor gave way.

Nevertheless, the townsfolk had to receive soldiers into their homes. Mme. Martin took advantage of the reestablishment of postal communications to send a detailed account of these lamentable days to Lisieux.

"About three o'clock on Monday, every door was marked with a certain number of enemy soldiers to be billeted there. A tall sergeant came and demanded to see over our house. I took him up to the first floor and told him we had four children. Happily for us, he made no attempt to go up to the second floor. Finally, he assigned us nine, and we cannot complain. In our neighborhood small shopkeepers, who have only two-storied houses, are being sent fifteen, twenty and even twenty-five.

"I am not putting myself out over them. When they demand too much, I tell them that it is impossible. This morning they brought in enough meat to feed thirty people, and we are now in the middle of having it cooked for them.

"We have been obliged to give up the entire first floor to them, and to come down to the ground floor. If I told you everything, I should have to write a book. The town refused to pay the sum demanded and we were threatened with reprisals. Finally, the Duke of Mecklenberg contented himself with 300,000 francs and an enormous quantity of material. All the cattle in the district have been seized. Now there is no more milk to be had anywhere. What will little Céline do, she who drank a litre a day? And how are poor mothers with infants to manage? There is no more meat in any butcher's; in short, the town is stripped. Everyone is weeping except myself."[9]

What Mme. Martin does not say is that she and her husband knew how to combine, in their supernaturalised patriotism, a courage capable of facing danger with a human sympathy that excluded all hatred. Thus it was that among the nine soldiers billeted in her house, she noticed one more humane and refined, whose face seemed to suggest that he was feeling the separation from his family. She did not hesitate to speak to him, and even to give him some little dainties secretly, for which he showed himself touchingly grateful.

As for M. Martin, he set himself to prevent depredations and to ward off abusive requisitions from his shop. A German having attempted to steal an article of

[9] Mme. Martin to her sister-in-law, Jan. 17, 1871.

jewelry, he intervened energetically, overcame the man's resistance, threw him out of doors, and lodged a complaint. When, on the following day, he heard that another soldier had been shot for a similar offense as an example, he went again to the military authorities and begged that the life of the man whom he had reported might be spared. In the face of the enemy, this true Frenchman kept the warm, kind heart of the father of a family, still more refined by the charity of the Christian.

The trial was no less cruel to this officer's son, accustomed since he was a toddler to the stories of the "Napoleonic Legend." "My husband is upset;" notes Mme. Martin on January 17, "he can neither eat nor sleep. I believe he is going to be ill."

On the same day she wrote these lines a mysterious incident occurred, which restored confidence to the Catholics. When she learnt of it from the newspapers, she could not restrain herself from at once calling to her husband to tell him the good news. "The Blessed Virgin has appeared at Pontmain. We are saved!"

In fact, after a short delay the religious authorities were to confirm this first report. In the little town of Pontmain, six kilometres to the south of Landivy, on the evening of January 17, 1871, in a starlit sky, some children had perceived a beautiful lady clothed in blue, who could only be Our Lady, whilst an invisible hand had traced beneath her feet in golden letters: "Pray, children, God will hear you soon. My Son will show mercy." On the same day, at Saint Brieuc, the arch-confraternity of *Our Lady of Hope* made a solemn vow to its Patroness to obtain the grace that Brittany might escape the wave of invasion, whilst at the Parisian sanctuary of *Our Lady of Victories*, public prayers, also rendered more solemn by an official promise, were said for the cessation of the war. Now during the same night of the apparition the 20th division, commanded by General Schmidt, was preparing to enter Laval which was covered by only a small force, when it received without apparent justification the order to retire. The advance was stopped and the withdrawal begun. Ten days later, the armistice was signed, to be quickly followed by the preliminary negotiations for peace, and then by the Treaty of Frankfort.

It needed nothing less than that Heaven should thus smile upon France to restore the optimism of the household in the *Rue du Pont Neuf*. It had paid its share of the cost of the war in material losses. The house was "in a dreadful state," debts could not be recovered, and business was suffering for the time being. However, the methods of order, economy, and industry, which reigned habitually in the house, repaired the breaches without delay.

The moral wound was deeper. M. Martin mourned for beautiful Alsace which he had found so enchanting in his youth, and Strasburg, the gem of the Rhineland, and its storks and nests, and its lofty spires. When the pretty song of Soubise came out; "*It is a bird that comes from France*," he placed it in the front rank of his favorites in his repertoire. In his case patriotism was not a passing emotion. He believed in his country, her greatness, her mission. He suffered—and his wife expressed their common indignation in a letter—when, on the very morrow of disasters, and to help pay the war indemnity, at Lisieux and Alençon people could think of nothing better to do than organise, with much advertisement, a riding competition, followed by a masqued ball . . . the dance on the tombs!

The House Amidst the Storm

During the following three years, the correspondence of Mme. Martin testifies curiously to the general unrest and the anguish of believers. Stunned by defeat, France was seeking to regain her balance. The adherents of the Comte de Chambord, Orleanists, Republicans, disputed the sovereign power. The Parisian masses, who emerged from the siege with nerves on edge and as though devoured by the fever of the blockade, raised the Government of the Commune against Thiers, and prolonged the insurrection for over two months, even to the massacre of the hostages, the sinister exploits of the "pétroleurs," and the terrible repression that followed. Under cover of many misunderstandings, a wave of anti-clericalism was slowly breaking over the land, whilst the social question remained unsolved and was to furnish an easy field for Marxist propaganda.

In certain conservative circles men felt as though a great fear was passing by. Among the militant Catholics it was a sort of pseudo-mystic impulse, and was accompanied by a by-product of a harvest of prophecies, entirely beyond the control of the clergy. On the other hand it was also the time when, with the support of Monsignor Guibert, there rose on high the national vow which was to issue in the erection of the sanctuary of Montmartre. It was the period of grandiose manifestations of faith, when men recalled the heroism of the zouaves of Charette, when they prayed for the Prisoner of the Vatican, or sang: "*Save Rome and France, in the name of the Sacred Heart!*"

All this effervescence promptly found an echo at Alençon. Nobility and upper middle class, who held the reins of authority, seemed pursued by the haunting fear of a revolution. They wore themselves out in sterile debates over the white flag. As for the fire of the

Catholic faith, its activity was all on the surface, sparkling rather than warming; a matter of outward protesting rather than interior living. In the drawing rooms, it drifted side by side with certain traces of the Voltairean spirit, like a mouldy relic of Gallicanism. One can even come across belated adherents of the Old Catholics who refused to accept several articles of dogma. On the other hand, the caste prejudices, tenacious in this provincial region, called forth a reaction in the shape of the rancor of the lower elements. A dividing line was being drawn which was soon to set "the two Frances" in opposition.

In such an atmosphere and at such a time it is not without interest to see how the supernatural sense of the Martin family reacted to all this. When informed of the outbreak of "the bloody week," the mother writes to Lisieux on May 29, 1871: "I feel very well as far as bodily health is concerned, but not in mind, especially this morning. All that is happening in Paris fills my soul with sorrow. I have just learned of the Archbishop's death, and of the sixty-four priests shot yesterday by the Communards. I am utterly dismayed." [10]

On the stock exchange shares went down forthwith; funds were frozen, it was impossible to realise their fortune. It mattered little. "When this tempest has passed, we shall gather up the fragments that remain, and live on that little." [10] It was highly necessary, however, to consider the children. The forebodings were so black and so precise that at the price of heavy sacrifices they took measures to obtain the immediate payment of the drafts. Predictions were going the round clandestinely which fixed certain dates for the

[10] Mme. Martin to her sister-in-law, May 29, 1871.

tragic course of destiny. At first, Zélie's womanly
sensitiveness was impressed, but as the fateful dates
went by, she became more and more sceptical and her
sound common sense was not long in making fun of the
auguries. "I am quite decided not to take any notice
of any prophet or any prophecy. I am beginning to be
very incredulous. I say, 'God alone knows the moment
and the hour.' Others believe they see something and
see nothing." [11] She resigned herself "to wait for the
end of the ball of thread," in order to form a judgment
on events, though at the same time she "wished that it
were not so slow in unwinding."

She lets drop in places a hint of her monarchist
aspirations, and is indignant with such as have dared
to state that Henry V might have compromised with
his convictions and adopted the principles of the
Revolution. Nevertheless, far more important than the
question of political régime was that of the interests of
Christ and the Church. It was those which they discussed so earnestly in the family conversations in the
evenings. In May, 1873, M. Martin writes to his
daughter, Pauline: "Pray hard, my dear little one, for
the success of the pilgrimage to Chartres, in which I am
to take part, and which will gather a great many pilgrims from our fair France at the feet of our Blessed
Lady, in order to obtain the graces of which our fatherland stands in such great need, if it is to show itself
worthy of its past." There were twenty thousand who
thus crossed the plain of the Beauce to reach this cradle
of our devotion to Mary, where the druids raised an
altar "to the Virgin who should bear a Child," and
which is dominated from the one solitary height by
"the incomparable spire that can never fall." The

[11] Mme. Martin to her brother and sister-in-law, July 21, 1872.

numbers surpassed all expectations; there were not
enough beds and many had to sleep on straw or remain
in the church. M. Martin spent the night in the sub-
terranean chapel, where Masses followed one another
from midnight to mid-day. He returned home with his
heart filled with hope.

Besides those who prayed there were the pessimists
who, while they awaited the catastrophe, sought to
escape from their terror by enjoying themselves, and
threw themselves headlong into the pursuit of pleasure.
In a letter to her sister-in-law, of March 1873, Mme.
Martin scourges them in her own way:

"You will be amused at the account of a fancy dress ball,
given by Mme. Y. which has made a great stir at Alençon.
Everybody is talking about it. It was magnificent, admirable, unique! Nothing has been seen like it since Alençon
has existed.

"Mme. Y. was a queen, and had a gold crown with a veil
spangled with stars. Mme. O. was a Folly. She wore a dress
of yellow muslin, which was so tight as to make her utterly
ridiculous. When she appeared in this get-up, and saw how
rich were the dresses of the other ladies, she did not know
where to hide herself.

"I learnt all these details from persons who were present
at the notorious ball, which ended at five o'clock in the
morning. As a finale, they had a grand dinner, after which
all the guests went to bed.

"It was necessary to strengthen the floor of the ball room
with props; otherwise the dancers would have fallen into the
room beneath. I forgot to mention that these rooms were
decorated with garlands of flowers and trails of ivy. It is a
pity to go to so much trouble and expense to be made a
laughing stock."

The House Amidst the Storm

Here is now the other wing of the diptych, not less neatly portrayed, which shows the class war. The letter dates from after the removal to the *Rue Saint Blaise.*

"A curious adventure took place recently in connection with a lady whose barouche was standing opposite to our house, outside the Prefecture. The coachman wore gorgeous livery lavishly trimmed with fur. A discontented individual carrying a canvas sack in his hand was just passing by. He stopped for a moment to survey the coachman and then the lady inside the carriage. Then he turned to the open door, undid his bag and threw the contents into her lap.

"At once, she cried out in terror. The coachman came to her assistance, the passers-by ran up. There they saw her convulsed in a nervous attack, and swarming over her were about twenty frogs. They were even on her head; in fact she was covered with them.

"The wretched assailant watched her struggling when the policeman arrived on the scene and asked him why he had done such a thing. He quietly replied, 'I had just caught these frogs to sell, but when I saw this aristocrat, with her coachman all decked out in furs, I preferred to give her a good fright, rather than sell my frogs.' They took him to the gaol; he did not try to escape."

Confronted with this growing antagonism, which was digging an abyss between the "haves" and the "have nots," if we would learn the opinion of the Martin household we may read between the lines of this account, wherein humorous censure is tempered with the gentle philosophy of the Gospel. Mme. Martin is referring to a gala performance at which M. de Cissay was to honor the guests with a speech.

"Two hundred letters of invitation were sent out to the "great ladies," and cards to the ladies not so "great," and care was taken to draw the line between the two categories.

The Story of a Family

"There was one whose son was one of the leading actors, and who had only a card, who said 'If they will not let me enter with those who have letters, I will take my son away and he shall not take part in the play.'

"However, she did not enter with them and did not dare to withdraw her son, but the result was a general discontent among the recipients of the cards.

"To forestall disturbance, today a small celebration was held without any social distinction being made. These gentlemen are really hard put to it to please everybody. It is true that the "great ladies" would not come unless the first places were reserved for them, and on the other hand it offended the mothers whose children were performing, to be relegated to the back places. But it is all in vain; it is only in Heaven that the poor will have the "highest places"; there is no question of it on earth!"[12]

What worried this Christian couple was to see the widespread increase of irreligion. The Pope was a prisoner at Rome and subjected to the insults of the Freemason clique in power. Mme. Martin, who on September 5, 1871, had written: "I firmly believe in the speedy triumph and reestablishment of the Holy Father in his territories," knew the agony of disillusion as year after year went by. She notes anti-clerical incidents at Alençon. On the Assumption, 1873, fanatics passed by, jostling in a threatening manner those who were walking praying through the streets. A civil funeral caused a scandal—the leading local authorities had been seen around the coffin, the Mayor had been a pall-bearer and the Member for Parliament had delivered a speech. Then, on the return of a pilgrimage from Lourdes there had been a sort of counter demonstration. M. Martin, who was coming back radiant, bringing as booty two pieces he had broken off the rock of

[12] Mme. Martin to Pauline, April 29, 1877.

The House Amidst the Storm

Massabielle, emerged first from the station, wearing the little red cross, to be greeted with insulting remarks and laughter. He daringly made his way through the obstructing crowd, but several fellow pilgrims, less fortunate, found themselves taken to the police station on a charge of having taken part in an illegal procession.

Faced with social war and the increasing persecution, should not practicing Catholics who realised the danger "go to the people?" An earnest officer who had fought in the war of 1870, the Count de Mun, proclaimed this to every shade of opinion, in the crusade that he was leading all over France in favor of the *Catholic Clubs.* Was it owing to the impulsion of his stirring eloquence that Alençon was aroused in its turn? A club was soon established in the parish of *Notre-Dame*, at no. 34, *Rue de la Gare.* Opened on November 25, 1875, and named after the brilliant orator, this enterprise of which the Abbé Dupuy, chaplain to the Lycée, took over the direction, bore at first rather a local urban character. Among its founders was M. Louis Martin, whose name is to be found in the dusty volumes in its archives on the list of the first pioneers of Catholic Action in the town society.

*   *   *

Throughout so many changes of all kinds, besides the father, whose serene and grave portrait will occupy our attention later, we see the ideal figure of the mother becoming ever grander and imposing itself increasingly. How can we fail to admire this woman with delicate health, prematurely marked by an inexorable malady, a sufferer from neuralgic headaches, often feverish, whose face, as she owns, is frightening some days, who bore nine children in fourteen years, knew six deaths in sixty-four months, not to mention the illnesses which she had to nurse in her official capacity; who added to the cares of housekeeping the direction of a lace-making business, and declares at moments of special stress that she was up from four-thirty in the morning until eleven at night; who had finally endured the partial wrecking of her home, and the shocks of an economic crisis, without ever weakening in her trust or losing her good humor?

It often happened that she acknowledged her weariness and cast a longing glance to that cloister which she had once longed to enter. The temptation never lasted long. She had embarked upon her life and would go on to the end, faithful to the convictions she had expressed to her brother some weeks before the death of her first baby boy.

"I have much trouble over this wretched *Point d'Alençon*, which puts the crown upon all my misfortunes. It is true I gain a little money, but, oh dear! at what a cost! It is at the cost of my life, for I believe that it is shortening my days, and unless God protects me in a special way, it seems to me that I shall not live long. I could easily console myself over that, if I had not children to bring up. I would gladly welcome death as one welcomes the soft, pure dawn of a beautiful day.

"I often think of my saintly sister and her calm and tranquil life; she works, indeed, but not to gain perishable goods; she is amassing wealth only for Heaven, whither all her longings tend. And I, I see myself here bent down to earth, taking a vast deal of trouble to amass money which I cannot take with me and do not want to. Of what use would it be to me up yonder?

"Sometimes I find myself regretting that I have not done as she, but at once I say to myself: 'I should not have my four little girls, my charming little Joseph!' No, it is better that I should be working where I am and they should be there! Provided I reach Heaven, with my dear Louis, and see them all better settled than I, I shall be happy enough like that, and ask no more." [13]

The last sentence depicts her to the life. She is crucified to the happiness of her family. It would be only if her husband should pre-decease her and all her daughters be settled in life that she might, as she owns to Pauline, consider the project of ending her own days at the Visitation. For the present she is the slave of the household, *lutz de case*, as they say in Italy; "the light of the home." To this primordial duty she is sacrificing what to her is sweetest, long hours of prayer, and the thrilling tasks of external apostolic work.

Her life is centred on *l'abandon* to the will of God. She expresses this in phrases which might have been borrowed from her little Thérèse.

"When I set up my business in *Point d'Alençon*, I made myself ill over it; now I am much more sensible, I worry over it much less, and resign myself to all the tiresome things that happen or may happen. I tell myself that God allows it to work out thus, and then think no more about it." [14] All have their troubles; the happiest are not those who have fewest trials; the wisest and simplest way in all that, is to be resigned to God's will, and prepare oneself beforehand to carry one's cross as bravely as possible . . . "God gives me the grace not to be afraid. I am very tranquil . . . God is a good Father, and He never sends His creatures more than they can bear." [14]

It was the daily sight of such magnanimity that led Marie and Pauline to say in the course of their evidence

[13] Letters of Mme. Martin to her brotner, Dec. 23, 1866.
[14] Mme. Martin to her brother, Feb. 14, 1868.

in the Process of Beatification and Canonisation of their sister: "Our mother was gifted with intelligence beyond the average, and with extraordinary energy. Difficulties were nothing to her." As for the Visitandine, after acknowledging to her brother that she feared lest her dear Zélie should succumb physically beneath the repeated shocks that tried her, she adds: "However, what reassures me a little is her spirit of faith and her truly incredible and prodigious courage. What a valiant woman! She is neither cast down by adversity nor uplifted by prosperity. She is admirable."

Mme. Martin never asked herself all these questions. She was haunted interiorly by the presentiment of her approaching end. She was not unaware that there was some anxiety felt on her behalf, but she vigorously rose above it. "Several people think that I have not long to live," she writes; "I would wish that they were mistaken, for I have no time to die. For the moment, I have too much work on hand." And then, before the eternal dawn must not the prophetic intuition of Sister Marie Dosithée be realised? Must not the *great saint* yet come, who was to be for such a mother the recompense of her martyrdom and the masterpiece of her love?

CHAPTER 6

THE LITTLE FLOWER OF THE FAMILY

The Rue Saint Blaise—awaiting Thérèse—birth
and illness of Thérèse—illness of Marie—
"unfolding of the flower."

FOR some years M. Martin had wished to spare his wife the overwork involved in keeping up a large establishment and the difficulty of two businesses. At the beginning of April, 1870, his nephew, M. Adolphe Leriche, who had recently come into a rich inheritance, decided to buy the jeweller's business and the house in the *Rue du Pont Neuf*.[1] The Martins searched in vain for another house provided with a large garden which the mother desired as a playground for her daughters. The war broke out and rendered all such moves difficult. Finally, they had to fall back upon the property in the *Rue Saint Blaise*, which they had inherited at the death of M. Guérin, and which had again become vacant.

His wife testified that M. Martin arranged everything well. He wanted her to have a pleasant home and saw to the smallest details of the fitting up. Is not a house a sort of reliquary, where the past becomes encrusted or, to put it better, is enshrined in order to

---

[1] M. Adolphe Leriche was the son of François Leriche and Fanny Martin, second daughter of the Captain, who died at the age of twenty-seven.

vivify the present? Is it not "the stone vesture of the household," its material covering, the "home," as they say across the Channel, where even with the minimum of comfort, one should savor the joy of being together, where everything should speak to the eye, the portraits hanging upon the wall, the pictures recalling impressions gained in travel, the crucifix which has received the last kiss of an ancestor, the statue of Our Lady received as a wedding present, that carpet wherein the taste of a loved one is expressed, that piece of furniture in which so many memories of long ago are locked up? If, from want of a coherent and bold housing policy, there are in France too many hovels which impart a leprous aspect to our great cities, nevertheless to adorn, care for, and cherish their houses is one of the most honorable traditions of the middle classes.

It was not until July 1871, that M. Martin migrated from the parish of *Saint-Pierre-de-Monsort* to that of *Notre-Dame*. His mother, however, retained the apartments she occupied in the house where her grandson now settled. Let us enter the *Rue Saint Blaise*, so named from an ancient devotion in Alençon to the glorious Armenian martyr. An historical mansion attracts the traveller's attention. Approached through a royal court of honor, it is a remarkable example of the style of Louis XIII, the *Hôtel de la Préfecture*, which once sheltered the piety and almsdeeds of a spiritual daughter of the Abbé de Rancé, the Duchess de Guise, before serving as the residence of the royal commissioners and subsequently of the administrators of the department.

Just opposite, at no. 42—formerly 36—a stone tablet points out to the pilgrim the house in which Thérèse of the Child Jesus was born. It is modest and incon-

The Little Flower of the Family

spicuous in its red brick; the front room on the ground floor is lighted by two windows provided with exterior shutters; the first floor, pierced by three French windows with elegant fanlights, opens to a balcony, the iron railing of which runs the entire length of the house front, and a single dormer window on the roof lights the topmost room. Formerly detached on its right hand, and separated by a railing from the neighboring buildings, on its left it joined a building as quiet as itself.

At first sight it looks small for a large family, for the additions planned by M. Guérin were never built. On the ground floor are three rooms, opening into one another; the drawing room, dining room and kitchen. On the first floor are three bedrooms, two of which look on to the street; on the second, one bedroom and an attic. A tiled passage leads to the small yard, where is a rustic stone washing place. The yard is prolonged by a narrow passage, contrived between the high walls of the adjacent houses, and gives entry into a square patch of ground—too limited, alas!—made attractive by fruits and flowers, beds both round and semi-circular, and also by climbing pear trees trained on the walls. Encroaching on the garden there was a simple shed, and a building that sheltered a linen room, an outside lavatory, and a lumber room. The living space was reduced, but the elder girls would be there only in the holidays, and then they would draw more closely together and it would be more homey.

When we cross the threshold, we are surrounded by an atmosphere of silence and recollection. Memories crowd upon us from every side. Here is the front room —both sitting room and office—where Mme. Martin, as in the days of her youth, settled herself at the second window to ply her needle on the traced vellum and to

The Story of a Family

receive her workwomen. Here is the steep staircase, from which Thérèse used to call to her mother from every step. Here is the room in which she was born, today enlarged by an oratory. In the garden her father put up a small swing for her. There was the alcove in the shade where she used to count her "sacrifices," the wood-shed where the firewood was stored; the chicken house where Céline with agile hand caught and played with the white fowls belonging to her younger sister.

It is the penetrating charm of French family life that we savor in these surroundings. Everything is calm, fresh and tender. The father put a marble tablet over the door on which were engraved those words: *Louis Martin, Maker of Point d'Alençon*, but that simply meant that, freed now from his own business, he would henceforth take a larger share in that of his wife and thus lighten her work. But there was no workroom, no display of goods to attract strangers. Apart from the comings and goings of the lacemakers every Thursday, they were perfectly private here.

* * *

The cradle was ready. The "great saint" so much desired could come; the last strophe of the poem of home life, wherein lights and shadows had alternated without the parents' hearts losing their freshness or their capacity for wonder. Around them, doubtlessly the wiseacres whispered "eight children, four early deaths, the mother's health endangered . . . was it not time to stop?" At times, M. Martin worried. The mother reassured him. "Do not fear; God is with us." It was the *leitmotiv* of her spirituality that God never gives us more than we can bear. And then, she was over forty, her husband nearly fifty. What a rejuvenation to live over again in middle life the emotions of their early married days! The coffin of their first Thérèse was scarcely closed than she longed for another Thérèse wherein the former might live again. "The good God has gone to the wrong house," she writes to her sister-in-law, who had told her of her own hopes, "for I, who have lost my last little one, would be so glad to have another. But no, I shall have no more. It is useless now to wish for it. I shall never get over the death of my little Thérèse; it hinders my sleeping at nights." [2]

A friend tactlessly undertook to recall her to a sense of realities. "No doubt, God saw that you could never manage to bring up so many children, and so He took four to Paradise." Mme. Martin reacted at once and uttered her supernatural protest at the suggestion. "I do not see the matter in that light . . . God is Master, and He has not to ask my permission. On the other hand, up till now I have borne the fatigues of motherhood very well, trusting to His providence. Moreover, what would you have? We are not on this earth to enjoy great pleasure. Those who look to do so are highly mistaken, and it is notorious that they are disappointed in their hopes." [3] Happy maternal courage, splendidly rewarded! If M. and Mme. Martin had confined themselves to being what the world calls "sensible," their crown would have been shorn of its finest gem. God's designs were to brush aside men's poor calculations and recompense the blind faith of these admirable parents. It was the child of their eventide of life, the ninth, who would set the seal upon their glory.

2 Mme. Martin to her sister-in-law, May 29, 1871.
3 Mme. Martin to her sister-in-law, May 5, 1871.

The Story of a Family

A letter of July 21, 1872, announces the good news:

"I must let you know about a happy event which will take place probably at the end of the year, but which interests only myself at the moment. However, I would rejoice if I knew that I could rear this little being who is to come to our home. She shall not leave it as long as she and I live. I am better than last time; I eat well and am never feverish. I hope the child will be born safely. The trouble is not always at the same door; however, God's will be done!"

On December fifteenth she again tells her sister-in-law of her great joy mingled with fears:

"I am expecting my little angel any day, and I am very perplexed for I have not yet found a nurse. I have seen several, but they are only very moderately suitable, and my husband could not make up his mind to take any of them. It is not a question of money, but because we are afraid of introducing unsatisfactory persons into our home . . . If God would grant me the favor of being able to nurse my child, it would be only a pleasure to rear her. For my part, I am madly fond of children. I was born to have them, but it will soon be time to finish with that. I shall be forty-one on the twenty-third of this month; it is old enough to be a grandmother!"[4]

She retired into herself during that happy time of waiting that has so well been called "advent" and whilst she wondered about the future she seemed to hear a voice uniting with her own. "Whilst I was awaiting her," she wrote later of her child to Mme. Guérin, "I noticed something that had never happened with my other children. When I sang, she sang with me . . . I tell it to you in confidence; no one would believe it." [5]

[4] Mme. Martin to her sister-in-law.
[5] Mme. Martin to her sister-in-law, Jan. 16, 1873.

The Little Flower of the Family

"Pious feminine auto-suggestion," those will say who dread the shadow of the marvellous. A touching intervention from Heaven will be the verdict of the simple. In any case, a delightful symbol of the union of virtue and grace that was being secretly prepared in the shelter of the mother's womb, between the harmonious soul of Thérèse and the vibrant soul of her mother.

"Did it then leap within thy womb, burden adored?
Did tiny angel flutter tiny wing?
You spoke within; the cradle calls her,
And her image laughs in curtained flower."

Hell endeavored to disturb this peace. One evening when she had remained alone on the ground floor of the house to finish some spiritual reading, Mme. Martin was thinking about the diabolic vexations from which certain great servants of God have suffered. "Such outrages will not happen to me," she thought, with a sort of relief; "only saints need fear them." At the same instant, she felt an enormous weight come down upon her shoulder, like a monstrous grip; it might have been the claw of an animal. Terrified for a moment, she pulled herself together, with a prayer of trust, and recovered the pure serenity of her union with God.[6]

Thérèse might make her appearance. In this mysterious bearing, of which only mothers know the intimate gestures, she had drawn with her physical life those contacts, those instincts, that ineffable predestination

[6] It is not within our province to judge the preternatural character of such a phenomenon, nor the authenticity of the interior locutions which, on several different occasions, suggested to Mme. Martin certain decisions. She herself never questioned herself on this matter. She attached to them only a secondary importance. It is in conformity with the divine will, and not in manifestations always subject to distrust, that true holiness consists.

The Story of a Family

which predisposes a child towards good before its birth, and orientates it towards God, as Sully-Prud'homme sings again, in one of his best sonnets:

> "If every soul be kindled from a mother's soul,
>   Flame from her glowing heart, light from her eye,
>   As torch takes fire from touch of torch,
>   This child will gentle, wise and lovely be."

It was on Thursday, the second of January, 1873, at half-past eleven at night, that she was born who would speak of herself as "a little winter flower."

Forthwith, the mother voiced the prayer wherewith she greeted every new-born child: "Lord, grant me the grace that she may be consecrated to You, and that nothing may ever come to tarnish the purity of her soul. If ever she is to lose it, I prefer that You take her at once." Marie and Pauline, then home for the holidays, were told by their father in the middle of the night, but they had to wait until morning for the pleasure of kissing "the benjamin," whose prettiness won their hearts on the spot.

The news was scarcely known outside the house than there was a ring at the door. Timidly a boy handed in a paper addressed to the parents, on which were written these words:

> "Smile, grow up with speed.
>   All summons thee to joy;
>   Gentle care, tender love.
>   Yes, smile at the dawn, bud just unclosed,
>   Thou shalt be a rose some day."

It was the graceful gesture of the father of a family,

The Little Flower of the Family

whom M. Martin had one day met with his wife and son, famished, turned out of doors, sheltering in the porch of the Prefecture. Moved by such "shamefaced poverty," for the family had known better days, his wife had brought them in, fed them, gained their confidence, whilst he exerted himself to find a lucrative position for the unfortunate unemployed father. The latter that day expressed his gratitude in a particularly touching way.

Marie-Françoise-Thérèse had as godmother her oldest sister, Marie-Louise, who was just on the verge of thirteen, and as godfather a boy of the same age, son of a friend of her father's, Paul-Albert Boul. The absence of the latter caused the baptism to be deferred until Saturday, the fourth of January, not without alarming the mother. In the arms of the faithful family servant, Louise Marais, the child was carried to the north side of the sumptuous church of *Notre-Dame*, the baptistry of which, like that of Poissy made famous by St. Louis, that day acquired a new prestige from this event and a new adornment. The sacrament was administered by the Abbé Lucien Dumaine, a personal friend of M. Martin, who was to give evidence at the Process of Beatification.[7]

[7] The piety of the Saint's clients has surrounded with marks of honor the spots hallowed by her twofold birth—to the life of nature and that of grace. The house in the *Rue Saint Blaise* has been detached on the left side and united to the neighboring house by a railing surmounted by a cross. On the right a chapel has been erected beside it, which opens into the room where she was born by means of a cast iron grille, the intervening wall having been pierced. This is situated on the first floor behind the guest room. There we see the bed over which is a copy of Our Lady of the Smile; beside it stands the little chair of the Saint, and opposite, in a glass case, her first clothes. The pilgrim's attention is drawn to a double inscription in French and English, the latter designating Thérèse by the gracious name of "The Little Flower of Jesus." Until 1912 the house was occupied by a former Scottish Presbyterian minister, the Rev. Alexander

The Story of a Family

The mother insisted upon herself writing the letter to Lisieux informing them of the happy event. She was proud of her bonny little daughter, her weight, her pretty face, already so expressive. "This child is named *Thérèse*, after my last little one. They all tell me she is very pretty, and she smiles already. I noticed it the first time on Tuesday. I thought I was mistaken, but I could no longer doubt it yesterday. She looked at me quite attentively, then she gave me a delightful smile."[8]

Alas! the next letter was less optimistic. After having tried to nurse Thérèse herself, a task she regarded as a duty and a pleasure, Mme. Martin had to abandon the attempt. "I am very anxious over my little Thérèse," she writes to her brother on January seventeenth. "I fear she has some intestinal malady, for I notice the same alarming symptoms as in my other children who died. Must I lose this one too? I am in anguish. I have scarcely slept for more than a couple of hours, for I am continually occupied with the baby who, for some time, has been very restless during part of the night."

The child grew worse and a fatal issue was expected in forty-eight hours. An urgent request begged the prayers of the nun at Le Mans. Urged by some inspiration, Sister Marie-Dosithée advised them to entrust the life of her niece to the care of the great Doctor of Geneva. She promised, if he cured the infant, to call her ordinarily by her second name, "Françoise," and summoned Mme. Martin to ratify the promise by at

Grant, and since his death in 1917 by his widow. In 1928, a chapel was added to the shrine, which was shortly afterwards entrusted to the nuns of the Carmel of St. Joseph.

As for the baptistry of *Notre-Dame*, it has been enriched with an altar and a statue of the Saint, by a window portraying an idealist conception of the rite of Baptism, and a memorial tablet, above which in a species of reliquary, is a considerable portion of the baptismal robe worn by Thérèse.

[8] Mme. Martin to her sister-in-law, Jan. 16, 1873.

once making this change. The latter was clinging to the patronage of the Reformer of Carmel, and was not going to give way except as a last resource. Moreover, before any intervention of the nun-aunt, there had been a perceptible improvement. And then, what could it matter to the gentle Francis de Sales if they renamed the child? She refused, ànd thus, at the same time, enriched hagiography with a second Thérèsian chapter.

After some quiet weeks, the enteritis made its appearance afresh at the beginning of March, and the temperature rose. They feared for the worst. The correspondence is full of cries of distress. "I often think of those mothers who have the happiness of nourishing their children themselves, whilst I have to watch them die, one after the other."[9] Mastering her weariness, the brave woman remained on her feet day and night, fighting for the life of Thérèse. The doctor's opinion was decided: only natural feeding could save the child.

The mother thought of "Little Rose," to whom she had entrusted her two baby boys, and whose honesty and robust health gave every confidence. It was then too late for her to set out alone.

"The night seemed long," she writes, "for Thérèse would take scarcely any food. All the gravest symptoms which had preceded the deaths of my other cherubs were showing themselves, and I was very sad for I was convinced that, in the state of exhaustion she was, I could do nothing more for the poor darling. So I set off at daybreak for the nurse, who lives at Semallé, about six miles from Alençon. My husband was away and I did not want to entrust the success of my enterprise to anyone else. On the lonely road I met two men who rather frightened me, but I said to myself, 'I should not care if they killed me!' I felt death in my soul."[10]

[9] Mme. Martin to her brother, March 1, 1873.
[10] Mme. Martin to her sister-in-law, March, 1873.

The Story of a Family

Mme. Taillé raised some difficulties. She could not leave her husband, "Father Moses," and her four small children, the youngest of whom was only a year old, nor could she forsake the treasure of the cottage, the white cow with brown markings, named appropriately "Redskin." They argued, they parleyed, and ended by coming to an agreement. "Little Rose" would come and spend a week at Alençon, then she would take Thérèse to her own home. The master of the house, who had given way only ungraciously, soon regretted his consent and sent his son to order his mother to return, but the lively peasant rated him soundly, and continued her way to the *Rue Saint Blaise*.

At the sight of Thérèse the nurse shook her head. All this upset was quite useless. The child was doomed. She would no longer take any food. The end was near. But we may leave the mother to speak.

"As for me, I went up to my room at once, knelt down before the statue of St. Joseph, and asked him to obtain the grace that my little girl might recover; at the same time, resigning myself to God's will, should He see fit to take her. I do not often cry, but my tears fell whilst I was uttering that prayer.

"I scarcely dared to go downstairs; at last I made up my mind. And what did I see but the child feeding greedily! She did not cease until one o'clock; then she rejected a few mouthfuls and lay like one dead on the nurse's lap.

"There were five of us around her. All were shocked. One of my lace-workers was there crying, and I felt my blood freeze. The baby did not seem to be breathing. We bent over her, trying in vain to find a sign of life. We saw none, but she was so quiet and peaceful that I thanked God she had died so easily.

"At last, after a quarter of an hour, my Thérèse opened her eyes and began to smile. From that moment she was

The Little Flower of the Family

completely cured. Her healthy look returned, as also her liveliness. Since then, all is as well as could be.

"But my baby has gone away. It is very sad to have brought up a child for two months and then be compelled to entrust her to the care of strangers. It consoles me to know that God so wills it, since I have done my utmost to nurse her myself. So I have nothing with which to reproach myself on that score.

"I should have preferred to keep the nurse in the house, and so would my husband; he did not want the others, but he was very willing to accept this one, for he knows that she is an excellent woman.

"With all my heart, I hope that you will never see your children in this condition. One does not know what to do; one fears one is not giving them the right treatment; it is a continual agony. To know what it means one must have gone through it. I doubt whether Purgatory could be worse. We shall suffer there, it is true, but at least we shall know what to do. However, there is one more heavy trial over."[11]

The poor mother was not at the end of her troubles. The honor of giving birth to a saint is dearly bought! Thérèse had reached Semallé in the Norman *Bocage*. The little house of the Père Moyse was one of the most rustic; consisting of a ground floor and garrets, the whole hastily constructed in stone and mud with a thatched roof. The proximity of the shippon, the inevitable dunghill, the fowls wandering about enveloped the dwelling with a country odor which was mitigated by the many scents of the meadows and the healthy perfume of cut hay and fields of grain. Inside the dwelling everything was neat and clean. "Little Rose" knew how to keep house. Her own urchins were well cared for, and the nurslings whom she took from time to time received the same treatment and the same

11 Mme. Martin to her sister-in-law, March 1873.

caressing as the children of the house. How could Thérèse help but revive? She grew plump, her cheeks became rosy, her lungs breathed in pure air.

Three weeks had hardly gone by, than a fresh internal attack declared itself. Her mother, urgently summoned, arrived with all speed, accompanied by the doctor. On the way she gave herself up to melancholy thoughts. "I noticed," she writes to her sister-in-law, "a fine mansion with magnificent grounds, and I said to myself, 'All that is nothing; we shall not be happy until we and our children are all united on high, and I made the sacrifice of my child to God.'"[12]

The immediate danger was averted but there was still anxiety as regards the future. Mme. Martin concludes with the gentle resignation of humble souls accustomed to master their sorrows. "After all, I have done everything in my power to save the life of my Thérèse; now if God wills otherwise, I will try and bear the affliction as patiently as possible. I have need, indeed, to summon up my courage. I have already suffered much in my life. I would wish you, my dear ones, to be happier than I." From Antigone to Iphigenia, from Epictetus to Marcus Aurelius, all the heroines of ancient drama, all the champions of Stoicism pale before this great-hearted woman. To find greater simplicity allied to greater magnanimity in a martyrdom of soul, we must look higher—to the *Mother of Sorrows* —whence Mme. Martin learned the secret of her strength, on Calvary where the tenderest of mothers offered to God the best of sons.

* * *

The parents had not seen the last of their anxieties. Holy Week of 1873 opened for them with a cross of a

---

[12] Mme. Martin to her sister-in-law, March 30, 1873.

The Little Flower of the Family

most unexpected character. Hitherto they had been stricken in their youngest children; they were menaced in their firstborn—her for whom the father had cherished a secret preference and who was his living image. On the eve of Palm Sunday, Marie, then thirteen, had to be brought home to them from Le Mans. Isolation was necessary. She was threatened with typhoid. The Alençon doctor confirmed the diagnosis.

Gloomy presentiments filled her mother's imagination, of which she tells her sister-in-law:

"Although she was not very ill on Saturday evening when she reached home, I felt struck to the heart. I cannot get rid of the idea that she will die of it. For a long time I have been uneasy over her future. She has an extraordinarily tender heart. She has not been able to accustom herself to a boarding school, for she cannot bear the privation of not seeing us. She has told me things in this connection that cut me to the quick.

"I am doing all I can to comfort her and make her hope for her speedy recovery. Yesterday I was telling her that it would be she who would keep house and bring up her little sisters when I am dead. It was very unfortunate that I spoke of that, for she only cried and cannot imagine my dying before her. I greatly fear the good God may hear her prayers.

"However, let us hope He will not permit so great a trial as that we should lose this child. My husband is utterly wretched; he will not leave the house; this morning he installed himself as nurse, for I was compelled to receive my workers, since it was Thursday. But it makes him ill to hear her moaning and takes away all his courage.

"Good-bye, dear. Pray for us in order that, should God require such a sacrifice, we may have the strength to bear it.

"This morning Marie made her Easter duties. She received Holy Communion at five-thirty, in perfect dispositions and with an angelic expression."[13]

[13] Mme. Martin to her sister-in-law, April 10, 1873.

The Story of a Family

The graph of the temperature chart soared in the characteristic arrow-heads. For fear of contagion, Pauline had to spend her Easter vacation at the Visitation. It was a heart-breaking separation for the two sisters, who were united in the most confidential friendship, and also for their mother, who always owned to a certain predilection for her second daughter, and called up all the resources of her ingenuity in order to console her.

Towards the middle of April, the crisis drew near; heavy languor by day, delirium at night, high fever, and that during five weeks. Nothwithstanding the capable assistance of the nursing Sisters, Mme. Martin felt worn out with fatigue. On Good Friday she spent "a grim night," listening to her child murmuring incoherent words in a dull, strange voice. She and her husband did not leave the patient, and remained up for twenty-four hours on end, defying weariness. "I am sure," she declared, "that under such circumstances one needs a special grace of God not to succumb." [14]

The temperature remained exceptionally high; the weakness increased and degenerated into exhaustion. Thanks to worn-out nerves, Marie had attacks of sensitiveness, when she would accept no attentions save from her mother. Caprices, if you will, but which the mother, at such a time, bore without complaint, even had she collapsed at her task.

M. Martin, who was suffering agony at his daughter's dangerous state, resolved to do violence to Heaven to obtain her recovery. He took up his staff and in the beautiful early May days went about eighteen miles on foot, to a sanctuary on the Chaumont ridge, to implore her cure from a thaumaturgus who, popular devo-

[14] Mme. Martin to her sister-in-law, April 13, 1873.

132

The Little Flower of the Family

tion claimed, cured all sorts of fever patients. He set out fasting and returned without having broken the fast. It was not too high a price to pay for his child's restoration. His faith won the intervention from on high. Soon the patient was convalescent. He returned to his favorite recreation and brought home a choice fish to tempt her appetite and, notwithstanding the maternal remonstrances, did not cease to load her with dainties of all sorts.

On May 13th Mme. Martin sent a last bulletin to Lisieux, reporting that Marie was rapidly regaining strength. On Ascension Day, she went out for the first time. At Whitsuntide, Pauline at last came home. The whole family were united at the altar to thank God, and they prepared a joyous expedition to visit their benjamin, in her peasant retreat.

* * *

Thérèse lived outside the family circle, but she was already its sun-beam. Week by week in her mother's letters we can follow the first awakening of her rich nature. She had recovered from the attack of the twenty-ninth of March, and with the spring she revived. The open air, the light, the healthy odor of the fields, the scent of the flowers, the country scenery, the healthy, Spartan life of the farms of Lower Normandy, all developed country instincts in her. Only "Little Rose" and humble folk like her, found any favor in the baby's eyes. One day, when her nurse had left her at the *Rue Saint Blaise* in order to go herself to church, there was such a scene of cries and tears that Louise, the maid, had to beg the good Mme. Taillé to return immediately after Mass. The latter, without more ado, left the church half-way through Mass, not without annoying Mme. Martin, whose conscience was delicate to the point of scruple. On May fifteenth, it was a very different matter. Thérèse would not be appeased until she was taken to the Alençon market place where the farmer's wife had a stall. "As soon as she saw her nurse, she looked at her laughing, and then did not utter another sound. She remained like that all day, whilst the latter sold her butter with all the good country-women." [15]

Should Thérèse happen to arrive in the middle of the lace-workers' visits, Mme. Martin would entrust her to one to another. "She was very willing to see them," her mother writes, "even more so than I, and kissed them several times." [16] Peasants, working-women dressed like "Little Rose," there was all the society she wanted! Away with fine ladies, their rich clothes and geegaws! One came into the room. "As soon as I saw her," continues the mother with a spice of mischief, "I said to her, 'Let us see whether Baby will go to you.' Very surprised, she replied, 'Why not? Very well, try.' She stretched out her arms to the little one, but the latter hid her face, crying out as though she had been burnt. She would not even let Mme. T. look at her. We laughed much at that. In short, she is frightened of people fashionably dressed."

It was at Semallé that Thérèse was at home. "She is sunburnt. Her nurse wheels her in the fields, perched on top of bundles of grass, in a wheel-barrow." [17] She carried her off in her apron, when she went to milk the cow and, now and then, to have her arms free, tied her on to the back of "Redskin," whose peaceful disposition

---

[15] Mme. Martin to Pauline, May 22, 1873.
[16] Mme. Martin to Marie and Pauline, Nov. 30, 1873.
[17] Mme. Martin to her sister-in-law, July 20, 1873.

The Little Flower of the Family

accommodated itself well to the light burden. This open air régime strengthened and invigorated her.

Mme. Martin, who saw with joy these signs of recovered health, watched no less closely those of the development of the intelligence. A lisped word, a gesture, a smile, is it not a whole world to a mother? The answer is unreservedly optimistic. "Little Rose" says one could not find a more delightful child . . . She will be very attractive later on, and even pretty. You need only put her on her feet beside a chair, and she stands very well and never falls. She takes her little precautions for that, and seems very intelligent. I think her disposition will be charming; she is always smiling and has an expression as though she were predestined in a special way." "My little Thérèse has been walking alone since Thursday. She is as sweet and good as a little angel and has delightful ways. You can see that already; she has such a sweet smile! I long to have her home." . . . She is a charming child, very sweet and very forward for her age." . . . "I am very happy to have her. I think she will be the last. She is a lovely child and already graceful. I admire her little mouth, which the nurse told me was 'as big as an eye.'"

On April 2nd, the baby girl, now fifteen months old, returned to brighten the home by her presence. It was not yet time for education, properly so-called; it was that of the first gentle influencing, the directing of the instincts, of those impressions which a gentle firmness makes upon the half-awakened will. To give the rein to nature is to prepare the spoilt child; to hold it in is to awaken the child of God. M. and Mme. Martin did not mean to shirk their duty as regards this earliest training. They wished to attend to it themselves. All here seemed to indicate that the task would be easy. This last fruit of their union had introduced into their life, as it were, a second youth. It was the last seal upon their mutual devotion; their common expression, the clear mirror wherein they both found each other. If Marie strikingly recalled her father's features, if Pauline exactly reproduced the face and personality of her mother, Thérèse truly seemed to have synthesised in herself, physically and morally, the twofold contribution of the outstanding traits of both. Her whole being cried out to them:

"You mingle both in me; look, I am you;
Your faces, voices, souls, your thoughts."[18]

The child had exquisitely winning ways, which made news for her mother's letters to the absent schoolgirls.

"Here comes Baby, to kiss me and stroke my face with her little hand. I see she is interested; she wants 'a pecam,' that is, a pin. The poor little mite will not leave me; she is continually at my side, and loves to follow me about, especially to the garden. When I am not there, she refuses to remain without me, and cries so that they are obliged to bring her to me. I am very glad she is so fond of me, but it is inconvenient sometimes."[19]

As for M. Martin, he doted upon her whom he already called his "Queen," and did not fail to spoil her a little on occasion. She was not eighteen months old before he put up a tiny swing for her at the entrance into the garden, and was not afraid to settle her into

[18] Lamartine.
[19] Mme. Martin to Marie and Pauline, June 25, 1874.

The Little Flower of the Family

it. "She behaves in it like a big girl," writes her mother, who was less at ease. "There is no fear of her letting go of the rope: Then, when it does not go high enough, she calls out. We tie her in front, to prevent her from falling, but, in spite of that, I am uneasy when I see her perched up there." [20]

A special providence watched over her infant days, if we may judge from the following incident, which the mother's pen recounts with satisfaction:

"I had recently a curious adventure with the baby. I am accustomed to go daily to the half-past-five Mass. At first, I did not dare to leave her alone but, seeing that she never woke up, I ended by deciding to leave her. I put her in my bed and drew up the cradle so that it was impossible for her to fall.

"One day, I forgot to place the cradle. When I came back, I could not find my little Thérèse. At the same moment, I heard a cry, and saw her sitting on a chair that was close to the bed. Her head was resting on the bolster, and there she was, only half asleep, as she was uncomfortable.

"I could not understand how she had fallen, sitting, on to that chair. I thanked God, on seeing that she had come to no harm. It was truly providential. She ought to have rolled on to the floor. Her good angel watched over her, and the Holy Souls to whom I pray every day for her, protected her. That is how I account for it; you can explain it as you like." [21]

Already, Thérèse was learning to fold her hands, look at the tabernacle, and lisp a greeting to "the good Jesus." Mme. Martin lived again with her, in deep

[20] Mme. Martin to Marie and Pauline, June 25, 1874.
[21] *Ibid.*

emotion, that most sublime of scenes; the mother bending over her child, surrounding it, enveloping it, clasping it to her, in order to carry it to God in one single movement; as though she would make all her own soul to pass into the soul of her little daughter and plunge it into the divine.

CHAPTER 7

THE SPIRIT OF THE HOME

In what sense was the family *bourgeois?*—the
spirituality of the home—family virtues,
affections and relations.

OUR story thus far has taken on the appearance
of a monograph, wherein the innumerable events
that marked the stages of the life of an ideal
French family have been recorded as they followed one
another day by day. It is time to sound the hidden
well-springs, to search out the love which, beneath the
outward appearances, vivified the inner life of those
concerned; in a word, the spirit of the home.

Their native district and social circle had imparted to
the Martin parents a certain permanent mold. With
its 17,000 inhabitants, among whom aristocratic land-
owners, leading officials, wealthy business men, both
active and retired, predominated, peaceful Alençon,
which ranked as the capital of the region, furnished an
excellent example of the provincial town, conservative
and traditionalist.

"It does not set itself up as a model," admits one of its
historians.[1] "It does not hide its defects but it does not make
a parade of its merits. If it happens that its folk still mis-

[1] René Jouanne, archivist of the Orne Prefecture.

take haughtiness and aloofness for real good-breeding, appearances for realities, a rudimentary culture for true knowledge; if the spirit of intolerance and envy sometimes springs into life, as apple trees in May; these are organic blemishes, such as all small towns know, to whom nothing that is human remains alien, and which cannot conceal the solid qualities that are the effects of its very shortcomings: a slow, steady prudence that avoids dangerous innovations, a praiseworthy aptitude for thrift, a healthy balance of all its faculties, which safeguard order and interior peace."

If their intensely Christian spirit saved the subjects of this account from falling under the first portion of this description, how can we deny them all the positive content of the last lines?

By origin, education and financial position they belonged to what is commonly called the *bourgeoisie*—the middle class; not those of the upper ranks, which then supplied the leaders of capitalism, the highest positions in the liberal professions and the State services, but the lesser ranks that constitute the heart of a nation's middle classes, themselves considered as the centre of its stability and the reservoir of its fundamental virtues. It happens today—and the result has been a happy reaction—that men have seen fit to attach a prejudicial meaning to this word *bourgeois*, to such a degree as to decry as *embourgeoisment* a settling down to an easy life, without originality and without ideal. It behoves us, therefore, to use it here only in its good sense, to express those healthy, solid qualities which were formerly reckoned among the elements of French greatness: simplicity of manners, a cult for work, a spirit of economy, a care to balance the family budget, provide for the future and settle the children in life. Its ideal is easy, honorable circumstances, a well-kept house, probity in business, a sense of proportion, discipline, organisation, method.

Need we add that in the cases of M. and Mme. Martin the Gospel ideal elevated what might otherwise have remained earthbound? There was nothing about them of the parvenu, who ostentatiously displays his valuables, and endeavors to dazzle his neighbors with his newly acquired tinsel. Nor was there anything of the pharisee, comfortably entrenched in the egoism of the *Beati possidentes*. They liked their children to be well dressed; they added extra dainties to the menu on feast days and when they had guests. Clothes and household linen were always clean and the furniture chosen in the style of the day. But all useless expense and ostentation were ruled out of court. They lived modestly according to their station, nothing more.

We must see how wittily the mother rallies the young women whose heads had been turned by the forthcoming ball. "Would you believe it? Some of them are having dressmakers from Mans to make their dresses fearing lest those at Alençon might reveal the secret before the day! Is not all that laughable?" [2] She thus writes to console her sister-in-law, then undergoing a severe trial. "Mme. Y. appears to be much happier than you; she lives only for luxury and pleasure. She gives dances at Mid-Lent, and yet I would rather see you with your troubles than think of you, like her, forgetting the things of Heaven for the short-lived delights of earth." [3]

The wisdom of the race is hidden in these words of the wife: "Under what illusion do the majority of men live! Do they possess money? Forthwith, they want

[2] Mme. Martin to her sister-in-law, March 27, 1870.
[3] Mme. Martin to her sister-in-law, March 30, 1873.

honors. And when they obtain these, they are still discontented, for the heart that seeks anything but God is never satisfied." The contact with the fire of the Christian purified, refined and supernaturalised the Alençon temperament. To understand this family life, we must examine the spirituality of the home.

It was governed by three principles: God's supreme rights; faith in His providence; a trustful, happy, acquiescence in His will.

Apart from God there is no truth; to ignore God is folly; everything must be arranged *sub specie aeternitatis*—in view of eternity. These principles keep coming back as the *leitmotiv* in the correspondence of Mme. Martin. On this point we are informed by Céline: "She had a great spirit of detachment from earthly things and a contempt of the world. Her longings were concerned only with those things that are eternal. I can hear her yet reading out poetic passages from her books, and always it was with a touch of melancholy, for she felt exiled here on earth."—"My father and mother," declares Pauline, in the Process of Beatification, "possessed a profound faith. When we heard them talking together of eternity we were led, young as we were, to look upon the things of the world as pure vanity."

"True happiness is not to be found in this world; we waste our time seeking it here," writes Mme. Martin. "Yes, apart from God all is vanity," the Saint of Carmel will echo. Let us make no mistake. Here we have the key to the training of the children. Like the Maid of Domrémy, it was indeed from her mother that Thérèse "learned her belief."

And it was in the school of the home that she learned

The Spirit of the Home

to adore the ways of God. Providence orders all things with wisdom, power and love, for His greater glory and our greater good. To trust Him blindly was the best policy. To her Visitandine sister, who was worrying over certain business troubles that had come upon M. Guérin, Mme. Martin answered in a letter worthy of a mistress of novices and led their brother himself to profit thereby.

"I have told him not to break his head over all that, and that there is only one thing to be done: pray to God, since neither she nor I can help in any other way. But God, to whom it presents no difficulty, will bring us through as soon as He sees that we have suffered enough, and then you will recognize that you owe the successful issue neither to your own capabilities nor to your intelligence, but to God alone, as I do with my *Point d'Alençon*. This is a very salutary conviction, as I know from experience.

"You know how liable we all are to pride, and I often notice that those who have made their fortune are, for the most part, intolerably self-sufficient. I do not say that either you or I would have come to that, but we should have been more or less soiled with this pride. Then it is certain that unvarying prosperity draws men away from God. Never does He lead His chosen by that road; they must first pass through the crucible of suffering in order to be purified. You will say that I am preaching, but such is not my intention. I often ponder over these things and I am telling them to you. Call that a sermon now, if you like."[4]

No, there is no question of a sermon for another's benefit. We have here the voice of a soul, the summing-up of its daily meditations, or rather, since in this the

[4] Mme. Martin to her brother, July, 1872.

couple were as one, the accepted teaching of the household, a teaching that worked out into a practical rule of life and issued in its logical outcome: abandonment to the divine will.

To these stalwart Catholics, life was something like those pieces of lace, the perfection of which is the result of long and patient asceticism. From all eternity, the divine Artist had traced out the design. Grace, like an invisible thread, had, with its inspirations, pricked out the pattern. It remained only to follow out the smallest details closely, and avoid breakages and knots. The simple worker toils at the piece from day to day, resigned to take care of a detail, without understanding the whole development of the design. The master worker repairs, adds finishing touches, regroups, assembles, and the marvel results; the outcome of obscure labor wholly informed by love. Foolish indeed would be he who wished to improvise, to substitute his plan for that of the Creator. Mme. Martin had experienced that on her own account, and relates the little incident charmingly:

"I had said to God, 'You know that I have no time to be ill.' I was heard beyond my hopes and I boasted of it to myself a little. Then He seemed to answer, 'Since you have no time to be ill, perhaps you will have time for much trouble?' And I assure you, I have not been spared. You see, in this world it is like that. We must carry the cross in one way or another. We say to our Lord, 'I don't want that.' Often He hears us, but often, alas! for our unhappiness. It is better to take patiently what comes to us; there is always joy beside the pain."[5]

It was not that they shielded themselves behind

[5] Mme. Martin to her sister-in-law, Oct. 1, 1871.

The Spirit of the Home

gush, when faced with adversity, or that they affected indifference or stoical insensibility. Their hearts bled, their eyes wept, they cried out under the affliction, but always, whether it were a question of separations, illness, bereavement, material uncertainty or spiritual suffering, the divine will had the last word: *Fiat!*

Still less were they playing at practicing high virtue. In the mother's letters we find avowals of this kind, but there was no false humility there. Mme. Martin was the last woman in the world to pose. "Oh dear! how tired I am of suffering! I have not a grain of courage left. I am impatient with everybody." . . . "Before desiring sanctity for others, I should do well to take the road thither myself—a thing I don't do!" . . . "I often say during the day: 'My God, how I long to be a saint!' and then I do not labor to become one!"

*   *   *

The whole life of the household was regulated according to God. His will was law, without gloss and without appeal. The observance of Sunday and that of the fasts and abstinence days of the Church was carried to the verge of scruple. Not only was the shop inexorably closed, an unusual thing at that time, since the *Code* made no regulation upon the matter, but except in case of absolute necessity all travelling and all purchasing was forbidden on the Lord's Day. The maids were required to buy all necessary provisions the previous day, bread and milk included. So much the worse for the children who, when there were feast-day celebrations in the town, endured the torments of Tantalus as they contemplated with envious eye the stalls laden with tempting wares which, for them, had become untouchable! Their father himself set the example. Tempted one day by a grindstone in a hawker's shop, he confined himself to saying to the salesman, "Take my order for a stone like that. I will come back tomorrow, as I buy nothing on Sunday."

The wife saw in this a pledge of divine favor. Writing to Lisieux, where they had had some business mishap, she expresses her hope that all will soon be set right.

"What gives me this confidence, which nothing can take from me, is, above all, the edifying way in which you keep Sunday holy. All those, perfect or imperfect, who faithfully observe the Lord's Day, succeed in their undertakings and in the end, by one means or another, become rich. I am so convinced of this that I often say to the children, 'One day, your uncle will be a rich man.' They reply, 'How do you know, Mother?' I answer that I do know, and they are much astonished. Marie replies, 'Then you are a prophet, Mother?' Well, the future will show whether I am mistaken, but I do not believe it."[6]

The future confirmed this expectation by means of an inheritance that suddenly established M. Guérin in a brilliant position. As for Mme. Martin, she owns with charming humility that she was less rigid on this point than her husband. "When, for instance, I need a roll for my children, I buy it. But very often I admire Louis' example and say to myself, 'There is a man who has never tried to become rich . . .' I can only attribute the easy circumstances he enjoys to a special blessing, the reward of his faithful observance of Sunday."[7]

Still more meritorious was their inviolable respect for the fasts and abstinence of the Church. On this point the father was uncompromising. On a fast day he let his guests do honor to the menu and contented himself

[6] Mme. Martin to her sister-in-law, Sept. 29, 1875.
[7] *Ibid.*

The Spirit of the Home

with a frugal collation. It was very upsetting to the mistress of the house! Hence she used all her epistolary diplomacy to incline her visitors to choose days exempt from all restriction.

Although not a strong woman, she showed herself almost fiercely intransigent where the laws of the Church were involved. "We are in the season of penance," she writes during Lent in 1875. "Happily, it will soon be over, for I suffer so from fasting and abstinence. It is not that it is a very hard mortification, but my digestion is so poor, and I am so cowardly, that I would not observe it at all if I listened to nature!" [8] It is true that to keep up her courage there were three daily sermons from the two Lenten preachers, but—she adds playfully—"not one of them preaches well and it is an extra penance."

The following year the moral strengthening was more efficacious but her physical strength was failing. "Au revoir, Pauline; we shall soon meet. Only twenty-one days, but twenty-one days very hard to spend, for I must fast. It is very tiring. Last week, I thought I should be obliged to give it up. I had such pain that I could scarcely bear the weight of my dress, and I suffered thus all morning. I had decided to give in, but the Capuchin Father preached a sermon in the evening that restored my courage." [9] In December, 1876, consumed with cancer, she went to Lisieux to consult a specialist, who had to pronounce concerning the feasibility of an operation. It was Embertide. She sent word to her brother, who was prepared to welcome her warmly. "You know it is a fast day, and I am fasting for I am not ill enough to dispense myself." We see her

[8] Mme. Martin to her sister-in-law, March 14, 1875.
[9] Mme. Martin to Pauline, March 26, 1876.

also, and this sort of mortification cost her very much
more, impose restrictions upon her correspondence during Lent. Rigorism, some will say. May it not be, perchance, that it is we who are lax or degenerate?

The truth was that in the cases of these two, there
subsisted a wholly ascetic side to their characters, betraying the old attraction to the religious life. M. Martin's ordered life retained something of a monastic
flavor. He abstained from smoking, from sitting with
his legs crossed, eating between meals, sitting close to
the fire without necessity. On Good Friday, he ate
only at mid-day, refusing all food in the evening. If he
were working in the garden on fast days, and his daughters brought him some refreshment, in order to make
him accept it they had to remind him that the law of
fasting did not forbid taking a drink. It was with joy
that he buried himself during three days in retreat at
the monastery of the *Grande Trappe*, at Mortagne.

On her part his wife added voluntary mortifications
to the "hairshirt" of her daily duties. "On her return
from daily Mass," states Céline, "I used to notice that
she gave the others a good lunch, but herself took only
some soup, which she ate standing, by stealth and in
haste. She attended to her occupations with extraordinary thoroughness and was the last to go to bed at
night." Under the guidance of the parish priest of
Monsort, she aspired to lead a life of perfection. She
belonged to several pious associations. In particular,
she became a member of the *Archconfraternity of the
Agonising Heart of Jesus*, of which she said, all the same,
though her humility renders the avowal suspect, that
it could not make her better, since she fulfilled the
obligations involved so badly.

Since her youth she had regularly visited the monas-

The Spirit of the Home

tery of the Poor Clares, close to her home, at no. 3, *Rue de la Demi-Lune*. The relics of the "Good Duchess," Margaret of Lorraine, were venerated there, and she had brought the *Poor Ladies* to Alençon. It was there that Mme. Martin used to come to the parlor to confide her troubles and beg for novenas and prayers. In this chapel she had made her profession as a Franciscan Tertiary, and she regularly attended the meetings of the Chapter. It was from having accompanied her often that Léonie came to dream of one day wearing the habit of the daughters of St. Clare. More than any other, Thérèse's mother was prepared to understand and live this Tertiary Rule, which confers upon the secular life the benefit of the religious life and, in the words of Lacordaire, makes of the nuptial chamber a cell and of the world a Thebaid.

* * *

Let us penetrate into this inner sanctuary of the family circle. We shall there find the "liturgy of the home" held in honor, which expresses the aspirations of the household collectively. They remembered the Master's promise: "Where two or three are gathered together in my name, there am I in the midst." It was in common or, better still, "united as one," that they called upon the Lord. Our Lady's statue became the spiritual meeting place, and, so to speak, the sign of their living unity. There every morning Thérèse knelt to say her childish prayers. Our Lady looked down upon the elder girls' room. Marie, thinking the statue too large, and out of proportion in the small chamber, would have liked to replace it by a smaller one, but her mother protested. "When I am no longer here, my dear, you will do what you like, but so long as I live this statue of our Blessed Mother does not leave this room."

The Story of a Family

At the beginning of May the statue was made the centre of what amounted to a real oratory. A background was constructed of leaves and flowers, mixed with branches of hawthorn which, in return for a liberal alms, a poor woman cut for them out in the country. Lights and baskets of flowers were arranged at Our Lady's feet; nothing was considered too good for her. Mme. Martin wished to see her emerge from the wreaths and petals, and delighted in their fresh beauty.

The eldest daughter, to whom belonged the privilege of arranging this shrine in her own room, declared frankly: "My May shrine was so pretty that it could stand comparison with that at *Notre-Dame*. It was quite a business to arrange it at home. Mother was too exacting; more difficult to please than Our Lady! She must have the white hawthorn branches reaching to the ceiling; the walls covered with greenery etc." How gladly the youngest gathered the best roses from the Pavilion, the cornflowers and marguerites growing beside the country lanes! She kept some for St. Joseph's statue, before which her mother loved to pray. It was thus that, quite spontaneously, she felt enveloping her a love for the things of Heaven.

> "I loved from dawn of infant days,
>   Mary and Joseph oft to praise.
> E'en then, my soul upsoared in raptured gaze.
>   To mirror deep within my eyes
>   The skies!"

The Church's feasts, that sacred drama inspired by the mysteries of our Saviour's earthy life, of which Chateaubriand sang in the *Génie du Christianisme*, the transcendent value of its aesthetic appeal, infused beauty into the evening conversations. The Church

The Spirit of the Home

calendar had a soul for those Catholics of the old school. They lived its cycle as the year went round. They made the lives of the saints their favorite reading, and in the middle of the 19th century, we find parents faithful to the practice, now so esteemed in the circles of our young adherents of Catholic Action, of reading some good biography in order to discuss it together and draw mutual profit from it.

Their whole existence as a family turned on the life of their parish. The parents began the day by hearing the half-past-five Mass at Saint Pierre-de-Monsort and later, when they moved house, at *Notre-Dame*, unless, a mission or some special occasion took them to the church of *Saint-Léonard*, or to the chapel of the Poor Clares. Whether they had been up late at night, or be Lent ever so hard, and the mother confessed that at times it cost her something, they rose at five a.m. The neighbors who heard the sound of a door being shut in the silent streets, would say, "Oh, it is only that holy Martin couple going to church. We have still some time to sleep." According to the circumstances, they communicated once or several times in the week, and every first Friday of the month. M. Martin had long been a member of the *Society of the Blessed Sacrament*. In his room, the favorite picture was an *Ecce Homo*. The reception of our Lord in the Eucharist and the contemplation of Him in His sufferings, helped him to make an offering of his work and a sacrifice of every trial.

The whole family was present on Sunday at High Mass, Vespers, and when there was a mission or any other special sermon, at evening service. The degenerate faithful—if these two words can be coupled together—will perhaps be inclined to label such proceed-

ings "fanaticism." Must not such a régime bore anyone
to death and inspire a horror of religious practices? If
Thérèse's parents could return to earth, they would
doubtlessly retort that, after all, such practices were
worth as much as obligatory attendance at the cinema,
or listening-in late at night to the radio, and that nobody was any the worse for the church going. If they
were ignorant of the topical songs of the day, they were
fond of religious airs, the only ones that speak to the
heart and dispose men to prayer. As for secular music,
they appreciated it in its place, but objected to its in-
trusion into the sanctuary. Referring to some May
Devotions embellished with some polyphonic music of
very doubtful taste, Mme. Martin writes: "To tell the
truth, I do not care very much for this ceremony. One
hears the most impossible settings, and such cooings
that it is impossible to understand anything; one might
be at a café concert, and it irritates me. Formerly it
was so much more devotional, but it seems we are going
in for progress!" [10]

They had the simple, honest faith of the artists who
carved on the porch of *Notre-Dame* a magisterial page
of Scripture, and reproduced chapters of the Bible in
gleaming stained windows. Public worship was a matter neither of obligation nor of routine, still less a
burden, but a need, a repose and, to put it shortly, a
festival. Now and then, they would take part in some
pilgrimage to *Our Lady of Victories*, to Séez, Chartres,
or Lourdes, and come back enriched with memories
which would form the subject of conversation at home
for some time. Often, such expeditions were in thanksgiving, or to pray for a recovery. The father, sometimes
accompanied by one or other of his daughters, accom-

[10] Mme. Martin to Pauline, May 14, 1876.

plished this mission as a religious service belonging to him. The mother did not suggest going with them. "For my part," she once wrote, "travelling does not appeal to me. There is only one journey for which I should feel much attraction, and that is to the Holy Land. I think, however, that I shall visit it only at the general judgment in the Valley of Josaphat. I shall try and see everything whilst I am there!" [11] At least she did her best to share spiritually in these pious journeyings and to associate all her little circle with them. Thus, little by little was formed the common "spirit" of that Christendom in microcosm which the family should be.

* * *

Such a household could not but radiate its beliefs. The days of Catholic Action with its various movements were yet to come. Collective good works were just beginning; we have seen the part which M. Martin had taken in founding the Albert de Mun Catholic Club. Already, for all that, Catholics were moving in a militant atmosphere. Polemics were in full swing; around Church and school could be heard the muttering of the storm; secret societies were preparing an offensive which in half-a-century, would laicise the whole of public life, and drive God from the public conscience. The only counter measure then possible was the witness of a profound, loyal, earnest conviction, inspiring a delicate and disinterested charity or, to speak better, that of an integral faith that unified a man's entire existence and developed towards both God and man.

Thérèse's father did not know the meaning of human respect. No matter who might be with him, he raised his hat when passing a church, greeted priests and reli-

[11] Mme. Martin to her sister-in-law, Sept. 7, 1875.

gious, knelt down if the Blessed Sacrament passed by. His motto was that of Ozanam: *Do not make yourself be seen, but let yourself be seen!* It frequently happened that he silenced blasphemous language by some simple, courteous remark. He did not hesitate to take it upon himself to remove the hat from a certain wag, a would-be "strong-minded" personage, who, with his cap crammed down on his head, seemed to be sneering at the procession of the Blessed Sacrament, and contemptuously surveying the monstrance. If M. Martin did not like religious controversy, he did not shrink from it when the good of souls was in question. His daughters recalled how eagerly, on one such occasion, he had quoted the celebrated saying of Napoleon at St. Helena: "I have known men, and Jesus Christ was not a man." In concert with his wife, whose charities gained her access to many a house, he took measures to secure that all the dying in the neighborhood had the last sacraments. He considered it an honor to escort the Blessed Sacrament to the poorest dwellings. Mme. Martin describes one such scene that occurred at the house of an indifferent neighbor where, by sheer force of kindness, she had succeeded in bringing a priest.

"I have been present at a ceremony that I shall never forget. I saw the poor, dying woman, who is about my own age, leaving so many children who greatly need her. They were all there crying. One heard nothing but sobs on every side. She had received Extreme Unction, and we were expecting the end at any moment, and she was suffering terribly. For a fortnight she had spent the nights up, for she could not bear to lie in bed for more than a few minutes. Her two youngest children, Élise and Georges, are at home. I keep them in the afternoon, and they play without troubling me . . . Oh, how sad is a house where there is no re-

The Spirit of the Home

ligion! How awful death seems! In the sick-room there was not one sacred picture to be seen. There were plenty of pictures, to be sure, but all of subjects anything but religious. However, I hope the good God will receive this poor woman into His mercy. She has been so badly brought up that there is much excuse for her."[12]

M. Martin himself made all arrangements for the funeral, whilst his wife strove to surround the orphans with every motherly care.

When an obstinate sinner proved recalcitrant despite every effort, the entire family joined forces to effect this difficult capture. St. Joseph was requested to intervene by means of a novena. Several such victories were obtained by dint of prayer. The parents knew no purer joy; they even persisted in applying their suffrages to souls whose seeming final impenitence had baffled their hopes.

M. Martin's influence extended to a whole circle of friends in the town, grouped around M. Vital Romet, several of whom, but for him, would perhaps have relished only worldly pleasures. He led them to attend the meetings of the Catholic Club, to add dignity to the parish ceremonies by their earnest cooperation, to visit the poor and enroll themselves with him in the Conference of St. Vincent de Paul. It was among them, likewise, that he recruited members for the work dear to him beyond all others, of the *Nocturnal Adoration of the Blessed Sacrament.*[13] He would not have missed his

---

[12] Mme. Martin to Pauline, Nov. 7, 1875.

[13] The *Adoration Nocturne*, which was one of several movements which came into being at the period, with the object of making reparation for the irreligion in France and particularly for outrages against the Blessed Sacrament, blasphemy, profanation of the Sunday etc. was founded in 1848, at *Notre Dame des Victoires* at Paris. It owed its origin to the zeal of the celebrated Jewish convert and Carmelite, Père Augustin du Saint Sacre-

monthly watch before Our Lord exposed, amidst a little group of adorers, for an empire. On All Saints' Eve, 1873, worn out with fatigue, he wished, notwithstanding, to be present at the tryst with his Lord. When the usual prayers had been said, he left an intimate friend to take his watch and went up to bed at once. His haste was fortunate. The dormitory was filled with thick, suffocating smoke; two beds were on fire. Had it not been for his energetic action, the fire would have destroyed the sacristy and, perhaps, have reached the church.

What he liked about the Holy Hour was the thanksgiving, wherein he could express his longing to praise God. He saw the finger of Providence everywhere. At the sight of the Creator's works, his soul burst into song, marvelled, went into ecstasies. He would have wished to communicate his song of praise to the whole earth. It was for this that he had so desired to have a son a missionary. He consoled himself for this disappointed hope by setting aside annually a generous contribution to the *Society for the Propagation of the Faith*.

*　　*　　*

The supreme argument of the apostolate is "the contagious charm of charity," the "See how these Christians love one another," which since the days of the Primitive Church, in the midst of an idolatrous or neo-pagan world has ever conquered right-minded men. In this respect, M. Martin was exemplary. He never showed himself other than kind and benevolent, abstaining from judging his neighbor and systematically giving him the benefit of the doubt. Like his patron,

ment, formerly the musician Hermann Cohen. Subsequently the Augustinians of the Blessed Sacrament took over its direction. It spread to Tours, thanks to the influence of the "Holy Man," M. Dupont, and then over France generally.

The Spirit of the Home

St. Louis, he highly appreciated the beatitude promised to the peacemakers, and on more than one occasion, aided by his physical courage and natural daring, he did not hesitate to separate ruffians fighting with knives.

Mme. Martin used to acknowledge that she found more difficulty in repressing the vivacity and mastering the first movements of an astonishingly rich and ardent temperament. Especially did she reproach herself for that shrewdness which made her discover in the twinkling of an eye, the "human side," of which Pascal speaks; oddities, follies, weak points, and prompted her to sketch an amusing picture of them for her own circle. There was hardly any malice in it; it was rather mischievous teasing and social wit. None the less, she did blame herself and humbled herself without any excuses.

"And I," she writes to her brother, "who was mean enough to make fun of Mme. Y! I deeply regret so doing. I do not know why I cannot like her. She has never done me anything but good and has rendered me services. I, who detest ingratitude, can but detest myself, for I am nothing but a real *ingrate*. Also I want to change once for all, and I have begun already some time ago. I have seized upon every occasion to speak well of that lady. It is all the easier to do that since she is an excellent person, worth more than all those who laugh at her, beginning with myself." [14]

Is it not true that here we have a failing acknowledged with a thoroughness rarely found in conventual Chapters of Faults?

An incident of a different kind will allow us to judge of the patience of the Martin couple. A disagreeable neighbor had a ditch dug too near to the intervening

[14] Mme. Martin to her brother, Dec. 25, 1871.

wall enclosing their property. The danger was pointed out to him; he became angry. For the sake of peace they yielded. The fatal collapse resulted. He now raged and took legal proceedings to force his victims to refund him half the cost of repairing the damage. The bad faith of the plaintiff was so obvious, that the magistrate himself was indignant. Unfortunately a few centimetres were wanting to the fallen enclosing wall. An expert had to be called in and the law offers many a resource to those skilled in sharp practice. There was a risk of being involved in the meshes of a lawsuit. Was this upset going to make the defendants lose their serenity, obviously bullied as they were? Here is how the mother comments upon it to Pauline: "We have come to this; I do not know how it will end. I am not concerning myself about it very much. We can but accept contradictions patiently, since we must suffer in this world. If only it enables us to avoid a little of Purgatory, we shall bless M. M. in the next world, for having made us undergo some of it in this life. But I prefer that it should be he who should do us this wrong, rather than that we should have to reproach ourselves with having caused him a quarter of the trouble." [15]

We may gather from this, how patiently they treated their debtors who were in difficulties. More than once, with timely monetary loans, they came to the help of business men threatened with failure. As for doing good to those in need, the Saint's autobiography tells us to what a degree charity was held in honor in her home. "We must give alms, in order to go to Heaven," the mother loved to repeat. Céline writes on this subject: "Like my father, she showed great charity to the

[15] Mme. Martin to Pauline, March 26, 1876.

The Spirit of the Home

poor, whatever might be their distress, and that without ever sparing herself trouble or setting limits to her generosity. I have often seen in our house unfortunates whom she sheltered and provided with clothes." The faithful maid, Louise, attests that her mistress often sent her to poor folk "with soup, bottles of wine, and two-franc pieces." "And nobody knew about it," she adds, "except us two." When the floods occurred at Lisieux, a liberal contribution to the relief fund was sent at once.

Nor was it a matter of merely giving in money or kind, or agreeing to a certain percentage being deducted from the family income and assigned to works of charity. They gave personal service; when needed, they went to inconvenience. This charity had its gracious, or heroic gestures—its *fioretti*—about which there seems to cling a breath of the early Franciscans. Thérèse, who had a prodigious memory, remembered how, on the twenty-third of May, 1875, when she was but two and a half, when Léonie made her first Communion she had seen a little fellow-communicant of a poor family, whom Mme. Martin had dressed in new clothes, sharing in the family festivities, and occupying the place of honor at the evening meal. When they travelled, they did not urgently seek the most comfortable places. On one occasion the mother politely recalled to a sense of what was fitting a neighbor who showed annoyance when the railway carriage was invaded by a woman carrying two tiny children. When they reached the terminus, together with her husband, she insisted upon accompanying the poor woman to her home, and helping her with her children and luggage. It was after midnight when the Martins reached their own house.

The Story of a Family

M. Martin once found at the railway station an epileptic, completely destitute of resources and dying of hunger. He took off his hat, put in a generous alms, and did not hesitate to go round and make a collection. Many coins were dropped into this new-fashioned begging bowl, and the sick man, in tears of joy, was able to have treatment at last and return home. Another still more meritorious incident happened in a crowded street, where the good samaritan found a workman fallen to the ground drunk, his bag of tools lying beside him. The passers-by glanced at him and turned away, not at all anxious to expose themselves to the drunken grumbles of the individual. M. Martin leaned over him, took his arm, lifted him to his feet together with the bag, and supported him to his home, though he gave him a serious talking-to on the following day.

He loved to spend himself without casting a thought to what people might say, or to his own danger. He was an excellent swimmer and had several rescues to his credit. He became an amateur fireman in case of need. Thus he went alone to the assistance of an old woman and dragged her out of the flames. At home, knowing his intrepid courage, they would tremble for his life, and when he was late in returning, they would dread lest he had come to some harm.

No doubt, it was in recognition of some outstanding benefit that some rhymer once addressed to him a doggerel verse wherein the gratitude is more evident than the poetry:

"Great and noble heart! Who ever knew better than he how to offer a supporting and protecting hand to such as implored it? Nothing could change his lovable simplicity.

The Spirit of the Home

Loyalty was ever his motto. To all he showed himself affable and generous. In stormy days none ever sought his help in vain."[16]

He was no less ready to undertake the peaceful but tedious negotiations with government departments, in order to obtain admission to the Home or the hospital of sick tramps and such like. Mme. Martin relates an incident of this sort to Pauline with some feeling:

"We had been for a long walk through the fields. On the way back, we met a poor old man of good appearance. I sent Thérèse to give him some money. He seemed so touched and thanked us so profusely, that I could see he was in a very pitiable state. I told him to follow us, and that I would give him a pair of boots. He came. I gave him a good dinner, for he was dying of hunger.

"I could not tell you all the miseries he was enduring in his old age. This winter, he had had his feet frost-bitten. He slept in an abandoned hut; he was in want of everything and used to go and crouch against the wall of the barracks, in the hope of receiving a little food. Finally I told him to come when he liked, and that he should have something to eat. I wish your father could get him into the Home for the aged; he is so anxious to go. We are going to arrange the matter.

"This meeting makes me very sad. I cannot help thinking of the poor fellow, whose face yet brightened up so happily at the few coins I gave him. 'With those, I shall eat soup tomorrow; I shall go to the public soup kitchen. Then I

---

[16] "Mieux que lui, qui jamais sut, grand et noble coeur,
A qui l'implore offrir un appui protecteur?
Rien ne peut altérer son aimable franchise.
Toujours la loyauté composa sa devise.
Il sait être pour tous affable et généreux.
Nul ne l'implore en vain aux moments orageux."

shall buy some tobacco and have a shave.' In a word, he was as happy as a child. All the time he was eating he would take up the boots, look happily at them and smile."[17]

Mme. Martin was not satisfied until, after many a fruitless attempt, her husband succeeded at last in obtaining the poor man's admission to the Home for Incurables, at which the beggar shed tears of joy.

Her charity would expose her to inconveniences of a different sort. She had entrusted Léonie to the care of two former school teachers, who had donned a religious habit without authorization, and she discovered that these were exploiting and cruelly starving a little girl of eight, Armandine V. whose education they had undertaken. After having for some time secretly fed the child, Mme. Martin made her speak and, secure in the evidence she possessed, decided to intervene. Since the shrews remained unmoved, the child's mother was informed, then the parish priest of Banner, and at last the local magistrate. With consummate hypocrisy, the accused tried to stir up public opinion. Armandine, threatened with reprisals and rendered bewildered by alcohol, denied her previous statements. The matter became more embittered. Finally, a public exposure decided the case for the right. The child was restored to her family and the Superintendent of Police concluded by saying to Mme. Martin, hitherto more dead than alive: "I place this child under your protection, and since you have been kind enough to take an interest in her, I will do also for the future. It is so pleasant to do good!"

The victory was won but it had been paid for with a sharp fright and was to have a very painful sequel. The

[17] Mme. Martin to Pauline, May 14, 1876.

The Spirit of the Home

intrigues continued. There was a danger lest the child should lapse into vice. Mme. Martin, who had offered in vain to pay for her at the *Refuge*, ends her account in words of poignant sadness:

"As you see, Pauline mine,

'On earth all is not roses,
Hope's sweetness, nor joy hour by hour,
At morning the bud uncloses,
At eve, oft the faded flower.'

"But to tell you the truth, I have made up my mind to it. I have been through so much already, in all sorts of ways, that a sort of protective armor has formed around my sensitiveness. Such is not yet the case with your tender heart, little girl, so you feel more keenly the least pinprick; but by dint of being pricked you will end by not feeling the pain."[18]

Does not disinterested charity, carried to this point, attain to the high standard of that majestic description drawn by St. Paul in his first Epistle to the Corinthians?

*   *   *

Need it be mentioned that in this domaine M. and Mme. Martin knew how to respect the hierarchy of values? The inner circle of the family affections was that wherein they showed the greatest earnestness. They possessed a certain "patriarchal" sense—alas, this word has an ill sound today!—which rendered them very keenly alive to the duties created by ties of blood. Repeatedly, the father pilgrimaged to Athis-sur-l'Orne, to pray at the tomb of his forbears and learn all the news of his relations. The grandparents were by right the guests of the home, and the children were trained to put up with the innocent vagaries of old age and to

18 Mme. Martin to Pauline, Nov. 7, 1875.

The Story of a Family

show the old folk honor and attention. The fact that these latter were able during long years to live in the same house, or share the life of their children without this ever causing the slightest difficulty, shows the quality of this filial piety.

It was with the Lisieux relatives that the warmth of intimate friendship was revealed most clearly. Thanks to the companionship of a wife endowed with exceptional gifts of character, Isidore Guérin had become a splendid type of Catholic and apostle. The many vexations which he experienced at the head of his chemist's business, and the drug factory, which he had added to it, never damped his courage. He had put himself into the hands of Our Lady of Victories; he expected her to help him effectively, and in due time he received such help. During times of doubt and cant, the words of Scripture sufficed to tranquillise him. He was soon to become a member of the Council of the Fabric of St. Peter's cathedral, and to cooperate in founding the Conference of St. Vincent de Paul and the Catholic Club at Lisieux. Subsequently, he became the promoter and the financial supporter of the *Bonne Presse*. In one letter Mme. Martin alludes to an altar of repose which her brother erected in 1876, and which stood out in rather startling fashion against a background of light and greenery, on which shone resplendent a great cross in variegated colored lights, surrounded by this inscription:

Plus on l'outrage, plus elle brille. "The more it is outraged, the brighter it shines!"

Gesture and motto depict the man.

This transformation of the former mocking and light-hearted student into the militant Catholic seems to have increased tenfold the love his sister had ever borne him. She no longer needed to guide, still less to scold him. She remained eager to help him in his material affairs. She inquired about his business, worried over his yearly balance sheets, and when he fell ill burst into tears—she who could not cry. For her young sister-in-law she procured maids whom she had herself first "tried" and trained. On his side, with exquisite tact, M. Martin arranged some matters of succession and at his own loss realised certain investments so as to secure the credit of his brother-in-law when the latter was in a temporary difficulty. He even took certain measures to help start the drug factory. When on March 27, 1873, this latter was destroyed by fire, a letter from Alençon expressed the distress of both, whilst at the same time sounding therewith the note of Christian hope.

"I am terribly upset"—again it is the wife who writes—"to hear your news about the fire. When I think of all the trouble which my brother had taken to set the factory going, and now to see his labor destroyed in an instant! You need great faith and resignation to bear this reverse of fortune without murmuring, and with submission to the will of God. For my own part, I am feeling its effects; added to the troubles I already have, it has taken away all my courage. It is true that we each have our cross to bear, but there are some upon whom it weighs more heavily, and you, my dear sister, have already begun to see that life is not all roses. The good God wills to detach us from earth, and draw our minds Heavenwards."[19]

Happier circumstances call forth mutual confidences. In February, 1868, Jeanne Guérin was born, to be followed by the little Marie in August 1870. All this correspondence is like a romantic cycle. The babes are

[19] Mme. Martin to her sister-in-law, March 30, 1873.

announced, arrive, grow up and sometimes die. Their doings and words fill the whole stage; their parents scarcely appear. "Two young mothers discover their children!" might well sum up these hundreds of letters, wherein everything concerning the home has a profound echo; the hopes, fears, disappointments and agonies; the layette in preparation, the forthcoming baptism, the duties of godparents undertaken on both sides with the full sense of their religious responsibility. Then the pretty faces wake; there is the mutual communication of fresh discoveries, of gifts exchanged and the enthusiasm they call forth. It is good to see these high-minded women encouraging each other to bear their glorious burden with a smile on their lips. "Children come," reads a letter from Alençon, "if you have as many as I, you will need much self-sacrifice, and the desire to enrich Heaven with chosen souls." From Lisieux, where the family medical authority lived, they reply by sending the proper remedies and advice to the poor mother, busied in attending to her patients.

When death digs a grave at the very foot of the cradle, these intimate exchanges of news reach a very high level. To her brother who, as we have seen, had had the sorrow of losing a son just after birth, Mme. Martin sends these lines:

"My heart is as oppressed as when I lost my own children. I see you all in tears around that dear little being, dead under such grievous circumstances; and yet, God has granted you a great grace, since there was time for it to be baptised. Now, dear brother, we need courage, and I do not think you lack that. You have sufficient energy and faith to bear the afflictions of this life.

"I received your letter just as I was about to sit down to table in company, for we had guests. . . .

The Spirit of the Home

"When I saw our visitors enjoying themselves during lunch as though nothing untoward had happened, I felt very bitterly. Do not think, however, that it was Louis' fault, for he felt very deeply for you in your sorrow, and is continually speaking of it.

"We were going over in memory all the sufferings and trials that your poor wife must have endured during the last six months, and we grieved over this sad result. Yes, it is hard indeed, yet, all the same, dear brother, do not murmur. God is Master. He may allow us, for our good, to suffer much more, but His grace will never fail us. . . .

"If you can write once before I go to see you, I shall be very pleased, and let me know particularly whether the child was alive when it received Baptism. The doctor should have administered clinical Baptism. When a child is in danger, that is always the first thing to do."[20]

Better even than letters, visits poured balm into the wounds. What a pity it was that the journey was so long, the railway so inconvenient, business so absorbing! They held high festival at Alençon when the "Lexovians" arrived. The best bedroom was reserved for them. The children danced for joy and their mother shared their childish glee. As for the visit to Lisieux, it was the great event in Mme. Martin's life. She talked of it; she lived in anticipation for six months in advance. To be free on the date fixed, she would work until midnight for a whole week. What delighted her there were not the parties, the fireworks at the *Jardin de l'Étoile*, still less the excursions to Trouville. It was to be immersed in the repose of a completely fraternal atmosphere, far from business papers, lace-workers and lace. Her great longing was to see the two households, brought together in the same city, form but one single family community though beneath two separate roofs. This

[20] Mme. Martin to her brother, Oct. 17, 1871.

167

The Story of a Family

was to be realised after her death by the removal to *Les Buissonnets*. She would know only the gracious prelude, in her too short visits to the Guérin family.

*   *   *

The relations with their servants and employees were almost on the same plane as the family affections. Mme. Martin herself has expressed her theory with respect to this question. On March 2, 1868, she writes to her brother: "It is not always high wages that assure the attachment of servants. They must feel that they are liked; we must show them marks of kindness and not be too stiff with them. When people are fundamentally good, we may be sure that they will serve us with attachment and thoroughness. You know I have a quick temper, yet all the maids I have had have liked me, and I keep them as long as I wish. The one I have at present would be ill if she had to go away. I am certain that if someone were to offer her two hundred francs more, she would not leave us. It is true that I never treat my servants less well than I do my children. If I tell you this, it is not to set myself up as a model; I assure you I do not think of that, for everyone tells me I do not know how to treat maids."

The word *familia*, by which of old the household servants were designated, here applied in its true sense. The maids were members of the "family." The rule was to choose them carefully in order not to be exposed to contact with undesirables, and then to show them full confidence. The children were taught to show the maids deference and obedience. Perhaps, indeed, the parents carried this too far. Certainly they showed themselves too complacent with Louise Marais, who spent eleven years under their roof. Faithful unto death, but of domineering character and peevish humor, she often tried their patience by her blunt speech and nagging, and gradually she arrogated to herself an almost tyrannical authority over the little girls. The eldest alone escaped this. "I am perfectly free," she would retort to every bullying injunction. As for Léonie, we shall see how she suffered from this system of over-submission.

Marie attests that her mother was extremely considerate. Never would she have given the servants leavings from the table. She took those herself. Utterly incapable of husbanding her own strength, she was very anxious not to overwork her employees. She worked harder than they; rose earlier; retired later. Were they sick? She nursed them like her children. She was seen during the three weeks at Louise's bedside day and night, when a very severe attack of articular rheumatism confined the maid to bed. It was only when the attack was over that she sent her, in a carriage, home to her family to complete her convalescence. She would have considered it an unworthy proceeding to get rid of the patient by sending her to hospital or burdening her parents, who could not afford it.

On occasion she tried to educate her. Here is her own account of the failure of one of her lessons. "M. de G., our neighbor, was buried yesterday, which event has greatly affected Louise. She cannot understand how anyone can die 'when they are so happy on earth,' and I believe she would readily sacrifice her part of Paradise in order to be eternally here below as happy as are the rich, who, she imagines, live in perfect happiness. It was in vain that I told her they were no more happy than others; she refuses to believe it." [21] A veritable scolding was needed before Louise would call in the

[21] Mme. Martin to Pauline, July 16, 1876.

priest to her old father, and had it not been for Mme. Martin's indignation, he would have died without warning after a life of indifference.

As we may see, nothing concerning her servants was a matter of indifference to this admirable woman. In her house the maid did not feel herself either a hireling or a stranger. Louise Marais herself, and Virginie Cousin, who was three years in their service as maid, and after her marriage as a lace-worker, wept at Mme. Martin's death and bore witness to her great kindness and sense of social justice. Truly, it was in her parents' school that Thérèse of Lisieux learned to sympathize with the sufferings of the lowly, to grieve over their humiliations, and appreciate their eminent dignity as children of God.

*   *   *

Such a home compels respect. Does it radiate joy? Does there not hang about it that sickly, heavy odor, such as comes from carpets and easy chairs stored in too small a lumber room; that dreary, stale atmosphere which suggests the sacristy, the museum, and the dining room of an old-fashioned presbytery? . . . "Old rags, old papers!" whisper the malicious.

Let us enter no. 36 *Rue Saint Blaise*. Songs and shouts meet us from all sides; the cheerful faces and incessant movement soon reassure us. It is not the heedlessness, the headlong rush to artificial distractions, the escape from the home at any price. The world had not yet been thrown as a prey to the caterers for pleasure who give themselves up to the commercial exploitation of man's lowest instincts and degrade him under pretext of amusing him; the supreme corruptions of the "diversions" of Pascal. The problem of leisure received a domestic solution. It had the due—not excessive—

The Spirit of the Home

place proportioned to the energies that had to be repaired after the stage of work. Spontaneously the educative element entered in. It charmed, rested, relaxed the mind; it drew the family nearer together, and made it one. In the etymological sense of the term, leisure is *re-creation*, in which the whole personality draws new inspiration and as it were, achieves something.

At certain hours the father gave himself up to his favorite relaxation. He settled down on the banks of the Sarthe, or the Briante, and made war on the trout and pike. He was a really keen billiard player, which often led him to say to his daughters, in the half serious half playful fashion he was fond of using, "Here on earth, we have a good game to play!" Sometimes he joined his friends in their country houses at Lanchal, Grogny, or Saint-Denis. In the early days of their married life, he and his wife had been present without much enthusiasm at some society entertainments. The way in which Mme. Martin would enumerate the actors in these soirées, from the entertainer to the lap-dog, each duly playing his part, the fashion in which she jokes about the songs and the dresses, show plainly that her heart was not in these things. Once the children began to come, they retired into their own home circle. Is it not the privilege of large families, merely by their own movement to engender high spirits, gladness and life, to renew themselves ceaselessly, in a word, to be self-sufficing? The little ones contributed the unforeseen element of their awakening faculties; the older children, their ingenuity; the parents their sense of organisation and their abnegation in the service of all. Apart from the meetings of the Catholic Club, the Martin family spent Sundays and holidays together.

In order to amuse her daughters, the mother did not hesitate to lay aside her needle for a while.

The Story of a Family

"I have been amusing myself like a child, and playing Patience," she writes, "and paid for my childishness. I had to send off an urgent lace order, and so was obliged to make for lost time and sit up until one o'clock in the morning."
. . . "There has been an exhibition of toys and a complete dolls' dinner to inaugurate the pretty china dinner service. It lasted nearly two hours. Never have the children enjoyed themselves so much. Pauline said this evening, 'Oh, what a pity the day is over; I wish it were this morning again!' I do not quite share her opinion, for I have had a hard time. For three days I have been alone with all these little pickles."
. . . "I have promised the children to celebrate St. Catherine's Day on Sunday evening. Marie wants fritters, Pauline cakes, the others chestnuts. As for myself, I dearly want some peace!"

The father was an incomparable play-fellow. No one ever knew better how to come down to the level of the youngest children. He expressed that in his own way: "I am a big child with my children." After his hard reading, he would supply himself with large, gilded marbles, which he would roll before the wondering eyes of his little daughters, make miniature toys, perform turn after turn of conjuring tricks and give his "Queen" a ride, sitting on his foot.

Very shrewd, witty and cheerful, he had the social gift for conversation, playful remarks, anecdotes, proverbs, society accomplishments. His voice was rich and harmonious and delighted the listeners with its sonorous, full tones. He liked reciting good poetry . . . at least as long as he was not asked for humorous sketches seasoned with Norman patois; he possessed and bequeathed to Marie and Thérèse a real gift for mimicry. He could imitate intonations and words of the Auvergne dialect, bird songs, drums, and military bugle calls, all with an accuracy, a cadence and expression which gave the illusion that it was the real thing. Above all, he cherished a real cultus for the old French songs and had an immense repertoire. He imparted a mysterious attraction to Christmas Eve when, sitting by the fire before the blazing yule log, with the shoes put ready in a row near by, the family were waiting to attend Midnight Mass. His daughters lovingly kept a manuscript collection of these airs which their father was wont to sing of old. *Compère Guilleri* keeps company with *Les Compagnons de la Marjolaine*, *Le Juif errant* with *Les Montagnards* and *La Plainte du Mousse* and *Le Fils de la Vièrge*. It is, as it were, a venerable witness to an age of moral health, when the productions of the France of yore had not yet yielded place to the music hall songs and doubtful jokes.

When the Norman countryside turned green, the family sought recreation out of doors. On Sunday after High Mass or Vespers, they made their way to those flowery lanes which Thérèse has described so happily. "I can still feel the impression made on my childish heart at the sight of the fields bright with cornflowers, poppies and marguerites. Even at that age I loved far-reaching views, sunlit spaces, and stately trees; all nature charmed me, in a word, and lifted up my soul to Heaven." [22] On their walks it was her special duty, and very proud she was thereof, to give alms to any poor by the wayside. They liked to visit the Blessed Sacrament in some lonely church, or they would say a prayer before the calvaries set up in the centre of the country churchyards. The mother's favorite walk beyond all others was by the winding path which, following the course of the Fuie, ran between high hedge-walls of

[22] Autobiography, C. I.

white or pink hawthorn, and led to the cemetery and its graves.

During the holidays the outings most appreciated by the small ones had as their goal the Pavilion, that chalet which M. Martin had furnished in the *Rue des Lavoirs*. No party gave them so much pleasure as those afternoons when they romped freely round the old fir and the walnut tree amid the flowers and fruit. If the father did not produce his fishing tackle, he retired with his books to the ground floor room with the rustic furniture: the farmhouse clock, the armchair, the folding table and perhaps best of all the two framed water colors over the fireplace, which testified to Pauline's budding artistic talent. The mother would bring her needlework and talk to her daughters while they picked strawberries, made posies, or worked at the small garden patches which had been assigned to each of the three elder girls. When tired with their games the sisters came, one after another, to settle themselves closely on the straw-seated bench; the picnic basket was opened, and there was a fresh outburst of laughter and joyous exclamations. Was there not a whole education in this simplicity that led them to delight in little things, in the family circle, without having useless recourse to the fallacious attractions wherewith those who cater for the leisure hours of the public think proper to cheer the incurable boredom of worldly folk?

* * *

The key to the puzzle was that they loved one another as it behooves Christians to do. *Charity is the soul of the home*. To be sure, it furnishes no material for the stormy adventures of dramatic passion. This crystal clear spring would be found disconcerting to sceptics, eager for erotic novels. It would cause shoulder-

The Spirit of the Home

shrugging among those who no longer believe in love from having seen it so profaned. We know the caustic sayings with which Gallic wit has stigmatised marriage. "A duel, rather than a couple." [23] . . . "They study each other for three weeks; love each other for three months; quarrel three years, and put up with each other for thirty . . . and the children begin it over again!" The source is abundant and the words do not want for realism. They are the low-water mark of a decadent age. Rather than smile at these sacred things, thoughtful people who would see their fatherland live again, might well take a lesson from the home in the *Rue Saint Blaise*. These believers of the *élite*, who had begun by abstaining from conjugal relations altogether, recall the fresh affection which united the King of Charity, Louis IX, to Margaret of Provence. Between the married pair was an unbreakable link—Christ. Their hands had been joined after having been first clasped in His. They knew that marriage is a sacrament of the living, of which they are themselves the ministers, a permanent sacrament, the grace of which would vivify their whole existence. The community thus founded is spiritualized in its very essence. It takes on something of a priestly tone. Far from withering love, holiness continually recreates it, making of it a masterpiece of mutual understanding, disinterested devotion, complete self-giving and self forgetfulness. Their joint life was not egoism in the married state—that they would have held in horror—nor a "mystical" escape out of marriage—a noble temptation, perhaps, which they had had —but a joint ascension *in* and *by* marriage. Thus did they realize in its fulness the plan of the Creator.

[23] "Un duel plutôt qu'un duo." It is impossible to reproduce the play on the words in translation.

The Story of a Family

The love they bore each other had nothing about it of the "quintessential," sublimated, etherialized to the point of seeming dis-incarnate. It kept all the fervor of the days of betrothal, all love's delicacies, the confidences of a supernatural friendship. The wife admired her husband. After four and a half years of married life, she writes of him. "I am always very happy with him. He makes my life very sweet. My husband is a saintly man. I wish every woman had such; that is my New Year wish for them!" She felt his necessary absences and indemnified herself by settling her own business matters and telling him all the little items of domestic news. She was so delighted at the thought of his return, that she owned she could not work. Without him, even journeys to Lisieux lost their attraction; a proof of this is provided by a letter dated August 31, 1873, which we cite at length as attesting this union of hearts.

"My dear Louis,

"We arrived yesterday afternoon at half-past-four; my brother met us at the station and was delighted to see us. Both he and his wife are doing everything to entertain us.

"This evening, Sunday, there is a pleasant party in our honor. Tomorrow, Monday, we are going to Trouville. Tuesday, there is to be a big dinner at the house of Mme. Maudelonde and perhaps a drive to the country house of Mme. Fournet. The children are in raptures, and their happiness will be complete if the weather is fine.

"But for myself, I find it hard to relax. Nothing of that interests me! I feel just like the fish you take out of the water; they are no longer in their element and must perish.

"This would have the same effect on me if my stay had to be very prolonged. I feel ill at ease. I am not in my niche,

The Spirit of the Home

and that overflows into the physical sphere and I feel almost ill. However, I reason with myself and try to master the feeling. I am with you all day in spirit, and say to myself: 'Now he is doing such and such a thing.'

"I long to be with you, Louis dear. I love you with all my heart and I feel my affection doubled by being deprived of your company. I could not live apart from you.

"This morning, I heard three Masses. I went to that at six o'clock, made my thanksgiving and said my prayers during that at seven, and came back for the High Mass.

"My brother is not displeased over business. He is doing quite well.

"Tell Léonie and Céline that I send my love and kiss them both, and that I will bring them a keepsake from Lisieux.

"If possible, I will try and write tomorrow, but I do not know what time we shall return from Trouville. I am in a hurry, for they are waiting for me to go visiting. We shall arrive home on Wednesday evening, at half-past-seven. How long it seems till then!

"I embrace you as I love you. The little girls wish me to tell you that they are enjoying themselves at Lisieux and send you a big hug."

More soberly, for he did not much like letter writing, M. Martin shows the same tenderness. We quote this note of October 8, 1863.

"Dearest,

"I cannot arrive at Alençon before Monday. The time passes slowly, for I long to be with you.

"I need not say I was very pleased to receive your letter, except that I see by it that you are over-tiring yourself. So I recommend calm and moderation, above all in your lace work. I have some orders from the *Compagnie Lyonnaise*. Once more, do not worry so much. With God's help, we shall manage to keep up a nice little home.

The Story of a Family

"I had the happiness to communicate at *Our Lady of Victories*, which is like a little heaven on earth. I put up a candle for all the family intentions.

"I kiss you all lovingly, whilst awaiting the pleasure of being with you again. I hope Marie and Pauline are being very good!

"Your husband and true friend who loves you forever."

Such love knew nothing of anxiety and touchiness. It was neither easily offended nor jealous. It was strong, peaceful, compact of confidence and security. The husband left the management of the interior of the home to his wife; that is to say, she had complete freedom in the domestic arrangements and housekeeping. His undoubted capability did not extend to this department. Left to himself, with his indifference to material comfort he would have neglected himself and lived on a morsel of bread and something ready cooked from the pork shop. His wife lovingly saw to everything. Never the slightest cloud came between them, such was their perfect unity of outlook. M. Martin exercised authority after the manner of a patriarch whose character alone inspired respect and submission. On one point only—his repugnance to being separated from any of his family—did his wife have to practice diplomacy in order to lead him to decisions which she considered wise: a sojourn of the little girls with their uncle; a spiritual retreat at Le Mans for Marie. Here her acute sense of psychology gave her so much discernment that without any jarring note, she induced her husband to fall in with her views. Doubtless, it was in course of some discussion of this kind, rather warmer than usual, that little Pauline, then aged seven, ingenuously asked her mother: "Mamma, is that what

The Spirit of the Home

people mean by being unhappy together?" The query was long a subject of amusement to the happy parents. "We have only too good reason to watch ourselves very carefully, my dear Louis," exclaimed Mme. Martin, when she informed him of Pauline's confidential inquiry.

As for the children, they felt they were surrounded by a love both tender and strong, accompanied by a genuine respect. The deaths of their four little ones had rooted deeply in the parents' hearts the conviction that they were but trustees of God's authority, and that to Him alone belonged the sovereign rights over His creatures. Purified in the crucible of suffering, marked with the seal of the Cross, their love had been detached from all self-seeking; it no longer sought to do aught but serve.

Sister Geneviève[24] tells us that M. Martin who, in the manner of the day, had used the plural form of respect —*vous*—to his own parents, would have liked his daughters to do likewise in their own home. The mother having objected that she would feel they loved her less, he yielded readily, and the singular form became the rule. Not that this detracted in the least from the veneration in which both parents were held. In her deposition at the Process of Beatification of her angelic sister, we find these carefully weighed sentences of Mère Agnès de Jésus: "My parents always seemed to me to be saints. We were filled with respect and admiration for them. Sometimes I asked myself if there could be others like them on earth. I never saw any such around me." It was more than filial piety; it was a real cultus. In their anxiety to show the same affection to both father and

[24] Céline took in religion the name of Sr. Geneviève de la Sainte Face; Pauline that of Sr. Agnès de Jésus.

The Story of a Family

mother, as children Marie and Pauline had an ingenious way of joining their names in their prayers: "God bless Papa-Maman!", or, reversing the order: "Help Maman-Papa." Thus the equality of authority was completely safe!

Each departure for school caused real grief. They never became accustomed to living apart from one another. In Marie's private papers we read some comments which are eloquent in this respect, on the day following her first Communion, which she spent with her parents.

"So I had found Father and Mother again; I who suffered so at being separated from them. It seemed like being in Heaven to be with them, but it was a very short-lived Heaven, for they had to leave us that same evening. So my happiness was far from being perfect. We went for a country walk. Soon I found myself in a field full of marguerites and cornflowers. But to gather them I had to let go of darling Father's hand, so I preferred to stay with him. I kept looking at him and at Mother . . . In my little nine-year-old heart, there was an abyss of tenderness for them . . . However, it would be impossible to say how I felt being parted from my parents. It would be vain to attempt to describe this suffering."

The return for the holidays was the signal for delirious outbursts. Marie lived every incident over in anticipation. For her younger sister's benefit she imitated the bell announcing their mother's arrival at the convent, the puffing of the engine, the calling of the names at the intermediate stations, and finally the arrival at Alençon, the embraces, the expressions of pleasure. There were real transports of gladness. Pauline owned that once, when taken home by a friend, her heart al-

The Spirit of the Home

most stopped beating when she caught sight of her own home; she thought she would collapse with emotion and had to stop for a moment to avoid fainting.

Between the little girls there reigned the most intimate affection. Léonie's moods provoked some storms, it is true, but the father's intervention soon restored fair weather. He had a horror of arguments and quarrels. "Peace, children, peace!" he would call out when tempers became warm and shrill voices were raised; and he would speak so quietly that the jangled nerves would calm down as by miracle. They would not willingly have hurt him on any account.

Christ was King of the home. Father Matteo Crawley had not yet preached his crusade of formal enthronement of the Sacred Heart in the home, but the spirit was there. Nazareth, Bethany, lived again in this home, where the divine Heart set its seal upon the union of souls, inspired every thought, and presided at every undertaking. God could not have prepared ground more favorable to the development of a saint. Having known the sweetness of that family atmosphere, Thérèse would sing in after years:

> "O what tender memories cling
> To childhood days, life's opening Spring,
> To guard my innocence 'neath sheltering wing
> My God o'er spread me from above
> With love.

CHAPTER 8

HOME TRAINING

Educative principles and method—training of
Marie and Pauline—Léonie: the "problem
child"—Céline: a child developing.

IN THIS family the training of the soul completed
that of the body. To bestow the natural life was the
lesser work; above all it was a question of bringing
to birth and promoting the growth of children of God.
That is the object of education; the supreme science,
too often unrecognised; the *ars artium*, that bends all
its energies to reproducing the divine image, not in
plastic material but in the spiritual substance.

Mme. Martin's correspondence reveals this concern
for right education in the highest degree. For her a
child was not a plaything with which to amuse herself,
nor a creature that has become an object of dread because no one knows how to train it. It was a trust received from the Creator's hands; she must serve it by
uplifting it, and she must not fear to aim high. The
prayer uttered over each newly born infant, "Lord,
may it be consecrated to You; take it now, rather than
it should be lost," emphasises how high was the ideal.
She wished to fashion Christians and saints.

Both parents possessed the sense of authority, its object and its limits. They knew that it is lost by negligence, discredited by the abuse of power; that it can be frittered away and torn to shreds by divisions. They understood how to increase its value in practice by the force of example. A child is an intuitive little being and terribly logical. It submits completely to the authority of its parents when it can admire them at its leisure and recognize them as its good genii. If the father could allow himself, in the mildest sense of the word to "spoil" his daughters a little; to favor Marie, his "best beloved," and to grant the least desires of Thérèse, without these effusions of tenderness ever having lessened the obedience and respect that were due to him, it was because the holiness of his life and the nobility of his character invested him with a sovereign prestige. He lent himself to the wishes of his "Queen" with a good grace, but she has told us that a look, a word from her "King" was for her a commandment not to be discussed. Céline declares likewise: "Never did I hear one of us at home say one disrespectful word to our parents, nor even an off-hand one. If we except Léonie's outbursts of moodiness, we never questioned an order received; it never even occurred to anyone. We obeyed from love."

There lay the secret of this training, in which a touching sensitiveness was combined with such astonishing firmness. Whilst M. Martin could be angry when there happened to be any question of calming any outbreaks of "nerves," he excelled in ferreting out the wiles of feminine vanity in his eldest daughter, and recalled the maid to her duty when she risked over-indulging little Céline by continual coaxing, or giving in to her whims. He was not "Papa," to be coaxed or tyrannized over; he was "Father," in his august majesty, and he did not

The Story of a Family

think it beneath his dignity to occasionally practice the "art of being Grandfather."

The mother supported him by her watchful care. The parental front was never broken in this model home. In the home circle itself and in its natural extension, the school, carefully chosen for its religious character, it tended to constitute an environment, tradition, a climate that inclined the children to goodness spontaneously. Thus they prevented evil, which is still the best way of curing it. Persons who were 'suspect were rigorously avoided. Without showing herself meddling or distrustful, simply because she was there, because she kept an eye upon everything, sharing the amusements and work of her girls, Mme. Martin kept all danger away from them. Soeur Geneviève relates two incidents that show to what lengths their mother carried delicacy in this respect. Shortly after the birth of Thérèse, the little family took it into their heads to play at Baptism. To make it more interesting, Louise, the maid, had the idea of dressing up Céline, then aged four, as a boy, to play the part of godfather in the improvised procession. Today the matter would seem very innocent, but we are dealing with 1873, and it was not yet fashionable to set to work to destroy modesty. The mother, who could not endure either make-up or travesty, and was careful never to permit anything unbecoming, insisting always that the girls' frocks should reach below their knees, showed herself very displeased at this masculine exhibition. She stopped it at once and severely reprimanded the maid.

She perceived by instinct and showed up pitilessly anything that might tarnish their innocence and purity of heart. Having allowed a girl several years their senior to share her daughters' games, she saw her entice

Home Training

one of the small ones into the garden for some mysterious tête-à-tête. Guessing at some wrong design by her suspicious manner and reprehensible gesture, she reproved her severely and sent her home without more ado. Then, with the utmost tact, she questioned her own child, explained the reason for such severity, and put her carefully on her guard against any pernicious influence. Later on, taking her on her knee, she had to prepare her herself to examine her conscience before Confession. As for the delinquent, she was so upset by the lesson that she completely amended her evil tendencies and subsequently entered a convent.

The soul of this training was confidence. Having suffered in her own youth from the régime of glacial and crushing restraint which her own mother had imposed upon her, Mme. Martin resolved at any cost to spare her own girls such a trial. She desired them to be expansive, open, trusting. The taciturnity affected by Léonie in her trying moods disconcerted and troubled her. She knew the temptations of a soul hermetically sealed, the danger of being driven back upon oneself. Her letters show how she applied herself to know all her children thoroughly, so as to treat each soul according to its needs.

It was through love that she drew forth a confidence or an avowal. Towards her elder daughters she behaved as their best friend; for the younger, she was tenderness incarnate. Nothing could be more pleasing than the picture she draws of Céline's winning ways:

"If you knew how endearing she is! I have never had a child like her for attachment to myself. She is so sensitive that however much she may wish to do something, if I tell her it makes me unhappy, she stops on the instant. She is very pleased when she is dressed to go out. It is particularly her pretty white hat that attracts her attention. But if at the moment of departure, I say with a pretence of sadness, 'So you are going to leave me?' immediately she leaves the maid, comes to my side, and hugs me with all her might. 'No, no, not leave Mamma; go away,' she says to Louise. Then when I tell her brightly to go, she looks me in the eyes to see if it is really true that I no longer mind, and begins to jump for joy."[1]

Ever loving, Mme. Martin was never weak. She did not allow stubbornness or childish caprice. "Do not be uneasy if your little Jeanne has a temper," she writes to her brother. "That will not hinder her from being an excellent child later on, and becoming your comfort. I remember that until the age of two Pauline was the same. I was wretched over it, and now she is my best. I must tell you, however, that I never spoiled her and, little though she was, I never let anything pass unchecked. Without making a martyr of her, I nevertheless made her obey."[2]

Self-love is the great enemy that renders all training unavailing and squanders God's gift. When speaking of the precocious intelligence of one of her nieces, Mme. Martin adds this remark; in which there is a hint of warning: "The only drawback I can see is the pride which that may one day engender in her. Children who are idolized by everybody have to combat this defect more than others, unless it is repressed by the parents."[3]

The family régime included a certain minimum of austerity. Language had to be chastened; vulgar words were strictly forbidden; good manners were considered

---

[1] Mme. Martin to her sister-in-law, May 5, 1871.
[2] Mme. Martin to her brother, Feb. 3, 1869.
[3] Mme. Martin to her brother, Feb. 8, 1870.

the outward vesture of innocence, politeness as the overflow of charity. Punctual as a soldier, the father insisted upon regularity, the mother watched over cleanliness and orderliness. At table the children had to behave themselves; no grumbles at dishes they did not much like! "Those who do not eat their soup do not have stew," the father would cut short all objections. They must eat plenty of bread on pain of being taxed with sauciness. In Lent the menu was subject to certain restrictions. In short, the whole organization of daily life incited energy and promoted a spirit of mortification.

The mother had a gift for stimulating generosity. Her method was to make use of everyday happenings in order to teach her children to overcome themselves. Young folk do not grasp theories, or lofty, abstract motives, as they do essentially concrete ideas. "The child does not like too wide horizons. To the fairest spots in all the world, he prefers an insect, a flower, a tiny path."[4]

To mold her daughters' characters, she used the small coin of the duties of one's state of life, putting before them essentially supernatural motives in order to persuade them to fulfil these faithfully: this or that sinner to convert, to console our Lord, to win Heaven. This is what they learned from her to describe as "setting pearls in their crowns." The expression became current coin in the household. The rosary of good deeds —pratiques—of which we read in the Saint's autobiography, took its origin from this inspiration. To obtain the grace that Grandfather Guérin, then recently dead, might soon enter Heaven, Marie, escorted by her mother, faced the dentist's forceps with a valor beyond

[4] Jean Aicard.

her nine years, and even regretted that the said dentist did not extract the aching teeth. "It is a pity! Poor Grandpapa would not have been in Purgatory." When Thérèse, having voluntarily taken up some catechizing, wished to initiate two little girls, of whom the elder was not six, into right conduct, "instead of promising them toys and sweets," she spoke to them "of the everlasting rewards which the Little Jesus will give to good children." She was merely repeating the lessons learned of old at her mother's knee.

A whole code of rules for bringing up children could be compiled from Mme. Martin's letters. Her daughters rendered this testimony to her at the Process of Beatification: "We were not spoiled. Our mother watched very carefully over her children's souls, and not the smallest fault ever went unreproved. Her training was kind and loving, but attentive and thorough." Do not such eulogies call up the shade of Isabel Romée, in the valley of Domrémy, and can we not apply to the humble flower of Carmel what Michelet wrote of Jeanne of Lorraine: "She knew all that her mother knew concerning sacred things. She learned her religion not as a lesson, a ceremony, but in the simple and popular form of a beautiful story, told in the evenings; as a mother's simple faith . . . What we receive with our blood and our mother's milk is a living thing; it is life itself."

* * *

Marie and Pauline were the first to profit by this spiritual transfusion, this "impregnation" with their mother's principles. Their characters showed marked contrasts: the elder, independent, very quick to react when her liberty was touched, but extremely sensitive, a foe to all complications, upright and candid, with original witty sallies and, withal, occasionally showing a shyness that led others to regard her as uncouth and enigmatic. The younger possessed a vivacity that needed restraining but, sympathetic and lively like her mother, she presented as did the latter that harmonious combination of brilliant and solid qualities which fits an individual to exercise authority. Both girls possessed gifts of heart and head, and were united in a friendship that rendered them inseparable.

From their early childhood, they had been placed in a novitiate of self sacrifice. Marie recalled with satisfaction her first act of unselfishness; when she gave up to her little sister a wonderful little saucer made of orange peel, "in order to have another pearl in her crown." "Mamma," she had called out forthwith, "shall I go to Heaven (*le cel*)?" She was completely taken up with the love of the good God and her family affections. She disdained to bow to passers-by, as she did not want it to appear as though she were trying to attract attention. When her mother reproved her, she replied bluntly: "It does not matter whether people like me or not. So long as you love me, that is enough." More than once, like a painter drawing a miniature, Mme. Martin portrays her daughters. "My eldest is becoming a very good child. One can see that she is trying to correct her little defects, and then she is so affectionate. When she notices that she has hurt me, she bursts into tears. Pauline is very well behaved and wins all hearts, but you never saw a child so exuberant." [5]

Marie related this reminiscence of the short time spent at school with the Sisters at Alençon. "In the same class with me were some naughty and very badly

[5] Mme. Martin to her sister-in-law, Oct. 1869.

brought up girls; nay more than that . . . The mistress noticed nothing wrong. As I would never hide anything from Mother, I told her all I had seen and heard." Madame Martin, happy at the horror felt by her small daughter for the slightest hint of what was seriously unfitting, profited by the occasion to train her conscience and encourage her to be perfectly truthful with her confessor.

"She once told me this story," continues the witness, "which made my hair stand on end. 'There was once a child who did not dare to acknowledge her sins, and when she came to confession, the priest saw the head of a huge serpent coming out of her mouth. Then it immediately disappeared. At last, one day she had the courage to tell everything, and not only did the big serpent come out altogether, but also a multitude of little ones; for when we have driven away the big one, the little ones go away by themselves, as if by enchantment.' I remembered that and not for anything in the world would I have wilfully concealed a sin."

In October, 1868, Marie and Pauline entered the boarding school of the Visitation at Le Mans. There were scenes of crying. "You cannot imagine," owns Mme. Martin, "what it costs me to let them go from me, but we must make sacrifices for their good." Marie echoes her by telling us that the separation was real torment to her. "Oh, if I had not had my aunt, whom I did not want to hurt, I should never have remained seven years behind those grilles." Not that this hindered the boarders from working steadily. Their mother was satisfied that, not without pride, "Marie is an excellent pupil; Pauline can learn anything she wants to and she is very diligent. She is the most advanced among the children of her age . . . One day,

Home Training

when Marie spoke to her during study time, she replied, 'Don't let us waste time for it costs Father and Mother's money.' Both of them are doing us credit." [6]

Not that the picture is without its shadows. The sudden sallies of the elder and the quick outbursts of temper of the younger girl would call forth reprimands from their aunt, whose influence was to have a profound effect upon both. At Mans as at Alençon, perfect truth was the rule. Marie honestly acknowledges her smallest misdemeanors. When some ribbon was conferred upon her as a reward, and someone whispered that she had received it "only by indulgence," she refused to wear it. "I will not wear anything," she explained, "that I have not really deserved."

The parents collaborated with the school, but they had no idea of shirking their own responsibilities. They followed the reports received, commended the successes, reminded the girls, just as they would have done at home, to receive Holy Communion on great feasts and certain other liturgical occasions; recommended intentions to be prayed for, and above all enlivened their absence by sending all the home news, so that they should retain their family spirit and not feel at all exiled. The mother's accountants were so attractive that the mistresses passed them on from hand to hand.

With the same tact, the parents re-orientated their eldest daughter, when the latter, on her return to Mans after the typhoid, formed such an intimate friendship with a schoolfellow belonging to the nobility that she lost her liberty of heart through it, and became ambitious for show and riches for herself. M. Martin made no mistake with respect to the significance of this evolution. One day when he was walking with Marie in a

6 Mme. Martin to her brother, Jan. 3, 1872.

191

The Story of a Family

modest family property known by the name of Roulée, he saw the girl hasten to gather a bunch of flowers, and noticed that she emphasised the action by remarking, rather mysteriously, "I am going to take these flowers back to the convent in memory of Roulée." "Oh, is that it?" he remarked shrewdly, "and then you will create a little fuss with your friends by showing them the flowers from your place in the country!" Marie felt that he had read her thoughts. Very annoyed, she threw the bunch into the grass . . . and they began to talk of something else!

The best antidote for dreams of grandeur was the permanent submission to the duties of one's state. When Marie left school at fifteen and a half, her mother forthwith made her take her share in the housekeeping. She was already haunted by the presentiment of her approaching death, and eagerly initiated this daughter who would inherit the heavy task. The girl refers to this. "In the afternoon, I did sewing with Mother. When she saw that I was talking whilst letting my needle lie idle, she told me I must learn to work while I talked."

Under these circumstances, Marie developed admirably, and quickly got over the crisis of sentimentality which had nearly spoiled her charming simplicity. She remained the spontaneous creature whom Thérèse her goddaughter, would one day portray in some acrostic lines:

"Of old, I saw her in her independence,
  Seeking true happiness in freedom wide."

She had a horror of merely following the crowd. She rejected indiscriminately the tyranny of fashion in clothes, the requirements of social etiquette, certain traditional forms of piety. She recoiled at the idea of a religious vocation, and refused to use the prayer beginning: "St. Joseph, father and protector of virgins," because she considered it reserved for such as hankered after a veil or a *cornette*. On the other hand, marriage did not attract her any more than did the religious life. What she wanted was her "autonomy"; "I am my own mistress."

Gently, her mother influenced her, studied her, and recalled her to a sense of realities.

"There is Marie dreaming of going to live in a fine house, opposite the Poor Clares, in the *Rue de la Demi-Lune*. She talked about it all yesterday evening; one would have thought it was Heaven. Unfortunately, her desires cannot be realised. We must stay where we are; not for all her life, but for my part I shall leave this house only at my death. Although your sister has so little worldliness about her, she is never content where she is. She is ambitious for something better; she must have beautiful rooms, spacious and well furnished . . . When she has something different, perhaps she will feel its insufficiency still more."[7]

These lines which tended to strengthen Pauline's convictions, explain the line which Mme. Martin took with her children. She did not reduce them to silence, nor did she stifle objections; she let them speak, she liked them to express their minds fully; then, imperceptibly she rectified their judgement, when hasty or erroneous, by appealing to the standpoint of faith.

Her daughter was not allowed to go to evening parties given by people who were too wealthy.

"That arouses unhealthy envy." On the other hand, she

[7] Mme. Martin to Pauline, Jan. 16, 1876.

was allowed to attend certain more modest gatherings which could not turn her head. So much the worse for anyone who was shocked, be it even the Visitandine aunt. "So I am to shut her up as in a convent? You cannot live in the world like a hermit. We have to pick and choose in all that the 'holy nun' says! Firstly, I am not displeased that Marie should have a little distraction. It makes her less blunt; she is quite uncivilized enough already!"[8]

What did disconcert her for a while was to see her daughter systematically hostile to the outward manifestations of religious fervor. She asked advice of Sister Marie-Dosithée, whose "pious preaching," as her niece called it, proved of no effect. Marie, fundamentally pious enough—she went to Mass daily—disliked making herself conspicuous, and that led her into singularity. Her mother did not lose courage. In 1876, she sent her to attend an "old girls" retreat at the Visitation, and in 1877 repeated the experiment, despite her husband's hesitations, who had little liking for separations or expensive journeys. "Money is nothing where there is question of the sanctification and perfecting of a soul. Last year, Marie returned quite transformed. The good fruits still remain, but it is time she renewed her provision." This time the result was decisive. From the girl's account, her mother guessed what her future would be. "I am very satisfied with Marie. The things of this world do not penetrate as deeply into her heart as do those of the spirit. She is becoming very devout. I think she will become a religious. I would wish her to be a saint."

As for the second daughter, her favorite, whom M. Martin called familiarly, "little Paulinus," her mother carried on her training chiefly by letter. These missives

[8] Mme. Martin to her sister-in-law, Nov. 12, 1876.

are the most touching and the most unconventional, almost the most lengthy, for the child demanded—except in Lent—her four pages, closely written. Mother-love overflows in their delightful phrases. "I cannot say how happy your last letter made me. I have seen all the efforts you are making, in spite of your impulsive temperament, to please everybody. I am infinitely thankful to you for that. I love you too much for my love to be easily satisfied." [9]

Her mother was not unaware of the little girl's good qualities and her ability in her studies; hence she does not emphasize this point. She feared the spectre of vanity and self-complacency that scholastic success might raise. Piety would serve as an antidote. It was her one care. She speaks very freely on the subject in the tone of an intimate friend talking confidentially.

"I have not forgotten the 8th December 1860, but I cannot think of it without laughing, for I was exactly like a child asking for a doll from its mother, and I behaved in the same way. I wanted to have a Pauline like the one I have, and I dotted the *i*'s, in case our Blessed Lady should not understand what I wished. Of course, the first requirement was that she should have a beautiful little soul, capable of becoming a saint, but I also wanted her to be very attractive. As regards that, she is scarcely pretty, but I think her beautiful, even very beautiful. She is as I wanted her to be! This year again, I am going to find our Lady early in the morning. I want to be the first arrival. I shall give her my candle as usual, but I shall not ask her for any more little daughters. I shall only pray to her that those she has given me may all become saints, and that I may follow closely, but they must be much better than I." [10]

[9] Mme. Martin to Pauline, Nov. 7, 1875.
[10] Mme. Martin to Pauline, Dec. 5, 1875.

The Story of a Family

Could anything be more charming, and more calculated to form character than these motherly confidences?

*   *   *

The task of bringing up children has its crosses.
Sometimes a parent is confronted with rebellious na-
tures, equally restive against constraint and persuasive
arguments. Léonie Martin was of the number. A certain mental backwardness, physical deficiencies caused
by an uninterrupted succession of illnesses, had hindered her development and an inferiority complex had
further helped to produce a child whom it was impossible to govern and almost impossible to understand.
Many a time her mother expressed the suffering thus
caused her: "This poor child makes me very anxious,
for her character is undisciplined and her intelligence
under-developed" . . . "I cannot analyze her character; moreover, the most learned would be at their wits'
end. I hope, all the same, that some day the good seed
will spring up. If I see that, I shall sing my *Nunc
Dimittis.*" [11]

Mme. Martin was counting upon the pedagogical
talents and the virtues of her sister at Le Mans, but a
first trial of Léonie as a boarder failed lamentably. The
child was too capricious to submit to school discipline,
too excitable to adapt herself to the common life, and
too backward to follow the normal school course. Yet
the same aunt was by no means pessimistic. Under the
rough, unattractive surface, she discerned the germs of
solid qualities, and wrote to this effect:

"She is a difficult child to train, and her childhood will
not show any attractiveness, but I believe that eventually
she will be as good as her sisters. She has a heart of gold,

[11] Mme. Martin to her brother, July, 1872.

Home Training

her intelligence is not developed and she is backward for her age. Nevertheless, she does not lack capabilities, and I find that she has good judgement and also remarkable strength of character . . . In short, by nature she is strong and generous, quite to my taste. But if the grace of God were not there, what would become of her?"

The mother received this prediction joyfully, but in the immediate present the child whom her aunt called "the child of destiny" and at times dreamt of seeing join her in the convent, seemed rather a "bundle of thorns." The death of Hélène had deprived her of the gentle companion who might have helped to develop her satisfactorily. She had private lessons but scarcely seemed to profit by them. Neither reproofs nor caresses had any lasting effect upon her strange character. Her good moments were few and her amendments short-lived.

In January, 1874, in order to prepare the child for her first Communion, they gave her another trial at the Visitation. At first it seemed promising. Sister Marie-Dosithée took Léonie under her special care. After a few days, seeing that corrections simply glided off this unstable nature, she changed her tactics and began the system of kindness and perfect confidence. The effect was magical. For a few weeks there seemed reason to think that the battle was won, then all the hopes were shattered. The natural defects returned more violently than ever, accompanied by inattention and unruly behavior. Léonie had fallen back into what she herself would one day qualify as her "detestable childhood."

In April it was necessary to inform the poor mother, who came to fetch her daughter. She made no attempt to obtain her another chance, for she held that "when children are difficult, it is for their parents to have the trouble of them." But her disappointment was not the less painful.

"As you may think," she writes to Mme. Guérin, "this has much upset me; it is not too much to say that it has caused deep grief which will be lasting. My one hope of reforming this child lay in my sister, and I was persuaded that they would keep her. But despite the best will in the world, it was necessary to separate her from the other children. As soon as she is with companions, she seems to lose control of herself, and you never saw anything like her unruliness. Well, I have no longer any hope of changing her nature save by a miracle. It is true that I do not deserve a miracle but I am hoping against all hope. The more difficult she seems, the more I am persuaded that God will not let her remain like this. I will pray so hard that He will grant my petition. At eighteen months, she was cured of a malady from which she should have died; why did God save her from death if He had not merciful designs for her?"[12]

The rebellious child had become at one and the same time—mothers will easily understand this paradox—her greatest source of suffering, her chief preoccupation and the object of her most tender affection. She prepared her herself for her first Communion, helped her to learn her catechism, encouraged her to make little sacrifices and, to prepare her for the ceremony still further, took her on pilgrimage to the shrine of the Immaculate Conception at Séez. There was no doubt that Léonie did make an effort, and the joy of the great day was unclouded.

For all that, the unstable character was not permanently changed for the better. The spirit of contradiction seemed inborn in Léonie. At times she gave the

[12] Mme. Martin to her sister-in-law, June 1, 1874.

Home Training

impression of shutting herself in, barricading herself in her sullenness. After meals, she withdrew from the family recreations, remaining in the kitchen with Louise, who seemed to exercise a strange fascination over her. However, she would return to her mother by fits and starts, and practice unlooked-for acts of unselfishness, as when she obstinately refused a visit to Lisieux, for fear, as they discovered long afterwards, of thereby depriving Céline of the pleasure.

A mystery, only cleared up later, seemed to hang about Léonie and for her parents she constituted a living enigma. Her mother was not discouraged. She noted the slightest signs of improvement, she entrusted the child to Marie's special care, and the latter, who had left school, gained the happiest influence over her. She would appeal to her heart and hopefully note the successes obtained, precarious though these might be.

Some extracts from her correspondence show us at different stages, exercising the art of the educator at work on this unpromising material.

"I am not displeased with my Léonie. If only one could succeed in getting the better of her stubbornness, and rendering her character more flexible, we could make her a good daughter, devoted and not afraid to spend herself. She has a will of iron. When she wants something, she triumphs over every obstacle in order to gain her ends. But she is not at all religious. She says her prayers only when she cannot do otherwise. This afternoon, I made her come to me to read a few prayers, but she soon had enough and said: 'Mamma, tell me the life of Our Lord Jesus Christ.' I was not prepared to tell stories. It tires me greatly, and I have always a sore throat. However I made an effort, and told her of the life of Our Lord. When I came to the Passion, her tears burst forth . . .

The Story of a Family

"Here Léonie has come down to bring me her rosary and says, 'Do you love me, Mamma? I will not disobey you again.' At times, she has good moments and makes good resolutions, but it does not last . . .

"Yesterday, she had an odious day. At mid-day I told her to make some sacrifices to overcome her bad humor and that at each victory she was to go and put a counter in a drawer I showed her, and that we should count them up at night. She was pleased at that, but there were no counters! I made her bring me a cork, which I cut in seven little disks.

"In the evening I asked her how many 'victories' she could show me. There were none. She had been at her worst. I was displeased and spoke to her severely, telling her that it did not become her to talk about being a nun under these present conditions.

"Then came tears and she was really sorry. She flooded my face with her tears, and today there are already some disks in the drawer."

One thought upheld Mme. Martin in this task which was always to be begun again: the child of so many prayers and so much sorrow could not perish! And then, had not Sister Marie-Dosithée, whose supernatural intuitions came near to being prophecies, said of Léonie: "I cannot help thinking that, sooner or later, this child will be a Visitation nun."

*   *   *

To bring up Céline was a very different proposition, and one both easy and consoling. Mme. Martin began from cradle days. The child was hardly two when her mother noted uneasily her whims and signs of obstinacy. "She has been spoiled too much." Her many little ailments had something to do with it, as had also the indulgence of the maid, whose favorite she was. "She chatters like a magpie; she is winning and very quick. She can learn anything she wishes." In a fort-

Home Training

night she mastered the whole alphabet. If her sisters repeated a song several times, she would forthwith sing it in her turn, without a mistake in either words or melody. It behooved the artist to take up the chisel and prudently administer those touches whereby God is imprinted upon a soul. Here is one such characteristic instance:

"Céline is learning to read nicely but she is becoming a little imp of mischief. It must be said that she is only four years old and, thank God! I can manage her easily. Yesterday evening, she said to me, 'I don't like the poor.' I answered that Jesus was not pleased with that, and that He would not love her either.

"She replied, 'I love Jesus very much but I won't love the poor, never, never! What does it matter to Jesus? He is Master, but I am mistress also!'

"You cannot imagine how roused she was! No one could make her see reason. But her dislike for the poor had an explanation.

"A few days ago, she was standing at the front door with a little friend, when a poor child, who was passing, gave her an impudent, mocking look. That did not please Céline, who bade the child, 'Go away, you!' The latter furious, gave her a heavy slap and her cheek was red for an hour afterwards.

"I encouraged her to forgive the little one, but she had not forgotten the incident, and said to me yesterday, 'Mamma, do you want me to love poor who slap my face, so that my cheek is all red? No, no, I will never love them.'

"But the night brought her to a better frame of mind, and the first thing she said to me this morning was to announce that she had a nice bunch of flowers; that is was for the Blessed Virgin and our Good Jesus. Then she added, 'I love the poor very much now!' "[13]

[13] Mme. Martin to Pauline, July 9, 1873.

Mme. Martin gave the little one her first lessons. She found her so delicate, so often feverish, that she feared to send her to school and see her fade away like her sister Hélène. It was sitting on her mother's lap that Céline was initiated into the rudiments, but for all that, she was not "brought up in cotton wool," without rule or method. Little acts of sacrifice marked her way and strengthened her will.

When Marie left school, she was put in charge of Céline's lessons and devoted herself to her completely. "I could not have given myself more trouble, had I had twenty to teach." She had brought from Le Mans a chaplet of movable beads, to be used for counting special acts of virtue, and Céline persevered in the game. On her good days, she would count up to twenty-seven victories. The mother guided Marie in her difficult task with tact and moderation, and wisely showed her not to demand too much from her pupil.

"Little Céline is very good. She makes many little sacrifices to obtain her aunt's cure. Sometimes, however, she fails to keep them up. Yesterday evening, in spite of being asked, she refused to give up something to her little sister—I forget what it was—and Marie was cross and told her she only made the sacrifices she liked to make, and that, in that case, it would be much better if she made none at all. I told Marie that she was not right to discourage her thus, that so young a child could not be expected to become a saint all at once and that she must overlook some little things." [14]

The results proved satisfactory from every point of view, and Mme. Martin often returns to the subject. "I am very pleased with Céline; she is a very good child, says her prayers like an angel, learns her lessons well,

[14] Mme. Martin to Pauline, Nov. 8, 1876.

and is very docile with Marie. With God's grace, we shall certainly make something good of her . . ." "She is wholly inclined to good; it is in her very nature. She is sincere, and she has an instinctive horror of evil . . ." "Hers is a choice nature. She is already seriously concerned—Céline was then seven—to know how she should prepare for her first Communion."

Blanche of Castile studying the soul of Louis IX, did not bring to bear more clear-sightedness in watching, or more affection in encouraging or more virility in sustaining this progress upwards towards God in which we may sum up education.

CHAPTER 9

THE EARLY TRAINING OF A SAINT

The mother's testimony—moral physiognomy of
Thérèse—training in generosity—precocious
virtue and parental Pride.

A S A SCULPTOR, after feeling his way and making many a preliminary study, produces from the stone the masterpiece that will express his genius, so M. and Mme. Martin, having reached the eventide of their married life, were to chisel the masterpiece that would immortalise them. Thérèse was four and a half when her mother died but the latter's image was indelibly stamped upon the child's memory.

As she writes at the beginning of her *Story of a Soul.**
"God in His goodness, did me the favor of awakening my intelligence very early, and He has imprinted the recollections of my childhood so deeply in my memory that past events seem to have happened but yesterday. Without doubt He wished to make me know and appreciate the mother He had given me."

Her autobiography vividly portrays her mother, whilst Mme. Martin's letters show the saint's physiognomy on its true light. Abundant and regular, this correspondence which included eighty-two letters ad-

* This is the title by which the French version of the autobiography is known. Chapter I.

The Early Training of a Saint

dressed to the relations at Lisieux, and forty-seven to the daughters at the Visitation, constitutes our chief source of information concerning the saint's childhood. In it, there is no trace of any deliberate shirking of the truth or of involuntary blindness in the opinions expressed; it is with clear-sighted honesty and perfect tact that this capable woman, who can use her pen, analyses the characters which it was her mission to orientate towards God in their diverse tendencies, their defects, their progress and their natural temperaments.

To Isidore Guérin and his wife she writes in a more sober tone, with Pauline, who wanted long letters, she adopts a lighter tone, gives a wealth of detail; there is a singling out of the striking anecdotes, even a certain exaggeration of some of these, which, unless the reader is careful may lead him to lend to a child's words a significance greater than they warrant. Thérèse agreed upon this point at the close of her life. But in both cases there is the same sureness of touch and care for honesty. There is also something pathetic and solemn when, as death draws nigh, the mother bequeaths to those who will carry on her work with the younger ones her whole mind with respect to these latter and, as it were, depicts their portrait for the last time. Once more, what testimony can be of equal value to this?

*　　*　　*

The last to arrive in the home, Thérèse was its joy and crown. "How glad I am to have her," cries Mme. Martin, "I believe I love her more than all the others, doubtless because she is the youngest." . . . "Oh, how I should grieve were I to lose this child! And my husband adores her . . . It is unbelievable all the sacrifices he makes for her by day and by night." The elder sisters are not less enchanted.

The Story of a Family

"If you knew," writes Marie to Pauline, "how roguish and sharp she is! I am filled with admiration at this little dear. Everyone in the house devours her with kisses. She is a poor little martyr. But she is so used to caresses that she now scarcely pays any attention to them. Thus when Céline sees her air of indifference, she says to her in a reproving tone, 'One would think that all this is merely *Mademoiselle's* due!' And you should see the face of Thérèse!"

Was she a spoilt child? She might have become such had it not been for her parents' watchfulness and the happy combination of qualities which predestined her to good. Gifted with an astonishingly precocious and shrewd intelligence, before she was three years old one informal lesson sufficed to teach her the alphabet. She remembered stories and songs with a disconcerting facility. Allowed to be present at Céline's lessons—it was impossible to separate her from the latter without tears—she remained silent as long as was required, occupied in threading beads, but her small head was busy. She seized upon many a piece of information and they would be not a little surprised to hear her, aged four, explain such expressions as "Almighty," or "my poor little Pâtira," and season her remarks very appositely with pithy Norman words that made her father smile: "We must not have the cheek to think that Papa will take us to the Pavilion every day!" "Without seeming to do so," she will acknowledge later, "I paid attention to everything that was done and said around me; it seems to me that I judged of things then as I do now." Her mother could write to Pauline, "She has such an understanding as I did not see in any of you."

Her sensitiveness was no less keen. She responded to acts of kindness by similar acts. She recognised herself

LITTLE THÉRÈSE
at the age of
three and a half

*"She was afraid of
the photographer," her
mother said, "and
could not give her
customary smile."*

LITTLE THÉRÈSE
and her mother

*From a sketch
by Céline*

Thérèse
at 8 years and her
sister Céline

Thérèse
at 15 years and
her father

*From a sketch by
Céline*

The Early Training of a Saint

that she "had a tender heart." "No one could imagine how much I loved Father and Mother, and being very expansive, I showed my love in a thousand ways." "She is a child very easily moved," remarks Mme. Martin. "Her eyes quickly fill with tears; a mere nothing suffices; the momentary departure of someone she likes; a shadow passing over her mother's face, regret for a recent peccadillo; if it be not a lecture from Céline, accusing her of 'bringing up her dolls badly and letting them have all their own way!' "

Let it not be thought, for all that, that her nature was flabby, and her humor pettish, always ready to burst into tears and anxious to be pitied. If the photograph taken at the age of three and a half shows her as grave and pensive, her mother is careful to attribute this to fear of the camera. "She who is always smiling was pouting." Yet who could fail to like this portrait which the family considered hardly a success! That grave but innocent expression, those firmly closed lips, the strong chin, are they not already eloquent—in a physiognomy so rich that, whether pose or instantaneous, no photograph could ever synthesise it all—of the wonderful combination of gentleness and strength that makes the charm of Thérèse of Lisieux? There is character in that child who was capable of remaining for hours together, controlling her impatience, when her needle had become unthreaded, rather than trouble Marie in the middle of a lesson.

Still more deserving of praise was that crystal-clear honesty that led the child to avow the smallest failings. Mme. Martin relates with satisfaction these spontaneous confessions which Thérèse mentions again in her autobiography, and which show her to us enumerating the pushes given to her sister, the sharp word, the broken vase and the torn wall paper, without pleading any extenuating circumstances, and awaiting the verdict like a criminal who wants to atone, but is sure of receiving a pardon that will touch her heart as much as the regret for her faults. The mother never wearies of sketching this portrait: "The little one would not tell an untruth for all the gold in the world." "My Thérèse is a charming little creature." . . . "As transparent as amber, very frank and very lively."

Was she faultless? To say so would be presumption, but let us guard against darkening the picture. The faults were very small. Mme. Martin, who studied her child's development in the smallest particulars, in order to transmit to Pauline the account in all its freshness, has only minutiæ to gather up, despite all her ingenuity as regards reprehensible manifestations. There is a sisterly dispute whilst Céline and Thérèse are playing with bricks. "I was obliged to reason with Baby— Thérèse was not yet three—who works herself into a pitiable state when things do not go as she wishes. She seems to think all is lost." [1] There is the incident mentioned by the saint herself of the two barley sugar rings, given her on a visit to Le Mans by her nun aunt one of which she discovered had been lost. "See," she concluded shrewdly, "how from childhood we have the instinct to safeguard our self-interest. Despite my sincere desire to share, quite naturally I assigned the lost ring to Céline, in order to keep the one that remained." There is—albeit the first movement was immediately repressed—the regret she felt when her mother bade Marie dress her in her prettiest frock, but one with long sleeves. "I should have looked much prettier with bare arms." Above all, there is the strongly etched picture

[1] Mme. Martin to Pauline, Dec. 5, 1875.

The Early Training of a Saint

of Thérèse at the age of three years and four months:

"As for the little puss, one cannot tell how she will turn out, she is so young and heedless. She is a very intelligent child but has not nearly so sweet a disposition as her sister, and her stubbornness is almost unconquerable. When she has said 'No,' nothing will make her change; one could leave her all day in the cellar without getting her to say 'Yes.' She would sooner sleep there."[2]

Certain pessimistic biographers have seized upon the above passage triumphantly in order to use it as a decisive argument to blacken the child's early characteristics, and credit her with a sort of fierce and proud obstinacy, the disciplining of which was the whole drama of her life. An exegesis which appeals, as it should, to parallel passages, that is to say which confronts the testimony with evidences of a similar kind, a criticism which, in addition, sets the said passage in its context, and in deciding upon its significance takes account, as did the saint herself, of a certain exaggeration of tiny incidents called for by the general tone of a correspondence destined to interest Pauline, will reach a much more measured interpretation. The fact remains that Thérèse never had to be shut in the cellar. Leaving out the unconscious incidents of her earliest years, when she showed herself obstinate it was not when either the love of her parents or that of God was in question. There was more nobility than stubbornness in her refusal to bow down her small person to kiss the ground in order to earn a halfpenny. The mother made no mistake and did not reprove her.[3]

[2] Mme. Martin to Pauline, May 14, 1876.
[3] "I had another fault, that of strong self-love, which Mamma did not mention in her letters. Here are a couple of instances:—One day, wishing no doubt to see how far my pride would go, she said, smiling: "Thérèse,

The Story of a Family

It remains to be said that the child was over sensitive, that she was not insensible to the promptings of self-love, that she was uncommonly strong willed and needed enlightening in order to make use of it to please those whom she ardently loved, her father, her mother and God. One day she will be able to say—and her use of the conditional tense shows that the hypothesis was never realised—

"With such a disposition I feel sure that had I been brought up by careless parents I should have become very wicked, and perhaps have lost my soul!"[4]

We have here an example of the principle that the corruption of the best is the worst, but faced with the wealth of gifts bestowed upon Thérèse we have the right to add that never did the training of a child present itself under a more promising aspect.

Such as Mme. Martin depicts her, this little fair girl, eager and merry, with the aureola of her silky curls and the bright depths of her blue eyes, had something about her both winning and impressive. She was not born a saint, any more than she was born an anæmic, colorless being. Let us say that, exceptionally gifted, she was capable of heroism but that, marked with the traces of original sin she could have led this wealth of gifts astray into the blind alleys of the abyss. The enlightened upbringing she received from her parents and sisters was to orientate her towards true greatness.

if you will kiss the ground I will give you a halfpenny." In those days the sum was a fortune, and in order to gain it I had not far to stoop, for I was so tiny that there was not much distance between my lips and the ground; but my pride was up in arms, and, holding myself erect, I replied: "No thank you, Mamma, I would rather go without the halfpenny." *Saint Thérèse of Lisieux, The Little Flower of Jesus.* P. J. KENEDY & SONS, 1926.

[4] Autobiography. C. 1.

The Early Training of a Saint

M. and Mme. Martin, used to the full the need of love so astonishingly evident in their youngest. Such an absorbing affection amounted almost to a servitude. Thérèse's mother willingly adjusted herself to it. She listened patiently to her childish questions; she graciously welcomed the "extravagances of love" which led the innocent sprite to wish that she could die. She never failed to reply: "Yes, little girl," to the calls addressed to her from each step of the staircase. In order to amuse his "Queen," the father on his part played with her as long as she wished and shared her delightful prattle. There was a prodigious evolution of affection in this child. She came to the point of no longer fearing hell, persuaded as she was that not even the good God Himself could drag her from her mother's arms. But, on the other hand, what an irresistible authority her parents acquired over her! When they appealed to her heart they could ask anything they wished of her.

It was the same motive, raised to its highest power, that carried her on towards God. Her conscience had scarcely awakened than she was taught to please her Father in Heaven. Several times a day, as she would own later, her mother would put on her lips the gracious formula: "My God, I give You my heart. Take it, please, so that no creature may possess it, saving You alone, Oh Jesus!" We know her disappointed remark on the morning when a friend took Céline and her home in the last days of their mother's illness: "Oh, it is not like Mother. She always heard our prayers!"

Thérèse was precociously associated with the scenes of collective piety which the family held in honor. These living examples fired her imagination and fed her devotion. She could not sleep unless she had said her prayers, and she must remember them all, and not forget to ask for "grace." M. Martin who was not initiated into all the rubrics of this childish liturgy, had plenty to do on the evenings when he presided in his wife's place. Upon occasion he was himself called to order by the little one, who had not seen him kneel down, as the rites required. "Papa, why don't you say your prayer? Have you been to church with the ladies?"

Every Sunday, on pain of an outburst of tears, she must go to Mass—*à la mette*—and pray—*prider;* that is to say, she was present at a portion of Vespers. One evening when, after a walk, she was brought home without the usual visit to *Notre-Dame*, she escaped by the door which happened to be open, made her way in pouring rain to the church, and when Louise caught her cried for over an hour. She was then two and a half. As she grew older, her liking for religious ceremonies increased, but a fondness for sermons would develop only later. "It was better than usual, but it was long, all the same," she sighed when, aged four, she returned from a sermon during the devotion of the *Quarant 'Ore.*

The mother was surprised at these good dispositions and profited by them to suggest to the child supernatural motives which greatly increased her enthusiasm. "This morning, Thérèse told me she wanted to go to Heaven and that therefore she would always be as good as a little angel." What could be easier thenceforth than to point out and cure her faults? There is nothing more suggestive in this connection than the incident told of by Marie. Unable to open the door of the room where Céline was having her lessons, Thérèse had lain down in front of it, thereby to testify to her unhappiness. When informed, her mother ordered that she should not be allowed to behave like that. "The next day," concludes the eldest sister, "the same thing happened again. Then I said to her, 'Little Thérèse, you hurt little Jesus very much when you do that.' She looked at me attentively. She had understood so well that she has never done it since." We see the method of education and its results.

They never allowed the slightest movement of unruliness to go unreproved. She liked to cut out letters in paper, or to make little necklaces; it was her favorite amusement. Granted; but every time she must ask permission to do so. It behooved her not to make a face or affect any pose in order to attract attention. Not even her "King" himself would tolerate that! He calls her to leave her swing and come and kiss him. "Come yourself, Papa!" is the mischievous retort. "You rude little girl!" ejaculates Marie. And behold Thérèse, overwhelmed with contrition mounting the stairs at a run to beg pardon.

She pretends to be asleep when Mme. Martin comes to give her the usual morning kiss. Then she hides herself beneath the bed clothes. "I do not want to be seen." On her part it was a game; nevertheless her mother leaves the room and shows her displeasure. The culprit comes, forthwith, her face bathed in tears, to be reconciled and throw herself into the mother's arms. The incident ends on a delightful note. "When she was so well received, she said to me: 'Oh, Mamma, if you would only cuddle me as you did when I was little!' I took the trouble to go and fetch her blanket, and then I cuddled her as when she was tiny. I looked as though I were playing with a doll." [5]

Rarely do we see such readiness to avow baby faults such vehemence in regretting them. Marie mentions

[5] Mme. Martin to Pauline, Feb. 13, 1877.

her surprise: "When she has said a word too much, or done anything foolish, she notices it at once, and has recourse to tears of penitence. Then she asks forgiveness endlessly. It is in vain that one tells her she is forgiven; she cries all the same. How innocent little children are! I am not surprised that God prefers them to grown-ups. They are far more lovable!" [6]

Was there a shade of diplomacy mingled with all this? Perhaps, but there was something much more. Strictly speaking, Thérèse could not bear to hurt anyone. What preoccupied her more than her restoration to favor was the need of making atonement and healing the wounds she thought she might have caused. Let us hear what her mother says on this subject in a letter to Pauline:

"She had broken a small vase, the size of my thumb, which I had given her that morning. As usual when she has any accident, she came at once to show it to me. I showed a little displeasure. Her little heart swelled . . . A moment later, she ran to me, saying, 'Don't be sad, Mother; when I earn money I promise you I will buy you another.' As you see, I am not near holding it . . ."[7]

The mother skillfully played on this acute sensitiveness. She taught her to do all to please Jesus. Thérèse was initiated very early into the art of self-sacrifice and self-conquest. In this respect she rivalled Céline in generosity. It was the theme of interminable conversations between the two sisters. From behind the garden wall, the echoes thereof reached the ears of a neighbor who, much puzzled, enquired of Louise concerning the meaning of this sybilline language. "Sacrifices! Sacrifices!"

[6] Marie to Pauline, May 10, 1877.
[7] Mme. Martin to Pauline, May 14, 1876.

The Early Training of a Saint

Soon the youngest had the satisfaction of receiving in her turn one of the celebrated chaplets of movable beads, and the future saint, who would exclude all "nicely calculated less and more," "from her spirituality, sets out on her career by putting her hand into her pocket a hundred times a day to count her sacrifices. Apart from the arithmetic, it is already "the little way." Great exploits do not belong to this age; here there is question only of those small mortifications with which the way of life may be thickly sown without any external sign appearing. "Thus," says the future Carmelite later, "I had formed the habit of never protesting when anyone took away my things; or if I were accused unjustly I would prefer to keep silent rather than excuse myself."

During a walk she had gathered an ample supply of flowers and was enjoying making them into bunches. Alas! her grandmother Martin fell in love with the wonderful bouquet and demanded it for her altar. The sacrifice was made immediately, and with such a good grace that Céline alone guessed the interior struggle and noted the tears that glistened on her sister's eyelashes.

Already Thérèse bore patiently the little trials of life. "Jesus has always treated me as a spoilt child," she would write shortly before her death. "It is true that His Cross has accompanied me from my cradle; but He has made me love that Cross passionately."

Without having penetrated as yet, save by intuition, into the mystery of Redemption, the future nun obeyed the urgings of that able novice mistress, Mme. Martin. When uncomfortable, or suffering physically, she was careful not to whine or look miserable, as though she

215

already realised that patience is the masterpiece of strength and self-surrender, the peak-point of love.

* * *

Surprising as it may seem, truth compels us to say that from early childhood Thérèse acquired real self-mastery, and that this home training carried out by gentle methods led her to a very high degree of "balance." Her mother was soon reassured concerning her future. She is "an angel of benediction." . . . "She is Marie's happiness and glory: the latter is unbelievably proud of her." "You will have no trouble in bringing up Thérèse," she confides to the elder girls. "She is so highly gifted; hers is a choice nature." Before she died, she draws this little picture, which has all the freshness of a pastel of Le Tour:

"She will be good; you can see the seed there already. She talks of nothing but God; she would not miss her prayers for anything in the world. I wish you could hear her reciting little fables. I have never seen anything so pretty. She finds out the expression and tone she should use, all by herself. But it especially when she says:

"Say, little one with golden head,
Where dwelleth God, think you?
O, everywhere in all the world,
Then in the heaven so blue."

"When she comes to the last words, she looks up with an angelic expression. One never tires of hearing her say it; it is so beautiful. There is something so heavenly in her expression that one is enraptured."

The opinion of the Visitandine formed after an interview in the parlor on Easter Monday, 1875, is not less

The Early Training of a Saint

encouraging. "Zélie brought little Thérèse to see me. The little girl is very sweet and exceptionally obedient. She did all she was asked, without having to be pressed, and was so quiet that she could have been made to stay without moving all day long. How pleased I was to see this dear little angel!"

At the Process of Beatification, the elder sisters attested upon oath how deeply they had been impressed by this dawning virtue. Marie states categorically:

"From her earliest childhood Sister Thérèse of the Child Jesus seemed to me as though she had been sanctified in her mother's womb, or as though she were an angel whom God had sent to earth in a mortal body. What she calls her imperfections or her sins were nonexistent. I never saw her commit the smallest sin." She herself supplies the qualification to this eulogy which may sound excessive at first, when she shows all the care the child took to correct herself. "There was no need to scold her when she was a child. It was enough to tell her that what she was doing was displeasing to God. She never did it again . . . Her sacrifices consisted in giving in to her sisters many a time. To do this, she made great efforts at self-discipline, for her character was then very decided."

Pauline portrays her for us as an affectionate and docile little girl, in the ingenuousness of her repentance and amendment. Léonie shows her surrounded by the special love of the whole family. "She was such a charming child! On her part, Thérèse never abused this special affection. She was as obedient, and more so, than the rest of us, and I never noticed that she assumed an attitude of superiority with respect to us."

As for Céline, the companion of her games and her first lessons, it is upon her sister's strength of character that she insists: "Before my mother's death, Thérèse was a very lively child. By nature she was proud and self-willed, yet only when there was no question of displeasing God; for from those early days, as she herself confirms, she took great care to please Him in all her actions and never to offend Him."

We have something still better than these testimonies: that which the saint, whose unfailing memory retained precise recollections of her early steps in life, renders to herself. After having drawn up the short balance sheet of her childish pranks and her dangerous tendencies, she is obliged to conclude in the most optimistic manner:

"Jesus watched over His little bride, and turned even her faults to advantage for, being checked early in life, they became a means of leading her towards perfection." . . . "Goodness had charms for me. It seems to me that my character was the same as it is now, for even then I had great self-command . . ." "It is true that even before the age of three, there was not the least necessity to scold me in order to correct me. A single word, said gently, was enough, and would have been enough all my life, to make me understand and be sorry for my faults."

And finally, we have this prodigious declaration which only an incomparably humble soul could allow itself to make: "Since the age of three years, I have refused God nothing."

We know the episode of the basket that Léonie had filled with her doll's clothes, and which Thérèse carried off without more ado, saying "I choose all!" The sentence uttered in a roguish tone and with no thought of selfishness—after all, it was only a matter of some scraps of material—was subsequently to signify for the saint the absolute nature of the divine call, the radical

The Early Training of a Saint

nature of the sacrifice. Was she not already living by its symbolism, the child who, leaning on the balcony of the house in the *Rue Saint Blaise*, looked towards the railway station, as she thought of "little Paulinus," and, at two years old, dreamt of following the second daughter of the family in her religious vocation?

So well supported, so clearly established by a consensus of witnesses, this precocity in her soul's ascension to God disconcerts certain hagiographers and plunges them into a curious uneasiness. They consider this style of ascesis too softening and not at all valuable as apologetic. What is a sanctity worth acquired from the mother's womb and not produced from the painful struggle between nature and grace? Is it not the most dangerous sort of historical falsification, undermining the very foundations of spirituality and rendering imitation impossible?

Let them be reassured. Perchance in all that there is but a misunderstanding, but a sufficiently serious one, concerning the very essence of perfection. If sanctity consisted in the absence of external defects, in the elimination or the complete domination of those movements which betray outwardly the evil remnants of the "old man," Thérèse would have been a saint, or nearly such, from childhood. God, who is master of His gifts, having magnificently endowed her, and her upbringing having done the rest. But such a view is in truth too narrow. Beyond this stage, there is the profound purification of the fallen creature, this refashioning, this revolution, this *change of heart*, in the Gospel sense, that in the opinions, intentions, acts, dissociates from what is divine the disturbing element, often imperceptible, the disintegrating ferment, the proud and sense-dominated *self*. All this hidden misery, this odor of corruption, we carry about diffused within us and for long even unawares, until, because He wills to cure it all, the Holy Spirit reveals it to us. Those natural roughnesses yield only to the chisel of the divine Sculptor that opens and cuts to the quick the heart that has become softened by self-surrender.

Albeit unfolding itself only in secret, such a development is no less poignant than the sudden conversions or the evolution of souls through breath-taking vicissitudes. Now this drama the innocent Thérèse lived to the full. Her autobiography narrates its episodes with a precision worthy of mystical theology. There are not here the cries, or the austere analyses of the *Dark Night*. The style is flowery, suggestive, overlaid; but for those who can read aright there is the same two-edged sword, dividing even unto the marrow, the will wholly surrendered to God's good pleasure. There is Thérèse's strength. What could a prelude traversed by storms add to the authenticity of those transforming operations?

There is something more to consider if we would understand fully developed sanctity. After all, the Blessed Virgin is of all creatures the most authentically, the most meritoriously perfect, and she, the Immaculate, did not pass through the winepress of the active and passive purifications. There must be enkindled in the soul, now completely pacified, the flame of love which refers the smallest actions to the sovereignty of the divine will, and confers upon them the maximum of zeal, earnestness, supernatural energy. Moreover, we must conceive of the cruel suffering of unsatisfied longing in a being whose capacities are limited; that burning of a love that surpasses the possibilities of the human heart to such a degree that the latter is consumed with anguish to the point of being overcome. It is that also, and supremely, which Thérèse sings in her autobiography, and which reaches its culminating point in the final outburst that closes the eleventh chapter.

As may be seen, it is useless to complicate her childhood, or to harden or darken her characteristics, to invent faults, in order to enhance her merit. Her greatness lies elsewhere; in her detachment from the things of sense, in her rising above all that is of earth; in the essential right ordering of the interior man; in the fulness of her self-surrender without change or complication. In a word, it lies simply in the Christlike transformation of the entire personality. There is ample scope for heroism. A vessel of election from her birth, Thérèse for all that was not a fully fledged saint, a "rose-water saint." We do not dim her halo, rather do we set her in her true light when, with Pius XI, we define her as "a masterpiece of nature and of grace."

* * *

To a Patrician lady of Campania who was showing her her jewels, Cornelia replied, pointing to her sons: "Here are my jewels and adornments." She aspired to go down in history not as the daughter of Scipio Africanus, but as the mother of the Gracchi.

With the grace of God in addition, and with less of pagan pride, was it not a similar sentiment that inspired Mme. Martin? On this subject, her eldest daughter relates a significant incident.

"I was then seven years old. One day, when we had put on dresses of dark blue cashmere, my mother sent for us all four, my younger sisters and me, to see us before we went for a walk. She looked at us for some time with a quiet satisfaction; then she said to us: "Go now, children." But she was careful not to compliment us on our frocks, which

I myself thought so pretty, in order not to arouse any vanity in us."

This mother, who cared so little to be conspicuous herself, who to Marie's despair thoroughly disliked anything fashionable in her own clothes, and laughed heartily at what she called "the slavery of fashion," took a pleasure in attending to her children's garments, although careful that these should be simple. Mothers will not be insensible to this sketch of Céline at sixteen months old.

"On Corpus Christi, I dressed her in the charming frock which her godmother had given her. If you could have seen how well she looked! Everyone admired her and I assure you I was proud of my daughter. With that, she wore a pretty hat with a white feather; in short she was delightful. We have taken a fancy for keeping her in white, and she always wears white frocks when she goes out. They are very simple but she looks so nice in them. I never dressed my other children so well."[8]

When she was expecting Thérèse to return shortly to Alençon, she prepared her outfit with equal enthusiasm. "I have already a sky blue frock in view for her. With little blue shoes, a blue sash, and a pretty white cloak, she will be charming. I am rejoicing in advance in dressing this little doll."[9]

Something would have been wanting to the ideal womanliness of this mother, if she had not shown a certain fondness for dress where her daughters were concerned. M. Martin, who used to tease her playfully about the clothes she bought, at the bottom shared her

[8] Mme. Martin to her sister-in-law, July 19, 1870.
[9] Mme. Martin to Marie and Pauline, March, 1874.

The Early Training of a Saint

pride. The fact was that, sure of having their little world in hand, over and above the beauty of the senses both caught a glimpse of a higher dignity of which the Roman matron could not conceive. They knew that according as it is brought up, so does a child become for its parents a recompense or a chastisement. By their joint effort they cultivated for God those souls He had entrusted to them. There lay their highest ambition and their only object in life.

CHAPTER 10

A MOTHER'S CALVARY

A soul's ascent—final onset of the malady—
death of the Visitandine—the reformation
of Léonie—Lourdes—last days, death
and funeral of Madame Martin.

W E HAVE related how in April 1865 Mme.
Martin felt the first discomfort, numbness and
local pain caused by a glandular swelling in
the breast, doubtless originally a simple adenoma, and
which the doctor did not think expedient to remove by
operation, but which sooner or later might degenerate
into cancer. For eleven years the evil lay dormant,
nevertheless frequent headaches, feverish attacks, a
lassitude which could not be accounted for, betrayed
the fact that her health was becoming increasingly undermined. With indomitable energy she triumphed
over her failing strength. She, whom Mère Agnès was
to describe as "self-sacrifice personified," never spared
herself.

Yet she never lost the thought of her approaching
end. How often her daughters would hear her repeat
the passage wherein Lamennais evokes the thought of
the departed with its musical rhythm poignant as a
charm: "The bee had regained its hive, the bird its resting place for the night; the still leaves slept upon their

stem; a sad, sweet silence enveloped the slumbering earth. Only one voice, the distant voice of the village church bell, rose and fell in the still air. It said: 'Remember the dead!' " [1]

It was with a kind of supernatural homesickness, as she thought of all her kindred in Heaven, that she wrote: "Oh, talk to me of the mysteries of that world where in desire I dwell already; in the bosom of which, my soul wearied with the shadows of earth longs to bury itself. Speak to me of Him who has created it and fills it with Himself, and who alone can fill the immense void which He has created in me."

It was not that she shrank from living. Such faintheartedness never even troubled her. "Despite my great longing to see again my four little ones," she explains on November 5th, 1871, "I prefer to be deprived of them longer, knowing that they do not need me, in order to remain with the four who are left to me and to whom, seemingly, I am still useful." Her only wish was to be ready to face as a matter of course that "beyond" which her great spirit of faith as it were rendered familiar to her.

In the meantime, she did not live in the clouds. Her spirituality was solidly attached to earth. She believed that God is Master, that He is infinitely good, that He loved her, and had Himself traced out the whole plan of her life in order to make her happy. To do His will was the only wisdom. She found that will in her family duties and professional tasks which for her so often took the shape of the Cross.

"It is not," she writes, "any desire to amass more money

[1] This passage is an extract from the work: *A Voice from Prison*, which the visionary of La Chesnaie wrote during his forced sojourn at Sainte-Pélagie, and published in 1840. Mme. Martin doubtless knew it in some literary anthology.

that moves me. I have already more than I ever wished, but I believe it would be folly to give up this enterprise when I have five children to settle in life. If I were alone and had to begin again to go through what I have endured through twenty-four years, I would prefer to die of hunger; for the very thought of it makes me shiver." [2]

In her modesty, she can add: "I have often told myself that if I had done the half of all that in order to win Heaven, I should be a canonisable saint!" Let us make no mistake; it was indeed supernatural charity and that alone, which inspired and sustained this incessant crucifixion to the duties of her state.

For all that, there were times, like the temptation which the Curé of Ars knew so well, when she longed to escape into a convent, there to end her "poor life." She was tormented by a passion for the more perfect way. One All Saints' Day, she spoke freely of it to her daughters at Le Mans.

"My dear little girls, I must go to Vespers to pray for our dear departed relatives. A day will come when you will go to pray for me, but I must try and manage so as not to have too great need of your prayers. I want to become a saint which will not be easy; there is much to burn up and the wood is as hard as stone. It would have been better for me had I taken the matter in hand earlier, while it was less difficult; but after all 'better late than never.'" [3]

Is the flight to God compatible with the material servitude from which she suffered to the point of anguish? She asked herself, she worried, and Pauline received these confidences:

"I am longing for rest. I feel my courage failing to continue the struggle. I feel the need of recollecting myself a

[2] Mme. Martin to her sister-in-law, Feb. 6, 1876.
[3] Mme. Martin to Marie and Pauline, Nov. 1, 1873.

little in order to think upon my salvation, which the worries of this world make me neglect. Yet I should remember those words of the *Imitation:* 'Why dost thou seek rest, seeing that thou are born to labor?' But when this labor absorbs you too much and you no longer have your youthful energy, you cannot help wishing to be freed from it, at least partially. However, I live in hopes . . . It seems to me that I shall be much better when I no longer make my *Point d'Alençon.* I shall have time to work at my perfection. Oh what a happy day for me when I shall be delivered from it." [4]

The nearer Mme. Martin approached the tomb, the more accentuated did this contest between Martha and Mary become. The complaint still comes from the active housewife, but who, overworked, longs only to join her nun sister, to secure, like her "the best part." "This morning at Mass I could not pray, and told myself that were I a Visitandine I should be strictly obliged to pray; then this thought helped me to react. It seems to me that if one is a religious, one is not sad like that. For one thing, one has fewer cares, and I am head over ears in them." [5]

The thought of the dignity of the religious life revived with a strange fascination. Mme. Martin was reading the first volume of the biography of St. Jane de Chantal. "I am overwhelmed with admiration," she writes, "it interested me all the more that I love the Visitation Order so much, but now I love it more than ever. I think how happy are those who are called to it." [6] When she began the second volume, the servant, Louise, burst out in her blunt speech: "We are going to have discourses on it during another fortnight." And the poor

[4] Mme. Martin to Pauline, Nov. 8, 1876.
[5] Mme. Martin to Pauline, July 16, 1876.
[6] Mme. Martin to Pauline, Dec. 5, 1875.

girl did not feel at ease in this sort of conversation. Would her mistress be petitioning for the black veil of the Visitation?

"I am doing nothing but dream of cloister and solitude," she confesses. "Really I do not know why, with the ideas I have, it was not my vocation either to remain unmarried or shut myself up in a convent. I should like now to live to be very old, so as to retire into solitude when all my children are brought up." [7]

It was her castle in the air. What woman here below has not had hers, be she queen or mystic? In her heart she was under no illusion. She had too steady a head to nourish herself on chimaeras. "I feel that all these ideas are hollow, so scarcely dwell upon them. It is more important to make good use of the present than think so much about the future." Here we have the prelude to Thérèse's song: *Just for today!* Heroically, without ever deviating from it Mme. Martin would obey the golden rule: *Flourish where God has planted thee!* It was in family life that she must sanctify herself and others.

*   *   *

In October 1876 there was a fresh warning. The swelling in the breast became abnormally enlarged, causing frequent shooting pains, a continual dull ache, and a numbness that spread until the whole side was affected. The fearless woman was not alarmed. "If God permits that I die of this, I shall do my best to be resigned, and to bear my disease patiently in order to shorten my Purgatory. But I hope that all will be well." [8]

[7] Mme. Martin to Pauline, Jan. 16, 1876.
[8] Mme. Martin to her sister-in-law, Oct. 1876.

A Mother's Calvary

The remedies suggested by M. Guérin having proved ineffective, urged by her husband Mme. Martin at last resigned herself to consult Doctor X. of Alençon. He was a conscientious physician, but an unbeliever and a man who did not mince his words. The diagnosis was as trenchant as a verdict of condemnation. "What you have there is very serious. It is a fibrous tumor." He spoke in veiled terms of an operation, only to advise against it immediately. He wrote a prescription but in reply to the patient's question: "What is the use of it?" answered frankly, "None. I do it only to please the patients." It was verily a hammer blow, and administered in the most brutal fashion, but Mme. Martin was grateful to the practitioner for his frankness. "He has rendered me one service," she was to write, "on the day when he told me the whole truth. That consultation was priceless for me." [9]

Her entourage showed less serenity. She testifies to this herself on December 17th, 1876, when, under the shock of the first emotions, she addresses a letter to her sister-in-law which has already something of the tone of a last testament.

"I could not help telling them everything at home. I am sorry now, for it was a heart-rending scene. Everyone cried; poor Léonie sobbed. But I told them of how many people had lived in this state for ten or fifteen years, and I seemed so little upset, doing my ordinary work as cheerfully as usually, perhaps more so, that I calmed them a little.

"However, I am very far from being under any illusions, and I can scarcely sleep at night when I think of the future. All the same, I am doing my best to be resigned, though I was far from expecting such a trial . . .

"My husband is inconsolable. He has lost his pleasure in

[9] Mme. Martin to her sister-in-law, June 14, 1877.

fishing, put away his rods in the attic and no longer cares to go to the Vital club. He is as though completely crushed . . .

"I am very anxious that this should not sadden you too much and that you should be resigned to the will of God. If He thought that I was very necessary on this earth, certainly He would not allow me to have this disease, for I have so often prayed that He might not take me from this world so long as I was necessary to my children.

"Marie is now grown up; her character is of a very serious cast and she has none of the illusions of youth. I am sure that when I am no longer here she will make a good mistress of the home, and do her utmost to bring up her little sisters and set a good example. Pauline also is charming, but Marie has more experience. Besides, she has much authority over her little sisters. Céline has an excellent disposition and is a very pious child; it is rare to see a child of her age show such inclinations to religion. Thérèse is really a little angel. As for Léonie, only God Himself can change her, and I have the conviction that He will . . .

"They will be very fortunate in having you when I shall be no longer here. You will help them with your good advice and, should they have the misfortune to lose their father, you would take them to your home, would you not?

"It comforts me much to think that I have good relations who will replace me advantageously in case of need. There are poor mothers far more unhappily situated than I, who do not know what is to become of their children, who leave them in need without any assistance. I have nothing to fear on that score. In short, I do not see things through dark glasses. It is a great grace which God is giving me . . ."

To satisfy the desire of her relatives, Mme. Martin went to Lisieux to see a celebrated surgeon of the day, Doctor Notta, the same who, six years later, attended little Thérèse. Taking all sorts of precautions, she reports to her husband the negative result of the visit:

A Mother's Calvary

"The doctor considers it very regrettable that the operation was not performed at the very first, but it is now too late. However, he seemed to think that I can go on for a very long time like this. So let us leave it all in God's hands. He knows what is for our good much better than we do. It is He who wounds and He who heals. I will go to Lourdes on the first pilgrimage—ever since the fatal verdict, M. Martin had urged this course—and I hope that Our Lady will cure me if that be necessary. In the meantime, let us be tranquil.

"I am rejoicing much at the thought of seeing you all again. How long the time seems! How I should have liked to return today! I am only happy with you, Louis dear." [10]

It was in the course of this painful journey that the valiant Christian, despite her ashy face, obstinately refused to be dispensed from the fast and abstinence on Christmas Eve. She likewise took a sort of pleasure in teasing her brother and distracting attention from the threat hanging over her. "How I wish that they would not talk any more about all that! What is the use? We have done all that we can, so let us leave the rest in the hands of Providence."

Her letters to Pauline are neither fewer nor less happily expressed than before. She enlivens them with amusing anecdotes, such as that of the dishcloth forgotten by Léonie at the bottom of a soup tureen, which gave the soup an unusual solidity. "It is like the little shoe of Auvergne," exclaimed Father, "it is not dirty but it takes up space!" The family recreations continued, as lively as of yore. Mme. Martin took her daughters to the fair; on carnival night, she made fritters before going to church for the sermon. She humor-

[10] Mme. Martin to her husband, Dec. 24, 1876.

231

ously laid the blame for her troubles upon Adam and Eve. Her cheerful energy soon dispelled fears and renewed hope.

Nevertheless, she meant to settle her affairs, and tried to give up her lace business. The negotiations might have been carried through only for a last-minute scruple. Had she not presented matters in too favorable a light? A timely delay would allow her to inform the purchasers further. It was fortunate for her that she acted so. An unexpected piece of information revealed that the professed admirers were but swindlers out to rob her of her money. The sale fell through. She would have to work to the end to carry out her orders. "I feel I need rest," she sighs, "but I shall hardly have any before that which is eternal."

Quietly, she observed the progress of her disease. The pain became sharper; a second swelling appeared close to the neck. What mattered it?

"God is granting me the grace not to be frightened. I am very peaceful. I feel almost happy and I would not change my lot for any other whatsoever . . . If God wills to cure me, I shall be very glad for, in my heart, I want to live. It costs me much to leave my husband and my children. But, on the other hand, I feel myself that if I am not cured it will be because perhaps it is more expedient for them that I go . . ."

"I have hardly cause to rejoice at seeing the time draw nearer, but I am like children who do not worry over the morrow. I always hope for the best." [11]

If she envisaged the end so bravely and calmly, it was without pose, without any air of dashing courage; she was not playing at heroism.

[11] Mme. Martin to her sister-in-law, Dec. 31, 1876.

A Mother's Calvary

"Great sufferings? No. I am not virtuous enough to desire them. I dread them . . . I am trying to convert myself but I cannot succeed. It is very true that we die as we have lived; we cannot divert the stream when we wish. I see this very clearly, I assure you; at times I feel discouraged. Yet they say that only a moment is needed to make a saint out of a reprobate, but I think it is a very little saint! However, there must be saints of all sorts.[12]

She was to be more than "a very little saint," this woman who found such peace in trustful self-surrender; whom we shall see dragging herself to the first Mass at *Notre-Dame* up to the end, or attending, morning and evening, the retreat sermons at *Saint Léonard;* who will never cease to ply her needle, to attend to her children, to cheer her relatives hiding beneath a smile the hideous ravages of the cancer, and the torture that became more and more unbearable. On these grounds, does she not deserve to take her place at the head of the line of those humble souls to whom tomorrow her Thérèse will carry the teaching of Spiritual Childhood?

*   *   *

In January 1877 we find her once again at Le Mans. She loved the parlors of the Visitation where she breathed the atmosphere of Heaven. "Nothing so delights me"; she wrote, "it is my greatest joy." This time it was to say farewell. Not that she had informed her sister of the gravity of her own state. To what purpose? The nun herself was nearing her end and seemed likely to precede her to the grave. For the last two years consumption had been completing the destruction of her physical frame; a swollen foot had now made it almost impossible to walk. Every morning, notwithstanding, having obtained the then unusual privilege of

[12] Mme. Martin to her sister-in-law, Dec. 31, 1876.

daily Communion, when able to rise she overcame her weakness by really extraordinary energy in order "to seek the good God," as she expressed it. She still remained that perfect nun whom Dom. Guéranger liked to quote as an example, he having frequently met her on his visits to the Visitation to which he was deeply attached.

At Christmas 1876, she had received the sacrament of Extreme Unction. This period of watching for eternity was marked for her with the peace of a beautiful eventide. Why should she be troubled? The past? She had declared that it seemed to her that never in her whole life had she deliberately committed even a small sin. The future? Monseigneur d'Oultremont, Bishop of Le Mans, was to reassure her completely on this head when he came to give her his last blessing. "My child, have no fear. Where the tree falls, there it lies. You are going to fall upon the Heart of Jesus, there to remain for all eternity. . . ." "I am not thinking even about the last sufferings or my death agony," she confessed. "I am so convinced that God will give me His grace that I have no anxiety." "I am afraid of nothing. Our Lord is supporting me. I have grace for each moment, and I shall have it to the end."

Mme. Martin who, insensibly, was also schooling herself to die, was able to admire these perfect dispositions at leisure. She had no secrets from her elder sister and showing her the confidence one gives to a spiritual director, she spoke for the last time of what was "the soul of her soul." She wished, however, to hide the heavy secret that weighed upon her. Why cloud over uselessly this beautiful waiting for the Beyond? She confined herself to giving her sister "her commissions for Heaven." Let us hear how she tells playfully of the most urgent of the requests to the one who would go before her.

"I said to her: 'As soon as you are in Paradise, go and find Our Lady and tell her, "My good Mother, you played a trick on my sister when you gave her that poor Léonie; that was not the sort of child she asked you for, and you must mend the matter." Then you are to go and find Blessed Margaret Mary, and say to her: "Why did you cure her miraculously? It would have been better to have let her die; you are bound in conscience to remedy the evil." ' " [13]

Sister Marie-Dosithée reproved her dear Zélie for this hint of irreverence, but she acquitted herself of the double commission; we shall soon see the proof. Was it a foreshadowing of the miracle? Lo and behold! Léonie herself took it into her head to set her aunt's diplomacy in motion. Despite Marie's sceptical smile, she wrote in her best writing:

"When you are in Heaven, please ask God to give me the grace to amend, and also to give me the vocation to be a good religious, for I think about it every day." Her mother never referred to this. Who could have put these ideas into her head? . . . "I dare to hope," wrote Mme. Martin to her sister-in-law, "that perhaps God has His merciful plans for this child. If it required only the sacrifice of my life for her to become a saint, I would make it with all my heart." [14]

It was on Saturday, February 24th, 1877, the eighteenth anniversary of her clothing day, in the forty-ninth year of her age, that Sister Marie-Dosithée gently passed away. A supernatural confidence surrounded

[13] Mme. Martin to her sister-in-law, Jan. 8, 1877.
[14] Mme. Martin to her sister-in-law, Jan. 18, 1877.

her to the end. "Oh Mother," she said to her Superior, "I can only love and trust and surrender myself. Help me to thank God for it."

During the preceding night, much moved, she had blessed from afar the two families at Alençon and Lisieux. Three weeks previously, she had written a last letter to her brother and sister, in which she had said, in particular:

"I have good reason to thank God for having given me such a good family. Thanks to you, brother mine, and to you, my dear sister. God alone will be your recompense. I have commended you to His keeping; I am at peace about you; you will succeed. But in your prosperity do not be high-minded; let your tastes and your style of living remain simple; give of your abundance to the poor, and you will see your last day come undismayed. Now, dear brother, forgive me; and I ask the same of you, dear Zélie, since I am not strong enough to write to you personally. But forgive me and receive my thanks. I have always loved you . . . Let us all be united in the Sacred Heart; you will find me always there, for I shall die there and remain there for all eternity."

This loss was keenly felt by Mme. Martin. With pious eagerness, she longed to have keepsakes of the nun; the crucifix she had kissed in her last moments, the *Ecce Homo* that was in her cell, the rosary, which she intended to use herself, once she became "ill for good." Increasingly undermined by her terrible malady, was it not the knell of her approaching end that the thin-toned bell of the Visitation convent was ringing? When she attended to her daughters' black dresses, and spread the long crêpe veil over herself, she felt a sharp sensation, as though she were preparing mourning for herself.

A Mother's Calvary

An unexpected event intervened to make her cling to life. Léonie was still for her "a very heavy cross to bear." Moody and undisciplined, blindly obeying the least injunction of the servant but systematically sulking over her mother's orders, she was the shadow on the family life. How often would Mme. Martin bid her in vain come out with her, or share her sisters' recreations after meals! Must she despair of this child?

Sister Marie-Dosithée, who had received the commission, lost no time in making her influence felt. Three weeks had not gone by since her death when the mystery hanging over this destiny was cleared up at last. Puzzled by snatches of conversation she had overheard, Marie had been watching more closely the relations between the child and the maid. She watched, she questioned, she forced avowals, in short she discovered the secret. Faithful to death, but of a violent character and utterly lacking in any notion of moral training, Louise had prided herself upon being able to rule the girl over whom nobody else could gain any influence. She made use of her domineering manner and literally terrified Léonie, who became her slave, beaten and content to be so. What was more serious still, more or less consciously the woman had set herself to destroy the authority of the parents; Léonie must obey her unquestioned, but her alone, on pain of a punishment she would remember. The intrigue had been carried on in so underhanded a way that the mother had been unable to discover it. In vain had she made every effort to gain her daughter's confidence. The latter had been forbidden to speak out. What such a system had made of a nature already difficult may be imagined. Before long Léonie had become a hypocrite and a rebel.

The Story of a Family

It is easy to picture Mme. Martin's indignation at this sudden revelation. She had nothing with which to reproach herself. Overwhelmed with work and cares, she had been obliged to leave considerable initiative to the maid who was, moreover, capability personified and apparently worthy of every confidence. The reaction was not less violent for that. So loving by nature, this mother recoiled with her whole self from a system of constraint that encouraged rebellion under color of breaking down resistance. "Brutality never reformed anyone; it only makes slaves, and that is what has happened to this poor child."

The sudden change was to be complete. Mme. Martin explains in a letter of March 12th, 1877, to Pauline.

"I believe I have obtained a great grace through your aunt's prayers. I had so often recommended poor Léonie to her since she went to Heaven, that I believe I am experiencing the effects of my prayers.

"You know what your sister was like: a model of insubordination, having never obeyed me saving when forced to do so. In a spirit of contradiction, she would do the precise contrary of what I wished, even when she would have wished to do the thing asked of her. In short, she obeyed only the maid.

"I had tried by every means in my power to win her. Everything had failed up to this day, and it was the greatest sorrow I have ever had in my life. Since your aunt died, I have implored her to win the heart of this child for me, and on Sunday morning I was heard. I now have it as completely as I could have. She will no longer leave me for a moment, kisses me till she nearly stifles me, does anything I bid her without question, and works beside me all day long.

"The maid has entirely lost her authority and it is certain that she will never again have any ascendancy over Léonie after the manner in which things have turned out. She, the

Marie, age 21

Pauline, age 21

Thérèse, age 13

Céline, age 20

Léonie, age 32

Saint Thérèse of the Child Jesus, surrounded by her sisters
From photographs of 1895-1896

Top: Pauline, Sr. Agnes of Jesus. *To her right:* Marie, Sr. Marie of the Sacred Heart.
To her left: Léonie, Sr. Frances Thérèse. *Bottom, to the right of the Saint:* Céline, Sr.
Geneviève of the Holy Face. *To her left:* her cousin, Marie Guérin, Sr. Marie of
the Eucharist.

A Mother's Calvary

servant, wept and moaned when I told her to leave immediately, but I no longer wished to have her in my sight. She has so besought me to let her remain, that I am going to wait a little yet, but she is forbidden to address a word to Léonie. I am now treating the child so gently that, little by little, I hope to succeed in correcting her faults.

"Yesterday she came for a walk with me and we went to the Poor Clares. She whispered to me, 'Mother, ask the enclosed nuns to pray for me that I may be a nun.' In short, all is going well; let us hope that it will last."

The obstacle that had barred all access to this soul having been removed, it was necessary to re-educate the child, and Mme. Martin undertook the task with the ardor of youth. All the principles that had guided her in the training of her other children she now applied with complete success. Never had she showed so much patience, so much gentleness. Some accused her of over-doing it; she did not care. Her husband and she had very decided opinions on the subject. Capricious and turbulent the girl remained. She would still sometimes quarrel with her sisters and lose control of herself. We pass over these peccadilloes. Allowances must be made. The essential was that she ceased to be shut into herself; she made sacrifices; she wished to please her parents and still more, to please God. She was "re-adjusted"; the rest would come in time. The mother is triumphant when she can write of her daughter:

"She loves me as much as anyone could, and with this love that of God is penetrating her heart. She has unlimited trust in me, and goes so far as to tell me her slightest mis-doings. She really wants to change her life, and is making many efforts that I can appreciate as no one else can.

"I cannot help thinking that this transformation is due to

the prayers of my saintly sister, for all was altered two or three weeks after her death. It is she also who has obtained me the grace to know how to act so as to win Léonie's affection, and I hope God will let me finish my task which is far from completed as yet. It takes time to conquer such a nature, and I see that this mission has been entrusted to me and that no other could fulfil it, not even the religious of the Visitation. They would send the child away, as they have already done." [15]

To cultivate this "ungrateful soil," as she called it somewhere, Mme. Martin, whose health continued to fail, asked of Heaven a respite. No one understood a mother's work as did she, and this task, glorious beyond all others in its humility, she now felt that she must continue with this daughter who had suffered from "a bad start."

"It is for this that I feel at present a longing to live such as I have not felt hitherto. I am very necessary to this child. After I am gone she will be too unhappy and no one will be able to make her obey saving the woman who has victimised her. But no! that she shall not do, for as soon as I am dead she must leave at once. I believe they will not refuse to carry out this my last wish. But I am trusting in God and I am now asking Him the grace to live. I am quite willing that He should not take away my disease and that I should die of it, but I beseech Him to leave me long enough here that Léonie may no longer need me." [16]

* * *

It will be remembered that the brave invalid had gladly welcomed the prospect of a pilgrimage to Lourdes. Her malady was becoming worse. The

[15] Mme. Martin to her sister-in-law, May 10, 1877.
[16] Mme. Martin to Pauline, March 22, 1877.

A Mother's Calvary

growth in the breast became increasingly painful. The blue meandering lines spread to the back and neck, showing that the ganglionary trouble was spreading. She dreaded lest discharge and hæmorrhage should ensue. Attacks of violent pain became more frequent; from the month of May the suffering became continual with phases of paroxysm. Had not the time come to launch the cry of distress to the Virgin of Massabielle?

Unlike her husband, Mme. Martin greatly disliked travelling. At that period it was not a recreation; in her state it would be even a severe penance. But it was well worth facing the trial to be cured. She would not go alone; she would be escorted by her three daughters, whose prayers would force the miracle. Moreover, she would join a pilgrimage. It would perhaps be less comfortable but it would be incomparably more pious. As no pilgrimage was announced from Alençon or Mans, she made enquiries in the dioceses of the West and ended by securing the last four tickets for the train leaving Angers on Monday, June 18th, at 7.50 in the morning.

The whole family began a veritable crusade of supplications and sacrifices as a prelude to this expedition. They mutually encouraged one another. "It is impossible," writes the mother, "that the Blessed Virgin should not let herself be touched. If you saw Pauline's letter! It gives me confidence. No, Heaven has never seen or will see more fervent prayers, more lively faith. And then, I have my sister in Heaven to do her part for me and my four little angels who will pray for me. They will all be at Lourdes with us." [17]

In her wisdom she took care to maintain this fervor within the bounds of submission. She reminds Pauline, "We ourselves must be prepared to accept the will of

[17] Mme. Martin to her brother and sister-in-law, June 7, 1877.

God generously, whatever it be; for it will always be what is best for us . . ." [18] For herself, she hovered between the hope of a cure and the presentiment of her end. She writes in a philosophic vein.

"I had a nice dinner," she writes on April 12th to her sister-in-law, "and all the time I was preparing it, I said to myself, 'However would they manage if I were not there?' It seems impossible that I can go away; then I think that I must remain and shall remain. I am like all those I have known, not realising their own state. Only others can see clearly, and one is amazed how the patients promise themselves an indefinite time whereas their days are numbered. It is curious indeed, but I am like all the rest."

To be sure, the Almighty might work a miracle. She had even a pretty thought quite in the style of her own Thérèse, for her brother, who had urged that God would only cure her for His glory. "But I say that everything redounds to the glory of God, but He does not think only absolutely of Himself. He would well work a miracle for me although no one in the world would know of it." [19] "The wisest course is to leave everything to Him. I am hoping much but I am quite resigned to accept what He wills. Thus if we do not succeed the disappointment will be less great."

It was on a Sunday—to the great regret of Mme. Martin, who never travelled on such a day—that she and Léonie left Alençon. They took the afternoon train, since they wished to keep the morning for their religious duties. After a halt at the convent of Le Mans, where they were joined by Marie and Pauline,

[18] Mme. Martin to Pauline, May 1877.
[19] Mme. Martin to her brother and sister-in-law, June 7, 1877.

A Mother's Calvary

and a second delay at the Visitation at Angers, where they received a moving welcome with the promise of the spiritual support of the community, they set out on June 18th, at the hour named, for the banks of the Gave. An unconquerable hope filled their hearts.

The pilgrimage was one series of disappointments. Mme. Martin felt cruelly the jolting and shaking of the train, though that did not prevent her from firmly declining a better seat in the corner of the carriage. She had to look after her daughters, two of whom were suddenly seized with train-sickness. Certain errors in the time-table complicated the journey. Some fellow travellers, desiring to make some coffee in the train, lighted a small stove and then upset the whole contrivance over the clothes and food of the Martin family. Since they were with pilgrims belonging to a strange diocese, they knew none of the hymns sung on the journey, and that hindered them from taking an active part in the collective acts of worship. At Lourdes they met with trials of another sort. The accommodation engaged proved to be quite impossible and they had to go in quest of another room. The food left something to be desired; Marie lost the rosary which had belonged to her Visitandine aunt; the mother tore her dress, was once nearly crushed to death, and had so serious a fall that she gave her neck a twist which set up sharp twinges of pain which never again left her.

Amid all these trying contretemps, would Our Lady smile and at last reward the agonising wait of the invalid? No; Heaven was shut. In the poor mother's heart everything seemed grey and overcast. She had no sooner arrived at the station, being at the end of her strength, than she insisted upon going straight to the Grotto although still fasting.

The Story of a Family

"When I reached the Grotto," she writes, "my heart was so full that I could not even pray. During Mass I was quite close to the altar, but I felt so prostrated that I could scarcely notice anything. I came out in a state of collapse and from there I went to the baths. I was afraid when I saw that icy water and the deathly cold marble, but I had to go through it so I bravely plunged in. Yes, but . . . I was almost stifled. I was obliged to come out almost at once. I should have taken things more quietly." [20]

Notwithstanding ever more earnest prayers, they continued to experience disappointments.

"I have been immersed four times in the baths; the last time two hours before we left. I was in the icy water above my shoulders, but it was less cold than in the morning. I stayed in over a quarter of an hour still hoping that Our Lady might cure me. Whilst I was immersed I no longer felt any pain, but as soon as I came out the sharp twinges returned as usual." [21]

"She consoled herself by begging the protection of the Mother of God for Léonie. She rubbed her forehead with the water, praying that the child might develop and become less introverted. Her faith as regards this matter was so deep that she had a sort of intuition that she was heard. In order to take her mind off her own suffering, she sympathised with that of others. She thought of the lamentable cases which had met in this land of miracles which is the city of Mary. "Our Blessed Lady," she concluded, "has left others besides myself to bear their trials."

"She had corresponded with Monseigneur Peyramale, the venerated parish priest of Lourdes, who had received Bernadette's confidence and heard her story, and she wished to visit him. He was absent, but she was received by an un-

[20] Mme. Martin to her brother and sister-in-law, June 24, 1877.
[21] *Ibid.*

assuming woman to whom she mentioned the deep impression the sacred place had made upon her. "Oh, Madame," was the reply, "I assure you notwithstanding that it is nothing to what it was. When one has seen Bernadette in ecstasy as I saw her, one has seen enough for a lifetime."

The housekeeper dried a tear and related how she had watched the daughter of the Soubirous kneeling on the rough slope of the rock several times, her face radiant with the luminous brightness of the "Beautiful Lady," and had seen the candle flame licking her fingers without burning them. This account, moving in its simplicity, remained one of the happiest memories of the pilgrimage.

When, to the sound of the Lourdes *Ave Maria*, they had to leave, Marie, Pauline and Léonie were as though bewildered under the blow of the immense disappointment. Mme. Martin set herself to revive their confidence. She showed herself infectiously cheerful, joined fervently in the hymns sung on the return journey, and in fine overcame her exhaustion so valiantly that she succeeded in hiding her real condition. She had not lost all hope of a cure but she was already looking beyond. When recounting all the incidents of this momentous week to her sister-in-law, she wrote: "Tell me, could we have had a more unfortunate journey? To be sure, there are great graces concealed beneath all that, and those will amply compensate me for these discomforts . . . The Blessed Virgin has said to us as to Bernadette: 'I do not promise to make you happy in this world but in the next.' " [22]

She spoke likewise to her husband who came to meet her at the station at Alençon with the little girls, and

[22] Mme. Martin to her brother and sister-in-law, June 24, 1877.

whose face bore traces of the strain of these anxious days, spent in awaiting the telegram announcing the hoped-for miracle. M. Martin's distress was painful to see and he was astonished to see his wife return "as cheerful as though she had received the desired favor." The brave woman soon succeeded in driving away the clouds by her happy manner. Life must go on as usual. They began again novenas and applications of Lourdes water. Who knew whether Our Lady might not yet give the lie to those sceptical folk who, when they visited the *Rue Saint Blaise*, showed their astonishment at the sight of such credulity?

As for Pauline, who had returned to school, a motherly letter reproves her affectionately for being angry because Our Lady of Lourdes had not made her "jump for joy." "Do not hope too much for joys on earth or you will have too many disappointments. As for me, I know from experience how much one may count upon joys in this world, and did I not hope for those of Heaven I should be a very unhappy woman." [23]

If only she had had no family, Mme. Martin would have eagerly looked forward to that return of the child to its Father, which is what death means to the Christian. She felt so keenly the suffering of exile, the homesickness for the true Fatherland, but there was her husband, to whom the prospect of losing her was already causing agony; and beside him the caressing Thérèse, the delicate Céline, and above all Léonie, sickly and difficult. It was when thinking of all that that she wrote to Pauline: "Well, I am still waiting for this miracle of God's loving kindness and omnipotence through the intercession of His blessed Mother. Not that I ask Him to take away my disease altogether, but

[23] Mme. Martin to Pauline, June 25, 1877.

A Mother's Calvary

only to spare me a few more years of life, in order that I may have time to bring up my children, and especially poor Léonie, who needs me so much and for whom I am so sorry.

"She is less favored than you others as regards natural endowments but, nevertheless, she has a heart that yearns to love and be loved, and only a mother can show her at every moment the affection she craves, and observe her closely enough to benefit her.

"The dear child shows me unbounded tenderness; she anticipates my wishes; nothing costs her anything, she watches me closely to find out what will please me; she is almost too anxious about it.

"But as soon as the others ask anything of her, her face clouds over, her expression changes in an instant. Gradually I am succeeding in making her overcome this, though she still forgets very often."

It was this same Léonie who, having read in the *Semaine Religieuse* the account of some "victim-soul," suddenly had the bright idea which should be the Eureka of a spiritual Archimedes: she would offer herself in her mother's place! No sooner thought than done! "I am going to die," she assured them. "The good God has heard me; I feel ill!" They laughed at her; she cried; then drying her tears, saw fit to ask for a pair of carpet slippers. The mother replied to her wayward child: "But since you are going to die, that would be a waste of money!"

With such self-mastery, fulfilling all her responsibilities, despite her suffering, Mme. Martin remained to the end the soul of her family circle.

* * *

But she had soon to acknowledge the frightening

progress of the disease which the journey to Lourdes had merely accelerated. She had begged her brother to warn her in good time when the end was approaching. Knowing her courage, M. Guérin considered it his duty to take her at her word. When on a visit to Alençon, he told her point blank in the middle of dinner.

"My poor sister, you must not be under any illusions. Set your affairs in order, for you have no more than a month to live." When M. Martin, stunned, reproached him in a friendly manner, he tried when alone with his sister to soften the rather brutal form of his announcement: "I am sorry I told you that for, after all, I do not know what the future may bring. God may cure you yet." But with surprising composure the invalid replied that she was grateful to him for speaking frankly, and that she did not fear death. After a pause, she only said sadly, "What will become of poor Louis with his five girls? However, I leave them all to God." Much affected, M. Guérin asked her to make her husband promise to move his home to Lisieux, where the children would find a second mother in their aunt. "Oh no," exclaimed Mme. Martin, "if I mentioned that to him he would not hesitate to consent in order to please me, but it would mean too great a change in his life. I fear he would be unhappy."

When her sister-in-law renewed this proposal, she answered her on July 15th: "Your letter has indeed touched me, as has that of my brother. Tears came into my husband's eyes. He is astonished at your devotion and I assure you that it comforts me greatly when I consider my departure from this world, to think of the help my dear children will have in you. As for going to live at Lisieux, my husband says neither yes nor no. We must leave it to time."

The last eight weeks were terrible. The patient's

A Mother's Calvary

neck seemed as though twisted and pierced with dagger thrusts. The slightest movement was torture to her and she saw herself faced with the distracting prospect of complete helplessness. The nerves were stiffened or shaken by attacks of pain that forced sharp cries from her. To crown all, for several days running she suffered from violent toothache and continual fever, which wore her out. Yet she remained still valiant; as she said, she "was learning her business" and learning how to change her position without requiring too much help from those around her. Though, alas, retaining all their sensitiveness, her limbs became increasingly stiff, and it soon had to be recognised that she could no longer dress or undress herself alone. "The arm on the bad side is useless but—let us notice this brave jesting—the right hand still wants to hold a needle." Only when near her end did she leave her eldest daughter to deal with the lacemakers. She was upheld by her faith. She knew that in the scheme of Redemption, suffering quickened by love holds a primary place. At this price, she was purchasing the happiness of the world beyond and drawing down a blessing upon her own family. She took refuge in God and, in His company, tasted the sweetness of the beatitude of "those who weep now."

In order not to disturb anyone during the nights, which were a real martyrdom, this mother, who thought only of others, refused to allow any of them to sit up with her, and installed herself alone in the room formerly occupied by Léonie. Marie became used to her moaning during the sleepless nights: "Oh, thou who hast made me, have mercy on me!" But when the girl got up to go to her assistance, the patient showed distressed surprise. "Oh, why did you disturb yourself, since there is nothing to be done?" M. Martin had to use all his authority to make her accept a nursing Sister, and even then she showed some sadness the evening when she saw the latter come in for the first time.

On July 27th, she addressed a last letter to her brother, after having had a severe attack:

"Yesterday I was calling out loudly for you, thinking that only you could relieve me. During twenty-four hours I suffered more than I have ever done in my whole life, so those hours passed amid moans and cries. I called upon all the saints in Heaven, one after another; no one answered.

"At last, since I could obtain nothing else, I asked only to be enabled to spend the night in bed. I had not been able to remain there in the afternoon. I was in a dreadful position and could find nowhere to rest my head. They tried everything, but my poor head would not touch anything. Nor could I make the slightest movement, even to take a drink. The neck was held from all sides, and even to move it, however slightly, caused me atrocious suffering.

"Well, I managed to stay in bed on condition that I remained in a sitting position. When sleep began to come, the imperceptible movement that I made doubtless woke up all the pain again. I moaned all night. Louis, Marie and the maid lifted me in their arms like a child . . . I cannot write more . . . I cannot see and I am incomprehensibly weak . . ."

It was the royal way of the Cross; it was also an ascending way. Gradually, Mme. Martin became detached from all earthly things. She still joined in the novenas for her recovery; in her short intervals of sleep, she dreamed of Lourdes, the baths and a miracle; she frequently applied Lourdes water. But already she was moving in the atmosphere of eternity.

On July 15th, she had written to her sister-in-law:

A Mother's Calvary

"You tell me not to lose confidence. I know very well that Our Lady could cure me, but I cannot help thinking that she does not will to do so, and I tell you frankly that I greatly doubt now whether there will be any miracle. I have faced the situation and am trying to behave as though I am to die. It behooves me absolutely not to waste the short time I have still to live. These are the days of salvation which will never return, and I want to profit by them. I shall gain doubly, for in resigning myself I shall suffer less, and I shall do a portion of my Purgatory on earth. Ask for me, I beg of you, resignation and patience. I have great need of both; you know I am hardly a patient person."

Her confessor, the Abbé Crêté, parish priest of Montsort, was amazed at seeing her so serene. Later he repeated how moved he had been when Mme. Martin had said good-bye to him in the confessional, and foretold to him when she would die. When, shortly afterwards, he was visiting her in her home, she spoke to him of her approaching end so simply that he could not help saying, "Madame, I have seen some brave women, but I never saw one like you!" "The good priest," adds the maid, Louise, who witnessed this scene, "was less calm than Madame."

It was in God that she took refuge; for her, He must ever "be served first." [24] On Sunday, July 22nd, she again rose at five o'clock to go to the first Mass. Marie, who accompanied her, after having tried in vain to dissuade her, has left some moving details concerning this dangerous expedition:

"She needed unheard-of courage and effort to reach the church. Every step she took caused pain in her neck; some-

[24] Words of St. Joan of Arc. *Notre Sire Dieu premier servi.*

251

times she was forced to stop in order to regain a little strength. When I saw how weak she was, I implored her to return home, but she would go on to the end, thinking that this pain would pass. Nothing of the kind happened. On the contrary, she had great difficulty in returning from church . . . I never thought I should bring her home alive. Oh, in what anguish I heard that Mass! Several people looked at us astonished, doubtless wondering how anyone could have made a sick person come out in such a pitiable state. But, cost what it might, she would go, thinking she was not ill enough to miss Sunday Mass."

Mme. Martin agreed that it had been rash on her part, but none the less she persisted a week later in repeating the imprudence by preparing to attend the High Mass. Since it was impossible to dissuade her, her eldest daughter had to resort to a ruse, purposely dressing her very slowly and in fact delaying until it was too late. On August 3rd, she wished at any cost to go to *Notre-Dame* for the last time. It was almost madness. When descending the front door steps, she tripped on one, and a shock of pain ran through her whole body, causing her to cry out. She had to pretend to be interested in several shop windows in order to finish this way of suffering without falling. Marie wrote to her aunt:

"On Friday she went to seven o'clock Mass, because it was the First Friday of the month. Father took her and without him she could not have gone. She told us that when she reached the church had there not been someone to push open the door, she could not have entered." [25]

Confined henceforth to the house, she solaced herself by prolonging her devotions to Our Lady and St. Joseph. Prayer was truly the breath of life to her. Her

[25] Marie to Mme. Guérin, August 9, 1877.

daughter would find her panting, her face blanched, almost livid, on her knees before the statue of Our Lady, saying the whole rosary. She tried to make her sit down. A slight smile was the answer. Why try to prolong this life that was slipping away? It was so sweet to use it up in the service of the heavenly Mother! During the bad attacks they would hear her talking to the divine Friend. "Oh, my God, You see my strength to suffer is leaving me. Have pity on me. Since I must stay on this bed of pain, without anyone being able to help me, I beseech You not to forsake me!"

In the early days of August, taking advantage of a passing respite, they arranged a little surprise for the invalid. It was the Distribution of Prizes at the *Visitation Sainte-Marie d'Alençon* (thus they pompously designated the lessons given to Céline and Thérèse by Marie). The "Head Mistress" describes it herself in a letter to Mme. Guérin of August 9th, 1877.

"I assure you it was quite beautiful. I had decorated the room with periwinkle interspersed with bunches of roses, and with wreaths of flowers suspended at intervals. I covered the floor with a carpet, and two armchairs awaited the presiding guests at the great ceremony; M. and Mme. Martin. Yes, Aunt, even Mother wished to be present at our prize-giving. What a pity you were not there! Our two little ones were in white, and you should have seen how triumphantly they came forward to receive their prizes and wreaths. Father and Mother presented the awards and I called up the pupils. I even read a report which Pauline and I had drawn up the previous night."

* * *

This pretty family celebration was the invalid's last consolation. The joys of earth were no longer for her.

The Story of a Family

Pauline came home to complete the family circle, and took over the interior management of the household. At another time, the mother would have enjoyed the pleasure of having all her little world around her. She had so wished that after Louise left they could manage without hired help. It would be so delightful to be all by themselves, with the older girls helping with the housekeeping and the care of the younger ones. "Must I see the dream of all my life vanish," sighed the dying woman, "just when it was about to be realised?" This vision distressed her. At times she would cry, as she looked at her daughters, one after the other. "Oh, my poor children! Then I shall not be able to take you out; you whom I wanted to make so happy!" To please her, mastering his sorrow, the father had to arrange to take them for a sail. But how could they enjoy themselves when such a mother lay dying?

From time to time, a shadow would come over her face, now drawn with pain. She was not thinking of herself. She was anxious about the backward child who, more than any of the others, stood in need of loving understanding and guidance. "If I had any regrets for life, they would be only for poor Léonie. Who will look after her when I am no longer here?" Marie burst out in reply: "Oh, Mother, I will; I promise you," and she would keep her promise, helped by the beloved mother who, from Heaven, was to complete the task she had begun so fervently on earth.

Mme. Martin was thinking equally of the two little girls. She charged Marie and Pauline to bring them up as good Catholics, and also recommended them to her brother and sister-in-law, who came to visit her at the beginning of August. Thérèse's autobiography describes the painful impressions made upon the little

A Mother's Calvary

ones in those days, when they were purposely kept from the room where their mother lay in agony, and taken every morning into exile at a friend's house. All their thoughts were with their mother. For her they saved a beautiful apricot, which she accepted gratefully even though she could not touch it. Céline has told how, shortly before she died, her mother let her see the violet swellings devouring the shoulder and neck. The child went away with death in her soul.

In Mme. Martin's life Pauline held a special place. Had her mother any presentiment of the future mission of her second daughter? Was it pride in seeing herself reproduced in the girl, or the intuition of her subsequent consecration to God? None of the other daughters had received on their mother's part similar marks of a confidence that bordered upon respect. Seeing her at her bedside when the end was near, she seized her hands, kissed them and said: "Poor little soul! What a vacation for you! And I, who was rejoicing so to have you home for good! Oh, my Pauline, you are my treasure. I know well that you will be a nun." In after years, when the family were together again in the shadow of the cloister, they loved to recognise in that gesture and those words the symbolical significance of a sort of spiritual investiture conferred by the dying woman upon her who would be the "little mother" of Thérèse and the Prioress of the Carmel of Lisieux.

All her offerings had been made, her farewells and her last recommendations, and Mme. Martin peacefully saw death draw nigh. On Thursday the 16th of August, after having celebrated the feast of the Assumption in suffering, she sent to her brother a last note, ending on a grand note of abandonment to Providence:

The Story of a Family

"I can no longer stand. I come down with difficulty. I go from bed to the armchair and from the armchair to bed. I have just spent two cruel nights. Two days ago, I was washed with Lourdes water and from that moment I have suffered much, especially under my arm. Decidedly Our Lady does not will to cure me.

"I cannot write more. My strength is at an end. You did well to come to Alençon when I could still be with you.

"What would you have? If the Blessed Virgin has not cured me, it is because my time has come, and God wills me to rest elsewhere than on earth."

During the following days the pain increased still more in a tragic crescendo. The nights were terrible and the remedies almost quite ineffectual. Marie writes of it to her aunt: "She has to get up every quarter of an hour, for she is suffering so much that she cannot stay in bed. The slightest noise tries her terribly. It is in vain that we speak very softly and walk about without our shoes in order that she may hear nothing. She hears everything, and her sleep is so light that the least noise awakes her."

The consolations of the Faith remained her one source of strength. The Superior of the Visitation, having recalled in a letter to Pauline that thought of St. Francis de Sales: "One ounce of virtue practiced in tribulation is worth more than a thousand in times of peace and joy," they quoted it to the patient, who pondered over it at length, made them repeat it several times and said it over and over to herself when enduring bad attacks.

The 25th of August was sacred in the house to a traditional family feast; they used to offer their good wishes to M. Martin in honor of his patron, St. Louis.

A Mother's Calvary

This year the poor father spent the day in the keenest anxiety. He had been up all night, alarmed by a hæmorrhage that exhausted the last remaining strength of the dying woman. "He was in such torment that he could not leave her," states his daughter. In the evening of the 26th, he went to *Notre-Dame* to fetch the priest and insisted upon himself accompanying the holy Viaticum. The whole family was gathered round the dying bed; their hearts made one in the same prayer. Thérèse has recorded this memory: "The ceremony of Extreme Unction has remained imprinted upon my memory. I still see the spot where they made me kneel. I still hear our poor father's sobs." [26]

The sacrament exercised its soothing effect, the suffering died down somewhat, and Mme. Martin fell into a sort of stupor. She was as though prostrated, her legs and arms swollen so that she could not move them, and she was unable to make herself heard. They had to watch closely the almost imperceptible movement of her lips in order to learn her thought, but her eyes were still eloquent. When next day, summoned by telegram, M. and Mme. Guérin entered her room, she greeted them with a smile, then gazed a long time at her sister-in-law, with a grave and supplicating look, as though to convey all the hopes she put in her and her immense gratitude.

It was on the threshold of Tuesday, August 28th, 1877, exactly half an hour after midnight, that Mme. Martin gently breathed her last, after a very short struggle. Warned by the nurse, her husband and brother reached her in time to receive her last sigh. They also called the elder girls who, reassured by the nursing Sister, had left their dying mother at nine

26 Autobiography. C. 2.

The Story of a Family

o'clock. Pauline, who had taken up her quarters in the little room in the garden over the linen room, went in tears to the two little ones, but not wishing to disturb their sleep she put off telling them the painful news until the next morning. M. Martin took Thérèse to the death bed. "'Come,' he said to me, 'Kiss your dear mother for the last time.' And without uttering a single word, I pressed my lips to the cold forehead of our darling mother." [27]

She seemed to sleep. Although she had nearly completed her forty-sixth year, one would have said she had been struck down much earlier. Emaciated and as though sanctified by suffering, the face had taken on a strikingly dignified and youthful expression. An impressive atmosphere of recollection and supernatural calm seemed to envelop the death chamber. M. Martin and his daughters could not cease gazing upon the peaceful countenance of her who, after having travailed, knew at last what it was to rest.

As for the youngest, she has left us her account of those sad days in her autobiography. She was then aged four and a half:

"I do not remember having cried much, and I did not talk to anyone of all that filled my heart! I looked and listened in silence, and I saw many things they would have hidden from me. Once I found myself close to the coffin, standing in the passage. I stood looking at it for a long time. I had never seen one before, but I knew what it was. I was so small then that I had to lift up my head to see its whole length, and it seemed to me very big and very sad." [28]

[27] Autobiography. C. 2.
[28] *Ibid*.

A Mother's Calvary

The funeral took place on Wednesday, August 29th, at nine o'clock in the parish church, where relatives and friends had gathered, and the burial followed in the cemetery of *Notre-Dame*, at Alençon. It was only in October, 1894, after M. Martin's death, that M. Guérin, wishing to unite in the tomb those whose life together had been a model of conjugal union, had his sister's body removed to the family vault at Lisieux. The granite tombstone, with its inscription, was then placed on a piece of vacant ground close by. Fifty-one years later, it was recognised intact, and set up in a conspicuous position in the garden of the Pavilion, where pilgrims like to find the remembrance of the mother of St. Thérèse of Lisieux.

Praises were not lacking to the memory of the dead. The parish priest of Monsort declared roundly that "there was a saint the more in Heaven." Mme. Guérin, who had both received her sister-in-law's confidences and profited by her experience and delicate services, would recall her outstanding merits once more in a letter addressed fourteen years later, on November 16th, 1891, to her Carmelite niece, Sister Thérèse of the Child Jesus.

"What have I done that God should have surrounded me with such loving hearts? I have but responded to the last look of a mother whom I loved, oh so dearly! I believed I understood that look, which nothing can ever make me forget. It is engraven upon my heart. Ever since that day, I have endeavored to replace her whom God has taken from you but, alas! nothing can replace such a mother. However, God has willed to bless my feeble efforts, and today He allows me to reap the affection of your young hearts. He willed that

that mother who had guided your first childish steps should be raised to a more sublime glory, and rejoice in the happiness of Heaven. Ah, my little Thérèse, the truth is that your parents are of those who may be called saints, and who deserve to beget saints."

Not less touching is the appreciation of her former mistress from one who had lived eleven years in the Martin family, Louise Marais. This servant, faithful above all, had been sent away under conditions we have seen. She begged for delay and was granted a respite until the death of her mistress, claiming that no other could look after the latter like herself. In truth, she did surround the sick woman with the most wholehearted devotion until the end. Afterwards she left, for the reforming of Léonie required the step, but not without carrying with her a regret that would never be effaced for her who had shown her so much consideration and kindness. In 1923, some months before she died, she wrote again to the Carmel of Lisieux:

"In my sharp sufferings, I invoke my little Thérèse and, at the same time, her good and holy mother; for if Little Thérèse is a saint, in my opinion her mother is one also, and a great one. She was sorely tried during her life and she accepted all with resignation. And then—how she could sacrifice herself! For herself anything was always good enough, but for others it was quite another matter . . . I should be too long if I told you of all her goodness and submission to the will of God."

Louder than all these testimonies, rises the voice of her own daughters, who have witnessed to her virtues on oath in the evidence they gave during the Process of Beatification of their little sister. And loudest of all,

A Mother's Calvary

this last-named speaks, she whose increasing glory was to constitute for the dead the most authentic title of nobility. Was ever a fairer portrait drawn of a mother than that verse written by Thérèse:

> "I loved my mother's gentle smile,
> Her pensive gaze would say the while;
> 'Eternity hath drawn me from exile,
> I go unto the God of love
> Above.'

CHAPTER 11

LIFE IN THE FAMILY CIRCLE AT LES BUISSONNETS

Settling in at *Les Buissonnets*—Lisieux—organisation of the household—the children's
education—family leisure—spiritual life.

THÉRÈSE has told us how, in the evening of
Mme. Martin's funeral day, whilst Céline took
Marie for "Maman," she herself made Pauline
her "little mother." Aged respectively seventeen and a
half and sixteen years, the two elder girls were admirably prepared to play such a part. Responding to
the last thought of the dead mother, Mme. Guérin
offered to guide them and invited her brother-in-law to
transplant his home to Lisieux. The house attached to
the chemist's premises, now enjoying great prosperity,
would be a second home for the orphans, where Jeanne,
already a thoughtful child despite her nine years, and
Marie the younger, a charming little pickle with brown
hair and black eyes, would welcome them as sisters.
The intimacy that united the two families would only
increase; on either side there were the same traditions
of simplicity, industry and uprightness. The Fournet
family cherished the memory of one of its members, the
Abbé Thomas-Jean Monsaint, sometime curate of
Orbec-en-Auge and subsequently of S. Roch at Paris,

who had been martyred during the massacres of September 2nd, 1792. In the old, solid building overlooking the cross roads of the *Place Thiers* and the *Grande Rue*, in the shadow of the lofty towers of the cathedral of *Saint Pierre*, they would breathe the bracing atmosphere of the Faith in all its purity.

For M. Martin a change of residence amounted to an uprooting. Everything bound him to Alençon; the countryside he loved, its poetic associations, his angling, his many interests, the seclusion of the Pavilion, his aged mother whom he could not think of taking away with him and, above all, the proximity of his family graves. His confessor and the many friends he possessed in the neighborhood were strongly opposed to an exodus which would cost him so much. They urged him to place his three younger daughters in a boarding school and bring out the two elder into society, where Mme. Tifenne and Melle. Pauline Romet would exercise a helpful moral guardianship over them. This prospect of a more worldly life scarcely appealed to the stalwart Christian, any more than did the thought of still further saddening their mourning by a new separation. He would prefer for his children the careful and happy training of home. As for the arguments concerning him personally, he refused to consider them. What added to his perplexity was that, out of delicate feeling, his wife had concealed from him to the end her desire that he should settle at Lisieux. When approached by M. Guérin, Marie refused to take the initiative from the same motive as her mother.

In His indecision M. Martin sounded his two elder daughters on the subject of eventually moving. "I am asking your advice, children, because it will be solely on your account that I make this sacrifice, and I would not wish to impose one upon you also." The girls protested in their turn that they attached no importance to anything but their father's happiness, but he soon discovered where their inclinations lay. His resolution was taken. At the beginning of September, Marie writes to her aunt:

"For our sakes, he would make any possible sacrifice; if necessary, he would sacrifice his happiness, even his life. To make us happy, he would stop at nothing. He has no longer a moment's hesitation; he believes that it is his duty and for the good of us all, and that is enough for him."

M. Guérin, who was only waiting for a sign, set to work at once to look for a house large enough for seven people, in the town of Lisieux, and not far from his own home; bearing in mind also the last wishes of Mme. Martin, who had wanted a large garden, in order to provide recreation for the whole family and healthy exercise for the little ones. Strong in the invisible help of the sister whom he had prayed to guide him, he considered twenty-five empty houses in the vicinity, and at last, in the parish of Saint Jacques, in the suburb known as "New World Village," he found the ideal property which, in a letter of September 10th, he described in detail to his brother-in-law, with the precision of a lawyer.

It was 764 paces from the pharmacy, 700 from the church. From the main road to Pont-l'Évêque, passing on the left the fine *Parc de l'Étoile*—since then given over to allotments—the walker reached it by a stony path that ran steeply up hill. If this path, narrow and shut in, was then wanting in comfort and today in attraction, it made it easier to escape the noise, dust and

Life in the Family Circle

traffic on the road, caused by the crowd of tourists flocking to Deauville. At the cost of some meandering, half way up, nestling in an islet of green, we reach the pretty Norman country villa, with its pleasantly symbolic name, once praised by Cardinal Touchet, *Les Buissonnets.*[1] "Not even *Les Buissons!* It is a name that suggests a picture—a mass of honeysuckle, hawthorn, hazels, laburnum and what not?—where in the moss a nest is hidden."

We enter the door opening in the wall and ascend a few steps. The house stands out attractively with its low façade, in red brick with white courses; its pilasters and cornices of cut white stone, its tall windows with carved wooden ornaments. The trees, flower beds and trailing creepers give it an air of freshness, the breezes caress it and the cheerful songs of the many birds sound all about it. In front is an English lawn, with masses of flowers framed in bushes, and the shade forms a natural alcove where it is pleasant to work on hot days. A rustic shelter encloses the well and the old fashioned pump. Behind the house is a garden on a higher level, where the grass lends itself to children's games, whilst the kitchen garden provided the head of the family with useful and healthy occupation. Here and there are mysterious hollows with the laurels and barberry; winding paths running beneath firs and white cedars. It was part of the dreamland with which Thérèse would be enchanted. At the back was the shed where her swing was put up, the wash-house in front of which was a

---

[1] Strictly speaking, in 1877 the house had neither name nor number. It stood "in the district of *des Bissonnets.*" Thinking the name ugly, the Martin children substituted in private the more harmonious one of *Buissonnets.* By a process of simplification, the name became extended from the district and the road to the house itself. Thérèse's autobiography fixed it finally and gave it world-wide celebrity. Even words can have a destiny.

small square plot which she would strew with ferns and periwinkles, the bed that sheltered some rarer flowers, the outer gate opening on to a path, by which barrels of cider and bulky articles were delivered.

Beneath its modern, surface prettiness, the house is relatively old. The rooms have low ceilings and are rather badly arranged, though the whole is attractive and spacious. The ground floor, which is sunk on the garden side, consists of a dining-room wainscoted in oak; a kitchen with a red brick open hearth, a small room and a lumber room. On the first floor are two dressing rooms and four bedrooms, those at the back opening straight on to the gravel path of the higher ground. On the second floor are three attic bedrooms, well papered and, at the top of the house with its sharp gable and blue and white dormer windows, an upper room, suitable for study and for prayer, looking out over an immense panorama, a pleasing equivalent of the Pavilion and known as the Belvedere.

Enthusiastic over his discovery, M. Guérin, who could not even sleep over it, urged his brother-in-law to come and decide on the spot and make up his mind at once. M. Martin hastened thither and at once won over, signed the lease without delay. Whilst he remained for some time at Alençon to settle up his affairs and dispose of the lace-making business, his daughters left the *Rue Saint Blaise*, after a moving farewell visit to the cemetery of Notre-Dame. The move took place on November 14th, 1877. The orphans spent the first night under their uncle's roof, he having met them and being anxious to do the honors of the town. It needed nothing less than the motherly welcome of Mme. Guérin and the caresses of Jeanne and Marie to soften the first pain of such an exile. Thérèse alone was quite

Life in the Family Circle

serene. "I felt no grief at leaving Alençon. Children like change and anything out of the ordinary, so I was pleased to come to Lisieux." [2]

Next day they inspected the new home, which seemed ideal to them all; then they proceeded to furnish it cheerfully and in good taste. The dining room, its parquetry floor immaculately waxed, was handsomely fitted with oak furniture of good style; a sideboard, ornamented with twisted columns and hunting scenes, a round table on a massive pivot, straight-backed chairs to which, in view of rare parties, were subsequently added two armchairs in the same style. On the mantelpiece was a gilded bronze clock bearing M. Martin's name. Thick curtains subdued the light, and imparted an air of gravity to the picture of the Nativity, which hung above the glass overmantle and the pleasing portraits of children hanging on the walls. The kitchen was supplied with the solid utensils characteristic of old fashioned homesteads. The smaller room was made into a sitting room where the family spent the evenings.

On the first floor, facing the street, they arranged M. Martin's bedroom with jealous care. There the furniture was of walnut, practical and elegant; his desk, armchair, table and large bed, from the tester of which the curtains fell in classic folds and imparted to it something of quiet melancholy. The two oil lamps, which would light up the evening meal on the day of Thérèse's first Communion, stood on either side of the crucifix, before which would rise so many prayers. The setting was comfortable—*bourgeois*—but the monastic spirit asserted its rights once more in the religious nature of the pictures, which were favorable to prayer: the *Ecce Homo!*, the Crucifixion, to which would be added in

[2] Autobiography. C. 2.

267

The Story of a Family

1888 Céline's painting of *Our Lady of Sorrows*. The closely curtained windows admitted a softened light. With this room, rather suggestive of a cell, the adjoining one, reserved to Marie and Pauline and which later on was to see the miracle of *Our Lady of the Smile*, formed a contrast, with its light woodwork and the soft muslin curtains draping the alcove. Of the rooms at the back, the larger one was assigned to Céline and Thérèse and the other to Léonie. They took care not to forget to furnish the Belvedere, which their intuition told them would so perfectly meet the need for solitude that was innate in M. Martin, and which the loss of his wife was to deepen.

On December 16th, Marie was able to write to her father:

"We are settled in *Les Buissonnets*. It is a charming dwelling, bright and cheerful, with this big garden where Céline and Thérèse can romp. The only items that leave something to be desired are the staircase and the lane leading to the house; which latter you would call 'the path to Heaven,' for it is narrow indeed; anything but a broad and easy way. What does it matter? All that is of very little importance, for we are only sojourners on earth. Today we have pitched our tent here, but our true home is in Heaven, where we shall one day go to join our darling mother.

"Meanwhile, Father dear, we are longing to have you with us; your absence already seems very long. When will your business at Alençon be finished? I am thinking of you all the time. I believe you will be happy here with all the little family around you. Yes, we shall try to be very good, and make your life pleasant in order to thank you for the great sacrifice you have made for our happiness. This happiness will be yours also, for we shall do everything to make it so."

M. Martin replied that he was urging the lace-

Life in the Family Circle

makers to complete their "pieces." He also was in haste to take possession of his new kingdom. Meanwhile he exhorted them from a distance:

"Pay attention to all your uncle and aunt tell you. You know the great sacrifices I have to make to procure you the help of their advice; so do not lose a single occasion of profiting by it. You, Marie, my grown-up daughter, my firstborn, you know how I love you. Very well; continue to devote yourself increasingly to your sisters. Take care that in watching you they have a good model to imitate. Good-bye children, I press you all to my heart, as I love you, and entrust you to your mother in Heaven."[3]

When the workers had finished their tasks, M. Martin sent out the last orders and gave up his lace business. Since his old mother expressed the wish to end her days in some neighboring country dwelling, he installed her not far away, at Valframbert, in charge of Mme. Moyse Taillé, the "little Rose" of Semallé. He used to visit her frequently until April 8th, 1883, when she died in peace at the age of eighty-three. It was in view of having to return often in future that he retained the Pavilion as a *pied à terre*, where the room on the first floor would serve him as a bedroom at night. At the end of November, not without regret, he finally left the dear house in the *Rue Saint Blaise*, and arrived at the *Buissonnets*, there to receive a royal welcome.

* * *

Lisieux, whither the Martins came unknown and which would derive such glory from their sojourn, offered to the unexpected guests a countenance shaded over by autumn fogs. It was no longer the clean, distinguished town, girded by the smiling countryside.

[3] M. Martin to his daughters, Nov. 25, 1877.

The Story of a Family

The valley where the Touques and Orbiquet unite is veiled in grey, heavy mists. The meadows that clothe the slopes of the hills appear as though overcome and sodden with rain. The tall factory chimneys trace spirals of sooty black in the lowering sky. The streams that wind in unreal looking network, take on the color of slate, and at times look as though flowing with ink. There are narrow alleys where, in these troubled waters, the washerwomen beat and wring out their clothes. Here and there industry has laid its hand. You hear casks and barrels being moved. There are times when the acrid odor of fermented cider seizes you by the throat.

There is another aspect of Lisieux, which the implacable war has, alas! ravaged and almost annihilated. Besides many blemishes, some authentic glories used to be revealed. The ancient Gallo-Roman city, *Noviomagus Lexoviarum*, which before Caesar's invasion served as the capital of the important tribe of the Lixoves, retained some noble memories of its stirring past. Whilst fragments of pottery, archaic implements and carved stones, witnesses of those primitive times, enriched the galleries where the lover of history strolled, the Middle Ages lived again in the wonderful open air museum which formed the heart of the city. The Rue de la Paix, the Manoir Carrey, the Place des Boucheries and the Rue aux Fèvres displayed the most varied types of the Norman dwelling house of the 14th to the 16th centuries. The half-timbered houses with their pointed gables, leaned curiously towards one another, as though to tell secrets or murmur prayers. Grinning monsters, grotesque figures jutted out from the hoary structures, with worm-eaten window frames.

Further along, an unexpected façade betrayed the

Life in the Family Circle

hand of the Renaissance. The Versailles style is inscribed in the classical lines of the former episcopal palace, which contains, as in a jewel case, the King's apartment, the glittering "Golden Room." The tradition of Le Nôtre inspires the public garden, with skillfully arranged rows of trees, and bright hedges forming a setting for noble terraces. The soul of the great prelates has deserted these haunts, but the cathedral of Saint Pierre remains, with its high, unequal towers, where Gothic unites with Romanesque without incongruity. Maurice Barrès boasted as an artist of this ex voto of stone, of such imposing austerity.

The deep, Norman spirituality of the close of the 13th century shines out in the impressive lengthening of the nave. To fill such a place, a whole people must have assembled together. It is here, in the pretty apsidal chapel, presided over by a statue of Our Lady and which, demolished by "acts of war," was rebuilt by Pierre Cauchon, that daily the Martin family knelt at Mass and frequently received their Lord. It is there, on the south side of the ambulatory, almost in the apse, in the oratory formerly dedicated to St. Joseph of Cupertino, and today to St. Anthony of Padua, that every Sunday the father installed Thérèse, in order that she might hear High Mass with her eyes fixed upon the high altar. After the Gospel, he would be seen holding the child by the hand to lead her to a seat not far from the pulpit, so that, notwithstanding the size of the building, she might not lose a word of the sermon. Seated in the churchwardens' bench, M. Guérin would start with pleasure when she, whom he used to call his little sunbeam, appeared out of the subdued light.

During the week-day walks, it was rather Saint Désir and Saint Jacques, or the humble Carmelite chapel that received the visits of the father and daughter. Despite an elegant porch, an impressive "glory" and an historic choir, Saint Désir furnishes but meagre food for aesthetic inspection, but Saint Jacques, with its monumental flight of steps, its strangely roofed square tower, its ageing buttresses, so friable and worn by the wind, is an imposing building and inclines the visitor to prayer.[4]

After all, however open the new-comers might be to the impression of the many reflected beauties, it was not artistic pleasure which they sought within those walls. Thérèse herself will accurately mention the wonders accumulated in the picturesque city by the master craftsmen; to these she will prefer the path that loses itself in the hollows through the fields, leading to the distant prospects softened by fog and mist, or on the hills with their green pastures. What the family sought at Lisieux was much less amusement than to forget the world. With the proximity of the Guérin relations there was the prospect of a quiet, pious and secluded life in the intimacy of the family circle. The isolation of *Les Buissonnets* seemed made on purpose to favor such a hope.

*   *   *

Life was promptly organised. M. Martin directed it from above. He set its tone, its spirit, its general line. He wanted order and exactness in everything and showed displeasure when, through inattention or negligence, anything was wasted, lost or spoilt. He desired that each of his daughters should have her fixed duties and learn how to keep a house well. He would not

---

[4] Of Saint Désir there remains today only a heap of ruins. Saint Jacques, very seriously damaged, has only just escaped total destruction and can be restored only with great difficulty.

Life in the Family Circle

tolerate a shadow of "masculinity," and considered that household duties remained the honored field for feminine talents. For the rest, he left things to his daughters and never interfered in matters of detail. During nine years it was Marie and after her departure for the convent Céline who held the post of mistress of the house. The posthumous action of their mother supported them. Her invisible presence reigned over the household. At her death, had not her eldest daughter felt, almost with a sense of physical shock, the invincible assurance that the departed woman was not wholly gone, and would return to help her to fulfil her mission?

To the superficial observer, the way of life at *Les Buissonnets* might have seemed rough. Modern comfort was unknown. There was obviously no question of electricity, gas or running water. There was never a bedroom fire. Meals were prepared in old fashioned style. The kitchen stove was heated with charcoal; in the open hearth the soup caldron hung by a chain from the pot-hanger. Joints hung from a spit and were roasted before the fire. In the winter evenings, to the wonder of Thérèse, M. Martin had potatoes baked on a hot stone. They liked the leaping flames and the crackling of the logs in the fire. The meals were very simple, excepting on great feasts which even "Brother Ass" has a right to celebrate. The food was wholesome and plentiful; no one was expected to be either fastidious or greedy. Chocolate was given to the younger ones at the early breakfast, but was replaced by good onion soup as soon as they were older. Coffee appeared at mid-day only on special feast days.

Apart from the Guérin family, guests were few. They knew nobody and they were unknown. There was no drawing room. The dining-room did duty for one, or the father's room when the former was unavailable owing to preparations for some dinner party. Four calls sufficed at New Year to greet relatives and intimate friends. These duly paid, they mischievously pitied the poor uncle and aunt, whose position condemned them to the social slavery of some sixty parties and visits. Idleness was ruthlessly banished. Study, needlework and accomplishments filled every moment of the day. M. Martin, who greatly admired the delicate miniatures and portraits on vellum or ivory that came from Pauline's brush, was particular when he went to Paris to bring her gold shells of which she made excellent use. He arranged for Céline to have drawing and painting lessons. He likewise procured for Pauline the skeins of fine guipure lace thread wherewith, at the cost of two years' diligent labor, she embroidered an alb which was a real masterpiece. It was first presented to the Abbé Ducellier, her spiritual director and one of the cathedral clergy; after his death, it was returned to her at Carmel, and it was worn by Cardinal Pacelli at the French National Eucharistic Congress in 1937.

At Lisieux, as at Alençon, the servants were treated almost as members of the family. They were faithful and left only "to better themselves," Victoire, after seven years' service to set up a laundry business; Felicité, after three, to be married. M. Martin was extremely good to them. On August 30th, 1885, when travelling in Central Europe, we find him writing to Marie, who was at the helm in his place, to look well after the maid and pay her wages punctually every quarter. Later, when a woman in their employ asked for New Year's Day free, he pleaded her cause with Céline, who rather hesitated. "Let her go. Be kind. Give her the day's holiday." Seemingly the experiment turned out badly, and a fatal celebration having led to the servant's return in a half-intoxicated condition, they had reason to regret their indulgence.

If any dispute arose between maids and children, on principle it was the latter who had to give in. The father would not allow them to fail in respect. Thérèse, whom Victoire could tease upon occasion—the story of the *Memorare* and the candle-ends witnesses to that—had to apologise to the servant under circumstances where plainly the small girl was not in the wrong.

What could be more touching than the homage rendered to their former employers by these devoted servants? From Paris, on May 25th, 1926, old Victoire Pasquier, indignant at certain malevolent insinuations concerning the circle at *Les Buissonnets*, protests with honest vehemence: "Those young ladies never went out alone, and when their father did not accompany them it was I who went with them. I always saw them very reserved and models of good style. There were not many families like them. I have been in service in all classes of society, but I have met only one other family to compare with them."

At the same date, Félicité Saffray spoke still more strongly: in a letter to the Carmelite sisters: "M. Martin above all was a saint, and so brave. He was afraid of nothing. Truly, there are few families such as you were." If it be true that no man is a hero to his valet, is not this spontaneous canonisation of an employer by an employee a convincing document?

* * *

The father watched very carefully over the education of his daughters. Trustful love remained its guiding principle. "He was as loving to us as he was hard to himself," attests Céline. "He was exceptionally affectionate and lived only for us. No mother could have surpassed him but, notwithstanding, he was never weak with us." Thérèse, in her turn, speaks in almost identical terms: "Our father's heart, already so affectionate, seemed to be enriched with a truly motherly love."

He could not make up his mind to submit the two younger ones to the discipline of a boarding school. We have mentioned already how he felt family separations. Had Sister Marie Dosithée been still alive, he might perhaps have turned to the Visitation convent at Le Mans when deciding upon a school, but her death having left him free, he sought and found what he wanted at Lisieux itself.

At the extreme west of the town, after crossing the Touques and emerging on to the high road to Caen, might be seen a group of buildings varying considerably in style, and overlooked by the porch and bell tower of *Saint Désir*. That stretch of land where, during the night between the sixth and seventh of June, 1944, an aerial bombardment sowed ruin and fire, in which twenty nuns perished in the flames, and destroyed all the material associations connected with the first Communion of St. Thérèse of the Child Jesus, was an historic relic. There in the year 1046, Lesceline, widow of William, Count of Exmes, translated to a domain granted by William the Conqueror the Benedictine nuns established since 1011 at Saint Pierre-sur-Dives. If the upheavals of a thousand years had left traces in the stones, only the blood-stained interval of the Revolution had been able to interrupt—and that for a very brief interval—the celebration of the Divine Office which is the essential mission of St. Benedict's daughters. The same could not be said of the school annexed to the abbey, at least after the 16th century. Closed

Life in the Family Circle

during the Terror, re-opened in 1808, that flourishing institution was included in the proscription of 1904, and replaced by a guest house for ladies.

In 1877, the abbatial status having ceased under the Restoration, it was a Conventual Prioress, the Reverend Mother Saint Exupère, who ruled the monastery. The school was in charge of Mother Saint Arsène, a connection of the Martin family. In 1880 there was appointed to succeed her a remarkable nun, an able teacher and skilled judge of character, Mother St. Placid. There were five classes, each consisting of two or three divisions and distinguished by the different colors, red, green, purple, orange and blue, of the girdles worn with the school frocks, and comprising about sixty girls belonging to the leading local families. Beneath its austere appearance, the house was marked by its family spirit, and its reputation was well established. Jeanne and Marie Guérin were at school there, and when the term opened in January 1878 M. Martin decided that Léonie and Céline should accompany them. Although Thérèse was sometimes invited for some special occasion, or festival, she did not enter as a pupil until October 1881.

Whilst Léonie became a boarder, Céline and later Thérèse arrived in the morning, shortly after eight o'clock, and returned home towards six in the evening. On their return, they often accompanied their cousins, escorted by the faithful Marcelline, a maid of the Guérins who subsequently entered religion with the Benedictines at Bayeux. M. Martin often took them himself and sometimes brought them home. He seized such opportunities to talk about their work and progress. Beneath a smiling face, he concealed very real strictness. When their marks were not good, he promptly showed his displeasure, and the thought of having displeased him would cast a shadow over the return to *Les Buissonnets*. Never would he have consented to contest the authority of the mistresses and no diplomacy could induce him to put the latter in the wrong.

Likewise, he insisted upon exactness and regularity. He did not like the girls to complain about small ailments, or seek such pretexts for absenting themselves from school. Céline has stated that during her eight school years, and in spite of being very delicate, she missed only two days. Did she suffer from violent earache? She left home with a bandage under her chin. If she had indigestion she took only a small piece of chocolate for her mid-morning lunch . . . One did not take a holiday for such a trifle.

Reared in Spartan fashion by their elder sisters, accustomed never to question an order, the little girls easily carried off the first conduct prize. They were required to be careful of their school equipment, and use economically the fixed number of pens allotted to them each month. They likewise received for dessert at midday lunch a certain quantity of jam, which had to last for the time allowed. If they failed to make it last out, so much the worse! At the "snack," half way through the morning, their fellow pupils helped themselves from the tray that was passed round the class room, to the strengthening glasses of wine and the biscuits, supplied abundantly by their parents. The Martins contented themselves with a small piece of dry bread, even though their feelings, if not their sense of taste, had to suffer keen mortification thereby. Nor were they allowed to follow the fashions in dress, if to do so flattered their vanity. Céline, who had a high forehead, would have liked to wear a fringe, a style then very fashionable. No doubt, a touch of complacency about her appearance prompted the wish. She was not permitted to indulge the weakness.

So austere a training bore fruit. Even Léonie improved rapidly, to the great joy of her father, who was prodigal of patience and encouragements in her case. It was soon evident that her mother's influence was following her from beyond the grave, with touching efficacy. Marie, who had taken her in hand, expressed her delight. She, who had written:

"I am hoping more from the protection of my holy mother than from my own poor efforts, to complete from on high the transformation of my poor sister . . ." was able to send a first victory bulletin soon after the arrival at Lisieux:

"I notice," she writes of Léonie, "that she has been changing daily for some time. Have you not noticed it, Father? My uncle and aunt already perceive it. I am sure it is our darling mother who is obtaining this grace for us, and I am persuaded that our Léonie will give us some consolation in the future."

The fact was that if the girl's studies remained incomplete owing to the accumulated delays, her gifts of heart developed wonderfully. On the testimony of Mother St. Francis de Sales, who had much to do with her during her four years with the Benedictines, her French essays were remarkable for the high tone of the thoughts expressed in them. At home, if she did not entirely rid herself of her former ungraciousness, for which frequent sick headaches were partly responsible, she nevertheless became sociable and let herself be carried along by the stream of family cordiality that made the charm of *Les Buissonnets*. Certain malevolent in-

The Story of a Family

sinuations which have depicted her as the neglected Cinderella of the household are quite contrary to the truth.

As for Céline who had become, as Thérèse expresses it, "a little romp full of mischief," she quickly adapted herself to school routine. With a fervor that can be gathered from her sister's autobiography, she made her First Communion after several days of retreat spent entirely with the nuns. Her satisfaction was complete when Léonie's school career came to an end, and the youngest of the family entered the abbey as a pupil.

*　　*　　*

After studious days, the relaxation of *Les Buissonnets* seemed more soothing. The spirit of the world did not cross the threshold. The father lived retired from business, absorbed in his mourning. A stranger to the town, he formed few friendships there. The family attended the dramatic performances and concerts given by the Catholic Club; they appreciated the affectionate friendship of M. and Mme. Guérin, at whose house every Sunday the children spent the evening in turn, according to a fixed rota, but they remained unknown to the drawing rooms of Lisieux.

A born guardian of the traditional family spirit, the father jealously excluded anything that might alter it. He allowed no newspapers into the house, except *La Croix*, and he permitted only the elder girls to read that. He was not partial to mixed games, and the undue familiarity between girls and boys that resulted from them. Delicate to the point of scrupulosity, he chose the places where they might take their walks, so as to avoid certain less savory corners, and put his daughters on their guard against some disturbing and suspect sights. They amused themselves at home, and

Life in the Family Circle

this self-contained recreation secured the moral independence of the household.

Every winter evening, when the table had been cleared and the dishes washed and put away, Thérèse's clear voice would sound up the staircase, "Papa, Papa, the lamp is lighted." They would hear the armchair moved in the Belvedere, and a measured step cross the floor. M. Martin would come down with cheerful face to the little sitting room arranged next to the kitchen.[5] The elder daughters sat there during the day and the whole family in the evenings. A game of draughts would begin. The father showed himself an almost unbeatable player. When by chance his attention momentarily wandered and he was driven into a corner, Marie, his favorite partner, would find some means by making a false move of giving him another chance. Then the *Liturgical Year* of Dom Guéranger, which M. Martin had given to Pauline when she left school, was brought out, the volume for the season being marked at the date, and a few pages were read which sometimes led to discussions. This would be followed by some work of general interest, or a novel borrowed from the parish library, and thus a fresh occasion was provided for the mutual exchanging of ideas.

Then came the last act of the day and the one that most delighted Thérèse, who would settle into her father's arms and cover him with kisses, whilst he would sing a lullaby to his "little queen." She carefully remembered these melodies and in later years, at Carmel, wrote new words and refrains for the settings, so composing the songs and verses wherein she expressed her ideal. She took no less pleasure in hearing him recite

[5] At the restoration of *Les Buissonnets*, in 1913, this room was made shorter by the construction of a passage leading to the garden.

The Story of a Family

one of La Fontaine's fables, Victor Hugo's *Antéchrist*, or the *Reflexion* of Lamartine. He had but to select from his large collection.

Did he wish to enliven the programme? He would pass to one of the popular songs of La Palisse, or he would make toys for her, cutting tiny carriages out of melon skins which sent the child into ecstasies. He also cut out cones in the pith of elder tree, which he weighted at the base with a little piece of lead. Thérèse amused herself by knocking them over for the fun of seeing them right themselves, whilst her father would playfully point the moral: "In the trials and shocks of life, you must imitate the *Tombi-Carabi*; rise up again after every fall and keep looking up!" When Christmas came, he carefully chose out the most picturesque Yule log, which burned slowly in the hearth to the accompaniment of some Breton lament, dazzling all eyes, whilst the chestnuts were roasted in the ashes. Recalling this scene at Carmel, the saint wrote:

"I loved to seek, each year of grace,
My wee shoe in the chimney place.
Wakened to run, with eager, glowing face,
Singing the Babe on Christmas morn
New born."

In the summer, after working in the arbor, they took their meals out of doors, in the scent of the roses. Then they were initiated into gardening or into very novel games. One day, having come into a small inheritance, M. Martin wished to give each of his daughters a hundred francs, and buried the precious packets here and there. Then he guided the searches of the "gold seekers" by the time honored indications: "Warm" . . .

Life in the Family Circle

"Burning!" . . . "Freezing!" etc. Blasé folk may smile at such proceedings, but is it not true that happy are the houses where hearts remain simple enough to enjoy these childish pleasures?

When he left Alençon, M. Martin had not done away with his fishing rod. He proudly exhibited to visitors at *Les Buissonnets* the rod of which the divisions telescoped into one another, the plaited line and his supplies of horsehair. At Saint-Martin-de-la-Lieue, where the kindly owner of the country estate had given him a permit which protected him from the thunders of the keeper, he teased the pike. At Saint-Ouen-le-Pin, where he had a relative living, he caught trout in two fish ponds. Not far from Deauville, at Touques, the tide brought him flounders and other salt-water fish. Mention is made of memorable catches of his: notably a carp 60 centimetres long. Pauline made faithful drawings of the victims which adorned the Belvedere as trophies, whilst the best of the catch went to augment the ordinary bill of fare of the Carmel.

One day, the peaceful expedition ended in flight. Hidden in the grass in a hollow of a meadow, a bull suddenly charged straight for the intruder who was trespassing on its domain. The fishing box was smashed to pieces. M. Martin who was standing and following the current, beat a strategic retreat to the hedge. Driven into a corner by the ferocious animal, he faced it bravely and several times went for it with his lines. A last leap, *in extremis*, saved him from being gored. "Children, I thought you'd never see me alive again," he confessed that evening on reaching home.

His daughters often went with him. They settled themselves on the grass, took out some needlework or sketched. Even the Abbé Lepelletier, the senior curate of the cathedral of Lisieux, was seen to join the party, to learn how to throw a line. He profited by it, in return, to give little Céline a lesson in perspective by doing a sketch in her album of Thérèse gathering flowers.

When the temperature was cool enough for walking, M. Martin took them all out. They went into all the surrounding districts: Ouilly-le-Vicomte, the woods of Rocques, Beauvilliers, and along the Rouen and Paris roads. They visited the shrine of Petit-Bon-Dieu, or climbed the calvary of Saint Pierre. They made their way to the pretty cemetery of Lisieux which terraces the slope of the hill with its crosses and its hedges of privet. On their way they would halt at the spot from which a wide panoramic view lay below them, and gaze out upon the hills and valleys that cross and recross as far as the eye can reach beneath their halo of purple mist.

In September real excursions were arranged. A break took the whole family the ten kilometres to Saint-Ouen-le-Pin, to the small house which Mme. Fournet, the mother of Mme. Guérin, possessed there. There they went on nutting parties, or long walks in a country studded thickly with castles, steeples, ruins dear to archaeologists, and had picnics in the fields with the rustic crockery adorned with quaint Norman designs. As though by chance M. Martin always had assigned to him a plate illustrated with a lean couple, a dog like a skeleton, and in front a maidservant standing of imposing stoutness, who is presenting herself for engagement. Below was the inscription: *Wages one hundred francs; no presents, but you will have absolutely the same food as ourselves!* It was there, among the flowers and

Life in the Family Circle

high trees, that Thérèse spent her convalescence after an attack of whooping cough.

The stays at the seaside were not less enjoyed. In 1878, 1885, 1886 and 1887, during the season Mme. Guérin rented a house for a month or two. The *Châlet Colombe*, at Deauville, the *Villa Marie-Rose*, the *Châlet des Lilas* at Trouville, received the visitors familiarly. The father came for a day every now and then; the girls accompanied him and stayed there one after the other or two by two. These resorts had not then become world famous. Artists were anticipating Parisian society. If already unusual costumes were inclined to desert the *Promenade des Planches*, in front the open sea, and overlooking the piers that dam in the estuary of the Touques and the small country houses buried in the rocky solitudes there were real, silent haunts where a prayerful soul could become absorbed in recollection and praise. When Thérèse was not with him, M. Martin took care to take home some souvenir for her; a shell or a choice fish. In 1880, the child, then aged seven, wrote in her exercise book: "Papa is at Trouville; perhaps he will bring me back some crabs. I shall be so glad, for it is so amusing to see the little black creatures become red when they are cooked!"

Journeys to Alençon were rarer. M. Martin went there every three months and stayed for two or three days. He lodged in the Pavilion and took his meals with the friends who had so regretted his departure. About once in two years, the elder daughters went to visit their mother's grave, but Céline and Thérèse were to wait until 1883 before they again saw the cemetery of *Notre-Dame*. These visits, which often lasted over a week, were enhanced by friendly and even brilliant parties at the houses of friends. Melle. Pauline Romet took the guests to her brother's mansion at Saint-Denis-sur-Sarthon; Mme. Tifenne took them to Grogny, in the Sarthe, to the country house of her sister, Mme. Monnier. The Rabinel family received them occasionally in their mansion of Lanchal, at Semallé.

However, although he made concessions to social usages, M. Martin preferred family pilgrimages to these outings. He liked to take his daughters to the shrine of *Notre-Dame-de-la-Délivrande*. In 1883, when the expedition was so tragically interrupted by Thérèse's illness, he spent Holy Week with Marie and Léonie in Paris; took them to the churches, and was present with them at the liturgical ceremonies on Easter morning at *Notre-Dame*, which were crowned by what he expressed as "a splendid *agape*." "At least eight thousand communicants, all men; Monseigneur Guibert gave Communion and Père Monsabré preached." In July, 1887, piloting Léonie, Céline and Thérèse to the exhibition at Havre, he wished first to kneel at the altar of *Our Lady of Grace*, at Honfleur. His whole life was so impregnated with the Faith, of which he was so proud, that he could not understand half-measures in God's service. Loyally, he gave Him everything, and in his household leisure time, equally with that devoted to work and even to prayer, was marked with the seal of the Eternal. It is by escaping on high that, by becoming holier, the soul is restored.

* * *

At *Les Buissonnets*, as at Alençon, the daily life was strengthened at the divine fountains. That unreasoned fear, human respect, or false modesty which forbids that near kindred should exchange confidences of a spiritual order was unknown. The reading aloud of the

Life in the Family Circle

Liturgical Year favored exchanges of opinion on spiritual matters; it put them in union with the soul of the Church. The evening conversation sometimes merged into a collective prayer, and it ended in that family prayer when Thérèse, taking her place close to her father, "had only to watch him to know how saints pray." This last act, crowning the day's work, took place in the room of the two elder girls. There the statue of Our Lady had been set up in the place of honor. Fearing lest it should be broken in the moving, M. Martin had thought at first of replacing it in its original setting in the Pavilion, but Marie, on the plea of the devotion her mother had always borne to this old Madonna, had insisted upon taking it, and the translation had been managed without mishap. Thus the tradition could be perpetuated in all its richness.

As soon as he arrived at Lisieux, the father had visited the presbytery of *Saint Jacques*, their new parish church, and wished to rent named chairs for the family. However, in that populous parish the church was so crowded that at the time there were not sufficient sittings free. During the intervening period, the Martins had become used to attending *Saint Pierre*, which was nearer and was the church of the Guérin family, and to this they remained faithful.

On weekdays, the girls gathered at 6 a.m. in the apse of the cathedral, in the pretty Gothic sanctuary which was the Lady Chapel. Their father took them, indifferent to storms, snow or frost. He preferred this first Mass. "It is the only one that servants and workmen can hear; I am there in the company of the poor." It was not without regret that later on he changed it for that at 7 a.m. in order to save the family having to rise too early. His communions, at first frequent, subsequently became daily. The Eucharist—the Thanksgiving par excellence—so perfectly satisfied his need of praising God! On the way home, to the *Buissonnets*, he remained absorbed, silent, taking no part in the remarks exchanged between the others. If any surprise were expressed, he would excuse himself in a few words "I am continuing my conversation with our Lord."

During the day, he was particular to say his rosary and make a visit to the Blessed Sacrament. In the Corpus Christi processions he walked, recollected, his eyes fixed on the monstrance, and was never so happy as when one of the dignitaries who held the cords of the canopy let him have his place close to the Host. Yet it was real torture to him, on account of his baldness, to walk bare-headed in the scorching sun.

Only one thing was wanting: the *Nocturnal Adoration* of which at Alençon he had been the most active member. He never rested until his brother-in-law, a churchwarden of the cathedral, arranged with the local clergy to establish the devotion at Lisieux. He likewise joined the various pious associations in the parish.

His relations with priests were marked by a consideration bordering upon veneration. He would not have allowed the slightest hint of joking or criticism at their expense. Céline witnesses that the children conceived such reverence for them that they considered them "like gods." This explains a certain astonishment felt by Thérèse when, during the pilgrimage to Rome she met them at closer quarters, and her remarks on this subject in her autobiography. M. Martin paid the customary yearly visit of courtesy to his parish priest. Once a year, and also on the occasion of a First Communion, he entertained his confessor, the Abbé Lepelletier at table, likewise the confessor of his elder daughters, the Abbé Ducellier, both of these curates at the cathedral and the latter subsequently its Archpriest; and finally, Canon Delatroëtte, parish priest of *Saint Jacques*, and the Abbé Domin, chaplain to the Benedictines. Apart from these, no ecclesiastic visited *Les Buissonnets*, its inmates sincerely considering themselves unworthy of such an honor, and the clergy respecting this delicate reserve. It is an instance of this that when the Abbé Ducellier came to thank Pauline for the wonderful alb she had worked for him, he hesitated for a moment at the door of the house and finally turned back.

A special mention must be made of the Reverend Père Pichon, who was later to assure Thérèse that she had never lost her baptismal innocence. In the course of several preaching visits to Lisieux, he contributed powerfully to determine Marie's vocation, for which the father remained intensely grateful to him. Thus he playfully called him: "The friend and director of the Martin family." In 1886, Marie learnt that after a residence in Canada, the Jesuit was returning to Europe, and asked her father to take her to meet him. "I cannot refuse my eldest daughter anything," was the prompt reply. They waited two days at Calais, then at Dover, for the boat that never arrived. It was at Paris, after several disappointments, that they found Père Pichon again. When, a disappointed Philothea, Marie complained about the faulty information which had led them on a wild goose chase, M. Martin retorted with his winning calm: "You must not grumble, Marie mine; God saw you needed this trial."

There we recognise that serene charity which was increasingly to become the outstanding characteristic of the holy old man. He, who would not have been a

Norman had he not possessed the spirit of economy in the management of his money, showed himself daily more eager to give. Every Monday, a group of accredited poor clients might be seen gathering at *Les Buissonnets*. They had their day; it was a touching tradition of his forefathers. That did not prevent the houseless tramp from seeking a refuge at any moment. Thérèse was titulary almoner, having begged for this office.

With a pat, she would quieten "Tom," who resented this procession of beggars. She sympathised with the hollow cheeked mothers, the wan babies with their suffering expression; she graciously became their advocate in order to increase the alms. How moved she was when a woman answered her: "May God bless you, little lady!" or when a pilgrim honored and generously helped by M. Martin, awkwardly traced a great sign of the Cross over her and Céline, as they knelt; a pledge of divine favors!

When they were out walking, and some unfortunate stretched out his hand beneath a porch, or in the shadow of a bell tower, it was again she who opened her father's purse in his favor; a proceeding to which, needless to say, M. Martin lent himself with a very good grace. We know the episode of the infirm old man who refused the coin proffer by Thérèse, and how she feared lest she had hurt him. Later on, it was at home that she relieved and helped the suffering. "She shrank from nothing; she kissed and fondled poor little children, even though they were dirty." Léonie, who relates this, might have added that the whole family obeyed their charitable impulses. She herself was seen, mastering her repugnance, to visit a dying woman covered with vermin, clean her hovel, change her garments,

Life in the Family Circle

comfort and cheer her with her advice and, when she was dead, prepare her for burial.

M. Martin set the example of such acts of personal service. He had no sooner arrived at Lisieux than he had himself enrolled in the Conference of St. Vincent de Paul. He had his special cases and looked after them diligently. Céline noticed him visiting a poor woman with a large family, on the outskirts of the town. He gave her a generous alms, enquired familiarly after the health of everybody, and seasoned his conversation with apt considerations on Christian patience and the forgiveness of injuries. It was obvious that he was the benefactor to whom they listened willingly, and to whom they looked for everything; their material and moral support. To his daughter's question: "Do you know this person, then?" he merely replied: "She is a much tried woman, whom her husband deserts for long periods, and to whom I am trying to do a little good."

At times, in his delicate good-nature, he would accede to indiscreet demands. The folk of the neighborhood had been impressed by his deep piety and the supernatural expression that brightened his countenance. With his open brow, his hair prematurely white at the temples, his grey beard, and especially his distinguished bearing which combined so well dignity and cheerfulness, he imposed respect. A mediaeval illuminator would have put a halo round his head. Without going to the length of beatifying him in his lifetime, several local tradesmen rather regarded him as their mascot. At all costs, he must buy something from them, in order to begin their day with good luck. And he allowed himself to be persuaded, laughing shrewdly at their superstition, and loaded his bag with a small ham, or some fruit which would very soon find a destination.

The Story of a Family

His liberality only increased with age. Writing from Constantinople on September 16th, 1885, he added a postscript to his letter to ratify some alms given by Marie: "Give; go on giving, and make people happy!" In this school Thérèse learnt that generosity without measure that would lead her to say one day: "Had I been free to manage my property, I should certainly have been ruined; for I could never have borne to see anyone in need without at once giving him everything he needed."

*   *   *

That charity which gives God to unbelievers had M. Martin's first preferences. The conversion of a sinner was the highest joy he knew. When he learns that a dear friend has taken the decisive step, at once he shows his delight: "I feel I must congratulate you, or rather thank God with you, and that with all my heart, for the great grace He willed to grant you last December; a date to be forever remembered! We shall know the real price of this grace only hereafter . . . Your family are making good progress. Let us hope that the wind will not change and that all may reach the port." [6]

In truth he had become increasingly possessed by the longing for God's glory. His wife's death, the departure from Alençon, had left him, at fifty-four years of age, relieved from business cares, cut off from his old associations, and yearning ever more for the things of the supernatural world.

"I live almost entire now upon memories," he writes to the same life-long friend. "These, which cover all my life, are so sweet that, despite the sorrows I have undergone, there are times when my heart superabounds with joy . . . I was

[6] M. Martin to M. Nogrix, 1883.

Life in the Family Circle

recently telling you about my five daughters, but I forgot to say that I have four other children who are with their saintly mother on high, where we hope to go and join them some day." [7]

He had to attend to the administration of his property, and did so with real practical ability, but instinctively steering clear of dealings on the stock exchange in which he might suspect unjust speculation and "jobbing." "I feel," he once confided to Céline, "that I could easily become very interested in the skillful management of my fortune; but the slope is slippery and I do not want to go too near this evaluation of perishable riches." Meanwhile, in this sphere as in others, he put his trust in Providence and Providence did not fail him. He never made a decision without consulting God in prayer. One day, when he was about to leave by rail for Bordeaux, in order to invest a portion of his capital in an undertaking that seemed perfectly safe, a sudden sprain confined him to his room. He saw in this a warning sign from on high, and on the spot informed his lawyer, who was to have gone with him, of his withdrawal. The company failed almost at once, and the consequence would have meant almost total ruin for his family.

The time not devoted to business, travelling, his daughters, good works, gardening, fishing or walking, M. Martin spent entirely in the Belvedere. It was there that he had established his general headquarters. From its colored glass windows, beyond the pink may, the golden laburnum, and the green curtains of elders and firs, he would gaze out over Lisieux, taking in in a single prospect its high church towers, its old houses in all

[7] M. Martin to M. Nogrix, 1883.

their richness, its soot-stained chimneys; and descried beyond, in the heart of the luxuriant vegetation that clothed the hills and vales, the *Refuge of Our Lady of Mercy*, that home where Thérèse would have liked to bury herself among the deficient and abandoned children. No stranger ever entered the Belvedere. M. Martin made of it a cloister, a cell, a desert, where when he chose he might imagine himself living as a hermit, independent of the world and lost in God.

What did he do during those long hours of seclusion? Prayed, thought, contemplated, his eyes fixed on the heavens, or wandering over the trees that swayed in the wind. He would sing softly some hymn or song that brought back all his youth. He received his daughters and listened to their confidences. Within reach, on his little table were some favorite books: the Gospels, the *Imitation of Christ*, *The Clock of the Passion*, of St. Alphonsus di Liguori, the *Pensez-y bien*, the *Golden Book* or *Humility in Practice*. On the shelves were treatises on the spiritual life, religious classics, the *Histoire du peuple de Dieu*, the history of the Empire, that of La Trappe, the life of the Abbé de Rancé, the four volumes of the *Études Philosophiques sur le Christianisme* of Auguste Niccolas, and works or lives of saints. He read, he commented, he annotated. It was with no small surprise that among his papers they found chosen citations from the Council of Kiersay denouncing the errors of Gotescalc. The student and the man of culture are revealed in this case to glean in all fields and to take only the best.

The more he advanced in life, the more the curiosity of the seeker gave way before the holy eagerness of the believer. "*Greatness crumbles, beauty fades, joy vanishes. Know thyself.*" This maxim, carefully noted down, became his whole philosophy . . . or this other, borrowed from Père de Pontlevoy: "Leave the *why* and the *how* of mere curiosity. In this you will never have the last word. But know the *why* and the *how* that matters. Why are you on earth? How do you go to Heaven?"

On this height, where he took refuge, and where the image of the Great St. Bernard returned to visit him, M. Martin gave himself up to the action of the Spirit. He escaped from contingent things, rejoined his wife and his dead, and at times intoxicated with spiritual joy, even to tears, spent himself in glorifying God.

CHAPTER 12

THE LITTLE QUEEN AND HER KING

A day in Thérèse's life—school at the Abbey—
First Communion—M. Martin in Central
Europe—Thérèse's "conversion"—her
real character—union of hearts at
Les Buissonnets.

IN THE life of M. Martin at *Les Buissonnets,* Thérèse played a leading part. Her character had suddenly undergone a change. Exuberance had given place to reserve, assurance to timidity. Her sensitiveness, rendered the keener by her mother's death, reacted to the slightest shock. She defined herself as "a very gentle little girl, but excessively inclined to cry." She was at her ease only in the warmly affectionate home circle, and everywhere else she felt awkward, out of her element and repressed. Her training was in the hands of a very loving father and a grown-up sister with a firm hand. No imperfection was allowed to pass uncorrected and once a decision was made there was no appeal from it.

"I do not remember," states Pauline, "that she once disobeyed me. She asked permission for everything. When my father invited her to go out with him, she always replied: 'I will go and ask Pauline's permission.' My father himself

The Little Queen and Her King

trained her in this submission, and if I refused she sometimes cried on his account, because he would have liked to go out with her, but she obeyed without protest."

What a freshness is in this prelude of sanctity! Here, sketched from life, is Thérèse's day. Immediately she awoke, she made the morning offering of herself to God, dressed promptly and ran to M. Martin's arms. He on his side, watched for the visit of his youngest more eagerly than did ever courtier of the *Roi Soleil* the royal levée. As soon as breakfast was over the room became her school room. Her lesson hours were permeated with the supernatural, from the alphabet illustrated with sacred pictures—the word "Heaven" was the first the child learnt to spell out—up to the connected reading, preferably from the Gospels, and the French dictation and composition, varied by exercises of which the themes were family life and the glories of the Faith. In the book, yellow with age, that contains these simple essays, we read such passages as this: "Our Lady went to the Temple when she was three. She was noticed among her companions because of her piety and her angelic sweetness. Everyone loved and admired her, but the angels more than all, for they looked upon her as their little sister. The Blessed Virgin is my dearest Mother, and usually little children are like their mothers."

The lesson over, Thérèse made one bound to the Belvedere, there to report her successes and amuse herself at leisure. When it happened that her marks were too low, there were endless regrets. The father felt the more punished of the two; he had to take his afternoon walk by himself, and to see him thus disappointed caused the small girl a grief that drove her own into the background.

The Story of a Family

Apart from these rare exceptions, after dinner the two might be seen gaily descending the path from the *Buissonnets*, walking in the public gardens, and sitting on the banks of the Touques, to conclude with a visit to the Blessed Sacrament in one or other of the churches or chapels. As they walked, they talked about the most varied subjects. The father replied patiently to the child's innumerable "whys?" and did not hesitate to touch upon subjects far above her age. He moulded her little soul, initiating her into all the finer shades of Christian behavior. He profited by incidents on the way, a crucifix to be reverenced as they passed, a poor person to whom she took an alms, to arouse her charity. It was after these conversations that she wrote:

"It is quite certain, Papa, that if you spoke like that to the great men who govern the country they would take you and make you king. Then France would be happier than it has ever been; but you would be unhappy, because that is the lot of kings; besides you would no longer be my king alone, so I am glad that they do not know you." [1]

Later on a delighted companion escorted them, gambolling along. Not satisfied with keeping rabbits with silky coats, Thérèse begged her father for a dog that would jump and frisk around her. M. Martin acquired a very fine spaniel which, under the name of "Tom," took his place in the embellishments of *Les Buissonnets*. The little girl heaped caresses upon him. He lay at her feet whilst she did her lessons. Was he sick nearly to death? She saved him by giving him, mouthful by mouthful, food which she had herself prepared. This good dog, trained like a page and as faithful as a knight,

[1] Autobiography. C. 2.

The Little Queen and Her King

went on hunger strike during his master's absence in Central Europe.

He did not forget his mistress when the latter entered Carmel in 1889; on a certain day when Sister Thérèse of the Child Jesus, then portress, was letting some workmen into the monastery, Tom appeared by chance at the enclosure door, and ran to jump up under the veil of the dear saint, who wept with emotion. For the time being, he frisked around the father and daughter, mounted guard in the porch of the church where they were praying and, in his fashion, shared their pursuits. When he took a dive into a pond decorated with water lilies, and soiled his fine white coat by rolling on the dusty road, he furnished M. Martin with a simile of a spotless soul suddenly ruined by sin. Tom growled readily, and passers-by, warned by his barking, would look appreciatively at the group. They could not but admire the elderly man leading by the hand a delightful child whose face, framed in fair curls, seemed lighted up by her two shining eyes.

They would return home, tired with walking and feeling the heat. The child was thirsty. It was sometimes an occasion for Pauline to suggest a sacrifice, which was made at once without hesitation. Was there not a multitude of sinners to be saved? Did not our Lord for our sakes refuse to touch a narcotic which would have dulled His pain? . . . Then Thérèse would valiantly set about preparing her lessons, and conscientiously finished her exercises. Then came recreation in the garden where she loved to play. She would dash off in pursuit of a butterfly, show her interest in the growth of an apple tree, planted by Marie, gather flowers, though not without hesitating and asking Céline "if it did not hurt them." Sometimes she interrupted her father's reading to serve him her savory *tisanes*, make him admire her "marvellous altars," lead him to the back of the shed where he lifted her into her swing, and then pushed her regularly higher and higher until she could see over the wall into the next house and note "Mother Godet's" white cap.

After the evening meal and the evening recreation together, the examination of conscience closed her day. Inspired by Pauline, it prepared her for her first confession, made to the Abbé Ducellier, which left the child such happy memories. Her soul at peace, Thérèse went to sleep alone and in the dark; she had been accustomed to be afraid of nothing. She was as much a stranger to fear as to caprice.

Sundays and feasts introduced a note of ideal happiness into this calm existence. God's service made all her pleasure; there was no need of excursions or special allurements. Despite her desire to follow her sisters to the Holy Table, the child found herself debarred by the rules of the period. With what holy envy did she watch her dear Céline receive our Lord sacramentally for the first time! She consoled herself by going to High Mass in the cathedral. Did the preacher mention Thérèse the Great? M. Martin would bend down over his daughter and whisper: "Listen carefully, little Queen; he is speaking of your patron saint."

"I really did listen attentively, but I must own I looked at Papa more than at the preacher, for I read many things in his face. Sometimes his eyes filled with tears which he strove in vain to keep back; and as he listened to the eternal truths he seemed no longer of this earth, his soul was absorbed in the thought of another world." [2]

[2] Autobiography. C. 2.

The Little Queen and Her King

After Vespers, the beautiful Office of Compline wherein peaceful trust mingles with the grave melancholy of the closing day, ended the religious celebrations. Then came the evening spent in the family circle. When it was Thérèse's turn to spend the evening with uncle Guérin the father who, though he suffered at seeing a vacant place at the table at home, did not dare to refuse such an invitation, made it a pleasure to call for the child and bring her home in the starlight. He watched her steps whilst she, with her head upraised gazed into the sky and, discovering Orion in the form of the slightly bent T, artlessly exclaimed: "Look, Papa. My name is written in Heaven." A child's speech which the future would ratify, but which was then but the ingenuous remark of one whose soul was already responsive to the beauties of creation, and too simple to construct any horoscope for herself.

At the end of the school year, came prize day. The shed was decorated with hangings and greenery. Before an improvised platform a circle of relatives and friends assembled. The girls played some comedy for the occasion, but the central event was the reading of the prize list.

"Although I was the only competitor, justice was none the less strictly observed, and I never received awards unless they were well merited. My heart used to beat with excitement when I heard the decisions, and in presence of the whole family received prizes at Papa's hands. It was to me like a picture of the Judgement Day!" [3]

Holidays brought increased opportunities for outings; games in the park with Céline and Marie Guérin; fish-

[3] Autobiography. C. 2.

ing expeditions, during which the father taught the child to throw a line. In August 1878 came a visit to Trouville, when for the first time she saw the majesty of the ocean, the work of infinite Power, and at sunset from the lonely spot of the *Roches Noires* admired the golden furrow reddening the horizon: "the image of grace lighting up the way of faithful souls here on earth." It was during these outings that M. Martin recalled to discretion some passers-by who admired aloud "that pretty little girl." His innate sense of wise training made him avoid with jealous care everything that might spoil her simplicity by nourishing self-complacency.

At *Les Buissonnets*, they organised games. Thérèse was not fond of dolls. She was amused to watch Céline admonishing hers, and laughed till she cried when her sister brought them to her "to kiss their aunt." Nor was she any more attracted to rougher amusements. Sister Geneviève remembered giving her a toy pistol on her feast day, and how Thérèse was amazed and embarrassed, so far was she from sharing the bellicose tastes of her "dauntless" playfellow. With his usual good nature, M. Martin settled the difficulty by giving the pistol to a small boy in the catechism class and procuring for his youngest a toy more suited to her inclinations.

It is in the room containing the toys from *Les Buissonnets* that we may take pleasure today in recalling the saint's games. There is the boxwood spinning top, the wooden trumpet, the varnished wheel-barrow, and the skipping rope. Here is the aquarium in which she watched the antics of her goldfish with delight; the cage into which she put the seed for her birds, the kaleidoscope that so puzzled her and suggested the pretty comparison on the sanctification of daily duty in the fire of love of the Trinity. On a small table are set the jug and cups in which she prepared her herbal infusions; the hamper of the fishing expeditions in which she packed her jam sandwiches; close by we see the furniture of her miniature sacristy. These humble objects are eloquent. They make the predestined child who developed here live again under the most lovable and accessible aspect.

We see her again in these surroundings, jumping about among the bushes, admiring everything, delighting in trifles, and mingling with all her recreations her love for her father and that other love for *"Papa le Bon Dieu"*—her Father in Heaven. "We were never bored," she would be able to say one day. She was truly the life of *Les Buissonnets*. Her name resounded so often among the trees that the parrot in a neighboring house learnt in his turn to cry "Thérèse! Thérèse!" rolling the R. She, so shy when taken into company, became once more herself, lively, spontaneous, and at her ease, when she was with her own people. Did the shadow of the head of the family appear at an open door? With a bound, she was off to him clapping her hands with pleasure. "Oh, how could I tell of all the affection which my beloved father lavished upon his little Queen?"

Her poignant anguish may be imagined when, from an attic window overlooking the garden, on a certain day when M. Martin had gone to Alençon, she had all at once "the prophetic vision" of the old man, advancing wearily, bent, his face clouded, humbled beneath the Cross. The image never left her again and it set upon the happy charm of the pretty Norman house, as it were, a tragic note of interrogation. Thenceforth, a mystery of suffering was hidden beneath the attraction of *Les Buissonnets*. The Queen trembled for her King.

* * *

It was in October 1881, that Thérèse replaced Léonie at the Benedictine school and remained there as a day boarder until Christmas 1885. Although she was only eight and a half, she donned the green girdle which was the badge of the fourth class in which she was much the youngest pupil. Her progress was not the less satisfactory. Endowed above the average, having much facility in learning, except as regards spelling and arithmetic, above all attentive and painstaking, she easily gained the first place. Mother St. Francis de Sales rendered this testimony to her:

"I followed Thérèse practically all the time she spent at school. As her class mistress, I noticed that she was always at her work. I never had to reprove her. With her the thought of God was habitual and everything in her lessons recalled this to her. It was particularly striking in her little essays, where she always introduced a supernatural note despite the childish simplicity of the matter."

The head mistress, Mother St. Placid, who had in common with Thérèse that she entered religion at fifteen years of age, seems to have described beneath a reserve mingled with awkwardness—the result of over sensitiveness—her pupil's deeper and brilliant qualities. She surrounded her with devoted and affectionate care. However, the child found it none the less painful to adapt herself to the school environment. Away from home, notwithstanding Céline's sisterly encouragement, she was no longer herself.

There were so many things at which she felt herself

incapable. Despite her liturgical training, in chapel she found difficulty in following Mass in a book; already the Holy Spirit was drawing her to pure contemplative prayer. At recreation, she did not like running and jumping, wielding raquet or mallet. She preferred to tell stories, to play at charades, to give honorable burial to the birds and to watch the little ones' proceedings. On the rare occasions when, on special holidays, she went to *Monte Cassino*, a property amid the vales and hills near to the abbey, which lent itself to wonderful games of Hide and Seek, she would loiter to examine nature or look down from the height over the city. The Thursdays spent with the Guérin children and their cousins, the Maudelonde family, brought her mortifications of the same kind. Notwithstanding all her good will, she could not develop a taste for round dancing and quadrilles. "The only thing that gave me pleasure was to go to the park. Then I was the first everywhere, gathering flowers in quantities, and knowing how to choose the prettiest. I excited the envy of my little playmates." [4]

She needed her father and the calm environment of the home. What a cry of joy there was when, at the end of the day, to her question: "Has Papa come this evening?" the portress answered in the affirmative. Even before she had finished dressing, Thérèse was dancing out of the cloakroom. "Come along quickly, little Queen," M. Martin would call from his side, when he saw her through the wicket. It was a joyous meeting that soon chased all troubles away.

The child related the results of her work, proudly showed her badges: the silver one when she had been first in French composition; the scarlet one when she

[4] Unpublished reminiscences.

had gained full marks. A small silver coin, which she at once put into her money box for the poor, crowned her efforts, but her best reward was the joy that lit up her father's face. There, as elsewhere, love presided over her education.

Home life remained her delight. She had her aviary, where doves, parrots, canaries, bullfinches and linnets met together. She could have added some chaffinches found in a nest during a walk, but she had a scruple in taking them from their mother. Instead she soon had a magpie, which she put in a large squirrel cage, given her by M. Martin. Chattering and thievish, after the manner of its kind, it soon became a nuisance. In its turn, it tried to say Thérèse's name. Sometimes they let it free, but it seized the chance to steal right and left and pursue, pecking at them the while, the two young sisters who, armed with a stick to ward off its excessive familiarity, chased it round the garden forty times, which in distance was equivalent to some two miles. The poor creature was to perish tragically, for it was found drowned in a tub of water.

One of Thérèse's favorite amusements was looking over her collection of pictures with Pauline. The artistic merit of these was slight, but their graceful symbolism has its appeal for her sensitive, unspoilt nature.

Good books, carefully chosen according to her age, completed her instruction. She was passionately fond of reading, but gave only a very limited time to it; and it was there often, as she says pensively, that she found matter for great sacrifices. "Because as soon as the time was over, I made it a duty to stop at once, even in the middle of the most interesting passage." [5]

Her father would gladly have had her taught draw-

[5] Autobiography. C. 4.

The Little Queen and Her King

ing at the same time that he directed Céline to painting. An objection from Marie caused him to give up the idea. Thérèse, who was longing with all the ardor of her ten years to be initiated into artistic work, confined herself to offering to God in silence her disappointed hopes. This episode proves decisively how, deeply cherished as she was, she could avoid the failings characteristic of the spoilt child. It was that which made the exquisite *abandon* of the hours of intimacy which, later on, she would sing in her poems, re-telling to her "king" the "prayer of a saint's child":

> "Remember thou in terraced Belvedere,
>   Oft would'st thou seat her gently on thy knee.
> Murmur a prayer, then drawing her near,
>   Would'st cradle her with soft-sung melody;
> Heaven she saw reflected in thy face,
> When, pensive, thou wert gazing into space.
>   'Twas of eternity thy song was wont to be,
>   Remember thou."

Trials enough were to ruffle the surface of this youthful happiness. First, in October 1882, came Pauline's departure for the Carmel of Lisieux. Notwithstanding the tender affection of Marie, who took Thérèse's education directly in hand, the separation from her "little mother" was such a violent shock to the child that her health suddenly gave way. Headaches, at first intermittent, became continual. They did not hinder her from gallantly keeping her place in the third class, with the purple girdle, in which at the beginning of the new term she was placed, in the second division. But in March, 1883, during M. Martin's absence, the terrible attack seized her, accompanied by convulsive tremblings, hallucinations and incoherent ramblings, which

brought Thérèse to death's door. The father's grief at
his return was unmeasured. His child had reached a
condition in which she no longer knew him, turning to
the wall with cries of terror when he came near her bed,
his hat still in his hand. Doctor Notta was called in,
but could only express his helplessness. "Science is
powerless confronted with these phenomena." It was
as though a hidden power pursued the patient with its
mysterious obsession. Thanks to a passing period of
calm, she was able, nevertheless, to be taken to see
Pauline on the latter's Clothing day. On the morrow,
she fell again into the implacable grip of the malady.

During this trial, which struck him in his most sensitive spot, M. Martin showed, the autobiography tells
us, "a wonderful resignation." He found an indescribable support in his brother-in-law. "Remember he told
his children, that your uncle and aunt are devoted to
you in a way that is far from common." Above all, he
anchored his hopes in Heaven. He had never ceased to
bear a filial devotion to *Our Lady of Victories;* many a
time he had turned to her all powerful supplication. At
the beginning of May 1883, he sent to ask for a novena
of Masses at the celebrated Parisian sanctuary. His
faith and that of his family stormed Heaven on this
occasion with a sort of violence that bore away the
miracle. On May 13th, in the majestic light of a feast
of Pentecost, the statue of *Our Lady of the Smile,* which
the family had honored with a veritable cultus during
twenty-five years, came to life and smiled at the child
in Marie's room, whither the patient had been moved.
Our Lady overcame the evil power that was raging
against Thérèse and finally restored her to health.
Radiant, the father addressed this triumphant bulletin
to a friend of his youth:

The Little Queen and Her King

"I must tell you that Thérèse, my little Queen,—I call her thus for, I assure you, she is a fine, tall girl—is completely cured. The numerous prayers have at last taken Heaven by assault and God, in His goodness has willed to yield." [6]

*　　*　　*

Thérèse did not immediately resume attendance at school except for some friendly visits. The school year was nearly over; the child needed to regain her strength. A new trial awaited her. By a divine permission, the brief confidences which she made at the Carmel concerning the supernatural favor she had received, the impression she felt that she had explained herself badly and, perhaps, led her questioners into error, plunged her at times into real anxiety. M. Martin judged it well to complete her recovery by distracting her mind. In the month of August, he took her with her sisters to Alençon, where Mme. Tifenne and Melle. Romet took them from one entertainment to another, from country house to country house, amid the spring glory of the Norman countryside.

In October 1883 we find her again at school in the third class. It was the year of her First Communion. It may be guessed how intensely the child prepared herself to receive the Sacrament. On Sunday she went to the Abbey, and remained there with her companions until after Benediction. On account of her state of health, she was excused from spending the month preceding the great day as a boarder, but every evening Marie provided for her remote preparation. "It seemed to me that all her heart, so great and so generous, passed into me," declares Thérèse in the autobiography.

The same book has told with inimitable charm of the

[6] M. Martin to M. Nogrix, 1883.

The Story of a Family

recollections of the week's retreat, during which Thérèse, as a boarder, saw Mother St. Placid approach her little alcove, lantern in hand, to kiss her forehead. The day —May 18th, 1884—was shorn of all exterior pomp on account of the recent death of the Prioress, Mère Saint Exupère. This homeliness must have pleased the child, captivated to tears with the divine banquet, which she dared to call a "fusion." She associated all her relatives with her overflowing joy. "Since Heaven was dwelling in my soul, when receiving Our Lord's visit I also received that of my darling mother." [7] After Vespers, when Thérèse pronounced the Act of Consecration to the Blessed Virgin, M. Martin took her to the parlor of the Carmel, where Pauline, now Soeur Agnès de Jésus, awaited her. By a touching coincidence, or rather a delicate decision of the Superiors, she had that same day made her Profession. The festival ended with the family meal in the dining room at *Les Buissonnets*. M. Martin, as moved as his child, gave her a pretty watch as a souvenir, and she fell asleep dreaming of the day that knows no eventide of the eternal Communion.

On June 14th, with an enthusiasm and a sort of intoxication which she could scarcely control, so vehement was her appeal to the Spirit of Love, she received the sacrament of Confirmation, at the hands of Monseigneur Hugonin, who came to celebrate Mass at the Abbey.

In October, 1884, she entered the orange class, the second. It was there, in the course of her retreat for her second Communion, that she was assailed by a dreadful attack of scrupulosity, which was to torture her morally during seventeen months and bring on piercing headaches. This "martyrdom," as she calls it,

[7] Autobiography. C. 4.

did not shake her courage. At the end of May, 1885, her aunt made her come and rest a little in the villa she had rented for five weeks at Deauville, which had been named for its proprietor, the *Châlet Colombe*. The girl overcame her own suffering to interest her cousin, Marie Guérin, whose sickly condition easily turned to listlessness and melancholy. Despite protests from Marcelline, the maid, who urged the distance and the need for sleep, Thérèse insisted upon going to an early Mass, and the May devotions in the church of *Our Lady of Victories*, of which the fine porch and slender spire could be seen below, on the opposite bank of the Touques, rising up over the houses of old Trouville.

* * *

In September 1885, with Céline, Thérèse made a second stay at the coast of about a fortnight; this time at the *Villa Marie-Rose, Rue Charlemagne*, Trouville. Mme. Guérin had taken advantage of M. Martin's absence in the Balkans to offer her nieces all the pleasures of the seaside.

Thérèse enjoyed this holiday only moderately. Her father was absent. The Abbé Marie, curate at *Saint Jacques*, had succeeded after much persuasion in securing him as a companion in a long tour in Central Europe, to the shores of the Bosphorus, and in Italy. As has been said, M. Martin was very fond of travelling. He liked the unforeseen element in it, the picturesqueness and even the discomforts. It was with an almost childish delight that at every departure he would sing an old refrain of the days of his youth:

"Roll on, roll on, my coach,
Here we are on the great high road."

The Story of a Family

This time in order to make him decide upon the journey and, moreover, to overcome Marie's objections to letting him go so far away, Pauline's explicit encouragements had been required, with the prospect which, however, subsequently fell through, of prolonging the tour as far as the Holy Land. On August 22nd, he had not yet left Paris when he felt homesick for *Les Buissonnets*. "If it is too trying for you," he writes to his eldest daughter, "write and tell me so frankly. Address the letter to Munich, *Poste restante*, and I will desert this good Abbé Marie." From Munich, where he climbed in the Bavarian Alps, and explored the Art galleries, he sent several descriptive letters, wherein he added confidentially: "I would dearly like to have you all five with me. Without you the greatest part of my happiness is wanting. Meanwhile, continue to pray for us."

At Vienna, it is quite another story. He there received their greetings for the feast of St. Louis. Every year on that day, they held high festival at home. The Belvedere was decorated with flowers and garlands and the five sisters went up noiseless steps to surprise their father amid his loved books. The youngest went with her complimentary address, Marie with her traditional gift of a beautiful black silk handkerchief, which lasted its four seasons. At mid-day they basted the puff pastry with gooseberry syrup; all was gladness and gratitude. This time it was in the Austrian capital that he received Thérèse's little note: "My darling Father; Pauline had written some pretty verses for me to recite to you on your feast day, but as I cannot, I am going to write them to you." The recitation was entitled: *Wishes of a little Queen for her King and Father's feast Day*, and the concluding verses were:

The Little Queen and Her King

As I grow up, I see thy soul
With God replete and so with Love.
And in my turn enkindled at the sight,
    Fain would I follow thee.

Fain would I be on earth
My King's great joy;
Fain would I, Father dear,
    Love God like thee.

Father, I beg your benison,
Your kiss upon my brow.
Much would I say,
But words are all too poor and I must cease.

The letter ends with these words: "Au revoir, beloved
Father. Your Queen, who loves you with all her heart.
                                        Thérèse."
M. Martin read and reread the message, dried a tear,
and abandoning himself to his memories, let his pen
run on, in his turn:

"I seem to see you all around me in the Belvedere, and my
little Queen reciting her little speech in her soft, pleasing
voice. It has so moved me that I wish I were at Lisieux, but
for good, to kiss you all whom I so love . . . However,
Marie, 'my big girl,' my firstborn, go on leading your bat-
talion as well as you can and be better than your old father,
who has already had enough of the beauty all around him and
is dreaming of Heaven and the infinite. 'Vanity of vanities
and all is vanity, save to love God and to serve Him only.' [8]
Your father, who loves you all and bears you in his heart." [9]

[8] *Imitation of Christ*, B. 1; C. 1.
[9] M. Martin to his daughters, Aug. 30, 1885.

The Story of a Family

He was dazzled at the sight of Constantinople which he reached in mid-September; the wide views, the archaic grandeur of its mosques, its exotic bazaars, the swarming crowds in the clear air, and the magic brilliance of the eastern sun. This feast for the eye drew him to prayer. "If I could make you share all my feelings, as I admire the great and beautiful things that are all around me! 'Oh God, how wonderful are thy works! . . .' I could gladly cry 'Lord, it is too much. You are too good to me!'" Through all the wonders which he delights to describe, the image of *Les Buissonnets* pursues him. "In a few weeks it will be no longer a dream, and we shall be together again for such time as God in His goodness sees fit to grant us."

After a call at Athens and a melancholy meditation amid the ruins of the Acropolis, we find him at Naples, "that enchanting city," whence he sends this note: "Well, dear daughters, be always my joy and consolation on earth; continue to serve God well. He is so great and marvellous in His works . . ." At last, on Sunday, September 27th, he is at Rome. It was one of the last halts in the itinerary and for M. Martin was certainly the peak point of the tour. On this spiritual height where beats the heart of Christendom, his spirit of praise, traversed at moments by a strange foreboding of the calvary awaiting him, magnifies the Lord:

"For me St. Peter's is the fairest sight in the world . . . It is certainly here that I feel most pleasure. Tell my Pearl— his pet-name for Pauline—that I am too happy and am on my guard, for that cannot last . . . I commend you all to God's keeping and pray for you daily at St. Peter's. The thought of your mother never leaves me. So long . . . soon . . . soon.[10]

[10] M. Martin to Marie, Sept. 27, 1885.

The Little Queen and Her King

The captivity of the Sovereign Pontiff saddened him. "That is the dark spot," he confides to Marie, "and that casts a shadow over one, despite everything else." When he left the Eternal City without having been able to obtain the favor of a papal audience, he owned jokingly that he felt "like a blinking black cat, in a corner in the rain." In his heart, he was satiated with the sights of earth and his soul was seeking higher and better things. It was with a thrill of pleasure that on October 6th, when about to set out for Lisieux via Alençon, he wrote from Milan: "Everything which I have seen is grand, but it is still the beauty of earth, and one's heart remains unsatisfied until it beholds the infinite beauty that is God. We shall soon have the joy of being together again. It is the beauty of family life that comes nearest to Heaven."

* * *

Thérèse had resumed her daily journey to the Abbey, but she went alone, for Céline, her inseparable companion, had completed her school course. The loneliness, the increasing headaches, the interior torment of scruples of conscience, little by little undermined the girl's health, though without altering her energy or affecting her success in class. During the course of the first trimestre of 1886, alleging her state of health, M. Martin removed her from school. It was a providential decision, if one thinks that the full course of studies would have kept Thérèse there until July 1888, and have prevented her from entering Carmel at fifteen.

The scholar remained deeply grateful to her mistresses. Although she had left school, she was allowed to receive the medal and blue ribbon of the Children of Mary, on the understanding that thenceforth she would come back twice a week to the needlework class, and be present at the conference on the first Sunday of each month.

M. Martin used to escort her to and fro; more than ever, she was his little confidante. Physically he felt he was ageing, but his heart became young again when he chatted with her and walked with her, giving her his arm. Henceforth he took her regularly to have private lessons at the house of a worthy teacher, Mme. Papineau. In her unpublished reminiscences, Thérèse sketches a portrait of this lady and her circle which is not devoid of humor.

"She was a very good soul, very well educated, but with a few of the characteristics of an old maid. She lived with her mother, and it was charming to see the little household made up of three, for the cat was one of the family, and I had to put up with her purring over my exercise books, and even to admire her good looks. I had the advantage of living in the intimacy of the family. As *Les Buissonnets* was too far for the rather aged legs of my mistress, she had asked if I might come and have my lessons at her house. When I arrived, I usually found only old Mme. Cochain, who would look at me with her large bright eyes, and then call, in a quiet and sententious voice, 'Mme. Papineau, Mlle. Thér . . . èse is there.' Her daughter would answer promptly in a childish voice: 'Here I am, Mamma,' and forthwith the lesson began."

On her part, with her talent for character training, marked with a touch of originality, Marie directed her goddaughter to self-mastery and the supernatural spirit of sacrifice. Attractive comparisons clothed the austerity of the divine requirements and led to these being welcomed without causing fright. When they were staying at Trouville, she made use of the sight of the fishing boats gliding lightly by and the silent swelling of the white sails on the ocean to initiate Thérèse into fishing for souls. "Let us go pearl fishing in our little boat. There are some very fine ones at the bottom of the sea on which we are sailing. When a sacrifice presents itself, spread your net quickly." At other times, she depicted for her the feverish struggle of men to gain a fortune that is but sham and rust. "And we," she concluded, "can at any moment and without much trouble amass treasure in Heaven. We can pick up diamonds as with a rake   And for that it is enough to do all our actions for the love of God."

Alas! Here the young sister's face clouded over. The vocation foreseen in former years by Mme. Martin took definite shape. Marie in her turn was aspiring to the honor of religious life. The whole family escorted her to Alençon, where she saw again, with the emotions of long ago, the Pavilion, the cemetery of *Notre-Dame*, whilst Léonie with an unexpectedness which stunned all her relatives, attempted without any previous preparation a first essay of monastic life among the Poor Clares. On October 15th, 1886, the eldest daughter, who had been a second mother, retired with her Pauline behind the grille of the Carmel.

Under her father's loving direction, Céline assumed the authority of mistress of *Les Buissonnets*. Thérèse helped her only occasionally, "to please God." She was still only thirteen and a half. Of delicate health and frequently obliged to interrupt her studies, she was deliberately left to these, her prayers and her childish amusements. She was scarcely initiated into household duties. Her loved godmother's departure had the effect of making her really give way. Who would tranquillise her conscience in future?

Utterly upset, under the interior impression of being

in an immense void, she turned to her family in Heaven, the four little ones who had gone before her into their fatherland. She reminded them that, had they lived they would have shown her special consideration, as being the youngest, and that their enjoyment of the Beatific Vision could not render them indifferent to fraternal affection. In short, she begged through their intercession the end of her moral torment. "The answer," as she says, "was not long in coming; soon peace came, flooding my heart with waves of happiness."

It remained for her to rid herself of that acute over-sensitiveness, and that exaggerated impressionability which led her to weep floods for the most futile causes. Our Lord took that miracle into His own hands, on that unforgettable day, December 25th, 1886. We know from the autobiography that scene called by Thérèse her "conversion," which stood out in her psychology after the manner of a *coup d'état*. M. Martin having shown some irritation at seeing the traditional Christmas shoe put out for a girl of fourteen, the latter mastered her distress and gaily proceeded to discover the treasures hidden therein. "The little Thérèse had just recovered, and forever, the strength of mind formerly lost at the age of four and a half."

The interior balance fully established, then it was that the desire for knowledge awoke in her. She set up her working table in one of the attics, facing the great trees of the public park, in what had formerly been Pauline's studio, and of which she made, as she expressed it, "a real bazaar; a collection of pieties, and curiosities, a garden and an aviary. Truly that attic was a world for me and, like M. de Maistre, I could have written a book called 'A Journey round my Room.' It was in that room that I liked to stay for whole hours, studying and thinking before the beautiful view out-spread before my eyes."[11] There amid the twitter of the birds, ear-splitting to others, melodious to her, she applied herself to certain subjects. On her own showing, the personal effort caused her to learn more in a few months than she had done in all the previous years. This curiosity in reading was not without danger but her piety saved her and during this period she developed prodigiously. For a long time, the *Imitation* had been her spiritual nourishment. She always carried it about with her, in her pocket in summer, in her muff in winter. She knew the whole text by heart. She eagerly devoured a work by the Abbé Arminjon, lent to M. Martin by the Carmelites. These *Conferences on the End of the present world and the Mysteries of the Future Life* marked a date in her spiritual development. "I copied several passages on perfect love, and the reception that God will give to His elect at the moment when He will become their great and eternal reward. I kept repeating the words of love that had enkindled my heart." [11]

Every morning saw her kneeling in the cathedral apse, in the Lady Chapel, where the daily low Masses are said. By a special favor, in which, notwithstanding the longing she felt, she left the initiative to her confessor, she approached the Holy Table several times in the week. Soon, before the image of the Crucified, rejected by so many, the thirst for souls arose in her never more to be quenched.

Pranzini would be the first to benefit thereby. This half-caste, of many tongues, having come originally from Alexandria, had, in order to rob a safe, murdered three persons, one of them a girl of eleven, in the *Rue*

[11] Unpublished reminiscences.

Montaigu, Paris, and was now drawing near to the guillotine with a horrifying cynicism. He had spent the days of his imprisonment in translating obscene books. A devotion to Mary alone had survived the wreck of his religious beliefs. At table at *Les Buissonnets*, M. Martin had spoken of this monster, his forthcoming execution and the incredible hardness of his attitude. Thérèse was filled with distress. Would not this be "her first child?" She implored his conversion from Heaven; she awaited it; she begged; she asked for a sign, be it ever so humble, be it a simple kiss to the cross. And on August 31st, 1887, at dawn, the doomed man, who had hitherto resisted grace and was already bound to the fatal machine, made a sign to the priest and before submitting himself to the executioner, repeatedly kissed the crucifix held out to him.

This episode took Thérèse out of the narrow circle in which she had lived, and launched her into the deep of apostolic conquests. Even at Carmel she remembered Pranzini and had Masses said for him. For the present she taught catechism to two little girls whose mother was ill; she succeeded in convincing a charwoman whose faith had weakened; she slipped medals of Our Lady into the clothes of the workmen; she interested herself in those dying in the district; she enlightened and upheld the supernatural fervor of Marcelline, the devoted maid of the Guérin family.

* * *

Tempered by trial, her character had precociously reached its full maturity. The photograph of her at thirteen, which survives, shows us an ingenuous, shy, attractive face, with an expression of wistfulness about the mouth; that which depicts her with her hair up, a few days before entering Carmel, is full of life and decision. But in both, the clear brightness of the large blue eyes, and the recollected look is indicative of a soul directly moved by the divine Spirit.

Some have used in reference to her the ugly words: "snivelling child," and "proud girl." Truth and not the futile desire to whitewash at any cost a personality that stands in no need of it, compels us to say that that is a caricature. It is true that Thérèse had a weak point: the excessive emotionalism which had been suddenly aroused at her mother's death and which she did not always succeed in controlling. But this infirmity—in the Pauline sense of the word—was for her rather an occasion of showing her strength of character. No one ever saw her disagreeable, sullen, morose or selfishly hugging her grief. Trials of all sorts fell upon her; moral perplexities, illness, scruples, without making her give way, be it ever so little, to discouragement or negligence. Céline has spoken explicitly on this point:

"It is important to note that even in her early girlhood's years, she was really strong despite her apparent weakness. This remarkable strength was evident to me from the fact that her sadness never hindered her from fulfilling her duty in the smallest matters. For my own part, at this period I never surprised her in an uncontrolled outburst, a sharp word, or any failing in right behavior. She mortified herself all the time and in the smallest matters. She seemed never to lose an opportunity of offering God sacrifices."

As for that craving for domination, which some have thought they detected in her, I own that I have found no trace of such in all the immense collection of documents which contain the accumulated evidence of witnesses who had minutely scrutinised her least acts and gestures. It is true that she sometimes mentions her

The Story of a Family

"pride"; she states hypothetically—and this detail is not devoid of interest—"I had all the more need of this austere training in that I should not have been indifferent to praise." We may conclude that she was aware interiorly, in a nature not yet *pacified* completely, of those revolts, those urgings of "self," of which St. Bernadette accused herself when dying. What it is essential to know is whether this instinctive self-love showed itself outwardly, or if she pitilessly suppressed its least movements.

Let us question thereon those who lived in close contact with her. Pauline states roundly: "She watched carefully in order to obtain control over her actions, and from early childhood had accustomed herself never to grumble or make excuses." Léonie speaks no less categorically:

"Everything in Thérèse's person breathed kindness and unselfishness. She always forgot herself in order to please everybody; when she could make others happy she was in her element. Her evenness of temper was so simple and seemed so natural that it might have been thought that her continual renunciation cost her nothing. She was pleasant and courteous. Everything about her attracted people. Pride and vanity had no place in her innocent soul. She was very pretty but she seemed unaware of it. During these years when we were living together at home, I never saw her looking into a mirror. She was delicately attentive not to humiliate or hurt anyone."

Céline, her chosen companion, states with the same decisiveness:

"Not only did Thérèse not impose her will upon others, but she did not even make it known. At home as at school, I always saw her submissive in everything. We never heard

The Little Queen and Her King

her raise an objection, argue or grumble, even in fun."
Marie says, on her part: "I never saw her disobey even in
the smallest matter. Hers was a deep and thoughtful character. I considered her too serious and mature for her age."
Jeanne Guérin supports this: "Thérèse was an ideal child;
very gentle, shy, and extremely reserved."

Have we not here an unanimity in testimony that
cannot fail but carry weight? Shall we reject its authority because of the family ties which may paralyse
its impartiality and prejudice the judgement of the
speakers? Let us continue our enquiry. Mother St.
Francis de Sales, of the Abbey, deposes: "From the
time when the Servant of God was my pupil, I noticed
in her an innocence and piety which inspired me with
a feeling of respect. From the standpoint of docility
and good conduct, she was perfect. In her relations
with her young companions the goodness of her character was evident. She never showed animosity, even
towards those against whom she might have had
grounds for complaint. I never saw her otherwise than
simple and humble."

The Reverend Père Pichon, M. Martin's intimate
friend, who visited their home several times, lends to
this verdict the support of his character as priest and
religious:

"What greatly struck me in that child was her simplicity,
her ingenuousness and her innocence. She was greatly loved
by her father and sisters though I never saw any weakness
on their part. But what was particularly remarkable in a
child of her age was that she referred absolutely nothing to
herself, and was entirely self-forgetful, never taking advantage of her position. She was shy and reserved and never
put herself forward. M. Martin bore a particularly tender
affection to Thérèse, whom he called his "little Queen." A

less spiritually gifted child than she might have conceived some self-complacency from this, and suffered as regards her moral formation, but I never saw the Servant of God take advantage of it."

Shall we listen finally to the verdicts of some humbler folk? Here is that of old Victoire Pasquier, for seven years maid at *Les Buissonnets*: "Little Thérèse was very well brought up, and I admired her for her sweetness and angelic ways. She was always obedient and a little angel of gentleness. She was very shy." Here is Félicité Saffray: "I have heard that some evil-minded people found fault with the dear little saint; she who was so gentle and so lovable, always afraid of hurting you! I was three years in service with M. Martin, and I can say that she never gave me any trouble." Here is Marcelline, the servant at the Guérins, who became Sister Marie-Joseph of the Cross with the Benedictines of the Blessed Sacrament at Bayeux: "At that time, her character showed itself as very gentle and docile. She was always charitable and affectionate to others."

Let him who will complain of so precocious a perfection; it is difficult to escape from such a chain of evidence. Thérèse herself adds the weight of her serene and uncontested word. Does she not say in Chapter V of her autobiography that divine grace helped her to dominate even the first movements of temperament? "The practice of virtue became to me sweet and natural. At first my expression betrayed the struggle, but little by little renunciation seemed to me easy, even at the first moment." One may prefer for its epic attraction a more arduous progress of a soul towards God. We must yield to the evidence of facts and not attempt to impose upon the Most High the restricted setting of our narrow concepts. There can be no doubt that we

The Little Queen and Her King

are here confronted with a real prodigy of preventing grace. It is not infused sanctity; it is, and that in a surprising measure, an equipment of gifts and virtues predisposing a soul to the attainment of sanctity.[12]

* * *

No doubt the reader will think that we have embarked upon a long digression and that the setting in its right focus of the true portrait of the youthful Thérèse belonged to her biography, rather than to that of her parents. "The mother's treasure belongs to the child,"[13] the Carmelite sang in her last poem, dedicated to Marie. Can we not change the expression and allege as our excuse:

"The Queen's treasure belongs to the King."
By restoring to her her authentic physiognomy, do we not contribute to the full revealing of that of her father?

With the house in the *Rue Saint Blaise*, the *Buissonnets* constitutes the ideal sanctuary of the French family. Since Nazareth and Bethlehem, have there been many places where there was more mutual love one for another? This father, who heroically consented to give to Heaven with his wife, four of his children, then to devote the five others to the religious life, was never so happy as when in his own home, surrounded by his daughters. With a touch of quaintness, he gave each a pet name wherein his affection placed a particular emphasis. Thérèse made them the theme of a poem. First, there was Marie, his "diamond," his firstborn, his eldest; she whom on account of certain tem-

---

[12] For this analysis of the saint's character we have made great use of the thoughtful psychological study published by Canon Moreau, of the Senior Seminary of Bayeux: *Ste. Thérèse de l'Enfant Jésus: son tempérament moral.* (Aux Éditions *Spes*.)

[13] This poem, entitled *The prayer of a Saint's Child*, will be found at the end of this book.

peramental features, he also called "the gypsy." Then came Pauline, his "pearl"; then "the good Léonie," and Céline, "the dauntless." As for the youngest, he had a whole heap of nicknames and diminutives, which we like to mention because they recall the upbringing of our saint in its most human aspect. She was formally entitled "the little Queen of France and Navarre"; she became now and then, "the orphan of the Bérézina," his "little thoughtless one," his "poor little one." When he danced her on his knee he would say to her old Auvergnat expressions with special emphasis, which defied translation into standard French. Recalling the memories of her First Communion, the Carmelite exclaimed: "I found many times by experience that very few children deprived of their mothers as I was, have been so cherished as I was at that age."

The daughters of this "admirable father," returned his affection. We must discern in the letters written to him by Marie from the convent, the deep love which, in the strict sense of the word, comes near to being a cultus. On August 24th, 1887, she sends her good wishes for his feast day:

"May God spare you still long years to your children who love you so, for, saving for Our Lord, are you not all their Heaven in this life? A year ago on this day, there were four of us to go up to the Belvedere, which we had decked with wreaths and flowers. Do you remember? Since then, two have left the nest, but they still have wings, and if they do not use them to return to the 'strange' land of the world, how joyfully they turn to you! Oh father dear, what is the song of your doves who have flown away? All their love, all their gratitude. May you, who have not hindered their flight Godwards, who have given them so generously, be blessed forever! May you receive the hundredfold in this world, and

The Little Queen and Her King

in the next may our beloved mother, who has gone before us, join us in blessing you, with the four little angels who are also yours. Five in the Fatherland and five in exile! The family above and that below are today only one to greet you."

Notwithstanding the fact that father and daughters lived at Lisieux almost unknown, having little contact with what is known as "society," it happened that observant witnesses caught a passing glimpse of the unique quality of this community of souls.

"I like to recall," acknowledges an old lady of Lisieux, "the good M. Martin and his "little Queen." I held him in veneration. I can see him still, with his soldierly bearing and saintly face, and his little Thérèse, so simple and pretty, on the arm of that incomparable father. I even remember her navy blue frock and beautiful hair . . . It seems only yesterday, so clearly has the delightful picture remained in my mind . . ."

The sisters' relations with one another were marked by the same supernatural charity. In vain has it been insinuated that Léonie, like a Cinderella, received exceptional treatment, colored with disfavor, if not with ostracism. All those who shared the life at *Les Buissonnets*, from the Guérin relatives to the maids, Victoire and Félicité, have protested indignantly against such calumnies. After her mother's death, Léonie's temperament became sociable. Without quite losing a certain tendency to isolate herself, more and more she took part in the family life. Thérèse in particular endeavored to spare her in every way any possible suffering which might have resulted from a certain intellectual inferiority.

The Story of a Family

"I was very touched personally," states Léonie in this connection, "by the very delicate feeling wherewith she behaved to me. I was then twenty-three and she only thirteen, but I was very backward in my studies. My little sister used to teach me, using great charity and exquisite tact so as to avoid humiliating me."

When the "solitary" remained in her room, where she soon gave way to sleep, her two mischievous younger sisters teased her in kindly fashion. Did they not see fit in her absence to turn her room into a nun's cell, and pin up on the wall large cards bearing austere texts, among which this figured prominently: "My eyes close to the light of day when I do not take a turn after dinner." We see that French mischief did not lose its rights of citizenship in the future saint.

Sisterly affection rose higher than this, however. It reached its summit in the spiritual friendship that united the two youngest. They had grown up side by side in a cloudless intimacy. The happy enthusiasm with which they exchanged gifts at New Year or on their feast days had to be seen to be realised. Thérèse rejected ruthlessly every calendar which on the date of October 21st, did not bear the name of Saint Céline.[14] As she herself enjoyed the patronage of the Foundress of the Reformed Carmel on October 15th, their father used to take them both to a shop in the centre of the town a few days previously. Then he paced to and fro outside whilst his daughters, each on her own and with much mystery, made for half-a-franc (it was in the days of gold ten and twenty franc pieces) a number of purchases. Each wished to surprise the other. At the end

---

[14] Céline's patroness was St. Cilinia, the mother of St. Remigius.

of December, the scene was repeated and the saint describes it with her usual freedom.

"The funniest thing was to see us buy our presents together at the bazaar. Having half-a-franc to spend, we had to purchase at least five or six different articles. It was a contest as to which could buy the most 'beautiful things.' In raptures with our purchases, we would impatiently await New Year's Day in order to present each other with our 'magnificent presents.' Whoever woke first hastened to wish the other a Happy New Year; then we gave our presents and each went into ecstasies over the treasures obtained with fifty centimes.

"The little gifts gave us almost as much pleasure as my uncle's beautiful presents. Moreover this was but the beginning of joys. That day we were quickly dressed and each watched out to be the first to run to Father's arms. As soon as he came out of his room, the house resounded with cries of joy, and poor dear Father seemed glad to see us so happy.

"The gifts that Marie and Pauline gave their little girls were not very valuable, but they also gave the latter great delight." [15]

With the years, the exchange of gifts was altered into sharing supernatural confidences. On the morrow of her "conversion" Thérèse writes: "Céline had become the most intimate sharer of my thoughts, especially since Christmas. Our Lord, who wished to make us advance in virtue together, drew us to each other by ties stronger than blood. He made us sisters in spirit as well as in the flesh . . . Very sweet is the memory of our intercourse. Every evening we went up to the Belvedere together and gazed at the starry depths of

---

[15] Unpublished reminiscences.

the sky, and I think very precious graces were bestowed upon us then." [16]

This upward progress in spiritual things to which the saint alludes in her unpublished reminiscences, vividly recalls that soaring flight which on the shore at Ostia bore away to God the spirits of Augustine and Monica. It was already the ascension together from the beauties of sense to the Uncreated Good which alone can satisfy our human restlessness.

The father also experienced this sort of ecstasy. He was now nearing the summit of the uphill road which was crowned by the Cross. He would soon experience the latter in all its humiliating nakedness. As we are delighted by a symphony in which the themes keep recurring indefinitely, so his musical soul savored for the time being the many deep joys of family life. His household may serve as a model. Perhaps modern readers may think it rather restricted, too much of a hothouse, too wrapped up in its secret riches. They would have preferred it to have reacted with greater regard for the outside world; to have been the enterprising family of which the members, without sacrificing their fundamental collective unity, go forth and work unceasingly for the Christian transformation of society.

Let us avoid falling into the snare of anachronism, and go back in thought to the year 1880. Apostolic work in the sense of Catholic Action was then just beginning to feel its way. Could it have been suddenly transferred into our age, what new aspect would the calm existence of *Les Buissonnets* have taken on? We can only conjecture. History deals with the real; it loathes the fictitious. It remains that, with the means

[16] Autobiography. C. 5.

and in the spirit of their period, and knowing moreover
how to combine strong spiritual life with works of
mercy, with apostolic work as opportunity occurred,
and participation in their parish activities, the household of M. Martin offered to his contemporaries and,
over and above, to succeeding generations, the finished
"testimony," and ipso facto, an influential one, of a
family one hundred per cent Catholic, in which the
Gospel, lived out in its fulness, led to the perfection of
love.

CHAPTER 13

THE OFFERING OF THE CHILDREN

The Parents' attitude to the Religious Life—
Pauline and Marie at Carmel—Thérèse's
vocation—the Pilgrimage to Rome and
the Papal Audience—Thérèse
enters Carmel—vocation of
Céline.

RENÉ BAZIN has spoken of those mothers who
have "a priestly soul" and pass it on to their
children with their natural life. Of M. and
Mme. Martin we may say that they had "the souls of
Religious." Their home furnishes a concrete example
of the influence of the family atmosphere in the development of that high vocation. This thesis, dear to the
Abbé Viollet, the zealous promoter of the *Association
of Christian Marriage*, has inspired the present work.
It is worth pausing to examine its significance in the
light of a particularly striking illustration. Not that the
divine choice must be subjected to the fatal play of
heredity and education. Grace upsets all our calculations. It can intervene in ways as disconcerting as they
are decisive. At times, the call of the Master goes seeking the disciples amid the mire. It is none the less true
however, that as a general rule the solemn seal that
marks the fisher of men, or the bride of Christ is the

The Offering of the Children

crown of a collective upward progress. There are few domains wherein the mysterious law of solidarity which presides at the evolution of the supernatural as much as of the natural order, shows out more clearly.

In their youth M. and Mme. Martin had both once cherished the ambition to give themselves wholly to God. As instruments of Providence, events or men had frustrated their plans. Would they on this account, as happens sometimes, harbor a secret resentment and, as it were, an unavowed hostility towards the priestly and religious lives? They were too noble for that. Rather did they nourish a cultus, tinged with a sort of nostalgia for such. The virginal prelude to their marital union had given them an understanding of that state that came near to being a personal experience of it. Perfect chastity remained an object of envy, and not being able to bind themselves solemnly to the service of God, they aspired to give Him all their children.

We have told of the earnest prayers with which they begged for a future priest, promised to the foreign missions, and how the deaths of the two little boys had shattered those hopes. The valiant Catholics accepted the fiat but, having labored to people Heaven, they aspired to people the cloister. At every birth, that was the subject of their first request, and it kept recurring in all their prayers. They were not of the number of those pusillanimous parents who dread sacrificing to God what they have no hesitation in handing over to a creature. When she read in the biography of Mme. Acarie how that Foundress of the Carmel in France had entered a monastery with her three daughters, Mme. Martin struck with admiration exclaimed: "All her daughters Camelites! Is it possible a mother could be so honored?" Mère Agnès de Jésus, to whom we owe this anecdote, was able to declare on oath at the Process of Beatification: "My parents wished that we might all be consecrated to God. They would have liked to have given Him priests and missionaries."

For all that, it should not be thought that they made their home a hot-bed, where vocations were cultivated in a row. Wrong-headed persuasion, indiscreet interference, produces hypocrites or failures, if not renegades. These true "educators" had too much respect for conscience and too much submission to the divine will to stoop to such proceedings. They would have seen in such a violation of the liberty of the soul as well as, at the same time, a sort of assault upon God's good pleasure. It is freely, and not by constraint or violence that the soul must enter the holy of holies. Mme. Martin did not hesitate to dismiss Léonie, who mingled with her youthful caprices and outbursts passing desires to don the religious habit. "When she tells me every day that she will become a Poor Clare, I put as much confidence in that as if it were little Thérèse— then aged two and a half—who said it."

It was with exquisite tact that this mother followed, step by step, the development of the divine seed in Pauline's soul. She did not want to hurry anything; she feared to awake too quickly a confidence which would fix thoughts that were still floating. She acted likewise with Marie, as she writes to the younger girl, on December 5th, 1875.

"I should not be surprised if one day she became a religious at the Visitation. Her tastes are not at all worldly; on the contrary, I am more anxious than is she, that she would be well dressed. One evening, quite lately, whilst saying my prayers after I had been reading the life of Mme.

The Offering of the Children

de Chantal, I thought all at once that Marie would be a nun, but I do not dwell on it, for as I have noticed happiness is always the contrary of what I foresee. Do not tell her this. She would think that I wished it, and truly I desire it only if it be God's will. Provided she follows the vocation He gives her, I shall be content."

The parents' part was to prepare the ground in which the seed might germinate; to provide the atmosphere that would favor its growth. We have shown with what watchful foresight they kept their children away from all pernicious influences; how they directed their piety and trained them to will in everything what God willed; how, finally, they encouraged them in the way of sacrifice. Such discipline rendered those children readily responsive to every request of grace. Souls accustomed to say *Yes* to duty are not likely to elude the supreme invitation if it makes itself felt.

Need it be added that everything in the home had inclined them to appreciate the religious vocation as an honor? As children, they had learned to venerate their Visitandine aunt. The parlors at Le Mans, at the Poor Clare convent at Alençon and the Lisieux Carmel filled their young imaginations with fresh, monastic visions. In the street, they were taught to bow to priests and religious. It was impossible to criticise a sermon without their father's breaking in to exalt the word of God. The mother, so ready with her wit, who did not forbid herself to remark upon the mannerisms of even some ecclesiastical orators, yet showed a wholly supernatural deference to the mission preachers, and in order to hear them imposed upon herself heavy extra fatigue.

Here is an anecdote from Pauline which further informs us with respect to the mother's great influence in this department:

335

The Story of a Family

"When I was very small, Mother used to take me on her knee and tell me stories from the lives of the saints. Once she told me that in Heaven only the virgins would follow the spotless Lamb, Jesus, wherever He went, and that they would be crowned with white roses and sing a song that the others could not sing. Then I told her that I wanted to be a virgin with a beautiful white crown, and I asked what color hers would be, for she had told me married people would not have white crowns. She replied that no doubt she would have a crown of red roses, and I cried out: 'Oh Mother, I will never marry, so as not to have a red crown in Heaven.'"

It was from having lived in such an environment that Thérèse felt growing up within her a mysterious attraction, calling her to "the Spouse of Virgins." As she was to write later: "Sometimes I heard them say that Pauline would be a nun; then, without knowing quite what it meant, I thought, 'I also will be a nun.'" At Lisieux it was M. Martin who, in his earnest piety, kept the spark alight. The saint tells how when she entered the Carmelite chapel for the first time, he whispered in her ear: "See, little Queen, behind that big grille there are holy nuns who are always praying to God." It is easy to imagine the torrent of questions that followed and how, reminding her of the seraphic Thérèse, the father proceeded for the first time to initiate the little girl into the meaning of the monastic life. The divine call is never so persuasive, so alluring, as when it borrows, even unknown to them, the loved voice of a father or mother.

Not that M. and Mme. Martin did not envisage with a certain sensible emotion the pang of separation. Faced with this prospect, the best controlled nature in the world does not fail to tremble. The mother who in

The Offering of the Children

places voiced her pride in the foreseen vocations of Pauline and Marie and who, on her deathbed spoke openly to the younger, could not help acknowledging to her sister-in-law in a letter of July 9th, 1876:

"In spite of my earnest desire to give them all to God, if He were to ask these two sacrifices now, although I should do my best, I could not make them without suffering."

It was her own offering which the magnanimous woman was to consummate. She was to die carrying to her grave the dream that had made her thrill with the purest of ambitions: "All her daughters Carmelites!" It was reserved for M. Martin to go to the end with the holocaust and with his own hands to sacrifice to the Lord, with a generosity that recalls the grandest days of the Ages of Faith, the whole future of his family.

*   *   *

From when they first settled at *Les Buissonnets*, the name of the Lisieux Carmel had occasionally been mentioned in the family conversations. It was a geometrical group of buildings, of dark red brick, with dormer windows piercing its slate roofs, situated in the *Rue de Livarot*. The conventual quadrangle was formed by two wings of buildings linked at one end by the whole length of the chapel, and on the other by the rounded bays of a cloister in the plainest style. An imposing granite crucifix dominated the garth. A small garden provided the recluses with a limited area of green whence, peaceful and secluded, there opened out that attractive walk between the chestnuts which would see Thérèse, in her declining days, writing serenely the final pages of her autobiography. High walls that partly followed the line of the river Orbiquet, shut off the austere recollection of the enclosure from the gaze of the curious.

The beginnings of the monastery had been heroic and worthy to take their place in the *Book of the Foundations* of the Saint of Avila. Two young women, belonging to Pont-Audemer, Athalie and Desirée Gosselin, having resolved to devote their modest fortune to founding a Carmel, where they could fulfil their desire for the religious life, Mgr. Dancel, Bishop of Bayeux, directed them to Lisieux and assigned them as their future superior, the Abbé Pierre Sauvage, a Sulpician and senior curate of *Saint Jacques*. This zealous priest succeeded in finding at Poitiers an old and fervent Carmelite community which agreed to further his project by training the postulants and giving two of its best nuns to guide them in the early days. So it was that on March 16th, 1838, four novices from Normandy and from Poitiers, two professed nuns in their black veils descended from the coach at Lisieux. Of the two latter, Sister Elizabeth of St. Louis became Prioress and Sister Geneviève of St. Teresa Sub-Prioress and Mistress of novices. A canvas-covered tilt wagon conveyed them in pouring rain to the *Chaussée de Beuvillers*, where, until they could find a suitable house, Mme. Le Boucher had offered to shelter them beneath the thatched roof of a humble dwelling that bore the stamp of Bethlehem.

On the following 5th of September, they moved to the *Rue de Livarot*, into an old but slightly larger house. The new convent was dedicated to Mary Immaculate. Later it was to receive the additional dedications of the Sacred Heart and St. Thérèse of the Child Jesus. The little family was sheltered, as it were, under the pro-

The Offering of the Children

tection of the "Holy Man of Groswardein,"† the Prince of Hohenlohe, who had sent it his episcopal encouragement and, with a genuine prophetic instinct, foretold that "a whole family would enter the Carmel of Lisieux, from whom would come all blessings upon it."

Under the rule of Sister Elizabeth and, after her death, that of Sister Geneviève of St. Thérèse, who, nearly always in office as Prioress, was to be the living rule and the soul of the community during forty-nine years, the community developed rapidly. Trials rained down upon it; poverty dogged its steps. It took forty years of struggle to provide the monastery with necessary ground and buildings. The primitive plan was completed in the main in 1877, when M. Martin settled at Lisieux.

For a considerable time the family at *Les Buissonnets* conceived a sort of reverential awe for that Carmel. The mortuary urns, sculptured on its gate posts had a chilling effect upon them. It was to the Order of the Visitation that Pauline's inclinations turned. She was already in communication with the Superior at Le Mans when, one day, February 16th, 1882, when hearing Mass in *Saint Jacques*, close to the statue of Our Lady of Mount Carmel, she suddenly realised, in such a manner as to preclude all doubt, that God willed her to be a Carmelite. At the convent in the *Rue de Livarot* she would replace an aspirant from Lisieux who had

† Alexander, son of Prince Charles-Albert of Hohenlohe, was born at Kupperzell in 1794, his mother being a Hungarian, Baroness Judith Rewiezky. He became a priest and subsequently Titular Bishop of Sardica, and Dean of the Chapter of Groswardein, in Hungary. He died at Voeslau, near Vienna, in 1848. His life was exemplary but his Ultramontane principles caused him to suffer from the Austrian government and the higher clergy of the Empire. He is best known for the many cures he wrought, so that he was revered widely as a thaumaturgus. Some would doubtless now be explained on psychiatric and similar grounds; others could not, but critical examination did not take place. (Tr.)

The Story of a Family

died on the eve of her entry. In addition this arrangement would allow her to continue to mother Thérèse.

Pauline told her father, who was in the Belvedere absorbed in his morning reading which soon led to mental prayer. He received the communication very kindly, only remarking that her delicate health and tendency to frequent sick headaches would perhaps scarcely stand the austerities of such an Order. However, confronted with the girl's decided and confident manner, he readily acquiesced in her plans. In the afternoon, meeting her alone on the stairs, he said with some emotion: "Pauline mine, I have given you permission to enter Carmel for your happiness, but do not think that there is no sacrifice on my part, for I love you so much." And he tenderly kissed her.

The autobiography has described for us Thérèse's anguish at this news, and how the comforting words and explanations lavished upon her by her "little mother" suddenly made her aware of the divine call: "I felt that Carmel was the desert where God wished me also to hide myself." After Pauline's admission the Prioress, Mère Marie de Gonzague, was informed of these aspirations of the child of nine, and was careful not to discourage them. There was such a light of purity and innocence in those deep eyes! The period of waiting would not be easy.

On October 2nd, 1882, M. Martin, accompanied by his brother-in-law and Marie, took Pauline to her new family. His mind full of the memory of his wife, whose hopes were crowned by such a day, he joyfully made his first offering to God. Thérèse was not present at this separation; the shock would have been too painful. Nor did she attend the Clothing ceremony, which took place on April 6th, 1883. All the same, in the early

The Offering of the Children

afternoon she who would henceforth be called Soeur Agnès de Jésus, dressed in her white bridal dress, came out of the enclosure, according to the ceremonial then in use, and embraced her family for the last time in the parlor. Thanks to a providential lull in her mysterious malady, which had then been afflicting her for several days, Thérèse came then to visit her dear "little mother," sit on her knee, hide her face beneath her veil and kiss her freely. She then left, whilst on her father's arm Pauline entered the sanctuary and, after the ceremony regained the enclosure door to go and don the monastic habit in the nuns' choir. Thirteen months later, on May 8th, 1884, in the evening of her First Communion day, the child returned with her father, radiant in her snowy white dress and veil, to confide her impressions to the sister who had that day made her Profession. On the following July 16th, the whole family was present at her Veiling.

Between these visits the two met rarely. The child—and this was a real heartache to her—had but a few minutes in which to tell her little secrets. Where were the long outpourings of *Les Buissonnets?* As for M. Martin, he came to love these spiritual conversations more and more. His soul, athirst for complete self-abnegation, appreciated the resounding words of the great mystics. With St. John of the Cross, he understood even better the nothingness, the *nada* of the created. Within the four chill, bare walls of the parlor, in front of the grille with its spikes, as it were, challenging the world, he felt something of the monk stirring within him. In the correspondence exchanged with Marie from Constantinople and Rome, he does not forget his "pearl."

"Tell my dear little Paulinus that I think often of

her, and thank God for having given her so high a vocation . . ."—"How it comforts me to see that she is so
perfectly happy, and that our Lord, even here on earth,
deigns to visit her as only He can! Let us thank God,
my Eldest, and pray with all our hearts that He may
also shower His graces upon our poor, dear Léonie."

The last words allude to new sacrifices looming ahead.
Gradually Léonie was drawing nearer the religious life;
Marie herself seemed to be coming under its invincible
attraction. It was true that, to a superficial observer
such a suggestion might have caused merely a shrug of
the shoulders. Of a lily-like purity but fiercely independent, there was nothing of the conventional nun
about .Marie. She clung to her liberty but, withal,
there had been the profound influence of her mother,
who had known how to discipline that original and
magnanimous character, and who from beyond this
world was continuing to act upon it. Marie had also
been surrounded by the spirituality of her father, who
so loved his eldest daughter; there was Pauline's in-
fectious example and their conversations together. To
put it briefly, on a certain day in 1882—Marie being
then twenty-two—she had provided herself with a
spiritual director in the person of Père Almire Pichon,
an eminent Jesuit belonging to Carrouges, near Alençon, who was a specialist in preaching retreats and
guiding souls.* It was in vain that she struggled. His
incisive words had gone to her heart. She made her
election on eight closely written pages. The conclusion
was blinding. She felt "caught in the nets of divine
mercy." "Then," she exclaimed, "Jesus has cast a special look of love upon me also!"

Before proceeding to act, she had to finish her mis-

* Père Pichon died at Paris, in the odor of sanctity, Nov. 15, 1919.

The Offering of the Children

sion in the family circle. The years went by. We are in 1886. Léonie, on her part, wanted to put out to sea. With Mme. Martin she had attended the meetings of the Franciscan Tertiaries at the Poor Clare convent at Alençon and she longed to enter the latter; but Céline was now turned seventeen and it seemed as though Thérèse's education was nearing its end. By this time Père Pichon, had returned from Canada, whither he had gone two years previously. He cut short Marie's last hesitations.

"The hour of sacrifice was about to strike for me," she writes. "I saw it draw near without enthusiasm. It meant saying good-bye to the father I so dearly loved. I must leave my young sisters. But I did not hesitate for one moment and I revealed this great secret to Father. He heaved a sigh on hearing such a revelation, which he was very far from expecting for he had no reason to think that I wished to be a nun. He stifled a sob and said to me "Ah . . . Ah . . . But . . . without you!!" He could not finish and in order not to distress him, I answered confidently: "Céline is old enough to replace me. You will see, Father, that all will be well." Then he replied: "God could not ask a greater sacrifice from me. I thought you would never leave me!" And he embraced me to hide his emotion.

The entry into Carmel was fixed for October 15th, 1886. As Pauline had done, Marie wished first to kneel for the last time at her mother's grave. The whole family went to Alençon on the 7th. It was during this visit that, with a precipitation which nothing had led them to foresee, and of which the future would show the imprudence, that Léonie asked and obtained on the spot her admission to the Poor Clares. Faced, so to speak, with the accomplished fact, M. Martin consented

343

nobly. He even endeavored by wholly supernatural arguments to mollify his eldest daughter, who did not hide her displeasure at this unusual haste which nothing justified. In fact, on the 1st of December of the same year, Léonie returned home. Her constitution was too weak to stand the mortifications of a particularly austere Rule. With much tact and charity, the father set himself to soften the disappointment to her.

As for his eldest, he took her to Carmel on the feast of St. Thérèse. On March 19th, 1887, on the morning of the feast of St. Joseph, with emotion he could scarcely conceal he offered her to God under the name of Soeur Marie du Sacré-Coeur. At the moving Clothing ceremony, Père Pichon, returned a second time from Canada, preached, dwelling upon the high dignity of the religious state. In a series of letters, which are real masterpieces of delicate affection, the novice tried to mitigate the pain of the separation for her father.

He showed munificent generosity to the convent. At Pauline's Clothing, he presented two handsome wall brackets for candles, in gilt bronze adorned with crystals. When Marie's turn came, he enriched the conventual treasury with two large reliquaries in the form of monstrances. He frequently added some extra treat to the always frugal diet of the community. It was for that he plied his fishing rod so fondly for hours. If his rods were not in action, he made a contract with the fishmonger or supplied himself at the fish auction. His eldest daughter well named him "Our Lord's procurator." She thanks him wittily that, after having surrendered to God "all the treasures of the boat"—his daughters—he has also assigned to Him, over and above, in the persons of His brides, his whole catch!" Above all, she blesses him for the *fiat* of that magnani-

The Offering of the Children

mous consent that has made the happiness of his dear Carmelites. "Oh you, best of fathers, who give to God without counting the cost all the hope of your old age; yours is the glory, a glory that will not pass away. Yes, beloved Father, we shall glorify you, as you deserve to be glorified, by becoming saints. Less than that would be unworthy of you."

*   *   *

Coldly considered and calmly carried out, Marie's vocation had been realised after the manner of an arranged marriage, wherein love would keep all its rights. By contrast, Thérèse's took the form of an irresistible surging of passion. She bore it in her heart like a wound. Carmel had become her overmastering thought; to sacrifice herself for the Church and for priests her only ambition. The active congregations were not without their attraction for her; the apostolate would be a joy. She decided it was more crucifying to act directly on the First Cause in the silence of contemplation. So, after having accepted eagerly from a fellow pilgrim on the journey to Rome the *Annales Missionaires*, she would abstain from reading it. "I have too keen a longing," she would explain, "to devote myself to works of zeal, and I want to hide myself in a cloister to give myself more completely to God."

She had access to excellent confessors. The Abbé Ducellier, curate at *Saint Pierre*, and later to return thither as Archpriest, after having been parish priest at Mathieu and at Trevières; Canon Domin, chaplain to the Abbey, the Abbé Lepelletier, also one of the cathedral clergy, who left only in 1888, to go to Luc-sur-Mer, and later to St. Stephen's Caen. All of them remained in the dark regarding her decision. Père Pichon,

345

director of both Marie and Céline, was the only one informed of all her plans. She revealed them to him during a visit he made to Lisieux. He encouraged them unreservedly, including the appeal to Leo XIII. "I thought," the future Carmelite confessed, "that in my case God was not making use of an intermediary, but acting directly." Now we find Him inspiring her to enter the monastery at Christmas 1887, for the anniversary of her "conversion," just before her fifteenth birthday! Marie rebuffed her in the name of common sense. Pauline, who knew her "child" better, strongly supported her. Céline, who had guessed everything, and was also thinking of entering religion one day, consented to let her little sister take precedence. The interviews in the Belvedere took on an indescribable fervor as a result, of which Thérèse would one day sing:

> "Then would our voices sweetly blend,
>   Our clasped hands pledge love to the end;
>   Our song the nuptial feast, whose joys transcend
>   Of Carmel and of Heaven; our theme
>   To dream."

It remained for the young aspirant to tell her "King." He was not yet sixty-four. Although he retained his soldierly and upright carriage, he was already an old man and his health seriously threatened. On May 1st, 1887, while on his way to the seven o'clock Mass as usual, an attack of cerebral congestion with a slight stroke forced him to return to bed. The paralysis affected the whole side but spared his intellectual faculties. Warned immediately, his daughters hastily rose. Despite everything, he insisted on being helped as far as the cathedral to sanctify the first day of Mary's month at any cost. On the way back, considering with

The Offering of the Children

Christian philosophy this warning from on high, he said: "My poor children, we are as frail as flowers. One evening we look splendid and in the morning an hour's frost has withered and beaten us down."

M. Guérin, once informed, intervened energetically. He compelled the sick man to return to bed and applied leaches. "The festive board is very small for so many guests," remarked the patient cheerfully. The danger seemed to be averted. During the year, two seizures of the same kind, although much milder and successfully treated at once, occurred. M. Martin lost nothing of his animation or his good humor, but he became still more absorbed in his solitary reflections, and at times his pallor and purple lips inspired his daughters with well-grounded fears.

Was this the time to confront him suddenly with the prospect of the most distressing of sacrifices, that of his "little Queen"? Certainly he might have expected to offer her to God later on. He had perceived the fine quality of that pure heart, but she was only in her springtime. She had been his favorite companion when, with step rendered slower by the recent attack, he took his daily walk in Lisieux. Must this gentle tranquillity be disturbed? Thérèse hesitated for some time. She prayed to God for light, and found strength to speak.

It was Whitsunday after Vespers. Impressed by the peace of the beautiful evening, M. Martin was resting in the garden behind the house with folded hands, watching the foliage of the high trees in the fiery glow of the sunset. The girl approached. From the traces of tears in her eyes, he guessed at some secret difficult to keep. "What is the matter, my little Queen? Tell me." Perhaps he had a presentiment, for at once he rose, as though to hide his own feelings, and walked, whilst still

The Story of a Family

pressing the girl to his heart. But only Thérèse can describe such a scene:

"Through my tears I spoke of the Carmel and of my great wish to enter soon. He, too, wept, but did not say a word to turn me from my vocation. He only told me that I was very young to make such a grave decision, and as I insisted and fully explained my reasons, my noble and generous father was soon convinced. We walked about for a long time; my heart was lightened and Papa no longer shed tears. He spoke to me as saints speak, and showed me some flowers growing in the low stone wall. Picking one of them, he gave it to me, and explained the loving care with which God had made it spring up and grow till now.

I fancied myself listening to my own story, so close was the resemblance between the little flower and little Thérèse. I received this floweret as a relic and noticed that in gathering it, my father had pulled it up by the roots without breaking them; it seemed destined to live on, but in other and more fertile soil. Papa had just done the same thing for me. He allowed me to leave the sweet valley, where I had passed the first years of my life, for the mountain of Carmel."

The father's acceptance bordered upon heroism; the world would pronounce it folly. This was clearly seen when his brother-in-law, M. Guérin, the first to be informed since he was the legal guardian of his nieces still under age, resolutely refused to give his consent, declaring that the project was rashly imprudent, and that to carry it out was to risk doing harm to the cause of religion. A change of heart, asked for in prayer, and the timely intervention of Soeur Agnès de Jésus, subsequently removed this opposition.

But it arose again and from another more dreaded, more insurmountable quarter; that of the Superior of the Carmel, and parish priest of *St. Jacques*, M. Dela-

348

The Offering of the Children

troëtte. This priest, austere and excellent, had set himself with a fierce intransigeance to establish the strictest observance in the community. Although there was no reference to the subject in the Constitutions, he maintained that no subject must be admitted until she was turned twenty-one. His manner was lacking in geniality. His countenance, with its stern features, tightly shut lips, seamed with deep furrows, betrayed his imperious disposition. When the Mother Prioress mentioned the young would-be postulant, he cut her short. The similar intervention of the venerated Mère Geneviève de Sainte Thérèse had merely provoked a stormy outburst. Who knows whether this authoritarian pastor did not feel somewhat sore towards these parishioners who were guilty of not attending "his" church?

Nevertheless, Thérèse faced the formidable personage. She pleaded her cause warmly. Labor lost! The refusal came, prompt and final. Only a decision from the Bishop could make the Superior relent. M. Martin, who with admirable disinterestedness, became his daughter's advocate and support in this affair, and undertook to accompany her in all the steps she took, did not know how to console her. A torrential downpour of rain when they emerged from the interview marked this first collision between administrative prudence and the supernatural urging of an extraordinary vocation.

It was decided to go to Bayeux, but some family events delayed the visit. At the beginning of July, M. Martin took the three girls to the Exhibition at Havre. Later, they spent another holiday, the fourth—that of July 1886 having been very short—at the seaside, in the *châlet des Lilas* at Trouville.

In the meantime, on July 16th, 1887, with her father's

349

The Story of a Family

consent, Léonie had made a fresh trial of religious life. The desire to spare her precarious health, and also the memory of Sister Marie-Dosithée and her own gratitude to the seer of Paray-le-Monial, who had cured her as a child, led her to the Visitation convent at Caen. She made a stay there of some months only, which prevented her from taking part in the pilgrimage to Rome, and before the end of the year had returned to *Les Buissonnets*.

As for Thérèse, her father had approached the Vicar-General, M. Révérony, to arrange an audience at the Bishop's palace. Thither she went with him on October 31st, after having been careful to put up her hair, in order to look older. Monseigneur Hugonin had held the see of Bayeux for over twenty years. He was a good-natured, scholarly man, who liked to find conciliatory solutions to problems. The request of the young girl from Lisieux must have seemed to him as imprudent as it was generous. He referred her to the Superior which, notwithstanding the instructions and recommendations of M. Révérony called forth a flood of tears. M. Martin had purposely let his daughter speak for herself, no doubt thinking that her precocious maturity would thus be the more evident. Did the prelate suspect that there was some hesitation on his part? Was he struck by his remarkable appearance, or impressed by the magnanimity of the sacrifice to which he was consenting? He tried to make the child understand that she ought to remain with her father for some time yet. "What was not the surprise and edification of His Lordship when my father took my part, adding respectfully that we were going to Rome with the diocesan pilgrimage, and that I should not hesitate to speak to the Holy

The Offering of the Children

Father if I could not obtain permission before then."[1]

No doubt, this intervention of M. Martin brought about the suspension of a decision which everything suggested would have been a negative one. It had the advantage of making the Bishop himself agree to the appeal to the supreme authority, and so prepared the final solution. "I shall speak to the Superior myself about you," concluded His Lordship, "and you shall certainly have my answer in Italy." The girl's frank simplicity and tears had touched him. He accompanied the visitors to the garden and listened with interest when the father told him of the fair curls which had been put up only that morning. As for the Vicar-General, he said aloud that "such a thing had never been seen before; a father as anxious to give a child to God as was that child to give herself."

* * *

The only remaining hope lay in Rome. M. Martin had just entered his own and his two daughters' names to take part in a pilgrimage, under the leadership of Monseigneur Germain, Bishop of Coutances, and organised thanks to the industrious zeal of his Vicar-General, Monseigneur Legoux. The diocese of Bayeux was to send an important delegation under the leadership of M. Révérony. The special train would convey one hundred and eighty-seven travellers, including a certain number of clergy; for the most part, the layfolk would belong to the Norman aristocracy. The *Lubin Travelling Agency* had settled the itinerary so as to combine the maximum of comfort with the highest artistic and religious emotions: no night travel,[2] a route passing

[1] Autobiography. C. 5.
[2] The Saint herself expressly says that they did travel by night. See Autobiography C. VII. (Tr.)

351

through places of historic interest and the finest scenery; visits to the most famous cities and the best hotels were to render this month's tour an enchantment to the eye and the heart. From the Catholic point of view, it constituted an event. It was in the early years of the anti-clerical spoliation in Italy; the Catholic world trembled at seeing the Pope a prisoner. The Golden Jubilee of Leo XIII called forth a display of fervent loyalty. This pilgrimage, which was the second organised in France, would be a striking demonstration of faith.

Before leaving, M. Martin, ever thoughtful, remembered his two daughters, whose voluntary seclusion would deprive them of so many delights. He copied for them these lines from the *Imitation*, and sent them as a farewell:

"What canst thou see elsewhere that thou seest not where thou art? Thou hast before thy eyes the heaven, the earth and all the elements. Are not all beings in the world composed of these? What canst thou see, in whatever place it be, which can long remain stable under the sun? Perchance thou thinkest thereby to satisfy thyself to the full: but thou wilt never come to an end thereof. If all that is in the world were present to thy eyes, would it be aught but a vain representation?"

For the Martins, the journey was a real crusade. There were those who whispered ill-naturedly that in taking his daughter to Italy, under particularly attractive auspices the father's underlying motive was to shake her vocation. They were very far from knowing him. On the contrary, the main object for him was to obtain the Pope's approval of Thérèse's plan. As for the latter, she knew all the risks she might run in those

The Offering of the Children

excited weeks; she commended herself to her Mother in Heaven and to St. Joseph, "Father and Protector of virgins." Her childlike serenity was not to be troubled.

The general assembling was at Paris. Three days before, on Friday, November 4th, at three a.m. M. Martin left Lisieux with his daughters. "We reached Paris in the morning," writes Thérèse, "and at once began to visit it. Poor Father tired himself greatly in order to give us pleasure. Thus we had soon seen all the sights of the capital." [3] We know that, of them all, the saint liked best the church of *Our Lady of Victories.* M. Martin had purposely chosen an hotel close to the famous sanctuary, so that they could pray there at leisure. There it was that the trouble which still, at times, had clouded Thérèse's mind, concerning the vision of *Our Lady of the Smile*, finally vanished.

On Sunday, November 6th, Mgr. Germain presided at the formal opening of the pilgrimage, in the crypt of Montmartre. The pilgrims heard Mass and received Communion in the chapel of St. Peter, and then, to the singing of the *Magnificat*, the procession made its way to the upper apse and thence into the open air, where the Bishop blessed the archivault of an arcade in front of the Lady altar.

The train for Rome left the *Gare de l'Est* at 6.35 a.m. on the following morning. Each compartment bore the name of a saint, and the family from *Les Buissonnets* were not a little surprised to find themselves assigned by Mgr. Legoux himself to the patronage of St. Martin; this resulted subsequently in the father's being frequently addressed as "monsieur Saint Martin."

Only seven out of the eight places were occupied, all by pilgrims from Lisieux, among them a curate of *Saint*

[3] Unpublished reminiscences.

The Story of a Family

Désir, the Abbé Moulin. Occasionally, the Abbé Le-
comte, curate at *Saint Pierre*, came to join in the conversation, without, however, the father's having, as
some imagined later, requested him to look after his
daughters. M. Martin would not have left this duty to
anyone. He was too particular, and also too proud of
his Céline and his little Queen to be willing to leave
them. On the rare occasions when he did not accompany them, he entrusted them to some friends, the
Besnard family.

The company was a select one. They might have
been transported into some Norman country seat.
There were those who displayed their titles of nobility;
others who were maneuvering to make brilliant matri-
monial alliances. Drawing-room gossip ran to and fro
from one carriage to another. There were times for
prayer, but they were rather limited. As the author of
the *Imitation*, in a disillusioned passage, says: there is
nothing like a long pilgrimage to reveal each one's little
foibles. It was a question as to who should secure the
best corner, the most comfortable seat. Was it not
necessary to take measures to spare one's strength and
keep in good form to the end? Then there was the
gentleman who was always complaining; the one who
was continually asking for information and directions;
the other who thought only about meals and amusements. All this "human nature" did not hinder them
from mixing, living together and thinking alike, but it
was at the price of certain collisions and in the watchful
observation of the defects of their neighbors.

The Martins passed safely through these annoyances.
They had no handle to their name, but they formed
such an attractive trio, and had something so disinterested about them that the hotel servants made mis-

The Offering of the Children

takes at times and were particular to show them marked respect. It was with simplicity and perfect courtesy that M. Martin mixed with this high society. The autobiography relates how he effaced himself to offer others the best place, or the most convenient room; how he set himself to cheer up a hypochondriac neighbor, more naturally inclined to criticise than to admire. Notwithstanding the lassitude which was noticeable at certain times upon his face, he always showed perfect evenness of temper, and bravely shouldered all the inconveniences in order to please others. No incident on the journey could upset his peace.

When they set out, he had settled his daughters in corner seats, so that they might comfortably enjoy the scenery. Urged to take part in the everlasting games of cards, they courteously declined the invitation, on the grounds of their scanty knowledge of card play.

"Presently their annoyance became evident, and then dear Papa began quietly to defend us, pointing out that as we were on a pilgrimage more of our time might be given to prayer. One of the players, forgetting the respect due to age, called out thoughtlessly: Thank God, pharisees are rare! My father did not answer a word, he even seemed pleased; and later on he found an opportunity of shaking hands with this man, and of speaking so pleasantly that the latter must have thought his rude words had either not been heard, or at least were forgotten." [4]

For him, this month spent wandering through the fairy land of nature and art, was a continual hymn of praise. As they crossed Switzerland, he cast a glance of envy in the direction of the Great St. Bernard, where the rosiest dream of his life had been dissipated in an

[4] Autobiography. C. VII.

instant. The night at Lucerne, the panorama of the lake of the four cantons, the crossing of the St. Gothard, urged him to praise God on the mountains. At Milan, he heard the Mass of Mgr. Germain, close to the altar, leaning against the chasse containing the body of St. Charles Borromeo. His devotions were prolonged whilst Céline and Thérèse climbed the 484 steps that lead to the roof of the Duomo. At Venice, he left them to ascend the Campanile alone, whilst he admired the treasures in St. Mark's. At Padua it was the memory of St. Anthony that chiefly moved and impressed him.

In the evening of November 11th, they reached Bologna, and the whole student body of that university city was on the watch to welcome the French. The reception was cordial, even a little rowdy, as was to be expected of youth. The local paper, *Il Resto del Carlino*, gave a sympathetic account of it the following day. On emerging from the entrance hall of the station, in the confusion caused by the reception, M. Martin became separated from his daughters. When Thérèse appeared, wearing on her breast the badge of the pilgrimage of which she was the youngest—the white ribbon with blue pin stripes and the medal bearing the head of Leo XIII —a lively young fellow made a bound, lifted her up and carried her in triumph, until abashed by her look of grave innocence he put her down.

It was harmless mischief and it would be puerile to make drama of it, nevertheless the young girl conceived a certain dislike for a town where it was impossible to go about without attracting groups of loungers, or rows of admirers; even to the little flower girls, who ran after her, proffering their nosegays and calling, "Bella signorina! Bella signorina!" It was true that she was attractive, this "Queen" of *Les Buissonnets*, in her black

The Offering of the Children

dress and her brown coat of heavy cloth, its nap curled to imitate fur, her felt toque, trimmed with similar material and adorned with a wing. The wealth of her silky hair was flowing and tied with a ribbon in the centre, and framed happily her dainty, childlike face. M. Martin enjoyed the sight of her. "When we were not in the carriage," she confides, "and I was separated from him, he would call me, so that I might give him my arm as at Lisieux."

From Bologna they visited the *Santa Casa*, of Loreto, where the father, "with his usual submissiveness," to use Thérèse's expression, took part in the general Communion in the basilica, whilst his daughters, "less submissive," preferred "the diamond to the jewel case," and wished to receive our Lord in His own house. On November 13th, in the evening, they were thrilled to hear the shout in the darkness, *Roma! Roma!* The Martins stayed at the *Hôtel du Sud*, in the *Via Capo le Case*, today given over to other purposes, where the room occupied by Thérèse has been transformed into an oratory. Unless there was some special ceremony, they heard Mass at the nearest church, *Sant' Andrea delle Fratte*, the sanctuary rendered celebrated by the apparition of the Madonna of the Miraculous Medal to the Jew, Alphonse Ratisbonne, on January 20th, 1842.

It was under a dreary sky that they visited the Eternal City. The rain fell almost continuously during six days. The Saint has described the expedition to the Roman Campagna, the prayer at the Catacombs of St. Calixtus on the Appian Way, the station at the basilica of Saint Agnes-without-the-Walls, finally the Colosseum, where, despite the danger, she and Céline climbed down among the ruins leading to the "little pavement marked with a cross," the scene of the martyrs' combats. On the way, Thérèse enjoyed the guides' speeches, the tone, delivery, and placid grandiloquence of which she mimicked wonderfully. She playfully noted the inversion of syllables made by one casual interpreter, who called upon them to admire on an ancient temple: "the little *cornichons* (sic) and the *Cupides* (sic) placed above."

The many warnings which forbade the weaker sex to enter certain sacred places, called forth from her a vehement protest.

"Every moment they were telling us: 'Don't enter here . . . Don't go in there . . . You will be excommunicated!' Oh poor women! How they are despised! Yet they love the good God, and in far greater numbers than the men! And during Our Lord's Passion the women had more courage than the Apostles, since they braved the insults of the soldiers and dared to wipe the adorable face of Jesus . . . Doubtless that is why He allows contempt to be their portion on earth, since He chose that for Himself . . . In Heaven, He will know well how to show that His thoughts are not those of men, for then the 'last' will be the 'first.' " [5]

Have we not here a tirade which, although lacking the fiery style of the suffragettes of another day, none the less portrays Thérèse as an unexpected patroness of right-minded feminism? M. Martin smiled at these indignant outbursts. He liked spontaneity and courage. The intrepidity of his daughters which had led them to venture rashly into the arena of the pagan circus to kiss the earth once crimsoned with the blood of the martyrs, roused in him a noble pride. He likewise allowed them to ascend the dome of St. Peter's, even to the globe crowning the cupola erected by Michael

[5] Unpublished reminiscences.

The Offering of the Children

Angelo, as a great tiara over the tomb of the Apostle.

* * *

The critical event of the journey was the papal audience. Thérèse desired and dreaded it at the same time. On November 14th, she wrote to her aunt:

"I do not know how I shall manage to speak to the Pope; unless God takes charge of everything, I do not know how I can do it. But I have such great confidence in Him that He cannot forsake me. I leave everything in His Hands."

On Sunday, November 20th, she put on the regulation black mantilla and, on her father's arm, crossed the threshold through the Bronze Door, went up the Scale Regia, and took her place in the Consistorial Hall, where an altar had been set up. Leo XIII was to say Mass. Although he was only in the first period of his pontificate, he was already an old man, very bent, yet possessing an astonishing youthfulness. He was in truth an imposing figure with his tall stature, his long, diaphanous hands, his fine, wide forehead, aquiline nose and sparkling eyes lighting up the face of an ascetic, luminously pale and extraordinarily expressive. Some magnetic influence seemed to be communicated from his person. He seemed the incarnate synthesis of genius and holiness.

He celebrated devoutly and with impressive recollection, made his thanksgiving during the Mass that followed, said by a prelate, then proceeded to his throne in the *Sala dei Pala frenieri*.[6] Following after the Bishop of Coutances, Canon Révérony offered to the Holy Father the homage of the diocese of Bayeux and also,

---

[6] *Hall of the Grooms.*

as a Jubilee gift, a lace rochet in the Louis XIV style, bearing the papal arms, as well as those of several Norman cities. This masterpiece had taken the workers 8000 days to make.

The queue of pilgrims then began to file past, kneeling one by one before the Pope, kissing his foot and receiving his blessing. The Vicar-General had taken care to warn them aloud that "it was absolutely forbidden to speak to the Holy Father." He confined himself to pointing out to Leo XIII any notable pilgrims, and it was thus that he paused to draw attention to M. Martin, as being the father of two Carmelite nuns. The Sovereign Pontiff, "as a pledge of particular benevolence," let his hand rest longer on that pilgrim's head, seeming thus, as says the autobiography, to mark him with a mysterious seal in the name of Christ Himself.

Still under the impression of this gesture, what was not the father's surprise after the ceremony when his Thérèse reached him weeping in distress! Infringing all the prohibitions, she had dared to address the Pope, who for a moment had bent down his head over her until he brushed her forehead. "Most Holy Father, in honor of your Jubilee permit me to enter Carmel at fifteen." The action annoyed M. Révérony, who by stating that the Superiors were considering the matter, had to some extent dictated the Pontiff's evasive reply. It was in vain that the girl insisted. The Head of the Church answered in a penetrating tone, emphasising every word: "Come, come, you will enter if it be God's will." And he raised his hand to bless her, looking at her fixedly, whilst the Noble Guard, led her away in tears.

Her grief was poignant. A letter to her "little mother" witnesses to it on the same day.

The Offering of the Children

"Oh, Pauline, I cannot tell you how I felt! I was utterly crushed; I felt forsaken, and then I am so far . . . so far! I feel like crying as I write this letter; my heart is so full. However, God has given me strength to bear this trial. It is very heavy indeed but, Pauline, I am a little ball for the Child Jesus to play with. If He wishes to break His plaything, He is quite free to do so. Yes, I will all that He wills . . . I have not written nearly all I wanted; I cannot express these things. I should need to speak to you, and then, you will not read this letter until three days hence. Oh, Pauline, I have only God all alone, all alone! Good-bye, Pauline darling. I do not say more. I am afraid lest Father should come and ask to read my letter, and that is impossible. He would be too much upset at seeing me suffer so much."

The truth was that M. Martin shared her trouble, and was actively pleading her cause in the proper quarters in the pilgrimage. Having remained in Rome during the excursions which a group of travellers made to Naples and Pompeii, on the 21st and 22nd of November, he seized the chance to visit a venerable Brother of the Christian Schools, who had given him a fatherly welcome two years previously, on his former visit. Founder and Director of the College of St. Joseph, Frère Siméon was one of those eminent Frenchmen who used their connections with the Vatican circles to work disinterestedly for the spiritual welfare of their fellow countrymen. M. Martin pleaded for his daughter. He told the whole story; Marie's vocation, Thérèse's plans, her set-backs, the notorious audience and its disappointing result. Much impressed, the religious took notes. "We do not see that in Italy," he exclaimed. Already he had offered to approach M. Révérony, when —quite by accident—the Vicar-General in person was ushered into the parlor. But here we must let Céline speak, since as soon as she heard of the interview she wrote off an account to her sisters.

"M. Révérony has been charming with Father. He seemed to be sorry for his share and in order to win forgiveness reminded Father of the special blessing he had received from the Pope, because he had been presented as the father of two Carmelites.

"Father asked him whether he had received any reply from His Lordship of Bayeux concerning Thérèse, and added: 'You had promised me to lend a hand.' What a kind father!

"M. Révérony was touched, I think, and begins to believe that the vocation of Thérèse is extraordinary. He even said: 'Very well. I shall come to her Clothing. I invite myself!' Father assured him of his gratitude and all sorts of amiable words were exchanged . . .

"I really think we made M. Révérony sorry for us. Thérèse was so sweet at the Holy Father's feet. She was kneeling, her hands clasped and resting on the Pope's knee, and her eyes were so imploring. It was a beautiful sight." [7]

It is possible that the Vicar-General of Bayeux had been invited by Leo XIII himself to facilitate the obtaining of the Bishop's consent to the girl's request. It has since been stated in Roman circles that that Pope never allowed a single supplication to pass without taking an interest in it. Whatever the case may be, the promise of the formidable canon was a light in the night. Throughout the journey, Thérèse had felt his penetrating eye watching her closely. The result of the scrutiny must have been favorable, for henceforth the attitude of the imposing personage towards her was to be wholly sympathetic. The case was the same with

[7] Unpublished letters. Archives of the Carmel.

The Offering of the Children

Mgr. Legoux, and many another notable ecclesiastic in whom her request, known immediately, had aroused a kindly curiosity.

We even find that the *Univers* of November 24th, under the heading *Roman Letter of the 20th November*, mentions the matter to the French public incidentally: "Among the pilgrims was a girl of fifteen, who begged the Holy Father to be allowed to enter a convent immediately in order to be a nun." The Norman press copied and elaborated the news, giving it a publicity which Thérèse had neither foreseen nor desired. At Lisieux, especially in ecclesiastical circles, no one had any doubt; obviously it was Thérèse Martin who was in question. Her confessor, whom she had not informed of her decision—she thought that God and her "little mother" sufficed to direct her—hastened to the Carmel, eager for explanations. No doubt he was mollified, for Soeur Agnès wrote to her uncle Guérin: "M. l'Abbé Lepelletier knows everything. He came to see us on Saturday. He is full of admiration and says the child is a privileged soul and destined for great things."

From Lisieux, comforting messages were sent off to Rome and delighted M. Martin. He was moved at reading these lines from Marie:

"I am still under the impression of the Holy Father's blessing. I am not surprised that he looked specially at you. Our Lord's representative on earth must have been inspired by Him to understand you, revered Father! He has blessed your white hairs—your old age . . . It seems to me as though it is our Lord Himself who has blessed you, who has looked upon you! There is nothing left now to see or savor in this world. I think after that there remains only Heaven. But is this not a happy image thereof? Till we meet, Father dear."

The Story of a Family

As for Thérèse, she received from her godmother the following comforting words which the future was to confirm so quickly:

"Did you notice the words the Holy Father spoke to you? 'You will enter if God wills.' There is a deep meaning there, my little Thérèse. Oh, if you only knew the mysteries it hides! It is as though He said to you: 'Child, if I will it, you will enter. If I will it, despite all the contradictions, despite all the *no's*, you will enter; if I will it minds will be changed tomorrow, for I hold them all in my hands.' No, Thérèse, there is nothing to fear; only to thank our Lord for. Let the little ball lie quietly in the hands of the Child Jesus. If she knew how dear she is to Him, how He longs to have her for Himself alone and how He will indeed have her, if He wills! Yes, Thérèse, the Holy Father bent over you to listen to you, and Jesus did so also. How lovingly He bends over His little toy! As you well know, up to now I scarcely paid attention to your desires. I was asking myself whether we were not trying to forestall God's time. But I know now that it is not so. He has shown us proofs of that and I am sure that His will will be done."

The pilgrims were already on the way home. They had left Rome on November 23rd, visited Assisi the following day—"the places made fragrant by the virtues of St. Francis and St. Clare—paid passing visits to Florence and the shrine of St. Mary-Magdalen de Pazzi, to Pisa and the Leaning Tower, of which the sisters wished to undertake the ascent. After gazing at the fairylike splendors of the Riviera, they crossed the frontier, travelled along the Côte d'Azur, with its reddish cliffs, its rows of palms, and pine woods raising their sombre masses showing up against the blue background of the sea.

It was during this last stage that we find Thérèse with M. Révérony. At Assisi, where she lost her way

The Offering of the Children

in the labyrinth of the *Sacro Convento*, he had taken her into his carriage "like a squirrel caught in a trap." He had talked to her very pleasantly about her beautiful vocation. When they were leaving Nice, M. Martin, still concerned to soothe his daughter's trouble, discreetly whispered to the Vicar-General: "If you would say something to Thérèse; you know she is still thinking of her little Lord at Christmas." A smile was the only answer, but finding himself shortly afterwards in a bus beside the future postulant, the canon, so dreaded only yesterday, leaned over kindly and asked her: "Well! Where are we going when we reach Lisieux?" "I shall go and see my sisters at Carmel," replied the girl, blushing. "We shall do what we can, shall we not? Yes, I promise you to do all I can." No more was needed to revive all her hopes. "Oh thank you!" cried Thérèse joyfully.

They visited *Notre-Dame de-la-Garde* at Marseilles, sang the *Magnificat* in thanksgiving on the hill of Fourvières, and the pilgrims dispersed as soon as they reached Paris in the night between the 1st and 2nd of December. The journey had ended finally in a certain uncertainty as to the future. To console his youngest, M. Martin suggested a longer pilgrimage, that which he had himself always had the ambition to make: to the Holy Land and its blessed spots, where all speaks of the Gospel, but the young girl was satiated with the beauties of earth. The only land she wanted was that bounded by the cold walls of the Carmel. She had scarcely left the station at Lisieux, than she took her troubles to her "little mother." The latter gave her a timely reminder of the promise of Mgr. Hugonin, and advised her to write to him again without delay.

M. Martin privately confided to Pauline that his two

daughters had not seemed to him at all out of their element in the aristocratic company. "I can assure you," he declared, "they were among the most noticed." For her part, Thérèse wrote: "I think we were well liked by everybody, and Papa seemed proud of his two daughters; but if he were proud of us, we were equally so of him for, in our eyes, there was not a finer or more distinguished gentleman in the whole pilgrimage than my dear "King."[8]

* * *

The weeks that followed seemed interminable to the generous child. Every day, restraining his own feelings in order to carry out his daughter's wishes, her father himself took her to the post office to watch anxiously for the answer so long awaited. It did not arrive until January 1st, 1888, by means of Mère Marie de Gonzague. The Bishop left the decision wholly and simply to the judgement of the Prioress. In order to consider the feelings of M. Delatroëtte, and also to spare the postulant the rigors of an immediate monastic Lent, the Prioress had decided to postpone the entrance until after Easter, which would be near the date of the Golden Jubilee of the foundation of the monastery.

This fresh delay was particularly painful to the girl, who was sorely tempted for a moment to profit by it to relax her fervor, and enjoy the legitimate pleasures of the world she was about to forsake. The light of the Holy Spirit soon showed her this snare of the evil one. On his side, M. Martin bravely bore these three months respite, of which each morning marked the implacable progress. He had never so enjoyed his Thérèse's company. He could not do enough for her. At the end of

[8] Unpublished reminiscences.

The Offering of the Children

February did he not bring her a little new-born lamb, all white and curly, which was the delight of the two sisters? Alas! the rapture was short. In the afternoon the poor little creature died.

The date of destiny was at last fixed for the Monday after Low Sunday, April 9th, on which day was kept the transferred feast of the Annunciation. The last meal took place the evening before, in the dining room of *Les Buissonnets.* At the oak table, lighted by the glass torches, M. Martin took his place with his three daughters and the Guérin family. Léonie was one of the party, for a breakdown in health had recently stopped her postulancy at the Visitation of Caen. Bitterly disappointed at this second failure, she had considered it her duty to warn her sister against the possible results of too hasty a decision. Thérèse thanked her gently. Her resolution had not been lightly taken. She was under no illusions. It was a will to complete self-sacrifice that was urging her on. Strong in the divine support, she would not give way.

She did not feel any the less the sharp pain of those last hours when she was leaving everything. "How full of anguish are those farewells! When one would wish to see oneself forgotten, the most loving words escape all around, as though to make one feel the sacrifice of the separation all the more." And elsewhere: "Papa scarcely said anything but kept looking at me lovingly . . . My aunt was crying and my uncle said a thousand affectionate things to me." All eyes were wet. She alone remained calm and completely mistress of herself.

"To leave home is to die to some extent"; what emotion in that last look around at the most familiar things!

367

The Story of a Family

"Lifeless objects, have you then a soul
That clings to our soul, and power to love?"

For the last time, Thérèse walked round the paths of the English garden, looked at her favorite flowers, gave a last caress to Tom and, having taken in with one glance "the gracious nest of childhood," went down the stony "way to Heaven." She who had been the life of *Les Buissonnets* left it.

All her family accompanied her and in silence entered the austere chapel with her.

"At the moment of Communion . . . I heard sobs on all sides. I did not shed a tear, but as I led the way to the cloister door my heart beat so violently that I wondered if I were going to die. Oh, the agony of that moment! One must have experienced it in order to understand. I embraced all my dear ones and knelt for my father's blessing. He too, knelt down and blessed me through his tears. It was a sight to gladden the angels, this old man giving his child to God while she was yet in the springtime of life. At length the doors of the Carmel closed upon me . . ." [9]

What Thérèse does not say is that M. Delatroëtte had been present at the scene and thought it his duty to pour a drop of gall into the chalice. Speaking loudly enough for the girl and her father to hear him, he had said drily: "Well, my Reverend Mothers, you can sing a *Te Deum*. As the delegate of His Lordship the Bishop, I present to you this child of fifteen, for whose entrance you have so wished. I hope that she will not disappoint your hopes, but I remind you that if it happens otherwise, the responsibility will be yours alone." Evidently

[9] Autobiography. C. 7.

The Offering of the Children

the Superior did not possess the gift of prophecy. He would return to a better mind later on.

When he returned to *Les Buissonnets*, M. Martin looked again at a favorite sacred picture in his missal, entitled *Vocation*, which Marie had left him as a keepsake. It portrayed the virgin chosen by God leaving her father's house, and preparing to set out on the great road running uphill to Calvary; her eyes fixed upon the Christ between two rows of crosses. Below was the commentary:

> "May all be sacrificed to this one object of my love,
> And on the last day of my pilgrimage,
> When death shall strike me, let it find in me the image
> Of a God crucified!"

On the other side was printed a long extract from the immortal pages inserted by Montalembert in the fifth chapter of his *Monks of the West*, on the day when, with heart heaving but proud, he returned from offering to the Father in Heaven his daughter, Catherine. The extract, and its poignant close is well known:

> "But who is then this invisible lover who died upon a gibbet nineteen centuries ago, and who thus draws to Himself youth, beauty and love? Who appears to souls with a splendor and fascination which they cannot resist? Who swoops down upon them all at once and makes of them His prey? Who takes, all living, the flesh of our flesh, and slakes His thirst with the purest of our blood? Is it a man? No, it is a God. There lies the great secret, the key to the sublime and sorrowful mystery."

The Catholic Faith has inspired nothing more uplifting.

369

The Story of a Family

On the day after his oblation, alone in that Belvedere still full of the smile and confidences of Thérèse, M. Martin wrote to a friend:

"Yesterday my little Queen entered Carmel. God alone could require such a sacrifice, but He is helping me so powerfully that amid my tears my heart is overflowing with joy." He was not the less profoundly disturbed. To someone who was astonished at his apparent Stoicism, and said to him: "Abraham did not outdo you. You would have done as he did, if God had asked you to sacrifice your little Queen." He replied quickly: "Yes, but I own I should have raised my knife slowly, hoping for the angel and the ram!"

A note from Céline, written on the 9th of April, had informed the monastery of his noble, Christian greatness of soul. The three sisters that day united might be reassured. He was bearing the shock heroically. Marie at once expressed her admiration and her gratitude:

"My incomparable Father,
What Céline tells us is worthy of you! Oh, what a father we have! I am not surprised therefore, that God takes all his children. He is too dear to His Heart for Him not to look upon both him and his with a very special love. How our happy mother must be smiling in Heaven; how she must rejoice to see her ship so well steered by you into the heavenly port . . . I cannot write more; my heart is too full. Our Mother herself cried when she read Céline's account."

*   *   *

More than ever, the conversations in the parlor at Carmel became for M. Martin a rest and a spiritual feast. He found again his Thérèse, wearing the traditional little black cap and over her secular blue dress, the postulant's black cape. Her childish grace had

370

taken on a sort of dignity. She seemed radiant. No hint showed externally of the trials of all sorts which already constituted her lot. The only thing that was clear was that she did not intend to elude the Rule or to do things by halves. Those in the world might perhaps think that she was "the plaything of the community"; the divine Bridegroom had placed her, from the outset, beneath the austere régime that makes saints.

On Whit Tuesday, May 22nd, she was chosen to crown with roses her godmother, Marie, who had just made her Profession. Two days later, M. Martin was present at his eldest daughter's reception of the black veil, and was able to hear for the last time the powerful preaching of Père Pichon, setting forth the greatness of the religious vocation.

The month of the Sacred Heart brought him a fresh emotion. Léonie, not at all discouraged by two vain attempts, was determined, sooner or later, to return to the Visitation, the object of her thoughts. But what would become of Céline when her old father should be no more? She had just refused without discussion a brilliant offer of marriage. Her piety seemed to be guiding her also to the cloister. She had not breathed a word to M. Martin, for she was resolved to surround him with her care until his death. A fortuitous incident led her to tell him everything.

On June 16th, 1888, being then just nineteen, having finished a picture, which today hangs in the father's room at *Les Buissonnets*, and represents Mary Magdalene at the feet of Our Lady of Sorrows, she went up to the Belvedere. Her father was there, sitting at his table. He admired the picture, the subject of which impressed him vividly by its pathos. He took the opportunity to propose to his daughter to take her to

371

Paris, in order that she might further develop her talent in the studio of some leading artist. It was then that Céline let out her secret. She owned that, since she wished in her turn to follow her sisters into the Carmel, she had no intention of exposing herself to occasions of sin in the very mixed company that frequented the art studios. At this revelation, which set the seal on his sacrifices, and realised to the letter the last wish of his wife, M. Martin was thrilled with a holy pride. "Come," he cried at once, "let us go together before the Blessed Sacrament to thank God for the graces He has granted to our family, and for the honor He has done me in asking for all my children. If I possessed anything better, I should hasten to offer it to Him."

His joy was so great that he immediately shared it with his dear monastery in the *Rue de Livarot*. "I must tell you that I made haste to thank God and make you thank Him, for I feel that although very humble, our family has the honor to be reckoned among the privileged ones of our adorable Creator."

There were those who, pitying him for the empty places made around him, saw grounds for pronouncing the repeated sacrifices inhuman. He knew by experience that his old age was not clouded over by them. Never had he felt the warmth and passion of his children's affection as he felt it in those humble messages that reached him from Carmel, written on scraps of paper and enclosed in poor turned envelopes.

It is Thérèse who writes: "How good you are to your little Queen! Not a day passes on which she does not receive some presents from her King! Thank you with all my heart, Father dear. If you knew how much your *Orphan of the Bérézina* loves you! But, no, you will know that only in Heaven."

The Offering of the Children

"How could a queen not love her king, and such a king as you; so holy and so good! Yes, you are certainly as holy as St. Louis himself . . .

"When I think of you, my darling father, I think naturally of God, for it seems to me impossible to see anyone holier than you on earth . . .

"When I think that in a week I shall have been four months at Carmel, I am astonished; for I seem to have been always here; yet on the other hand it seems that yesterday was my entrance day. How everything passes!

"My Jesus, the King of Heaven, in taking me for Himself, has not taken me from my holy king of the earth. Oh no! If my dear father wills and does not think me too unworthy, I shall remain forever the queen of his heart, and I shall try and glorify him by becoming a great saint." [10]

The letters of Marie and Pauline show the same tender sensitiveness, elevated and as it were, transfigured and sublimated by the same supernatural fire. Here filial love is truly *piety* or, to speak better, it finds its culmination in charity. After having written of Thérèse that the "queen" is really worthy of her title, that hers is "a perfection worthy of her King," the eldest turns to the latter. "I do not think that there are many others loved and venerated as greatly as you. I feel that my own heart becomes ever more tender towards you. If I could but give you all my happiness!"

On December 31st, 1888, she will say again:

"Your diamond would wish to crown you even here below! And after all, is not your crown begun? Are there not already at Carmel three jewels of it in the hand of the divine Artificer? Oh, how well He knows His craft! What wonderful work He

[10] Unpublished letters.

will do in our souls if we put no obstacles in the way! And then, the two pearls gleaming in *Les Buissonnets;* must they not be counted also! And our saintly mother in Heaven, and the four little angels departed? What a beautiful crown for the old white-haired patriarch! It is something to renew his youth!"

So many signs of divine favor make her tremble at times with gloomy forebodings.

"Oh, my darling father, I think of the treasure you have amassed for yourself and I am almost afraid. Oh, may God not think fit to give you this treasure immediately! One would think at times that He could not refrain from crowning His saints. But wait, Lord, You have Eternity!"

God was to wait. He crowns His saints only after having given them to drink, and that at length, from His chalice. M. Martin knew for an hour the halt on the summit of Thabor. It was but a brief stage. Soon he must climb, ere entering into his glory, the most painful of Calvaries.

CHAPTER 14

THE FATHER'S SACRIFICE

The prophetic vision—the offering—the great
affliction—the Clothing of Thérèse—the
sanctification of suffering—the *Holy Face*
—Profession and Veiling of Thérèse
—death of M. Martin.

SO FAR, everything in M. Martin's life, even suffering, had been bright. He was now to enter upon a dark phase and to know that interior darkness in which faith is purified. He was to experience that progressive decline of his mental faculties, that growing instability of his will power, which constitute the most depressing of afflictions. For some time he was to remain sufficiently lucid to sanctify the bitterness of this extinction of his personality, whilst his daughters were to find in it the supreme trial destined to launch them on the "royal way of the Cross."

This painful drama had a "Shakespearean" prologue, or rather, since here an allusion to profane drama is scarcely in place, let us say that it opened eight years previously with a prophetic foreshadowing as highly colored and overwhelming as the most tragic visions of Isaias or Ezekiel.

Thérèse was seven years old. It was early afternoon

in bright sunshine. M. Martin being away on business at Alençon, she was deprived of her daily walk and was making up for it by surveying the landscape from the upper bedroom behind the Belvedere.

"I was alone at a window looking on to the large garden, my mind full of cheerful thoughts, when I saw before me, in front of the washhouse, a man dressed exactly like Papa, of the same height and appearance, but more bent and aged. I say *aged* to describe his general appearance, for I did not see his face as his head was covered with a thick veil. He advanced slowly with measured step, along my little garden; at that instant a feeling of supernatural fear seized me, and I called out loudly in a trembling voice: "Papa, Papa!" The mysterious person seemed not to hear, he continued his walk without even turning, and went towards a clump of firs that grew in the middle of the garden. I expected to see him reappear at the other side of the big trees, but the prophetic vision had vanished." [1]

Marie and Pauline came running up upon hearing the child's cries of terror. They thought Victoire, the maid, had been playing some practical joke; she denied it. They searched among the bushes; there was no sign of anything unusual. Finally they judged it wiser to close the incident by telling the child to think no more about it.

"Ah, that was not in my power! Often and often my imagination brought before me this mysterious vision; often and often I tried to raise the veil which hid its true meaning, and deep down in my heart I had a conviction that some day it would be fully revealed to me. And you know all, dear Mother. You know that it was really my father whom God showed me, bent by age, and bearing on his venerable

[1] Autobiography. C. 2.

The Father's Sacrifice

*   *   *

At the stage we have reached, M. Martin's thoughts were turning more and more to the other world. He was possessed of sufficiently ample means and managed his money well, though in a calm, careful manner in which the business keenness of the Norman had little part. With a touch of mischief, Sister Thérèse of the Child Jesus reminded him by letter of certain speeches wherein he had envisaged the prospect of possible ruin without emotion. "In these dispositions," she remarked, "no misfortune could be alarming."

He liked to recall the passage from the Book of Wisdom which had become the subject of his frequent meditations:

"For venerable old age is not that of long time, nor counted by the number of the years: but the understanding of a man is grey hairs. And a spotless life is old age. He pleased God and was beloved: and living among sinners he was translated." [3]

Those who met him were aware of an indefinable impression of greatness. A supernatural peace emanated from his person, an august serenity that affected others and imposed respect. "That man is a real patriarch," someone said, merely seeing him go by. The Benedictine Dames at the abbey—and the photographs that remain fully justify this comparison—said he had also "a look of St. Joseph." "Indeed," adds Céline, to whom we owe this detail, "he looked the Just Man by

[2] Autobiography. C. 2.
[3] Wis. C. XXIV; V. 8-10.

377

The Story of a Family

excellence, and when I want to imagine St. Joseph I think at once of my father."

Whilst on the pilgrimage to Rome, Thérèse had verified her father's nobility of character and moral superiority. "Above all, noted his progress in the path of holiness; he had succeeded in obtaining a complete mastery over the impetuosity of his natural disposition, and earthly things were unable to ruffle his calm." [4] In support of this, she instances his long-suffering with respect to meddling or quarrelsome neighbors. "My mother and all who knew him bore witness that no uncharitable word ever passed his lips." [5] Soeur Geneviève states no less categorically: "His charity in easing the trials of his neighbor, and his charity in speech were equally remarkable. He always found excuses for the wrong-doing of others." One day when he was obliged to make legitimate representations to an unsatisfactory tenant who, although well to do, refused to pay her rent, the latter pursued him in the street with vulgar abuse and unseemly gestures. Céline was stamping with indignation; he remained perfectly cool. An angry woman does not reason; very philosophically, he left her on the street and withdrew without saying a word.

M. Martin had read the life of St. Francis of Assisi and, like him, he believed in treating his body as an enemy or, as says the Poverello, putting "Brother Ass" in his place. The ascetic in him never laid down his arms. Until the age of sixty-seven, he remained rigorously faithful to all the ecclesiastical fasts. In secret he enjoyed the *Lives of the Fathers of the Desert*, and drew

[4] In 1894 the total capital bequeathed to his family amounted to 280,000 frs. net personality. Reckoning in the dowries settled upon his daughters, and certain gifts of value, M. Martin, aided by his wife, had amassed a fortune of 360,000 frs. God had blessed also his temporal undertakings.

[5] Autobiography. C. 7.

thence fresh plans of campaign against himself. Marie, who had given him that work as a present, ended by taking it away from him, in order to put a stop to the results of what she called an imprudence.

However, it must not be thought that he was a hardened fanatic, compact of pious exaggerations. He was always the life of family gatherings. He had an artist's enjoyment of aesthetic pleasures. Whenever Marie Guérin appeared, his goddaughter, whom her father called his "little nightingale" and M. Martin himself "the Greek girl," on account of her expressive black eyes, she had to sing some romantic song to him in her melodious voice. He was sensitive to the beauties of the material creation, but he showed himself ever more ready to adore their Creator.

His devotion seemed to become more tender with the years. At Christmas, Soeur Agnès de Jésus heard him exclaim in the parlor: "A little Child! Oh, how could we not be drawn to God who has so humbled Himself! A little child is so lovable." He carefully copied out a prayer of St. Francis Xavier to the Five Wounds of our Lord, and one to the Holy Face, composed by Sister Mary of St. Peter, who had died in the odor of sanctity in the Carmel of Tours on July 8th, 1848, and whose influence was to have so powerful a repercussion upon the convent in the *Rue de Livarot*. If it be added that in the eventide of his life, M. Martin felt himself irresistibly drawn to the Blessed Sacrament, to the point of practicing daily Communion, one can only admire the providential disposition which prefigured in the father's soul the three essential aspects of the spirituality of St. Thérèse of the Child Jesus.

Since his youthful days M. Martin had made a sort of collection from his regular reading of chosen passages of spiritual writers, so that we have in his handwriting a whole anthology, where St. Augustine keeps company with St. Anselm, or St. Francis of Assisi or Bonaventure is neighborly with St. Ignatius and St. Jane de Chantal. A manuscript page found among his private papers seems to belong to the last period, when he had made his sacrifices. We give it in full. The orientation of his piety before the final shock of his cross can be clearly discerned.

"Men torment themselves and take so much trouble to preserve their life on the eve of their death, as if they had many centuries to live. They do likewise with all the things of this world; there is nothing that they will not do in order to render themselves immortal.

"Yet God mocks at their carefulness, and He knows the moment at which from all eternity he has decided that they shall cease to live.

"That does not exclude all kinds of carefulness, but worries, extraordinary and too elaborate precautions. Let us do our best and leave the rest to Providence.

"The Abbé de Rancé was right: it is in vain that the raging sea foams and roars, that the waves dash and howl, that the vessel is tossed about; if the breath of Providence swells its sails it cannot be wrecked, and nothing will prevent it from reaching the harbor."

.   .   .

"Oh holy Roman Church, mother of churches and of all the faithful; Church chosen by God to unite His children in the same Faith and the same Charity! From the depths of our being we shall ever keep unity with thee." (Bossuet, Sermon on the Unity of the Church.)

.   .   .

"Oh my beloved Saviour! when I first entered thy service I knew not the happiness there is in belonging to Thee; but today I know all that Thou art to me. That is why, taught

The Father's Sacrifice

by experience, I protest to Thee that I prefer the honor and joy of thy service to all the satisfactions of the world."

.   .   .

"Love God, then; cling to Him alone, and die of sorrow if you do not live by love." (St. Madeleine-Sophie Barat.)

As the years had gone by, M. Martin's tendency to contemplation had only developed. He was fonder than ever of his cell in the Belvedere, where he was seen for hours together enjoying the glories of summer or the softer attraction of the autumn landscape. In the last months at *Les Buissonnets*, Thérèse had remarked upon this growing attraction of her father for recollection and prayer. "He easily got over the contradictions of life. God flooded his soul with consolations. During his daily visits to the Blessed Sacrament, his eyes filled with tears and his face breathed forth a heavenly beatitude." [6]

Often the *Magnificat* ended in a *Nunc Dimittis*. Since his stay in Brittany, M. Martin had retained a certain deep-seated melancholy which, though usually repressed at times, found vent in short reflexions. "My poor little Queen," he would say, "he who enjoys life enjoys death." How often had he not recited the lyric complaint: "For the exile there are but tears and sad thoughts . . . Oh Fatherland! the Fatherland!" How striking was the tone in which he recited Lamartine's *Reflection!*

"Man, for a mortal time is nought.
  To mourn it were but folly; who hoards it hoardeth woe.
  Time is thy vessel, not thy dwelling place.
  Haste we to run unto the endless goal,
  Tread underfoot this world and live to die!

[6] Unpublished reminiscences.

The Story of a Family

Love, learning, pleasure, life,
This shadow of true good thy heart doth sacrifice,
As seed divine behind thee cast shalt flower more fair,
But in eternity."

A text he specially loved were those words of God to Abraham:

"I am thy reward exceeding great."

Would he go thus into his Father's house, intoxicated with the joy of his holocaust, lulled by his children's love, and glorified by their virtue? In the full strength of his twenty years, he had remembered this passage from a prayer of Fénelon: "Lord, when I consider thy yoke methinks it is too sweet; is it then the cross that I must carry, following Thee all the days of my life? Hast Thou not another chalice, more bitter, of thy Passion, to make me drain to the dregs?"

This foreboding of a great trial never left him. "God has shown only one road whereby to lead all men to the happiness which He destines for them. It is the way of contradictions and crosses. It is for the prince as for the shepherd, and the faith teaches us that He exempts no one therefrom." True M. Martin had known suffering, but it had been haloed with so much brightness. The claw of the prince of darkness had never torn him. He had been spared humiliation. Faced with such a destiny a scruple crossed his mind. After having watched his wife's sacrifice, the immolation of his daughters, ought he not to communicate in their thirst for perfection, share their apostolic zeal, take upon himself, as they had done, the burden of vicarious reparation? The struggle in his conscience culminated, in May 1888, in that scene recounted by Thérèse in the seventh chapter of her book.

The Father's Sacrifice

"Mother, you remember that day in the parlor, when he said to us: 'Children, I have just come back from Alençon, and there in the church of *Notre-Dame*, I received such graces and consolations that I made this prayer: My God, it is too much, yes I am too happy; I shall not get to Heaven like this, I wish to suffer something for Thee—and I offered myself as a . . .' The word *victim* died on his lips. He dared not pronounce it, but we understood."

His had long been a soul that loved to praise God; now he was to become a victim of praise. The consecration had been made in the same sanctuary in which his little Queen had been baptised. It had likewise been during one of her father's visits to Alençon that the child had had the prophetic vision of her "king" tragically veiled. Was the mystery about to be explained? Marie began to ask herself. "Very often, when thinking about Father, I had asked myself: How will this beautiful life end? I had a secret presentiment that it would close in suffering, though I was far from suspecting what this suffering would be." As for Thérèse, here is how she interprets the phrase in which he had enthusiastically ratified the vocation of Céline: "If I possessed anything better, I would hasten to offer it to Him." "That 'something better' was himself! And God accepted him as a victim of holocaust. He tried him as gold in the furnace and found him worthy of Himself."

* * *

Up to the age of sixty-four years, M. Martin's health had been proof against every trial. The fatigue doubtless the result of intellectual over-working—which had compelled him in his youth to abandon all thought of the religious life, had vanished after he had ceased to study without leaving any after effects. Since then, he had never needed medical attention save on the oc-

383

casion of a mishap when out fishing, towards the end of his residence at Alençon. Stung by a poisonous fly, he had neglected the bite. The infection had spread, and behind the left ear a painful sore formed which, ten years later, thanks to treatment equally barbarous and mistaken, spread until it was the size of the palm of his hand, and healed only very slowly. Except for this incident, he had been a stranger to medicine and doctors. He had retained good sight, a quick walk, an active mind and showed remarkable power of endurance under every kind of fatigue. It might have been augured that he would reach the age of his father, the Captain, struck down at eighty-eight by a stroke, or of his mother who had died at Valframbert on April 8th, 1883, at the same age as her century.

We have seen how the stroke of May 1st, 1887, soon followed by two milder seizures, came to disappoint these hopes. It was a case of what is commonly called cerebral congestion; the disorder being due to arterio-sclerosis which, by rendering the vascular tissues friable, disorders the flow of blood to the brain. These troubles are essentially mobile and variable in their effects, according to the seat of the mischief, its extent and duration. M. Martin was to run the whole gamut of them. Struck on one occasion by hemiplegia, he would subsequently recover the complete use of his limbs, to be later on immobilised and powerless when the lesions became permanent. At first his faculties were spared, but he would suffer their progressive decline when larger areas of the brain would become mortified in their turn.[7]

---

[7] A professional psychiatrist to whom we have submitted all the details of M. Martin's illness, together with developments which could not be included in a simple biography, has been kind enough, after an exhaustive

The Father's Sacrifice

The period of relative recovery that followed the first attack allowed of the pilgrimage to Rome. All the same, in the beginning of 1888, symptoms of a new morbid phase became evident; more marked lassitude, lapses of memory. Despite all the precautions taken by filial affection, Thérèse's father became aware of his state with brutal suddenness on a certain day when, owing to neglect, he found he had let his favorite parrot die. This incident upset him and alarmed him, since it revealed to him for the first time that his mental powers were failing. In the last days of her own life Thérèse would never recall it without emotion.

Still it was only in June 1888 that the latent malady suddenly awoke again. M. Martin had just pronounced his offering at Alençon; quite recently he had ratified that of Céline. The confidential talks wherein his youngest daughter related her discoveries at Carmel

examination, to supply his particularly authoritative opinion in the following note:

"From the age of sixty-four years, M. Martin showed several cerebral lesions, leaving after effects of a hemiplegic character, transitory at first, then definitive. The patient's age, the study of his antecedents the clinical appearance of the disturbances permit us to envisage as almost certain the retrospective diagnosis of cerebral arteriosclerosis. After a series of spasms or vascular obliterations, engendered by atheroma and scelerosis of the cerebral blood vessels, paralysis and other neurologic symptoms do not disappear but remain permanent, confining the patient to a quasi-immobility.

"Parallel with the organic disturbances, psychic disturbances develop, first with phases of regression, later implacably towards a final intellectual weakening. At first there were slight disturbances of the memory, forgetfulness, obsessions; then signs of delirium and hallucination, borrowing their themes from the deep affective tendencies of the patient's personality.

"By reason of the typical character of the disturbances recorded, on the one hand, and the frequency of the affection on the other, it seems hardly possible to consider another diagnosis."

Let us add, for the sake of completeness, that the synchronization observed between the cerebral accidents and the intolerable sufferings caused by the remedies applied to the sore on the head, of which we have spoken, led M. Martin's entourage to think that these sufferings were not unrelated to the congestive stroke.

caused him intense joy. And now, all at once, the signs of amnesia became more frequent. Certain hallucinatory phenomena appeared which took their color from the whole past life and religious spirit of the holy old man. Haunted by the anti-clerical peril which was beginning to loom over France, he feared for his daughters' lives, for the safety of the priests. The passion for travelling seized upon him in a keenly disturbing manner. He was pursued by a desire for the eremetical life. He longed to fly, to escape the noise of the world, to find some distant retreat where he could escape all eyes, meditate in peace and prepare for death.

Dominated by these fixed ideas, without giving any warning he left home on June 23rd, 1888, and for four days there was no word from him. It is easy to imagine the frantic anxiety of his children, who spent themselves in useless searching, and believed he must have fallen a victim to some accident or to foul play. It was during these days of anguish that Mère Geneviève de Sainte Thérèse, favored by Heaven with supernatural communications, revealed to Thérèse and her sisters, in order to remove their alarm, a consoling word heard by her in prayer from our Lord, and which was verified the following day. On June 27th, a telegram sent from Havre enabled Céline and M. Guérin to find their patient there, somewhat confused at seeing his plans so quickly spoilt but visibly glad to be restored to the affection of his family. During the absence of the latter, a fire broke out which destroyed a house near by and, to Léonie's terror, *Les Buissonnets* narrowly escaped a similar fate.

When they were all together again, after this twofold alarm, life was resumed as usual, but the constant underlying fear of a more decisive attack weighed heavily upon them all. First, on August 12th and then on November 3rd at Havre, whither he had accompanied Père Pichon to see the latter off to Canada, M. Martin had further paralytic strokes, which markedly affected his speech and for the moment seriously disordered his mind. Then it was that, with an instinctive gesture, the patient always tried to cover his head as with a veil. Are we to see therein, as did Soeur Marie du Sacré-Coeur, one of the details foreseen in the "prophetic vision?"

When the attack had passed, he felt at times the unspeakable agony of his threatened sanity. "Death alone has invincible attractions for me," he exclaimed, quoting a remembered poem. He had so longed to make his daughters happy. For their sakes he was planning to buy *Les Buissonnets* and even purchased an adjoining piece of ground. He also rented a châlet at Auteuil, where he made a short stay with Léonie and Céline. The future prospect was so pleasing of a peaceful old age surrounded with loving care! Then he remembered his gesture of willing oblation to God. Was he not betraying his vocation by remaining selfishly at home? And then, this weakening of his powers, these sick fears, were they not the prelude to a more complete detachment still; that which no human being can envisage without trembling, for it strikes at the very core of the personality, humiliating it by condemning it to a seeming annihilation? M. Martin knew these agonising terrors. He calmed himself by accepting them. "All for the greater glory of God," he liked to repeat. "Fear nothing for me, children, for I am the friend of God." This was said in the convent parlor, without a trace of unhealthy excitement, in calm faith.

The patient clung as of old to all his pious practices.

The Story of a Family

He was often absorbed in the thought of eternity. To the last, he retained a delicate sensitiveness as regards purity with an anxious care to mortify himself.

A trifling episode will show his readiness to deprive himself. Before leaving for Carmel, Marie had given him as a keepsake a brass crucifix which he carefully kept in his bedroom. Not knowing where it had come from, Céline expressed a desire to have it to wear at night. At first her father hesitated; he specially prized everything that had belonged to his eldest daughter . . . But during Mass, whilst reading the prayer of General de Sonis, which Céline had given him, he leant over to her and whispered: "I will give you my crucifix." Systematically, he set himself to give up earthly possessions, not hesitating to devote 10,000 francs to the erection of a new high altar in Lisieux cathedral. Greatly moved at such self-sacrifice and so many trials, the clergy at Saint Pierre regarded with veneration him who was familiarly known in religious circles of the town as "the holy patriarch."

*   *   *

One last consolation was reserved for M. Martin. With passionate interest, he was following Thérèse's vocation. He enjoyed the notes wherein she lavished affection and encouragement upon him. "Your Queen is always thinking about you, and praying all day long for her dearest King," she wrote to him on November 25th, 1888. "I am very happy in the soft nest of Carmel, and wish for nothing more on earth save to see you completely cured; but I well know why God is permitting this trial. It is in order that we may win Heaven. He knows that our father is all that we love most on earth, but He well knows also that we must suffer in order to merit eternal life; and that is why He is trying us in that which we hold dearest.

The long awaited hour was soon to strike. On January 10th, 1889, Thérèse was to receive the religious habit. The postulancy, lasting normally six months, had been prolonged in her case in order to consider the feelings of M. Delatroëtte. A providential lull in his malady allowed her father to be present at the ceremony. The feast was all brightness.

The Clothing rite, which has since been simplified, was then carried out with a pomp and circumstance which was peculiarly impressive. In her bridal dress, the postulant came out of the enclosure and entered the outer chapel with her father, followed by her relatives, who walked in pairs as at a wedding. After having been present in the sanctuary for the first part of the ceremony—Vespers or Mass, with a sermon—the procession re-formed to go to the sacristy. For the last time the betrothed of Christ kissed her relations, received the blessing of the celebrant, and recrossed the threshold of the enclosure door for good. Holding the hand of the Prioress and preceded by all the nuns carrying lighted candles, she then entered the monastic choir, where the Clothing ceremony, strictly speaking, took place. The faithful then approached the grille, standing around the officiating priest, who pronounced the liturgical formulae, whilst the Superior proceeded to dress the novice in the brown habit and white mantle.

It may be imagined how striking is this celebration, in which everything is symbolic. M. Martin followed it closely, in full possession of his mental powers, and with holy enthusiasm. Thinking of the exquisite work of the wife he had so loved, he had wished his daughter to wear a white velvet dress, trimmed with Point d'Alençon and swansdown. With her wreath of lilies and her long veil flowing around her, her long fair curls hanging over her shoulders, Thérèse really suggested a picture of St. Agnes.

"My father came to meet me at the enclosure door, his eyes full of tears, and pressing me to his heart exclaimed: 'Ah! here is my little Queen!' Then, giving me his arm, we made our solemn entry into the public chapel." [8]

Nothing was wanting to the gladness of that day. The offering was preceded by the Eucharistic Sacrifice, a perfect setting for an act of oblation. The Bishop of Bayeux, Mgr. Hugonin, was present in person, won already by the child's supernatural charm. Forgetful of the rubrics, he intoned the *Te Deum*, which expressed perfectly Thérèse's feelings of gratitude. And then there was "the little miracle" of the snow, the childlike longing of the humble "winter flower" divinely heard despite an exceptionally mild temperature.

"After the ceremony, the Bishop entered. He gave me many proofs of his fatherly tenderness and, in presence of all the priests, spoke of my visit to Bayeux and the journey to Rome; nor did he forget to tell them how I had put up my hair before visiting him. Then, laying his hand on my head, he blessed me affectionately. My mind dwelt with ineffable sweetness on the caresses Our Lord will soon lavish upon me before all the saints, and this consoling thought was a foretaste of Heaven." [9]

M. Martin rejoined his child in the parlor, and sur-

[8] Autobiography. C. 7.
[9] *Ibid.*

veyed her delightedly in her new Carmelite garb. His soul was as though sated with happiness. "It was his triumph; his last feast here below," writes Thérèse, who, further on, likens this day to our Lord's entry into Jerusalem on Palm Sunday. Alas! the curtain soon fell on this scene of rejoicing. The saint concludes with the melancholy reflection:

"As in the case of our divine Master, his day of triumph was followed by long days of sorrow; and even as the agony of Jesus pierced the heart of His holy Mother, so our hearts were deeply wounded by the humiliations and sufferings of him whom we loved best on earth."

*   *   *

The improvement observed in M. Martin's health was maintained throughout the month of January. When on a journey to Alençon, he confessed to Céline: "I am attached to life; it is not for myself but for my children. I want to buy *Les Buissonnets*. I shall arrange things for the best. I want to please you in everything."

A sudden relapse put an end to his plans. A new brain attack, which left the limbs unaffected but destroyed the memory and developed to a dangerous degree the obsession to run away, led M. Guérin to consider placing his brother-in-law in a mental home. In view of the impossibility of constantly watching the patient, who retained perfect freedom of movement, it was the only way to avoid some serious accident and perhaps also to prevent him from squandering his means.

For the sick man, who remained sufficiently aware of his state, with the ability to think about himself, the affliction would be poignantly bitter. On a former occasion, foreseeing such a prospect, when talking with Céline of another inhabitant of Lisieux condemned to such confinement, he had remarked with a shudder: "It is the hardest trial a man can undergo." His spirit of abnegation extended even thus far; he was not spared the bitter sacrifice.

What that terrible day, February 12th, 1889, was for father and daughters can be imagined; the distress of the last farewell to *Les Buissonnets*, the sadness of the brief visit to Carmel, where M. Martin did not see his nuns—the shock would have been too great but left at the turn, as he had so often done, the box of fish reserved for the community. To the Sister of the *Bon Sauveur* at Caen, who on receiving him told him that he would still have good work to do among so many unbelievers, the patient replied: "That is true, but I should prefer to be an apostle elsewhere than here. However, since God wills it! I think it is to humble my pride." And to the doctor he said: "I have always been used to command, and I see myself reduced to obeying; it is hard. But I know why God has given me this trial; I have never had a humiliation in my life; I needed one." "Well, this may count," the physician could not help replying.

The home of the *Bon Sauveur*, at Caen, which Barbey d'Aurevilly has introduced into literature in his story of the Chevalier Des Touches, constituted a veritable small town, containing 1,700 inhabitants, and comprising together with a large religious community, a boarding school, a day school, a school for the deaf and dumb, a medical dispensary, and buildings set apart for the nursing of mental cases. It justly prided itself upon being in the forefront of such institutions for the arrangements for the patients' comfort and its therapeutic equipment. Everything was done to assure to them the most up-to-date treatment with the maximum of freedom compatible with their condition. A spacious chapel, which stood conspicuous for its beautiful façade and slender spire, gave a soul to the buildings. Here philanthropy was left behind; it was divine charity which bore rule in these precincts.

M. Martin had to remain there a little over three years. He had refused the separate accommodation offered him, preferring from a motive of zeal to live in the company of the other patients, with whom, to the despair of his nurse, he would persist in sharing all the little dainties procured for him. No inmate of the *Bon Sauveur* was easier to manage. There was never a word of complaint. Always used to a certain austerity of life, he still expected to observe the laws of ecclesiastical penance. The religious surrounded him with respect and consideration. "You may rest assured," wrote the Mother-Assistant to Céline, that your dear patient is the object of most considerate care. "Mère Costad, who had charge of the department reserved for the five hundred male patients, tended him as though she had been his daughter, in memory of her own father, who had been similarly stricken. "In the short time he has been here," she said, "he has managed to make himself loved . . . and then, there is something so venerable about him. One has the impression that he is bearing a mysterious affliction."

He became the most assiduous visitor to the chapel. He communicated several times in the week, and even daily when well enough. The privation of the Eucharist constituted his hardest sacrifice. Apart from rare attacks, when an instinctive fear, accompanied by delirium, plunged him into a sort of night, he faced his situation calmly from the supernatural standpoint, and bravely resigned himself to it.

When his daughters invited him to join in the novena they were making to St. Joseph for his cure, he replied: "No, we must not ask that, but only that God's will be done." The false maneuver of a lawyer, who misinterpreted the directions of M. Guérin, and came to make the patient sign a perfectly useless deed renouncing the management of his property occasioned a painful scene which ended, likewise, in acquiescence in the divine good pleasure. "I really think," wrote Céline to her sisters, "that the more he fails, the more peaceful and holy is the expression of his face."

After Holy Communion, M. Martin's greatest joy was the arrival of his family. Leaving the *Buissonnets*, which would have ceased to be their home on the expiration of the lease, Céline and Léonie had, on February 19th, 1889, decided to take rooms near the *Bon Sauveur* at the orphanage of the Sisters of St. Vincent de Paul. In spite of the contrary opinion of their uncle, they remained there as long as it was possible for them, in virtue of a special authorisation, to see frequently the father who was everything to them.

The illness of a member of a household is a test of the unselfishness and strength of the family spirit. In this case, it proved perfectly conclusive. They remembered the counsel of Ecclesiasticus: *Support the old age of thy father . . . And if his understanding fail, have patience with him, and despise him not when thou art in thy strength: for the relieving of the father shall not be forgotten.*[10] Beneath the blow of the humiliation, the love only grew and became more delicately thoughtful.

It was only when they had to conform to the general

[10] Ecclus. III, 14-15.

The Father's Sacrifice

rule, which allowed only one visit per week, that the two daughters returned to Lisieux. On June 7th, 1889, they went to reside with their uncle. At this date, M. Guérin no longer lived in the *Place Thiers*. On the previous August 22nd, together with his Maudelonde relations, he had inherited the handsome fortune of one of his cousins, M. August David, formerly a solicitor at Évreux, and had sold his business and retired to a house in the *Rue Paul Banaston*. It was there, or during summer at the Château de la Musse, in the department of the Eure, that he divided his time between studies, good works, and his society duties. Céline and Léonie were welcomed by him as his own children.

M. Martin was delighted at this arrangement. On July 17th, the Sister who nursed him gave these touching details to the Prioress of the Carmel:

"We have talked at length of all his beloved daughters, and on hearing that Mesdemoiselles Léonie and Céline were in the country at La Musse, he exclaimed: 'So much the better. Tell them to stay there as long as their good uncle thinks fit. I do not want them to return on my account. I am well, very well, here.' This venerable old man speaks only of the greater glory of God. He is truly admirable. Not only does he never complain, but he thinks everything we give him excellent . . . It is touching to see his affection for his family."

On the darkest days, the latters of his Carmelites had the power to tranquillise him. He remained the great Christian whom the bare mention of the Faith sufficed to immerse in God.

Truth to tell, his condition deteriorated only slowly. He even knew several periods of improvement, which made it possible to hope for his return to his family.

The Story of a Family

Thus they passed through many alternatives of hope and disappointment. Then the malady tightened its hold implacably, to such a degree as to weaken the mental faculties considerably and attack the motor nervous system anew.

*   *   *

For a long time, at least intermittently, M. Martin retained sufficient lucidity to feel, accept and sanctify the most tragic of afflictions, that which, little by little, immerses the personality in darkness and chaos. Borne along by the stream of a whole life of generosity, he accepted the humiliation from the outset, and did not retract his offering. Even when he was delirious, expressions of self-surrender recurred upon his lips as a sort of instinctive homage rendered to the divine plan, in a nature ruled by the force of habit.

As to his daughters, the blow affected them deeply. We know how they worshipped their father. To stand by powerless and watch his faculties fail, to be obliged to entrust him to strangers, to suffer on his account from the tactless remarks which in such cases bystanders rarely fail to permit themselves, was for them an unspeakable torture, compared to which his death would have been sweet. The world discharged its poisonous arrows beneath a cloak of pity. In its eyes, M. Martin figured as a vanquished man who, forsaken by his family, was sinking amid the ramblings of religious mania. "A less austere virtue might have saved him from shipwreck. It is a clear proof that God does not ask all that!" The wiseacres had their opportunity.[11] We can

---

[11] Is it necessary to say that these malevolent insinuations were quite erroneous? In the successive departures of his daughters for the religious life, M. Martin had found only peace and greater reason to hope in God. To claim to establish a relation of cause and effect between these sacrifices nobly consented to and the malady that afflicted the saintly old man

The Father's Sacrifice

sense this painful surrounding atmosphere, reading between the lines wherein Thérèse expresses their common distress and common acquiescence.

"I remember that in the month of June, 1888, when we were fearing another stroke of paralysis, I surprised our novice mistress by saying: 'I am suffering a good deal, Mother, yet I feel I can suffer more still.' I did not then foresee the trial awaiting us. I did not know that on February 12th, one month after my Clothing day, our beloved father would drink so deeply of such a bitter chalice. I no longer said I could suffer more; words cannot express our grief; nor shall I try to describe it here."

Will not such a wound leave her shuddering and crushed, utterly stricken interiorly? Let us continue the quotation:

"The three years of my Father's martyrdom seem to me the sweetest and most fruitful of our lives. I would not exchange them for the most sublime ecstasies . . . Precious and sweet was this bitter cross, and our hearts breathed out only sighs of grateful love. We no longer walked—we ran, we flew along the path of perfection." [12]

To understand the mystery we should have to have been present at the conversations in the parlors where Léonie and Céline drew supernatural strength with their Carmelite sisters; we should have to go through

would be to betray the leading lines of his moral physiognomy and do violence to the facts. Nor is there any justification for alleging in this connection some excess of religious practice. The patient's piety was excellently balanced. There was no exaggeration, no tendency to sentimentality or illusion. If in his state of affliction he continued to react and speak as a Christian and an apostle, it was that the habits of the Faith were so deeply ingrained in him that they had, as it were, become second nature, and survived the partial ruin of his lucidity.

[12] Autobiography. C. 7.

all the correspondence exchanged between them. It is but one long cry of fervent acceptance or, rather, "since resignation is still distinct from the will of God," as Thérèse quotes from Mme. Swetchine, it is but one hymn of gratitude, amid their tears. In the plan of the divine Surgeon, sorrow like the shock of an operation, detaches from even legitimate joys; it forces us to look only on the heavenly side; it sets the seal of the Man of Sorrows upon us; it makes us share in His work of Redemption. Such is the *leitmotiv* of those heart to heart exchanges where the saint sets the tone with a hope that reaches to the point of heroism.

Recalling these hymns, shall we transcribe some unpublished strophes? Here at the end of January, 1889, the voice from *Les Buissonnets* addresses the Carmel:

"Dear little sisters; I am thinking of the words of the *Imitation* 'I will bestow infinite glory for one passing humiliation!' Oh, humiliations are our daily bread; but if you knew all I find hidden there . . . for me it is a mystery of love.

"I beg of you not to be troubled. Is it in vain that Thérèse has prayed? Is it in vain that I have put the oil from the lamp of the Holy Face in Father's forehead? No, a thousand times, no! I am certain that there is a wonderful plan in this which we cannot understand. I feel that our Lord is so pleased that we have unlimited trust in Him and find all that He does well done . . .

"No, I am not going to ask God to remove the humiliations, the contempt, the heartache, the anguish, the bitterness . . . But I am going to beseech Him to remove all that from our dear father. He can grant us that grace and I am sure that He will."

Here is the same voice, speaking from Caen on March 1st, 1889, after the patient had been transferred to the *Bon Sauveur:*

Louis Martin surrounded by his family, one year before his death

From left to right: Marie Guérin; Léonie; Céline, near her venerable father; M. Guérin; Madame Guérin; a friend. *Rear:* the Martin servants.

The Holy Face
of Jesus
of the Carmel
of Lisieux

From the
Holy Shroud
of
Turin

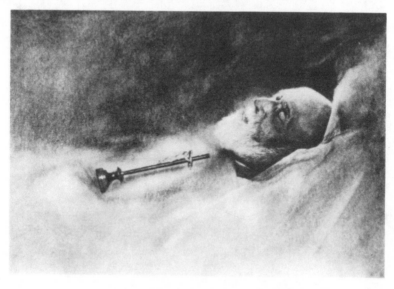

Louis Martin on his death bed
July 29, 1894

The Father's Sacrifice

"Little sisters, I want to rejoice in our tribulations, to do more: to thank God for the bitterness of our tribulations. I do not know why, but instead of receiving these afflictions with resentment and grumbling at them, I see something mysterious and divine in God's dealings with us. Moreover, has He not Himself been through all these sorrows? As for the world's opinion, I own it has no weight whatever with me.

"Oh, if you knew how I see God in all our trials! Yes, everything is visibly marked with His finger."

Six weeks later, as the trial is prolonged, the cry becomes more vehement. We can trace the temptation to discouragement, which finds its expression only to end in a *fiat*.

"My dear Sisters, what a sigh I am heaving from my inmost soul at this moment! My poor heart is broken. I cannot get used to seeing our dear father so ill; I remember him always as he was at home, when he used to talk to us like a real patriarch! He was so good!

"How God must love us when He sees us so afflicted! I ask myself why He is not impatient to take our beloved father to Himself; it seems to me as though He must make a great effort to leave him on earth! Some great good must be coming from it, for His glory, for Father and for us. Otherwise, He could wait no longer. Dear sisters, oh what a happy moment it will be when we are all united up yonder! How these sorrows make us yearn for our fatherland!"

Their souls were making progress in this school of suffering.

"Dearest sisters," writes Céline again, "surely Papa will have no Purgatory in the next world, but for us these sufferings are of such a nature as to revolutionise our souls, I think, and make us saints."

Léonie echoes all these opinions: "The best thing we can do is to throw ourselves upon the Heart of Jesus, and leave everything concerning us in His hands. Only there shall we find courage to bear the sorrows of life, which certainly are not wanting to us. But do not let us murmur. We are more than the friends of our Lord; we are His brides, at least by desire. In Heaven we shall see our darling father, brought so low here on earth, crowned with glory for all eternity. Let us be his crown and render ourselves worthy of such a father!"

The voices from Carmel take up the dialogue. In March 1889, Soeur Agnès de Jésus sends Céline this letter, full of supernatural peace:

"Let us be saints. Jesus is asking that of us . . . He must have it. He must have souls that are wholly devoted, wholly surrendered, wholly given over to His divine pleasure . . . Let us open ours wide, and allow Him to enter into the innermost sanctuary, or rather compel Him to come in. As the disciples at Emmaus said to Him 'Lord abide with us, for the day is far spent, and it is towards evening; let us not remain on the road where evil doers pass by . . . But why have You to be so pressed? Would Your companionship be so onerous?'

"And Jesus smiles and points to the Cross that never leaves Him . . . 'My children, many invite me as do you, but few keep me, because many love me without my Cross and very few let me set it up in their hearts. Yet that is the only means whereby I take my abode there forever. If love finds me, it is only suffering that keeps me.'

"Oh Lord, we will the Cross! Come in and abide with us! Here You are at home . . . It is another Bethany, wherein you will find faithful hearts. Here is an old man, white haired, stricken down, who yet can call himself Your friend; and a group of virgins whose Spouse You are; a Spouse of blood, but ever adored . . .

"Good bye, darling. Let us rejoice in suffering."

Soeur Marie du Sacré-Coeur thus sums up her impressions with respect to the father's affliction, foreseen by her long ago.

"When it came, one day during Mass, I saw so clearly how precious it was that I would not have changed it for all the treasures of earth. And what merits our dearest father must have gained . . . At that time, the story of Job occurred to my mind, and it seemed to me that it was Father's story and ours, and that Satan had stood before God once again and said: 'It is not surprising that your servant should praise you. You loaded him with good things. But strike him in his own person, and see if he does not curse your name!' But the name of the Lord was not cursed. On the contrary, it was blessed always."

As for Thérèse's thoughts, we shall find them expressed in her correspondence with Céline. Let us select some particularly suggestive passages:

"What a favor from Jesus, and how He must love us to send us so great a sorrow! Eternity itself will not be long enough to bless Him for it. He heaps His favors upon us as upon the greatest saints . . . Now we have nothing more to hope for on earth; 'the cool mornings are passed,' for us suffering alone remains! Ours is an enviable lot, and the Seraphim in Heaven are jealous of our happiness." [13] "How has Jesus acted in order to detach our souls from all created things? Ah, He has struck us a great blow, but it is a blow of love . . ." [14] "Do not let us lose this trial which our Lord sends us; let us not lose the opportunity to exploit this gold mine." [15]

[13] Letter to Céline, Jan. 1889.
[14] Letter of July 14, 1889.
[15] Letter of Feb. 28, 1889.

The Story of a Family

As Céline's confidante, Thérèse upheld her eager aspirations, and calmed her fears. In her Little Way she found wonderful intuitions. The tears might fall, nature might writhe and groan; the essential was to let God have the last word. "He who says *peace*, does not say *joy*, or at least sensible joy: to suffer in peace it is enough to will heartily all that our Lord wills . . . We should like to suffer generously and nobly; we should like never to fall: What an illusion! What does it matter to me if I fall at every moment? In that way I realise my weakness, and I gain thereby." [16]

When sorrow reaches its highest point, the thought of Heaven pours balm into the wound: "Céline, my darling sister, the shadows will soon disappear; the rays of the eternal Sun will thaw the frosts of winter . . . A little longer and we shall be in our true country, and our childhood's joys—those Sunday evenings, those outpourings of our hearts—will be given back to us forever." [17]

*　　　*　　　*

This spiritual ascension made together, urged on by the goad of moral suffering, justified Thérèse in inscribing February 12th, 1889, as among "the days of grace granted by our Lord to His little Bride," and to call it "our great riches." Mère Agnès de Jésus, however, invites us to explore further into the significance of this beatitude, when she says of the Servant of God: "It was at Carmel, during the time of our great sorrow

[16] Letter of March, 1889.

[17] Letter of April 26, 1891. From Canada, Pere Pichon sent to the devoted nurse his supernatural consolation:

"I drink in long drafts of your bitter chalice. The dear patriarch is forever present in my thoughts at the Holy Altar. Yes, yes, he has been chosen as a victim and that explains everything. Be proud of it and thank our Blessed Lord."

caused by our father's cerebral disease, that she became more attracted to the mystery of the Passion. It was then that she obtained the permission to add to her religious name that of the Holy Face."

This devotion was held in honor in the *Rue de Livarot*. The community of Lisieux had inherited it from the Carmel of Poitiers which, in its turn, had received it from that of Tours. It was through this connection that Mère Geneviève de Sainte Thérèse had in 1847 learnt of the revelations made by our Lord to Soeur Marie de Saint Pierre. She had carefully collected the promises in favor of those devoted to the Holy Face. The sixth, in particular, appealed to contemplatives: "like the pious Veronica, they shall wipe my adorable face, which sin outrages and disfigures; and in return I will imprint my features upon their souls." [18] The foundress hastened to take measures with the Bishop to erect the *Archconfraternity of Reparation*. She put up in the chapel the impressive picture which at that period was being propagated by the "Holy Man of Tours," M. Dupont.

It was on the threshold of her religious life that

---

[18] Sr. Marie de Saint Pierre—Perrine Eluère—was born at Rennes in 1818, entered the Carmel of Tours in 1839, and died in 1848. She was an exemplary religious and certain revelations she received with respect to this devotion, and especially to the need for making reparation for the irreligion, blasphemous writings etc. so prevalent in France at the time, led to the founding of the Archconfraternity mentioned. At the time there were several other devout persons of both sexes urging similar reparation. Gregory XVI approved the Archconfraternity in 1847. In Tours M. Dupont propagated the devotion to the Holy Face; in Paris the Nocturnal Adoration of the Blessed Sacrament was established and soon spread widely, whilst Théodelinde Dubboucher—Mère Marie de Jésus—founded the religious institute of the *Adoration-Réparatrice*. As regards the details of the revelations the special commission recommended reserve, and considered that the Sister's imagination may have played some part therein, but the actual devotion was to be recommended. Curiously, in the Poitiers Carmel a certain Sister Adelaide claimed to have had similar revelations in 1819. (Tr.)

Thérèse first realised the significance of this cultus. "Until then, I had not appreciated the treasures hidden in the Holy Face. It was my 'little mother' who revealed them to me. As she had been the first of us to enter Carmel, so she was the first to penetrate into the mysteries of love hidden in the Face of our divine Bridegroom." [19]

That had been only a first initiation. The crushing sorrow of 1888-9 shed a dazzling light upon this understanding of "the fellowship of His sufferings," and gave the devotion a precision. On the morrow of the "prophetic vision" of the father's phantom crossing the garden of *Les Buissonnets*, aged, bowed, his face veiled in dark shadow, Thérèse had had a presentiment that the anxiety thus aroused would sooner or later be explained. On the day that M. Martin was struck down, she lived again, this time in terrible realism, the former scene. Then, as her comprehension deepened, the connection forced itself upon her between that father, so revered, so holy, walking silently, bowed beneath his burden, and the *Just Man* by excellence, stripped of His glory, His face swollen, His brow stained with blood, become "like unto a leper." "As the adorable Face of Jesus was veiled during His Passion, so it was fitting that the face of His humble servant should be veiled during the days of his humiliation, in order that it might shine with greater brilliancy in Heaven." [20]

From the sorrow a light came forth that illumined Thérèse's whole spirituality. She turned for strength to Isaias, and in order to send it to Céline, copied out the wonderful earlier portion of the fifty-third chapter:

[19] Autobiography. C. 7.
[20] Autobiography. C. 2.

The Father's Sacrifice

"Who hath believed our report? And to whom is the arm of the Lord revealed?

And he shall grow up as a tender plant before him, and as a root out of a thirsty ground. There is no beauty in him, nor comeliness: and we have seen him, and there was no sightliness, that we should be desirous of him:

Despised and the most abject of men, a man of sorrows, and acquainted with infirmity: and his look was as it were hidden and despised. Whereupon we esteemed him not.

Surely he hath borne our infirmities and carried our sorrows: and we have thought him as it were a leper, and as one struck by God and afflicted.

But he was wounded for our iniquities: he was bruised for our sins. The chastisement of our peace was upon him: and by his stripes we are healed.

These tremendous verses, she pondered, fed upon, lived by. Always she saw the Son of Man in the depths of His abjection. She realised how His humiliations are the price of our salvation. Then her thoughts flew to the dear patient at the *Bon Sauveur*. She saw him again, through Christ, docile, recollected, abased in men's eyes but so dear to the Heart of God. His suffering took on another aspect, and she no longer saw it save as a chapter in the story of the Redemption.[21] Abasement is the condition of supernatural fecundity. What mattered the suffering of the wounded human tenderness? What did it matter what the world said? The Face set in thorns was the key to the mystery.

The capital importance of this "discovery" in Thérèse's existence can never be sufficiently emphasised; a discovery in the sense that, by an incisive ac-

---

[21] The doctrine of the Mystical Body must be borne in mind constantly in this connection. (Tr.)

tion of the Holy Ghost, it was graven in her inmost heart in fiery characters, as a vital principle, a truth known yesterday but not fully exploited. As the saint declares: "Those words of Isaias are the foundation of my devotion to the Holy Face or, to put it better, the underlying principle of all my piety." "The devotion to the Holy Face," writes Mère Agnès de Jésus, "was the special attraction of the Servant of God. However tender her devotion to the Child Jesus might be, it could not be compared to that she had for the Holy Face."—"That Holy Face was the meditation book whence she gained the knowledge of love . . . It was when meditating on the Holy Face that she studied humility."

This theme keeps recurring in her poems. She devoted one entirely to it. She inscribed it in her "armorial bearings," she made it the subject of a consecration for the novices and of a prayer for herself. She depicted it on chasubles. She always kept a picture of it in her breviary, looked at it during her mental prayer, pinned it to her bed curtains during her illness. With what conviction—despite a certain astonishment caused by this audacious act of faith—did she share in her sisters' initiative in erecting in the chapel of Carmel, beneath the picture of the Holy Face, at the close of the hardest hours of their trial, a marble tablet, today set in a shrine behind the high altar, on which was engraved in gold letters this cry of gratitude and filial *abandon* to God's will:

SIT NOMEN DOMINI BENEDICTUM

F.   M.

1888

The Father's Sacrifice

It was in the school of her childhood's companion that Céline, whom Thérèse called happily their father's "little Veronica," learnt in her turn to contemplate the Marred Face. When she entered religion, she was placed under the patronage of the Holy Face. Shortly after Thérèse's death, the Holy Shroud of Turin revealed its secret on the photographic negative, when she conceived and carried out the idea of painting and scattering throughout the world the august image which had impressed Pius X. In this chain of graces, who but can admire the hand of Providence unfolding His plan amid the changes and chances, and making an agonising misfortune the means of sanctifying those who love Him? [22]

* * *

It was in these dispositions that Thérèse approached her Profession on September 8th, 1890. The day before, she received a special blessing from Leo XIII, obtained by means of Frère Siméon, who retained a vivid recollection of the two visits of M. Martin to Rome.

The vows were pronounced in the Chapter House, in the hands of the Prioress, none of the clergy or relatives being present.

Nevertheless, the thought of the sick father was uppermost during the ceremony.

Thérèse had expressed the desire that, sickness carrying with it a blessing, the crown destined for her be rested on his august brow, marking by this symbolic gesture the part that he played in the oblation of his daughter. Céline carefully carried out this double rite. When decorating the statue of the Child Jesus, of

[22] These thoughts will be found developed in the first part of the admirable work of R. P. Petitot: *Sainte Thérèse de Lisieux: Une Renaissance Spirituelle.* (Desclée et Cie.) Trans. by a Benedictine of Stanbrook Abbey. Burns, Oates & Washbourne.

which she had charge, for the feast, the saint used the poor, old discolored candles used at her Clothing. Those "spoke more nearly to her soul" than the new ones, as she explained in a note to Soeur Marie du Sacré-Coeur, for "they began to burn on my Clothing day, when they were new and pink. Father, who had given them to me was there and all was joy. But now the rose-pink has faded . . . Are there here below any rosy joys still for your little Thérèse? Oh no, there remain only those of Heaven."

During the prostration on the carpet of coarse material which follows the pronouncing of the vows, she entrusted to God all her requests. In order to obey the order of Mère Marie-de-Gonzague, she prayed for her father's restoration to health, but in terms carefully weighed which left full play to the divine good pleasure. "My God, grant that Father may recover, if it be Your will; since our Mother had bidden me ask this of You." On the other hand, it was absolutely that she pleaded for the spiritual interests of her Confirmation godmother. "For Léonie may it be Your will that she may become a Visitandine; and if she has no vocation, I beseech You to give it to her. You cannot refuse me that." More earnestly still, she asked for herself: "a boundless, unlimited love," and "the martyrdom of the heart and of the body."

Was it a first answer from on high? Thérèse's Veiling had been fixed for the 24th of September. This is an additional rite, proper to the Carmelite ceremonial. The Bishop blesses the veil at the altar, and puts it upon the newly professed at the Communion grille. After the office the father advances in his turn to bless his daughter. With childlike confidence, Thérèse had been counting upon the presence of her "King." A passing improvement, recently noted in his condition, seemed to allow of his being moved. At the last moment, M. Guérin decided against this, fearing quite rightly that the shock might be too much for the old man . . .

For the "little Queen" it was a heavy blow. She admits it quite frankly to Céline, her usual confidante:

"It is true Jesus had already enriched me with many jewels but no doubt there was one of incomparable beauty missing: this priceless diamond He has given me today . . . Papa will not be here tomorrow, Céline, I confess that I have cried bitterly . . . I am still crying so that I can scarcely hold my pen.

"You know how intensely I longed to see our dearest father again: but now I feel that it is God's will that he should not be at my feast. God has allowed it simply to try our love. Jesus wishes me to be an orphan . . . to be alone, with Him alone, so that he may unite Himself more closely to me." [23]

To crown the disappointment, the Bishop of Bayeux, who should have presided at the ceremony, was prevented from coming. He delegated to replace him his own brother, Canon Jean-Baptiste Hugonin, who shortly afterwards succeeded M. Révérony as Vicar-General. These circumstances, and several others which, from motives of tact, Thérèse omits to mention in detail, turned this day of graces into a day of tears. "However, she remarks, "I found peace, still peace at the bottom of the chalice." [24]

*   *   *

Recent strokes having paralysed the lower limbs, it had become unnecessary to prolong M. Martin's sojourn at the *Bon Sauveur*. There was nothing more to

[23] Letter to Céline, Sept. 23, 1890.
[24] Autobiography. C. 8.

fear from his wandering mania and Léonie and Céline longed to look after him themselves. Yielding to their pleading, M. Guérin brought the patient to Lisieux on May 10th, 1892. Two days later, they took him to Carmel. He showed he really understood what was said to him, and was suffering only from being unable to express himself. Thérèse has described this pathetic meeting, the only one he had with his nun daughters during his illness: "Oh what an interview! You remember it, Mother! At the moment of parting, he raised his hand and pointing with his finger upward, he remained thus some time, being able to express his thought only by this one word, uttered in a voice full of tears: Heaven!!" [25]

Céline and Léonie were then living in the hospitable house in the *Rue Paul Banaston*, which Jeanne Guérin had left eighteen months previously, to accompany her husband, Doctor La Néele, to Caen. The old man spent a few days there, then they rented a house close by in the *Rue Labbey*. They had only to cross the street in order to enter the Guérin garden by the tradesmen's entrance. The manservant, Desiré, whose wife did all the housework, was exclusively for M. Martin's service. He was a fine young fellow, cheerful and devoted, who had two sisters religious at the *Providence* convent at Lisieux, and could combine hymns and jokes without difficulty.

M. Martin occupied a room on the ground floor. His poor legs were inert and as though fixed stiffly together. The arms remained free, though he had some difficulty in moving them. He had become very thin and trembled like a leaf, since he was also suffering from nephritis. As for his mental faculties, they seemed asleep, with

[25] Autobiography. C. 8.

waking moments in which he showed he could take an interest in everything. His face retained real expression still. He spoke little but at such times he never rambled.

On July 25th, Céline writes: "Father is much the same. I dare not say he is well, for he has had some very bad days; there have been sharp sufferings and fits of weeping which greatly distressed me. Today he is bright, so I breathe again. Yesterday he said to me: 'Oh, children, do pray for me!' Then he asked me to pray also to St. Joseph that he might have a happy death." When on February 20th, 1893, he heard that Soeur Agnès de Jésus had been elected Prioress, he answered with obvious pleasure: "They could not have chosen better." He also showed he was pleased when they bought an invalid carriage; the same which afterwards served for Thérèse during her last illness. In it he spent whole days under the trees in fine weather, listening to the song of the birds.

Visitors and passers-by liked this old man, whose sweetness and docility never failed, and who, even in his affliction, retained a kind of dignity. When, on Corpus Christi, 1892, the procession halted at the altar of repose erected in the vestibule of the Guérin house, the Archpriest of S. Pierre, after Benediction, came into the next room, where the family were all assembled, and rested the monstrance for a prolonged moment on the head of the revered invalid. Tears of emotion trembled in his eyes.

In the summers of 1893 and 1894, M. Martin accompanied his daughters to the Château de la Musse. It was some five miles from Évreux, in the civil parish of Armières, but nearer to Saint Sébastien-de-Morsent, an old aristocratic estate consisting of forty-one hectares, entirely enclosed. M. Auguste David, who owned that

The Story of a Family

he had committed a "folly" in so doing, had restored it splendidly. The clearing had been carried out thoroughly, so as to add the charm of a spacious park to that of the large woods. The house, of dignified aspect, was built on the top of a hill, overlooking perpendicularly the picturesque river Iton. From above the view was incomparable. On the right, the prospect stretched as far as the spire of Conches, more than fifteen miles away. On the left was a wide view of dales, hills and terraced slopes, rising towards Évreux. In front, on the opposite side of the valley, the thick wood echoed the baying of the hounds and the blast of the horns during the hunting season. "The distant sound of the soft and melancholy horn sounded in the twilight."

After the death of the attorney, who had made it his favorite residence, although his wife, whose tastes were more worldly, preferred to the solitude her town house at Évreux, her liveried servants and her brilliant parties, La Musse had descended to the children of Madame Fournet, who used it jointly, living there in turn. The Guérin heirs stayed there from May to August 15th, and the Maudelonde family during the hunting season until October.

So it was that, from 1890, Léonie and Céline lived there, one after the other with their aunt, and in June 1893 it was decided to bring their father himself. Mme. Guérin had not forgotten the last look of Mme. Martin, when the latter had entrusted her bereaved children to her. As for M. Guérin, the family spirit was innate in him with the faith of his ancestors. Both did everything in their power to ease the last days of their brother-in-law. The latter expressed his gratitude in his own way: "In Heaven I will repay you for this."

Céline was ever at his side, his consoling angel.

The Father's Sacrifice

Léonie, in whom a visit to Paray-le-Monial had, despite her two failures, rekindled the longing for the religious life, decided to make a fresh attempt. On June 23rd, 1893, she had entered the Visitation at Caen, and on the following April 6th, in the presence of her sister and the Guérin family, she had received the habit, with the name of Soeur Thérèse Dosithée.

With her noble generosity, Céline remained alone at her post. Something akin to a motherly instinct had been aroused in her for this invalid who looked to her for everything. Thérèse happily interprets her sister's feelings in this verse which she puts on her lips:

> "My youth I offered, glad to cheer
> My father through each lengthening year;
> He was my all—joy, treasure, child most dear;
> Full oft I held him to my breast
> Close pressed."

The time of spiritual outpourings was over. The patient must be spared the slightest emotion. He could no longer apply his attention; it was considered unnecessary to require religious practices from him. Notwithstanding, alone or helped by Desiré, he would sing hymns and canticles in a voice still good, although a little indistinct. Something intellectual survived the ruin of his memories and his old acquired knowledge. The musical talent of his niece, Marie, still retained its hold over him, and he never tired of hearing her play the *Reverie* of Rosellen. He would gladly remain with folded hands, in a sort of rapture gazing at the lovely scenery or listening to the confused murmurs that rose from the earth at sunset. Céline has sketched vividly for her Carmelites one of these restful scenes.

The Story of a Family

"I shall remember all my life his beautiful expression when, in the evening at dusk, in the depths of the wood, we stopped to listen to the nightingale. He listened . . . and with how expressive a look! It was like an ecstasy and something of Heaven was reflected upon his features. Then after a long silence, we were still listening and I saw the tears running down his cheeks. Oh, it was a lovely day!

"Since then he has been less well. This extraordinary consolation could not last, and yet, notwithstanding everything, how peaceful his last days are! Who could have thought it? Our Lord is dealing with him with ineffable loving-kindness."

*　　*　　*

La Musse, it turned out, was to be the last residence of M. Martin. On several occasions he had experienced the characteristic heart attack that ends this kind of malady. On May 27, 1894, it was thought advisable to have him anointed. A more serious attack occurred on Friday, July 27th. M. Guérin happened to be at Lisieux, where at that date he presided at the prize distribution at the boys' school as a rule. His wife hastened to the dying man, with Céline and Doctor le Néele. In the evening of the 28th they summoned the parish priest of Saint Sébastien, the Abbé Chillard, a former military chaplain, very popular at the Château for his originality and his interesting accounts of his many campaigns. He again administered the sacrament of Extreme Unction.

The death agony began on the following morning. Those in the house formed into two parties in order to hear Sunday Mass in turn. The first relay, with the doctor and Desiré, went to Évreux by carriage. Céline remained alone with her aunt by M. Martin's bedside. The oppression increased with a distressing death-rattle, and the limbs gradually grew cold. A little before

The Father's Sacrifice

eight o'clock, Céline repeated aloud the invocation: "Jesus, Mary, Joseph!" What was not her surprise to see the old man's eyes open and fix themselves upon her with a long look which bore, with all his old vivacity, an intense expression of gratitude and love! Was it one of those returns to consciousness which is sometimes noted on the threshold of the other world? Did God allow this consolation in those last moments as a final softening of the terrible trial? The fact remains that Céline believed she saw her father as he had once been.

The light was but passing. A few minutes later the breathing became gasping and then began to fail. M. Guérin, who had rushed to the Château, placed the crucifix to the already cold lips. At a quarter-past-eight, without a struggle, as a child peacefully falls asleep, M. Martin gave up his soul to God. He was nearly seventy-one. He who had so strictly observed the Sunday rest, had gone in the early Sunday morning to enjoy the everlasting rest; to begin the Mass of eternity.

In his *Life of St. Elizabeth*, when alluding to the monuments of mediaeval churches Montalembert has spoken of "those statues, so grave, so moving, so devout, stamped with the peace of the Christian death." A similar impression is left by the photograph taken of M. Martin on his death-bed. The face, thin and worn by suffering, seems as though haloed with a gentleness and a supernatural dignity.

The body was taken to Lisieux where the funeral took place on August 2nd, the feast of *Our Lady of the Angels*, after the Requiem at the cathedral. More moving still was the ceremony that united the family around Thérèse and her sisters in the little Carmelite chapel. Never, perhaps, was a father so mourned, or mourned with such hope.

The Story of a Family

The mortuary card which his daughters designed for the departed, according to the Archpriest of Saint Pierre, who had known him particularly well, was exactly expressive of his personality and life. On the front was a simple biographical notice beneath the Holy Face, surrounded by suitable texts: *Ought not Christ to have suffered and so to have entered into His glory?—Oh adorable Face, that fillest the just with joy for all eternity, turn thy divine glance upon us!—Lord, hide him in the secret of thy Face!*

On the back were quotations from Holy Scripture stressing the value of suffering, and the spiritual fecundity of a household wherein reigned a sense of duty and simplicity of heart. A saying of the dead recalled the joy wherewith, before offering himself, he had offered to God all his family, emphasising the essential virtue which had made his existence so peaceful and had surrounded him, even in the grave, with the glory of a unanimous chorus of sympathy and regret: "His charity was admirable; he never judged anyone, and always found an excuse for the faults of his neighbor."

*   *   *

It was at Alençon that the news of his death called forth the keenest regret. He had retained deep friendships there. Mme. Coulombe, owner of the Château de Lanchal, wrote to his daughters: "In spite of the difference in our ages, I took so much pleasure in your revered father's society. The fact is that saints such as he have something about them that attracts and pleases all around them; they are admired and loved."

The curate of *Notre-Dame* was to testify at the Process of Beatification concerning the reputation for fervor and uprightness which M. Martin enjoyed throughout the town; Père Pichon, who came into close contact with him after 1882, declared in his turn: "The father of the Servant of God was a veritable patriarch; always supernatural, a Christian of the old style. The modern spirit had not touched him." In June 1930, on her death-bed, Mme. Tifenne was to recall his memory: "I am recommending myself to M. Martin. He was so good; I loved him dearly."

Soeur Marie-Gertrude Bigot, formerly a native of Alençon, who entered the Visitation of Le Mans, sent her condolences to Carmel in the following words: "What saintly parents yours were! Mme. Martin, energetic, heroic, was indeed the worthy sister of our ever regretted Soeur Marie Dosithée, and her husband a holy man such as we rarely see. And what a model household! What diligence at work as at prayer!"

The sacrifice was deeply felt in the Guérin family. Under cover of an allegory, M. Guérin expressed his feelings in this passage of a letter addressed to Soeur Marie du Sacré-Coeur: "One day, God showed me an old tree, laden with five beautiful fruits not yet ripe, and ordered me to transplant it into my garden. I obeyed. The fruits ripened one after the other; the Child Jesus, as we are told in a legend of the Flight into Egypt, passed five times and made a sign. The old tree bent down lovingly each time and, without murmuring, let fall one of its fruits into the hand of the Infant God. What a wonderful sight was that new Abraham! What a great soul! We are but pigmies beside that man!"

Returning to the Château de la Musse in May 1895, Marie Guérin wrote to Céline who, in her turn, had entered Carmel: "I made my little pilgrimage as soon as I had alighted from the carriage. I have been in my uncle's room, and there all the memories came back to me. I saw it all again . . . I was overwhelmed with the impression that there, in that chamber, something so great had taken place; that there my uncle had seen God and had been so well received. It seemed to me that I was also going to see something of Heaven, and my uncle has given me this thought when thinking of the particular judgement: "Judge not, and you will not be judged!"

On the anniversary of his death, she returned to these impressions: "I cannot pass by that room without being seized, in spite of myself, with a solemn, calm feeling that speaks to me of the other world and fills my soul. That happens to me very often and without any preparation on my part. I am "seized"—it is the correct word to use. I do not know why but this anniversary, sad in itself, has not at all that effect upon me. I feel so sure that my uncle entered Heaven that day, that I have rather a feeling of happiness when I think of his deliverance. How happy he is now, but he has well deserved it . . . ! Tomorrow, I mean to ask many graces from him and I am sure I shall obtain them on that day. When one recalls, and has imprinted upon one's mind his beautiful expression, calm and full of such happy peace it is impossible not to be led to love God." [26]

But it belonged to the saint to render the supreme eulogy to the dead. It is in the eighth chapter of the

[26] Was it not fitting that in the place where he ended his days, there should be some memorial of him whom Benedict XV, in his discourse of August 14th, 1921, for the Promulgation of the Decree on the Heroism of the Virtues of St. Thérèse of Lisieux, would call "a true model of a Christian parent?" On May 11th, 1899, by common consent, the Guérin and Maudelonde families, all of whose children were settled, sold the property of La Musse which, after passing through several hands, became in 1932 a large sanatorium for tuberculosis patients. With the approval of the Director of this establishment, in July 1938, there was erected beside the Château, overlooking the Iton valley, a bust representing M. Martin with Thérèse beside him, her head affectionately bent towards him.

The Father's Sacrifice

Autobiography that Thérèse has related the posthumous action of M. Martin in favor of his valiant nurse who, freed from all her ties, longed only to fly to Carmel. "Alas! the obstacles seemed insurmountable. One day, when matters were going from bad to worse, I said to Our Lord after Holy Communion: 'Thou knowest, dear Lord, how earnestly I have desired that the trials my father endured should serve as His Purgatory. I long to know if my wish is granted. I do not ask Thee to speak to me, I only want a sign. Thou knowest how much opposed is Sister X. to Céline's entering; if she withdraws her opposition, I shall regard it as an answer from Thee, and in this way I shall know that my father went straight to Heaven.' "

"Oh infinite mercy and ineffable condescension! God, who holds in His hand the hearts of His creatures, and inclines them as He will, deigned to change that Sister's mind. She was the first person I met after my thanksgiving, and with tears in her eyes she spoke of Céline's entrance, which she now ardently desired. Shortly afterwards, the Bishop removed the last obstacles and then you were able, dear mother, without the least hesitation, to open our doors to the poor little exile."

To what purpose add fresh testimony to the funeral eulogies of M. Martin? Is there a higher sign of predestination than this mysterious action from the life beyond attested by the voice of a saint?

NOTE. In the appendix to this work there appear large excerpts from the sermon given by Canon Ducellier at the Clothing of Sr. Geneviève of the Holy Face. On this occasion the eloquent Dean of Trevieres gave what amounted to a funeral oration of M. Martin.

CHAPTER 15

THE CROWNING OF THE FAMILY

The family destiny—Thérèse's spiritual heritage
—family solidarity in the spiritual life—their
share in the glory of the Saint.

THE posthumous glory of the parents is the supernatural influence of their descendants. In this
respect, what household was ever more ennobled
than that of M. and Mme. Martin? "The whole nest
was blessed by them," Céline tells us, "of all their
fledglings they did not lose one." As we have seen, she
herself experienced her father's mediation when, her
filial duty done, she wished to join her sisters at Carmel.
The intransigeant M. Delatroëtte, who had vowed to
prevent the "scandal" of a whole family united in the
same convent, suddenly allowed himself to be won over.
It was the same with certain nuns whose opposition had
seemed insurmountable. In short, on September 14th,
1894, the girl entered upon her postulancy; on the following February 5th, she took the habit under the name
of Soeur Geneviève de la Sainte Face et de Sainte
Thérèse; on February 24th, 1896, she made her profession, and on March 17th of the same year Mgr.
Hugonin gave her the black veil, the Abbé Ducellier,
Dean of Trevières, preaching the sermon.

Would Mme. Martin's desire be granted: "All her

daughters nuns?" Léonie remained in the world, full of distress at her third failure. The system of excessive austerity set up by a Superior too much in love with strict observance, had ended in September 1895 in sending Léonie away from the novitiate, together with all her fellow novices! Received with fatherly kindness by her uncle Guérin, who had himself just devoted his daughter Marie to God, she had overcome her first depression and, side by side with her social duties, had arranged for herself an almost conventual life, watching for a favorable opportunity to take her flight once more to the monastery. There is something poignant in the letters wherein she expresses her disappointed hopes. When one thinks what this soul, thus haunted with a divine nostalgia, had once been, it is impossible not to hail in her the masterpiece of the training of the Martin parents. To fashion the heart of a saint constitutes for the father and mother a triumph which earns for them the homage of posterity. In God's sight, is there not an even more conclusive result, a more authentic victory, in having set right a rebellious character, and awakened fervor in one that had seemed as ground strewn with weeds?

Léonie was indeed the collective triumph of the family. Everything had played its part in her conversion: her mother's last offering, her father's patience, the prayers of the entire household. It was as though they all felt uncomfortable at knowing that she was lagging behind on the way of perfection. In the evening of her life, Thérèse confided to Soeur Marie du Sacré-Coeur: "After my death, I shall make Léonie return to the Visitation, and she will remain there." The prophecy was not long in being fulfilled. On January 28th, 1899, the obstinate postulant once more crossed the threshold of the Visitation of Caen. Falling into the Superior's arms, she cried: "I am here for good." On July 30th, she was clothed and, in memory of the dear saint recently dead, took the name of Soeur François Thérèse. On July 2nd, 1900, she pronounced her vows.

Her religious life which lasted forty years was to be an eager ascent of the way of spiritual childhood. "Thérèse is doing a great work in my soul in humility," she wrote. "The higher I see her raised in glory, the greater need I feel of abasing myself. I thirst to disappear; to be counted for nothing. What a grace!" When infirmities reduced her, in her own words, to the state of "a real crumbling castle," it was with a loving serenity that she carried the burden during several years. The death of a predestined soul crowned this long fidelity. "I have become so little," she confesses to her sisters in Carmel, "that I have the audacity to believe that I shall not go to Purgatory. . . . It is my extreme poverty that gives me this confidence, and I think with joy that when I leave the arms of our Mother, which are so dear and maternal, I shall fall quite naturally into those of Jesus and of the Blessed Virgin, my Mother in Heaven." On June 16th, 1941, in a last loving outburst, Léonie rejoined her family in Heaven. The nuns of her monastery venerate her and pray to her as a saint.

Soeur Marie du Sacré-Coeur had preceded her at the meeting place. The seed of her vocation had never ceased to grow in an indefectible rectitude. Her craving for freedom had been changed into a loving servitude. "I have found Jesus within these four walls," she wrote, "and finding Him, I have found Heaven." Dazzled by the "little way" of her Thérèse, who had at one sitting written for her the pages which, on the morrow would

The Crowning of the Family

constitute the wonderful eleventh chapter of the Autobiography, she had set herself to become ever more
simplified spiritually. The poor manual laborers were
her favorites. Did she not take into her head the idea
—and the important point is that she succeeded—to
initiate into the greatness of the Offering to the Merciful Love old Victoire herself, the devoted ex-maid of
Les Buissonnets?

Broken by rheumatism and crippled with pain, the
"dear godmother" retained to the end, together with
her witty originality, her valiant courage, without any
pose, and her passion for souls. She calmly faced the
divine tryst, which she liked to call "the day of great
mercy." On January 19th, 1940, she passed to her reward, as did her goddaughter, kissing her crucifix in a
last "I love Thee!"

Shall we extend yet further this retrospective survey
of the family destinies? The sick father had many a
time promised his brother-in-law a repayal of gratitude
when he should have reached the world beyond. He
kept his word. A special benediction seemed to rest
upon the household of M. Guérin. Called to the religious life from the time of her First Communion, Marie,
the younger daughter, had heard the call of Carmel on
Thérèse's Veiling day. Five years later, she entered and
in the afternoon of Céline's Veiling she received the
habit and the name of Marie de l'Eucharistie. On
August 15th, 1895, she was placed as a postulant under
the direction of her young cousin, who had been made
assistant novice mistress. Her unalterable patience
amid attacks of scruples and physical sufferings of the
sharpest kind, quickly perfected her in virtues. She
died on April 14th, 1905, after the manner of "little
souls," at the age of thirty-four, leaving as farewell

these words: "I am not afraid to die. Oh, what peace! We should not fear suffering . . . He always gives the strength . . . My Jesus, I love Thee!"

The same impression of peace had marked the end of Mme. Guérin, on February 13th, 1900. M. l'Abbé Ducellier, who assisted her in her last moments, said of her: "In the twenty-five years that I have been a priest, I have never seen anyone receive the last sacraments with such angelic piety. "Feeling death approaching, this noble woman had held in one hand the crucifix used by her saintly niece and in the other her own daughter Marie's Profession candle. "My Jesus," she uttered in a sudden last effort, "I love You. I offer You my life for your priests, as did my little Thérèse de l'Enfant Jesus."

As for M. Guérin, he had joined the ranks of the Carmelite Tertiaries and, in M. Martin's place and stead, had become the great benefactor of the community. Retired from business and enjoying a large fortune, the courageous fighter supported Catholic schools, prevented a Catholic newspaper of the district from suspending publication, and aided by his son-in-law, gave personal service by word and pen in resisting the first assaults of anti-clericalism against religion. He also died a holy death in his sixty-ninth year, on September 26th, 1909.

With the death of Doctor la Néele in 1916, and that of his wife, born Jeanne Guérin, in 1938, there remain no survivors of the inner circle of *Les Buissonnets* and the *Place Thiers* excepting Mère Agnès de Jésus and Soeur Geneviève de la Sainte Face, the two most important witnesses of Thérèse's life; Pauline, her "little mother," and Céline, "the faithful echo of her soul."

* * *

The Crowning of the Family

To the many chapters of this family history, with so many dramatic and happy pages, there was need of an epilogue with the attraction of an apotheosis. It came with the last cradle.

We may smile to see the efforts of a belated group of Voltaireans to present the thaumaturgus of Carmel as the anticipated creation of an ultramontane advertisement. If they are to be believed, a mystic is launched at Lisieux like a "star" at Hollywood, or a celebrity in the studios of the Côte d'Azur. These puerilities are not worth wasting time upon. Even though they be more worthy of respect and marked by evident good faith, we must distrust no less those over-simplified explanations which present sanctity as an improvisation of Providence. Would not "spontaneous generation" here resume its rights?

Facts, objectively considered, register such assertions as false. In the order of grace as in that of nature, although with more flexibility, free-will keeping the last word in short, the law of solidarity reveals its mysterious developments. It reaches its highest point in the immense Communion of Saints. In order to produce a choice flower, how many beds have been carefully cultivated! In order that a soul may reach the peak in triumph, how many previous half ascents! Save for exceptions, wherein the sovereignty of divine intervention is affirmed, it is in a party that we reach the summit; let us say more correctly, it is in a family.

Thérèse of Lisieux is not a legendary being who has suddenly emerged from the mist to enlighten the ways of men. She is a child from our midst. The fruit is all the finer from the fact that the tree is strong and healthy. She well expresses this when commenting upon her "armorial bearings": "The green ground is the blessed family in the midst of which the little Flower grew up," or in this appreciation of her parents: "God gave me a father and mother more worthy of Heaven than of earth."

How can we help recalling in this connection the prophetic encouragement of Sister Marie Dosithée, renewed after each of her sister's losses: "The measure of your sorrows will be that of the consolations reserved for you; for, after all, if, because He is pleased with you, God should give you the great saint you have so desired for His glory, would you not be well repaid?"

Thérèse's sanctity is the culmination of a long lineage in the work of perfection. Heredity conferred upon her, together with the spiritual fire and knightly instinct of her father, the perfect balance, the solid judgement, the never-failing wisdom which characterised Mme. Martin, and which would be so highly necessary to the "doctor" of the way of Spiritual Childhood."

She came, the ninth, to a home often visited by affliction; there she found, in the state of inborn tradition, the spirit of thorough generosity and the sense of sacrifice. As has often been pointed out, it is not merely by chance that the majority of saints have arisen from particularly large families. There is no better school for tempering courage and accustoming a soul to selfless generosity.

Training completed what birth had brought, and to refine this moral physiognomy a wonderful cooperation came into action. Each vied with the other. The mother contributed a sureness of touch to the working out of the pattern she clearly conceived, and made wise use of affective powers. Thérèse had but to draw her inspiration from her own childhood to become subsequently a peerless novice mistress. Pauline guided her ere she helped to develop her vocation. Marie reverently prepared her for her First Communion, calmed the spiritual anxieties of her adolescence, won her confidences as a young nun. Léonie called forth her generosity supremely when, thoroughly upset over her own vocation, she called to the rescue her sister's spiritual support. Céline shared her loving transports and, herself longing for complete self-sacrifice, waived her own right as the elder, and made it possible for Thérèse to enter Carmel at fifteen. Her father instructed his "Queen" in the secrets of union with God. Even the four little departed brothers and sisters helped her, at her request, by their prayers to overcome the scrupulosity under which she had so long labored. The Breviary lessons exactly express the truth when, eulogising the heroism of her virtues, they associate with her the entire family among whom her soul developed.

*   *   *

After this, is there any cause for surprise if we find in the saint's teaching, synthesised, plumbed to their depth, further developed by interior contemplation, the principles that ruled her family life? No doubt, she could say of her way of love: "It is our Lord alone who has instructed me; no book, no theologian has taught it to me . . . I have received no encouragement from anyone, save from Mère Agnès de Jésus." It remains true that God makes use of secondary causes for the accomplishment of His designs, and that the ideal family life in which she was nurtured predisposed Thérèse to realise in its fulness that transcendant family life which plunges the faithful soul into the "society" of the Three divine Persons. We do not weaken the divine originality of the thought by showing how it was remotely prepared on the knees of a truly saintly father and mother.

She who was to reveal to us the "asceticism of littleness" experienced the sweetness of being at home the ninth child, the very last, the benjamin. Without spoiling her, they lavished tender affection upon her; she was "devoured with kisses"; they hastened to help her weakness; they lovingly admired her childish grace. She was keenly aware of the power such weakness gave her. The lesson was not lost upon her. Transferred on to the supernatural plane, it taught her to recognise her powerlessness and to love her nothingness. It was because she had personally lived it that, from the verses of the Gospel, Thérèse grasped intuitively the sovereign power of childhood.

In order to open her heart to the confidence which is the very soul of her doctrine, she had likewise only to transfer to the infinite, in the heart of her Heavenly Father, that loving-kindness which she had read in the hearts of her earthly parents. Francis of Assisi was cast into the arms of God by the curse that shut him out from his family and home. Chased away, disinherited, rejected by his own parents, he sought a higher refuge. "Up till now, I have called Pietro Bernardone my father; henceforth I shall say: *Our Father who art in Heaven.*" By a diametrically opposite experience, Thérèse reached the same height. M. Martin was for her the living incarnation of condescension. From him she hoped for everything; pardon, support, encouragement. She delighted to feel his caresses. If such was the love of a man, what must be the boundless love of Him of whom Tertullian said: *Nemo tam Pater:* No other is a father to such a degree as He.

This deduction of her heart is triumphantly logical.

The Crowning of the Family

Ere long, it will make of the "little Queen" the theologian and martyr of the Merciful Love. The Carmelite will cry: "My Father—God!" *Papa, le Bon Dieu*, in the tone of the child who of yore called her father her "darling King." For her, prayer will not be something complicated, an outburst of fine phrases or great thoughts. She will talk with God as once she talked with M. Martin alone in the Belvedere, or in the meadows beside the river Touques. "I tell God quite simply what I want to tell Him, and He always understands me." She is moved to tears when pondering over the Lord's Prayer: "It is so sweet to call God our Father!" Céline testifies that "she loved God as a child loves its father, with unbelievably affectionate ways." She even made use of the affliction which clouded her father's mind to lose herself ever more in the abyss of eternal love. "God has taken from us him whom we loved so dearly; is it not in order that we may truly say: *Our Father who art in Heaven?* How comforting is that divine word! What vistas it opens up to our sight!"

The spontaneous fruit of this boundless trust was *abandon*. Thérèse had practiced it under the direction of her nearest and dearest. The primacy of the divine will, the joyous conformity to God's good pleasure, constituted, as we have emphasised elsewhere, the very foundation of the spirituality of the *Rue Saint Blaise* and *Les Buissonnets*. That serenity in sorrow, that refusal to contest God's rights, that horror of criticism and bitterness, in a word that fixed determination to adore the providential plan in everything, to bow to its hardest demands without understanding them, what a training in obedience for a supple and docile soul!

Let us add to this direct training, the reflections which the absolute devotion shown her by her parents sug-

gested to the child. Once more, she saw herself at the
foot of the staircase, trying vainly to climb the first
stair, or in front of the swing in which she wanted to
seat herself quickly. The father and mother hastened
at her call, showed concern for her trouble, and taking
her in their arms enabled her to overcome the obstacle
at a bound. What happiness to be very little, and so
the object of such care! Was it not wisdom to surrender herself unresistingly to the embrace of those
loved ones? And this is the beginning of the parable of
the divine "lift," which has become classic. Self-surrender, the handing over of one's whole personality to
the Sovereign Love, leads, sooner or later, to eminent
sanctity. Our Lord draws to Himself the soul that is
wholly *abandoned* to Him and trusts in Him.

One thing only is required of the other party to this
decisive agreement, and that is that the "little one"
should set herself by every means in her power, to
please Him. Not that it is necessary to envisage tremendous sacrifices, to dream of heroic deeds, and wear
herself out with corporal penance. Thérèse has very
decided views on that subject. Her philosophy dates
from long ago. She returns to her first steps. From the
age of three, they had taught her to make use, all day
long, of her "rosary of pious practices." They had
taught her to act from love, and that a "mere nothing"
done from love wins the Heart of Jesus more than
a spectacular performance. How often had she not
watched her father putting a clock together, her mother
"assembling" her *Point d'Alençon*, with the exactitude,
the patience, the care for detail that produces works of
art? This loving application to make a masterpiece of
everything was, so to speak, in her blood, together with
an instinctive distrust of mere show, a horror of osten-

Saint Thérèse of the Child Jesus

Design adopted at Rome for the great banner
of her Canonization, May 17, 1925

Saint Thérèse of
the Child Jesus,
Patroness of
Missions for
the entire world.

Decree of
Pope Pius XI,
December 14, 1927

Saint Thérèse of
the Child Jesus,
Secondary
Patroness of
France,
equal to Saint
Joan of Arc.

Decree of
Pope Pius XII,
May 3, 1944

The Crowning of the Family

tatious insincerity, a contempt for pinchbeck glory.

The Christian realism which bathed her childhood's tranquil days with God's sunlight, would tomorrow impregnate her whole life as a Carmelite, and that in order to uplift it to heroism. It was in her family circle that she had gained her aptitude to do the most ordinary things extraordinarily well. It was there that she found the talisman of which she wrote one day to her cousin Marie: "You ask me to tell you a means of reaching perfection. I know of only one: love." It was there that she learnt her attractive manner of expressing in similes, in concrete comparisons, in homely language, the highest secrets of union with God. As once upon a time Pauline had explained to her, by putting her thimble and her father's drinking glass side by side, the unequal and yet full satisfaction of every one of the elect, so she would find a ball, a top, a kaleidoscope, sufficient to explain the economy of the Kingdom of Heaven in its most arduous aspects. Until her last sigh, a far-off remembrance of the family circle with its homely scenes can be felt hovering over her thought and her behavior.

The Autobiography itself portrays exactly the life led by the subjects of this book. One December evening, in 1894, Thérèse had recalled those memories during recreation with her "little mother" and her godmother. Soeur Marie du Sacré-Coeur found them so enchanting that she urged Mère Agnès de Jésus to order the story-teller to set them down in writing. The Prioress allowed herself to be persuaded and on the eve of her feast day, January 20th, 1896, her child handed her the humble manuscript pages which constitute the first eight chapters of the Autobiography. When tuberculosis was gradually consuming the young nun,

The Story of a Family

Mère Marie de Gonzague, at the earnest request of Mère Agnès de Jésus, bade her take up her pen again to recount her impressions of religious life; and those were to be chapters nine and ten, which, in a conventual setting, would be a commentary on the precept dear above all to M. Martin, of love towards one's neighbor.

In September 1896, seeing her goddaughter failing more and more, and with a presentiment of her glorious destiny, Soeur Marie du Sacré-Coeur begged in a touching note her *ultima verba*.

"My darling little Sister,

I am writing to you not because I have anything to tell you, but in order to have something from you, from you who are so close to God, from you who are his privileged little bride, to whom He entrusts all His secrets . . .

"The secrets between Jesus and Thérèse are very sweet, and I would wish to hear them again. Write me a few words; it is perhaps your last retreat, for our Lord must be longing to pluck His 'ripe grape'; little Thérèse must be longed for indeed up yonder by Jesus and Mary, and Father and Mother, the four little angels and all the saints in Heaven whom she has taken for her family.

"Ask our Lord to love me also, as He has loved His little Thérèse. Oh, that little Thérèse! How she has grown! And yet she is still the little one, still the benjamin, still the darling child whom Jesus—as formerly our poor and dear father—is holding by the hand . . ."

The reply came "by return of post," as soon as the Prioress had given permission. It is this exposition of the Little Way, a gem without rival in the annals of holiness, that forms the sublime conclusion of the book.

Reading these glowing pages, the eldest sister experienced a feeling of sadness at finding herself far, very far from such heights. Could she, in her poverty aspire to

The Crowning of the Family

climb so high? A note of September 16th, 1896, informed Thérèse in terms of deep humility of these regrets and doubts. The very next day, another letter brought the grand focussing, that cry of impassioned faith in infinite Mercy which, whilst reassuring the dear godmother, would open up to souls who feel their spiritual penury the vista of perfection. "Oh, my darling Sister, I beg of you, understand me. Understand that in order to love our Lord, to be His victim of love, the weaker and more wretched we are, the fitter subjects are we for the workings of that consuming and transforming love . . ."[1]

The Autobiography, of which the letter of September 17th, 1896 is only an explanatory appendix, constitutes, as we see, in its genesis and its internal construction, a document of a family character. The prodigious book which would bring about so many conversions, direct so many vocations, and count among the outstanding successes of the publishing world, was originally but a handful of confidences and counsels, gathered up at the bedside of a sick nun by sisters eager to hear them. Men have often dreamed of an ideal picture of the French family. Why seek further? Our forefathers, with their simple, pure customs, would reply unhesitatingly: The Autobiography is such a picture.

*　　*　　*

Thérèse is not only a "doctor" but an "apostle," and again it was from home that she drew her first inspiration. M. and Mme. Martin had prayed so earnestly to obtain from God a priest, a missionary. Their favorite charity was the *Propagation of the Faith*. As she had learnt in their school to relieve the poor and "not to judge," so was she instructed by them concerning that

[1] Letter to Soeur Marie du Sacré-Coeur, at the end of the Autobiography.

433

eminent form of charity which is the longing to radiate Christ. She did not forget the sacrifices they made at home for the conversion of sinners. They had told her —and she herself would act likewise—that her mother had made the heroic offering in favor of the Church Suffering, in Purgatory. She remembered her youthful enthusiasm when she obtained *in extremis* the favor concerning Pranzini. Her Prioress allowed her to have a Mass said annually for the first-born of her converted sinners. "He was my first child," she exclaimed, "and after the exploits of his life he must stand in great need of it!"

She had entered one of those fervent convents, such as the seraphic Thérèse the Great had wished them, where zeal for God's glory energised the prayer of the religious. The missionary tradition had been held in honor there for half a century. As early as 1849, from the prison of Hué, where he was wearing the *cangue* and awaiting execution according to the sentence that condemned him to "the torture of the hundred wounds" Monseigneur Lefebre, Vicar-Apostolic of Cochin China, had set before the Lisieux community his plan of installing the contemplative life in his young mission. With supernatural magnanimity, Mère Geneviève-de-Sainte Thérèse entered into his views. The persecution, which reached its maximum severity under the Emperor Tu-Duc, long hindered the project, but they clung to it obstinately. On July 1st, 1861, Sister Philomena of the Immaculate Conception, professed nun of Lisieux, embarked at Marseilles with three companions. On October 15th, she founded at Saïgon the first monastery, and from this all the Carmels in the Far East have been successively founded.

Thérèse, whose imagination had so often been fired

by the stories of the pioneers and martyrs, and who had shut herself up in a cloister only the better to assist them in their conquests, preserved in her secret heart, as an unrealisable but abiding aspiration, her parents' former longing. She wanted a brother a priest and a missionary. On September 8th, 1890, at the time of her Profession, she begged God to give her a "vocation." And lo! two years before she died, obedience presented her with two "spiritual brothers," Père Roulland of the *Paris Foreign Missions*, whose ideal, compromised for a moment, had suddenly been confirmed on the actual day of her Profession, and the Abbé Bellière, then a seminarist at Bayeux, who was preparing to enter the institute of the *White Fathers*. For the nun, it was an overwhelming joy. "If, as I believe," she wrote to Père Roulland, "my father and mother are in Heaven, they must look down upon and bless the brother whom our Lord has given me. They so longed to have a son a missionary. Could they have lifted the veil that hid the future, they would have seen that it was in me that their longing would be fulfilled."

The prophecy would be realised still more fully than Thérèse conceived at this date. Her missionary vocation unfolded. She pinned the post-card of Su-Tchuen on the wall of the room where she worked. She painted for her brother a picture representing the Sacred-Heart shedding, drop by drop, from its wound on the guilty world the dew of Redemption, and in gold letters she wrote this as a commentary: "Oh divine Blood of Jesus, water our mission; make it bring forth chosen souls!" She eagerly read the life of Père Nempon; she read that of Blessed Théophane Vénard, and developed a real friendship for the gentle martyr. Soon there was question of sending her to the Carmel of Hanoï. For a time, this prospect further increased her fervor but, as she wrote shrewdly, "for that, the scabbard would need to be as strong as the blade, and perhaps the scabbard would be thrown into the sea before it reached Tonkin." What matter? God had always gratified her "immense desires." "If I go to Heaven soon," she writes in confidence to Père Roulland, "I will ask our Lord for permission to visit you at Su-Tchuen, and we shall continue our apostolate together."

One district was too little for her ardent passion. Soon it was over every continent and in the farthest isles that she would "come down" scattering her "shower of roses." It was of all non-Christian lands that the Church would make her the Protectress, side by side with Francis Xavier. To this universal protectorate of the Foreign Missions, entrusted to her by Pius XI, His Holiness Pius XII would on May 3rd, 1944 add an official patronage of that new "missionary country" which today is France.[2] M. and Mme. Martin must rejoice at their ease in eternity. They have not been disappointed of their hope. In giving all their daughters to God, they gave up the hope of posterity according to the flesh. Providence assigned them the glorious counterpart, a posterity according to the spirit, which would cause their memory to be blessed from generation unto generation.

*　　　*　　　*

Here we touch the loftiest aspect of the close solidarity that binds the influence of Thérèse to the calvary

[2] As is known Pope Pius XI had already proclaimed the Blessed Virgin, under the title of her Assumption, principal Patron of France, and St. Joan of Arc secondary Patron. The new patronage conferred upon St. Thérèse of the Child Jesus emphasises the missionary vocation of the Eldest Daughter of the Church, which should, according to Pius X (Allocution of Nov. 29th, 1911), carry, as in the past, the Name of Christ unto all nations and unto the Kings of the earth.

of her parents. Evoking the testimony of the victims of the first world war, and the weight it carries in the destinies of France, Jacques Debout, the poet of *Morts Feconds*, wrote:

"Their eyes are closed; others must open wide,
Close to the fallen tree grows out the shrub.
A night so dark calls for a mighty dawn
Tombs call to cradles."

The verse, bearing in mind only the restoration of the race after a terrible bleeding, is limited to a patriotic appeal to the responsibility of the family. In the supernatural sense, the formula is absolute. It expresses an intangible law of economy and of grace. *"Without shedding of blood,* cries the Doctor of the Nations, *there is no redemption.* In order to live unto God, to communicate the divine life, we must die to ourselves. The harvest of souls has as its necessary prelude,

"The sad, long slumber of the cast grain."

More than that, the destruction of the seed, its corruption, its death. That is the metaphor of our Lord Himself.

In this new light, let us look again at the grandiose panorama of the apostolate of St. Thérèse of Lisieux. In these modern times, she must teach again the way of spiritual childhood, become the mother of a legion of victims all immolated to the God who is Love. She must multiply her conquests throughout all nations, and reawaken faith in the sovereign Goodness. So vast a mission demands a prodigious capital to begin with, a sum total of sacrifices proportioned to the width of the field of action. Here it is that the collective intervention of the Martin family comes in. The mother pours into the treasury the sorrow of her bereavements, the spending of her strength at the bedsides of her sick, the self-abnegation of her whole existence, the agonies of her end in a serenity that never failed. The father contributes the Christian courage of his years as a widower, the *fiat* writ to the vocations of his five daughters, the oblation he made of himself in a last visit to *Notre-Dame* at Alençon.

Incited by such examples, Thérèse and her sisters entered upon their careers of self-abnegation very young. The rosary of little sacrifices passed through the hands of all, and earned a symbolic value. In the Martin family, *offering* became a traditional rite, a habit, a heart-felt need. Each new separation, that of the grave as that of the religious enclosure, made them savor more the sweetness and value of sacrifice.

It entered into God's plan to furnish them with heroic matter for this spirit of self-sacrifice, to make their sensitive powers tread the wine press, in order to associate them more closely with the work of salvation. For this design of mercy, the father was to become the instrument of Providence, a conscious instrument, since he presented himself at the altar of sacrifice. But who could suspect the implication of his holocaust, nor the infinite extensions of its repercussion? It was then a sombre drama, bowing down the head and all his own in a filial submission, in the midst of the most pathetic adversity. Thérèse expressed the thought of them all when, on July 23rd, 1897, she says: "In the hour of our great affliction, when it was my turn to say the versicles in choir, if you knew with what feeling of *abandon*, I used to pronounce the verse: *In te Domine, speravi:* In Thee, Lord, have I hoped!" Consumed by his malady, her "king" had become one of those helpless ones, humiliated and despised, at whom the world jeers but

The Crowning of the Family

whom Christ was to make use of in order to save sinning humanity. The paradox, the scandal, the folly of the Cross, was to be played out to the full once more. It is this simile that is expanded in a last confidence of the dying saint to Mère Agnès de Jésus: "What has been our humiliation for a moment will subsequently be our glory, even in this life."

Pius XI was thinking of all that when he declared to Mgr. Picaud, Bishop of Lisieux: "Say, and make others say that perhaps the spirituality of the Little Saint has been made rather too cloyingly sweet. Yet how strong and virile it is! St. Thérèse of the Child Jesus is a *great man*, whose whole teaching is one of renunciation." Captivated by the charm of the Carmelite, her flowery language, her smile—people of the world have readily extolled her as a prototype of perfection "reduced." The "little way" has become synonymous with the "broad way." Perhaps this biography will help to do away with this dangerous distortion, which is an insult to the Gospel. There are no roses without thorns at *Les Buissonnets*, any more than at the Portiuncula. The crucifix of Carmel places the physiognomy of Thérèse in its true light, just as the steep slope of Alverno casts its austere shadow over the winsome figure of the Patriarch of Assisi. It costs the saint and her parents heavily to draw so many hearts to the Eternal Love.

*   *   *

Is there not shining out from these souls that power of the Resurrection which we feel so strongly in our hearts when we approach the cemetery on the east side of Lisieux? It is picturesque as could be wished, this cemetery nestling amid the beauties of nature. To reach it, we must follow an ascending road, beneath a vault of greenery, between two rows of hoary-headed trees, mixed with knotty trunks and hollowed-out skeleton forms. On either side, the rich Norman meadow-land stretches out to the skyline, among the fields graze the fat cattle, and the broken shafts of the twisted apple stand out. It is there, at the end of the avenue, overlooking the valley of the Orbiquet, opposite the last wooded hill crests that surround the town, that a whole forest of crosses and mortuary chapels stretches out in terraces over the slope of the hill. The privet hedges with hazels at intervals preserve the straight line. The sombre hue of the rock shows up in places in the grassy slopes. We feel a sense of recollection pervading the place. Only the call of the cuckoo, the strident chirp of the cricket, or the trills of the birds flying about above, break the peace-giving silence where all noise dies away.

The Carmelite enclosure stands out half-way up. A statue guards it: that of Thérèse in ecstasy. On the plinth is a cry of gratitude taken from her Autobiography, at once her *Magnificat* and her *Nunc Dimittis:* "Oh, my God! You have surpassed my expectation, and I would hymn Your mercies!" Her body left this spot on that day of triumph, March 26th, 1923, but her spirit still seems to linger amid these wooden crosses that once overshadowed her coffin.

Her parents had preceded her in the autumn of 1894. After her father's death, M. Guérin had the mortal remains of her mother, their four young children prematurely deceased, their grandmother Martin and grandfather Guérin, translated, so that they might rest with those of the head of the family. The monument that covers the family vault is situated a short distance from that of Thérèse, only a little lower. It is impressive

The Crowning of the Family

in its austerity. On a pedestal, surrounded by a wrought iron chain, stands a heavy cross of granite. Slender white cedars form a solemn setting for it. Short inscriptions call for thought. *O Crux Ave, Spes unica!* . . . *"The memory of the just shall be blessed"* "Here rest the parents of the Saint of Lisieux, Thérèse of the Child Jesus."

There is something eloquent in the proximity of the two tombs. One likes to associate them in a common pilgrimage, and here ponder upon those lines which Thérèse addressed to her cousin Jeanne, to console her upon entrance into religion of the sister whom she dearly loved:

"Remember that God has promised the hundredfold to him who for love of Him has left father, or mother or sister . . . I know that these words are usually applied to religious, yet I think in my inmost heart that they were uttered also for the generous parents who, for God's sake, make the sacrifice of children they hold dearer than themselves." [3]

For M. and Mme. Martin, after so many and such hard trials, what a magnificent recompense! They are submerged in the glory that bears away their youngest child. To the official cultus which the Church has decreed to her, is added the homage rendered to the authors of her being in private devotion. The letters that come to the Carmel attest that this confidence of humble folk is often rewarded, as though God has willed to communicate to the parents a ray of the power so lavishly conferred upon their child.

On May 17th, 1925, in the evening of the canonisation of the "little Queen," whilst at Rome, for the first time since 1870, the façade of Maderna and the cupola

[3] Letter to Mme. La Néele, August 1895.

441

The Story of a Family

of Michael-Angelo were lighted up with their thousand lamps, the carillon of *Notre-Dame d'Alençon*, the bourdon of *Sainte Eulalie* of Bordeaux, and the timid country bell of *S. Denis-sur-Sarthon* vibrated in unison. Through these bronze voices, the virginal soul of the Flower of Carmel and the heroically faithful souls of those who deserved to give her to the world communed with one another in joy.

CONCLUSION

The Martin Home and its Contribution to the Needs of the Modern Family.

WHILST we were trying to describe the intimate life of the *Rue du Pont Neuf*, the *Rue Saint Blaise* and *Les Buissonnets*, a thought kept recurring to us. In the eyes of our fellow countrymen, would not this household appear to be an anachronism? Would there not be those who to describe it would make use of the word "jail" which the advocates "freedom" dared formerly to apply to the marriage union with its sacramental seal? Would not so lofty an example give them vertigo?

It is a fact that the modern man and woman have thought to break their chains by undermining the divine foundations of the family. The French Revolution gave the first blow of the pickaxe when it introduced Civil Marriage, which in practice denies the religious character of the conjugal contract. Once torn away from God, and committed to the hands of men, the institution has quickly succumbed to the wild storm of the passions. The very bases have been swept away. It was the logical result. By what right does any human

443

The Story of a Family

lawgiver claim to discipline the most imperious of instincts?

The unity of the house is *Slavery*. Is it not cruelty to reduce to this degree the innumerable urgings of a sensitive heart?

The indissolubility of the marriage bond is *Slavery*. How can we refuse to broken families the "safety-valve" of divorce?

The marriage bond itself is *Slavery*. Must love, "the child of Bohemia," know any law? "Your body is your own"; so runs the motto of the future.

The family is *Slavery*. It is an inconvenient incumbrance, which hinders the indulgence of the senses. An only child may be tolerated, to carry on the name! But away with those large families that impose abnegation where all should be licence!

The education of children is *Slavery*. Let the State see to it! Since Jean-Jacques Rousseau, has not the State been the universal father, responsible for the bringing up of the race?

The marital authority is *Slavery*. According to a certain type of feminist, the limitations of the sexes must give way. The type of the perfect woman is henceforth "the man spoilt"!

The pleasure of the couple, their absolute egoism, the precarious adventure: there we have the new morality, without obligation or sanction; the substitute for the stable contract and mutual giving of the parties, each to the other. Jules Guesde, in his *Socialist Catechism*, published in 1878, thus crudely defined it: "Ought not the family to be preserved? No, for up to the present it has been one of the forms of ownership, and not the least odious . . . The interest of the species, as much as the interest of the elements that enter into the com-

Conclusion

position of the family, demand that this state of things should disappear."

What humanity has become as a result of this philosophy, events have proclaimed with fierce eloquence. How is it possible to avoid war, when riches are piled up in a depopulated land, making of the latter, at one and the same time, a temptation and a victim that cannot defend itself? How can we avoid overproduction and unemployment, if the number of consumers diminishes from year to year? How look after the old, the sick, the infirm, if there are no longer the young to replace them? How train characters, find leaders, if the refusal to face life, by becoming universal, stamps out initiative, the willingness to take risks, and the spirit of enterprise? When all the stones are worn out and undermined from within, the building may stand for a time and retain its brilliant exterior, but it is inexorably on the way to ruin. A country is worth what its families are worth. It lives by their courage and it suffers with them. When they abandon it, the statisticians may inscribe in their graphs, as the inevitable result, decline, collapse, and the ultimate disappearance of the nation.

And will they, at least, have reaped the harvest of happiness when they have sacrificed their country? What have they gained by learning the art of loving in the schools of the "stars" who people the cinema, the radio and the stage? In the chronicles of the films, in the provocative pages of scandalous novels, crimes committed from passion form the escort of love. From all the hospitals rises the gloomy lament of those whom Brieux called the "Damaged Goods" of society. We are rapidly returning to the paganism in which woman was without honor, enslaved to men's lusts and to heavy

The Story of a Family

manual labor. Unbridled pleasure debases and darkens the mind. Humanism is effacing itself before sexuality.

Is not the gloomy destiny of the household of Karl Marx a mournful symbol of this enchantment? Of the three daughters of the doctor of Socialism, two perished as suicides, the first after having endured ill-treatment from a disciple of her own father, who was, moreover, a fervent follower of Darwin; the second, after having linked her fate with that of the militant Socialist, Paul Lafargue, who poisoned himself and her, leaving these words of explanation: "We are dying because life has no further joys to give us." The sentence is eloquent of the chaos of souls without God. Pleasure has driven away joy: passion has ousted love. Beneath its outward veneer of civilisation, this world, wherein men amuse themselves, is nothing more than a lethal chamber. Paul Bureau has drawn up an overwhelming indictment on this matter in his fine book: *L'Indiscipline des Moeurs*. He published it immediately after the last war. What would he say twenty-five years later?

On the ruins of the ancestral home, the idolatry of the State, stigmatised of old by Pius IX, has been established. There is much talk today of a crusade for the rights of human personality. Is not the family the cradle and the centre of personal life? Overturn that, and you remain fenced only by the "individual atom" and the Moloch State which subjugates and devours it. Only the family can resist this totalitarian power, which Nietzsche himself once called "the coldest of cold monsters." Back to the family, or else "All for the State." There is no other alternative. Pius XII affirms this when, in his messages, he claims "the living space for the family."

Having drawn up this balance sheet, which invites

446

Conclusion

the partisans of "free love" to be less cocksure, perhaps we shall be justified in proposing to our contemporaries, as a model, a home where there reigned supreme what is sometimes called, with a touch of irony, "the good old moral tradition."

* * *

In the Martin home, everything bowed to the law of God. They never sought to escape therefrom. The crucifix that looked down upon their family life was no mere conventional ornament. In every room in the house, it reminded them of the presence of the Master, His sovereignty, and the obligation to observe exactly the Ten Commandments and the Gospel teaching. There love was never something contraband or something that left free play to every instinct. A Sacrament in the strict sense, from the first it took on a quasi-religious character. The family was a sanctuary where God reigned; a school wherein souls made progress; a citadel wherein the race gathered and, if necessary, entrenched itself with its reserves of virtue. These constraints were felt, certainly, but that servitude had its greatness, its high dignity. Has it not been said of husband and wife that by vocation they are: "Two hands folded in an eternal adoration or bound in an eternal reprobation?"

It remains that the majority are put off by these high ideals. Hidden at the back of their minds, or bluntly expressed, the insidious objection rises: "In the last analysis, Thérèse's parents had voluntarily denied themselves every earthly satisfaction. They were slaves to family duty. Trials overwhelmed them from every side. We may grant that they gained posthumous glory, but none the less their life on earth was a calvary. Such is perhaps the way of heroes and saints, but hu-

447

manity in the main is not composed of saints or of heroes. Let us honor them and pass by."

The argument is specious, but it is unsound. I turn to the letters of Mme. Martin, the confidences of her husband, the recollections of their children. Everywhere and even amid tears, I find that it witnesses to a peace, an interior gladness which can spring only from true happiness. Work, sickness, death strike them repeated blows; joy always emerges. Obviously, when all is reckoned up optimism has the last word. We are here confronted with what is commonly called a happy home.

And the secret of this happiness? Is it the peace of a good conscience, the calm of union with God, the all-powerful aid of His grace? It is true, but also—and this is worth analysing, since it will weigh more with prejudiced minds—there was the development of human love and the overflowing joys of a home where life was not afraid of spending itself generously.

The love of the husband and wife was not less tender because it was stamped with the seal of duty. Far from weakening human love, divine charity deepens and elevates it to a purer essence. It safeguards it from the caprices and vagaries of the flesh. It initiates it into the mutual giving and taking and into unlimited devotedness. It is only egoism that destroys conjugal love. God is not jealous of it, for He is its first author. He asks only that men shall respect the end of this love. To love in order is to develop. To love in violation of the Creator's plan is to pervert nature; to "sabotage" a great thing; to devote the senses and the heart, after a passing intoxication, to disorder, corruption, and ultimate powerlessness.

We may say the same of the yoke of family responsi-

Conclusion

bilities, which our contemporaries hold in horror. M.
and Mme. Martin did not seek to escape these. They
faced them squarely, joyfully, generously. They took
their state such as it was, with its unavoidable burdens
and its sublime compensations. If they knew the sorrows of mourning, the Christian education which they
carried out in masterly fashion spared them the most
cruel of all afflictions—that of watching a loved child
weaken morally and collapse. Their children became
their pride, their consolation, their support. Each arrival brought to them a power of renewal and, as it
were, an added spiritual richness. Can we imagine the
power for happiness of such an addition; the sweetness
of feeling oneself surrounded to such a degree by gratitude and filial affection?

Granted, it will be replied, this family was a great
success. But a day came when the vessel was wrecked.
Human affections were lost at a monastery grille where
all the children were stranded. Has it not been said of
the cloister—and it is Père Petitot who cites the words
—that it is a place "where men come together without
choosing their companions, live without knowing them,
and die unregretted?"

Let us grant to the sons of Voltaire, who venture upon
this witticism, that religious Profession does involve a
real sacrifice of love. Not only does it do away with the
prospect of marriage, but it erects at least a moral bar-
rier between members of the same family. We think of
the emotion of the last kiss exchanged on earth between
Thérèse and her father. That is not all. In the convent
where Thérèse found again her two elder sisters, was she
to enter upon a close intimacy with them, which would
be a sort of compensation for her heart, a resumption of
the sensitiveness she had overcome? She herself informs

us on this point: "No, I did not enter this blessed Carmel in order to live with my sisters. On the contrary, I foresaw clearly that this must be a source of great suffering when one was resolved to allow nothing to nature." [1] The company she sought was that of the nuns who were least congenial to her. When her "little mother" became Prioress, of all the community it was Thérèse who enjoyed fewest interviews with her. When her cousin, Marie Guérin, entered the convent, although she had been deprived for a year of all intercourse with them in the parlor on account of certain circumstances, she abstained from approaching the enclosure door to see her relations. She accepted the prospect of severing all links with home and exiling herself in the Carmel of Hanoï. When the project was abandoned on account of her health, she consented to the eventual departure— more crucifying still—of Mère Agnès de Jésus and Soeur Geneviève for Saïgon.

"Oh," she writes, "I would not have said a word to keep them, although my heart was breaking at the thought of the trial that awaited them." [2] Some will protest at these words: "A barbarous asceticism, that drugs the affections!" In order to love God, must we become inhuman? With her sense of perfect balance, Thérèse sets all in order: "When it gives itself to God, the heart loses none of its natural affection. On the contrary, this affection becomes greater by becoming purer and more divine." [3] It is not a question of mutilating but of pruning. The sap is not dried up; the flow, for a moment restrained, rushes forth more powerful and more fruitful. To the phase of compression succeeds

[1] Autobiography. C. 9.
[2] *Ibid.*
[3] *Ibid.*

Conclusion

one of free expression, thus described by the saint: "Oh how glad I am that from the beginning of my religious life I deprived myself of it! I already enjoy the reward promised to those who fight bravely. I no longer feel the need of refusing myself these consolations, for my heart is fixed on God. Because it has loved Him only, it has grown, little by little, and now it can give to those who are dear to Him a far deeper and truer love than if it were centred in a barren and selfish affection." [4]

Adjusted, disciplined, set in its right place, sensible affection takes flight anew. It shows itself in those real masterpieces, the letters written by Thérèse to Céline and to all her family; in the farewells of the dying nun to Léonie and her uncle Guérin, and her predilection for the Blessed Théophane Vénard, a loving soul if ever there was one, in which connection she said: "I also love my family very much. I cannot understand saints who do not love their families!" That does not prevent her, however, about the same time, from advising her sisters elsewhere not to "lead a family life," that is, not to settle down comfortably into the too narrow limits of its natural affections. Everything must be subordinated to that final vision which is described in the fourth chapter of the Autobiography: 'When my thoughts run on in this way, my soul loses itself as it were in the infinite. I seem already to touch the heavenly shore and to receive our Lord's embrace. I fancy I can see our Blessed Lady coming to meet me, with my father and mother, my little brothers and sisters; and I picture myself enjoying true family joys for all eternity."

We are far here from the drying-up, or glacial indif-

4 Autobiography. C. 10.

ference, with which a certain sort of literature reproaches the monks and nuns of legend. Death itself does not stop the expression of such love. In a particularly delicate way, the saint's relatives would share in the Shower of Roses. Marie received a heavenly kiss from her godchild; during one night of physical torture she perceived her at her side, composing the poor limbs stiff with rheumatism, and replacing the blanket on the numbed shoulder. Léonie saw a luminous hand lighting up her breviary and rousing her fervor. Pauline and Céline smelt the fragrance of incense. After an unusually painful attack, Mme. Guérin declared to those around her: "I was suffering very much, but my little Thérèse has lovingly watched over me. All night I felt her close to my bed. Several times she caressed me, which gave me extraordinary courage."

In 1915, when Léonie, became Soeur Françoise-Thérèse at the Visitation, was summoned to Lisieux to give evidence before the ecclesiastical tribunal, sitting at the Carmel, the four sisters lived over again, entranced, their memories of Alençon and Lisieux. Soeur Marie du Sacré-Coeur recalls this indescribable meeting:

"We were all four sitting on the steps near the infirmary. The sky was blue and cloudless. Suddenly I lost all sense of time. The days of our childhood, the *Buissonnets*, all seemed to me one instant. I saw Léonie beside us and the past and the present were mingled in one single moment. The past seemed a flash to me; I seemed to live already in an eternal present, and I understood eternity, which is all entire in a single instant."

It was the soul of the family which recollected itself to enjoy in silence the sweetness of belonging wholly to

Conclusion

God. Living and dead were in communion in the dawning glory of Thérèse. Lights and shadows, labors, sorrows and joys, all were fused into a single gaze of gratitude and trustful self-surrender. The children gathered together sang, with the glory of God also the praise of the parents who had reared them in the school of sanctity. Whosoever, be he ever so imbued with modernism, could have penetrated the secret of this scene of family intimacy, would have spontaneously repeated the cry of astonishment of the pagans who beheld the Primitive Church: "See how they love one another!" It is the lesson bequeathed to the world by this ideal home: the supreme art of finding happiness in a love without egoism, wholly informed with the love of God.

THE PRAYER OF A SAINT'S CHILD

Rememberest thou that erstwhile here below,
  To care for us was thy sole happiness;
O hear thy children praying, and bestow
  Thy fond protection—deign each one to bless.
Thou findest in the heavens our mother loved at rest,
She hath been long already in country of the blessed.
    As in that sacred land
    Ye both together stand,
      Watch o'er us now.

Rememberest thou thy Mary, O so dear,
  Her ardent spirit closest to thy heart:
Rememberest how thy life she filled with cheer,
  As love and charm and joy she did impart.
For God thou wouldst renounce her presence sweet and mild,
Blessing the hand that offered such sorrow through thy child.
    Thy "diamond" most rare,
    Ever more radiant, fair,
      Remember thou.

Remember'st thy "fine pearl" so softly bright;
  Seeming a weak and timid Lamb to thee;
She leadest now the flock on Carmel's height,
  Counting on strength divine her strength to be:
Behold her, "Mother" now of thine own children here.
Come, guide her steps below, who was to thee so dear:
    Leave not thy heav'n on high,
    But be to Carmel nigh,
      Remember thou.

Remember'st thou that earnest, pleading prayer
  Offered for thy third child with fond intent,

The Prayer of a Saint's Child

God heard it! . . . earth for her was bleak and bare,
 A place of exile and of banishment.
The Visitation hid her far from worldly eyes;
She loved the Lord, and waves of peace arise;
  Her ever burning sighs,
  Her ardent, yearning cries,
  Remember thou.

Remember'st thou Céline, thy faithful one,
 Who was a ministering angel unto thee,
When the sad Face divine looked down upon
 Thy chosen soul, to test it gloriously.
Thou reignest now in heaven, accomplished is her task;
To Jesus she hath given the life His love doth ask.
  Protect thy child today.
  How often doth she say,
  Remember thou.

O then remember thou thy "little Queen,"
 When tender love o'erflowed her heart for thee;
Remember how her wavering steps would lean
 Upon thy guiding hand for surety.
Papa, remember thou, in childhood's happy days
Her innocence for God thou wouldst preserve always.
  Her ringlets fair and bright,
  Which gave thee such delight,
  Remember thou.

Rememberest thou in terraced Belvedere,
 Oft wouldst thou seat her gently on thy knee,
Murmur a prayer, then drawing her anear,
 Wouldst cradle her with soft sung melody;
Heaven she saw reflected in thy face,
When, pensive, thou wert gazing into space.
  'Twas of eternity
  Thy song was wont to be,
  Remember thou.

The Story of a Family

Rememberest thou that Sunday fair and bright,
    When, pressing her to thy paternal heart,
Thou gavest her a floweret pure and white,
    Permitting her for Carmel to depart.
O Father, dost recall how when her soul was tried,
Thy proven love sincere was ever at her side;
      At Rome as at Bayeux,
      Thou pointest heaven to her,
        Remember thou.

Remember'st thou the Holy Father's hand
    Laid in the Vatican upon thy brow;
The mystery then thou couldst not understand.
    It was the seal divine—we know it now.
Thy children look above in reverent prayer to thee,
They praise, they bless thy cross, thy bitter agony.
      Upon that glorious brow,
      Shining in heaven now,
      Nine lilies flower!

(This translation, as also that of all the other quoted verses of the Saint, is that made by the Carmelites of Santa Clara, California, U. S. A.)

APPENDIX

(Excerpt of the discourse given by Canon Ducellier, Dean of Trevieres [Calvados], at the Clothing of Sr. Genevieve of the Holy Face, February 5, 1895)

"My dear Sister, it seems fitting that at this time, when you are on the threshold of the Cloister, I speak for a moment about your vocation. It seems to me that I owe this to the memory of that venerable Patriarch, your well-loved father, whom we remember on this solemn occasion; I owe it to the edification of the faithful here assembled; indeed, I owe it to all. Those unworldly persons who suffer resignedly the deprivation of even that which is most dear to their hearts because it is asked by God, are very rare; it is truly meet and just that, when we meet such a person, we speak of him.

"First of all I should like to point out that the decision to take your place among these virgin Brides of Christ was agreed upon between you and God a long time ago. Seven years ago you spoke of it for the first time to him who rightfully merited all your filial devotion. There was some question, at that time, of whether or not to send you to Paris for further training at painting. More desirous of perfecting the art of painting, in your soul, the image and model of all perfection, our Saviour Jesus Christ, you seized the favorable moment for making known your wishes for the future. You knew, without doubt, that the venerable father in whom you were going to confide was, by his unusual sensibility, by the power and vigor of his faith, well worthy to receive it. As a matter of fact, scarcely had you spoken —in words that he could not possibly have anticipated—than he took you in his arms and pressed you to his heart. 'What am I that God should shower me with such honor!' he exclaimed. 'I am truly an exceedingly happy father.' And he asked you to come with him immediately to offer yourselves before the tabernacle. 'Come—let us go together to thank God for all the special graces he has given our family.' What cooperation with grace! The Sacred Heart of Jesus must have trembled with joy! The Sanctuary angels must have been filled with admiration at the sight of this father who, absolutely forgetful of himself came to offer of all that remained to him, his most cherished possession; this father whose fervent and valiant faith recalled to mind that of the Patriarchs of old.

"It was thus that this truly enlightened soul fully understood the great question of vocations. 'God does me the honor of asking for all my children. I give them with joy. If I possessed anything better, I would be eager to offer them as well.'

"Even though he had nothing better to offer—certainly nothing more dearly loved—he had at least one thing more intimate—himself. He had given everything; there remained only the offering of himself; he made that offer. 'God,' he said one day to one of your sisters with that charming simplicity characteristic of great souls, 'God grants me too many consolations. It is too much for this earth. I have asked the Lord to cease showering me with favors. One cannot get to Heaven that way. One cannot get there without suffering and I have offered myself . . .'

"Who of us can not see in these words the language

Appendix

of the great victims of Divine Love. 'I offer myself.' When these sentiments are expressed by those worthy of Him, God sometimes takes them at their word and, for their eternal glory as well as for the good of the entire world, he grants them their wishes in a way which disconcerts some of us, with our frail human wisdom, but which will one day be the admiration and the joy of the elect. He leads them along the road of sorrows as His Divine Son was lead to Calvary, to be ground under the pressure of unimaginable torments.

"My dear Sister, your saintly father offered himself as a sacrifice—God judged the victim worthy of Himself. Suffering, accepted with the heroism and tranquility of the Christian, which refers everything to God and accepts, in advance everything which comes from His paternal hand—Suffering came—pitiless—to crown with its diadem his noble brow. How well you understood then where your duty lay—by his side. You remained long years—night and day, until the last sigh, until the tomb. It is thus that the Lord, by allowing your father to grow in grace before Him and his angels —this father, whom you surrounded with every care and the most tender pity—brought about your preparation for the life of devotion and sacrifice that is the lot of the daughters of Saint Therese."*

---

*"Saint Therese"—that is, St. Teresa of Avila (1515-1582), great reformer of the Carmelite Order. —*Editor*, 1994.

If you have enjoyed this book, consider making your next selection from among the following . . .

Prices guaranteed through December 31, 1995.

Miraculous Images of Our Lady. *Cruz* 20.00
Raised from the Dead. *Fr. Hebert* 15.00
Love and Service of God, Infinite Love. *Mother Louise Margaret*. 10.00
Life and Work of Mother Louise Margaret. *Fr. O'Connell* 10.00
Autobiography of St. Margaret Mary 4.00
Thoughts and Sayings of St. Margaret Mary 3.00
The Voice of the Saints. *Comp. by Francis Johnston* 5.00
The 12 Steps to Holiness and Salvation. *St. Alphonsus* 7.00
The Rosary and the Crisis of Faith. *Cirrincione & Nelson* 1.25
Sin and Its Consequences. *Cardinal Manning* 5.00
Fourfold Sovereignty of God. *Cardinal Manning* 5.00
Dialogue of St. Catherine of Siena. *Transl. Algar Thorold* 9.00
Catholic Answer to Jehovah's Witnesses. *D'Angelo* 8.00
Twelve Promises of the Sacred Heart. (100 cards) 5.00
St. Aloysius Gonzaga. *Fr. Meschler* 10.00
The Love of Mary. *D. Roberto* 7.00
Begone Satan. *Fr. Vogl* 2.00
The Prophets and Our Times. *Fr. R. G. Culleton* 11.00
St. Therese, The Little Flower. *John Beevers* 4.50
St. Joseph of Copertino. *Fr. Angelo Pastrovicchi* 4.50
Mary, The Second Eve. *Cardinal Newman* 2.50
Devotion to Infant Jesus of Prague. *Booklet* .... .75
Reign of Christ the King in Public & Private Life. *Davies* 1.25
The Wonder of Guadalupe. *Francis Johnston* 6.00
Apologetics. *Msgr. Paul Glenn*. 9.00
Baltimore Catechism No. 1 .... 3.00
Baltimore Catechism No. 2 .... 4.00
Baltimore Catechism No. 3 .... 7.00
An Explanation of the Baltimore Catechism. *Fr. Kinkead* 13.00
Bethlehem. *Fr. Faber* 16.50
Bible History. *Schuster* 10.00
Blessed Eucharist. *Fr. Mueller* 9.00
Catholic Catechism. *Fr. Faerber* 5.00
The Devil. *Fr. Delaporte* 5.00
Dogmatic Theology for the Laity. *Fr. Premm* 18.00
Evidence of Satan in the Modern World. *Cristiani* 8.50
Fifteen Promises of Mary. (100 cards) 5.00
Life of Anne Catherine Emmerich. 2 vols. *Schmoger* 37.50
Life of the Blessed Virgin Mary. *Emmerich* 15.00
Manual of Practical Devotion to St. Joseph. *Patrignani* 13.50
Prayer to St. Michael. (100 leaflets) 5.00
Prayerbook of Favorite Litanies. *Fr. Hebert* 9.00
Preparation for Death. (Abridged). *St. Alphonsus* 7.00
Purgatory Explained. *Schouppe* 13.50
Purgatory Explained. (pocket, unabr.). *Schouppe* 7.50
Fundamentals of Catholic Dogma. *Ludwig Ott* 20.00
Spiritual Conferences. *Tauler* 12.00
Trustful Surrender to Divine Providence. *Bl. Claude* 4.00
Wife, Mother and Mystic. *Bessieres* 7.00
The Agony of Jesus. *Padre Pio* 1.50

Prices guaranteed through December 31, 1995.

Prices guaranteed through December 31, 1995.

Brief Catechism for Adults. *Cogan* 9.00
The Cath. Religion—Illus./Expl. for Child, Adult, Convert. *Burbach.* 9.00
Eucharistic Miracles. *Joan Carroll Cruz* 13.00
The Incorruptibles. *Joan Carroll Cruz* 12.00
Pope St. Pius X. *F. A. Forbes* 6.00
St. Alphonsus Liguori. *Frs. Miller and Aubin* 15.00
Self-Abandonment to Divine Providence. *Fr. de Caussade, S.J.* .. 16.50
The Song of Songs—A Mystical Exposition. *Fr. Arintero, O.P.* .. 18.00
Prophecy for Today. *Edward Connor* 4.50
Saint Michael and the Angels. *Approved Sources* 5.50
Dolorous Passion of Our Lord. *Anne C. Emmerich* 15.00
Modern Saints—Their Lives & Faces. *Ann Ball* 18.00
Our Lady of Fatima's Peace Plan from Heaven. *Booklet* .... .75
Divine Favors Granted to St. Joseph. *Père Binet* 4.00
St. Joseph Cafasso—Priest of the Gallows. *St. John Bosco* 3.00
Catechism of the Council of Trent. *McHugh/Callan* 20.00
The Foot of the Cross. *Fr. Faber* 15.00
The Rosary in Action. *John Johnson* 8.00
Padre Pio—The Stigmatist. *Fr. Charles Carty* 13.50
Why Squander Illness? *Frs. Rumble & Carty* 2.00
The Sacred Heart and the Priesthood. *de la Touche* 7.00
Fatima—The Great Sign. *Francis Johnston* 7.00
Heliotropium—Conformity of Human Will to Divine. *Drexelius* .. 11.00
Charity for the Suffering Souls. *Fr. John Nageleisen* 15.00
Devotion to the Sacred Heart of Jesus. *Verheylezoon* 13.00
Who Is Padre Pio? *Radio Replies Press* 1.50
Child's Bible History. *Knecht* 4.00
The Stigmata and Modern Science. *Fr. Charles Carty* 1.25
The Life of Christ. 4 Vols. H.B. *Anne C. Emmerich* 55.00
St. Anthony—The Wonder Worker of Padua. *Stoddard* 4.00
The Precious Blood. *Fr. Faber* 11.00
The Holy Shroud & Four Visions. *Fr. O'Connell* 2.00
Clean Love in Courtship. *Fr. Lawrence Lovasik* 2.50
The Prophecies of St. Malachy. *Peter Bander* 5.00
St. Martin de Porres. *Giuliana Cavallini* 11.00
The Secret of the Rosary. *St. Louis De Montfort* 3.00
The History of Antichrist. *Rev. P. Huchede* 3.00
The Douay-Rheims New Testament. *Paperbound* 13.00
St. Catherine of Siena. *Alice Curtayne* 12.00
Where We Got the Bible. *Fr. Henry Graham* 5.00
Hidden Treasure—Holy Mass. *St. Leonard* 4.00
Imitation of the Sacred Heart of Jesus. *Fr. Arnoudt* 13.50
The Life & Glories of St. Joseph. *Edward Thompson* 13.50
Père Lamy. *Biver* 10.00
Humility of Heart. *Fr. Cajetan da Bergamo* 7.00
The Curé D'Ars. *Abbé Francis Trochu* 20.00
Love, Peace and Joy. (St. Gertrude). *Prévot* 5.00
The Three Ways of the Spiritual Life. *Garrigou-Lagrange, O.P.* .. 4.00

At your Bookdealer or direct from the Publisher.

Prices guaranteed through December 31, 1995.

NOTE ON THE CAUSES OF CANONIZATION OF LOUIS MARTIN AND ZÉLIE (GUÉRIN) MARTIN

(Information received by the Publisher in April, 1994 from the Office of the Postulator General of the Discalced Carmelites, Rome.)

On March 26, 1994, Pope John Paul II proclaimed the "heroic virtue" of the Servants of God Louis Martin and Zélie (Guérin) Martin; they are now therefore known as "Venerable."

The Causes of canonization were first processed separately in the dioceses of Bayeux-Lisieux and Sées from 1957 to 1960 and were then transmitted to Rome.

These two Causes, now being processed according to the historical method and presented to the Congregation for the Causes of Saints in a joint study or "Positio," will be examined together so that, if the Church so decides, the Servants of God can be canonized together.

The faithful are invited to invoke Louis Martin and Zélie Martin together to obtain favors and miracles through their joint intercession. Information about favors received, as well as offerings for the expenses of these Causes, may be sent to:

> Postulazione Generale dei Carmelitani Scalzi
> Corso d'Italia, 38
> 00198 Roma
> Italia